NEW PERSPECTIVES ON
MARY E. WILKINS FREEMAN

Interventions in Nineteenth-Century American Literature and Culture
Series Editors: Christopher Hanlon, Sarah R. Robbins, Andrew Taylor

Available

Liminal Whiteness in Early US Fiction
Hannah Lauren Murray

Carlyle, Emerson and the Transatlantic Uses of Authority: Literature, Print, Performance
Tim Sommer

Crossings in Nineteenth-Century American Culture: Junctures of Time, Space, Self and Politics
Edward Sugden

(P)rescription Narratives: Feminist Medical Fiction and the Failure of American Censorship
Stephanie Peebles Tavera

New Perspectives on Mary E. Wilkins Freeman: Reading with and against the Grain
Stephanie Palmer, Myrto Drizou & Cécile Roudeau

Forthcoming

Melville's Americas: Hemispheric Sympathies, Transatlantic Contagion
Nicholas Spengler

The Aesthetics of History and Slave Revolution in Antebellum America
Kevin Modestino

www.edinburghuniversitypress.com/series/incal

NEW PERSPECTIVES ON MARY E. WILKINS FREEMAN

Reading with and against the Grain

Edited by
Stephanie Palmer, Myrto Drizou and
Cécile Roudeau

EDINBURGH
University Press

Edinburgh University Press is one of the leading university presses in the UK. We publish academic books and journals in our selected subject areas across the humanities and social sciences, combining cutting-edge scholarship with high editorial and production values to produce academic works of lasting importance. For more information visit our website: edinburghuniversitypress.com

© editorial matter and organisation Stephanie Palmer, Myrto Drizou and Cécile Roudeau 2023, 2024
© the chapters their several authors, 2023, 2024

Edinburgh University Press Ltd
13 Infirmary Street
Edinburgh EH1 1LT

First published in hardback by Edinburgh University Press 2023

Typeset in 10/12.5 Adobe Sabon by
IDSUK (DataConnection) Ltd

A CIP record for this book is available from the British Library

ISBN 978 1 3995 0447 8 (hardback)
ISBN 978 1 3995 0448 5 (paperback)
ISBN 978 1 3995 0449 2 (webready PDF)
ISBN 978 1 3995 0450 8 (epub)

The right of Stephanie Palmer, Myrto Drizou and Cécile Roudeau to be identified as editors of this work has been asserted in accordance with the Copyright, Designs and Patents Act 1988, and the Copyright and Related Rights Regulations 2003 (SI No. 2498).

CONTENTS

List of Figures   vii
Acknowledgments   ix
Contributors   xi

Reading Freeman Again, Anew   1
   Stephanie Palmer, Myrto Drizou, Cécile Roudeau

Part I: Kinship Outside of Normative Structures
1. Mary E. Wilkins Freeman's Neighborly Encounters and the Project of Neighborliness   25
   Jana Tigchelaar
2. "Her Own Creed of Bloom": The Transcendental Ecofeminism of Mary E. Wilkins Freeman   43
   Susan M. Stone
3. "Preposterous Fancies" or a "Plain, Common World?" Queer World-Making in Mary E. Wilkins Freeman's "The Prism" (1901)   60
   H. J. E. Champion

Part II: Violent, Criminal, and Infanticidal: Freeman's Odd Women
4. The Reign of the Dolls: Violence and the Nonhuman in Mary E. Wilkins Freeman   79
   Donna M. Campbell

CONTENTS

5 Transatlantic Lloronas: Infanticide and Gender in Mary E. Wilkins Freeman and Alexandros Papadiamantis 95
   Myrto Drizou
6 Redefining the New England Nun: A Revisionist Reading in the Context of *Pembroke* and Irish American Fiction 112
   Aušra Paulauskienė

Part III: Women's Work: Capital, Business, Labor
7 Hunger Strikes: Queer Naturalism and the Gendering of Solidarity in Mary E. Wilkins Freeman's *The Portion of Labor* 131
   Justin Rogers-Cooper
8 "It Won't Be Long Before the Grind-Mill Gets Hold of Him": Child Labor in Mary E. Wilkins Freeman's *The Portion of Labor* 147
   Laura Dawkins
9 Literary Businesswoman Extraordinaire 164
   Brent L. Kendrick
10 Deconstructing Upper-Middle-Class Rites and Rituals: Reading Mary E. Wilkins Freeman's Stories Alongside Mary Louise Booth's *Harper's Bazar* 182
   Audrey Fogels

Part IV: Periodization Reconsidered
11 Mobilizing the Great War in Mary E. Wilkins Freeman's *Edgewater People* 203
   Daniel Mrozowski
12 A Cacophony of Voices: Freeman's Modernism 219
   Monika Elbert
13 Underground Influence: Sylvia Townsend Warner's Pastiche of Mary E. Wilkins Freeman 236
   Stephanie Palmer
14 Untimely Freeman 253
   Cécile Roudeau

Afterword: Why Mary E. Wilkins Freeman? Why Now? Where Next? 272
   Sandra A. Zagarell

Index 286

FIGURES

Frontispiece	Mary E. Wilkins at sixteen. *The Critic*, New York, 5 March 1898, p. 156. Collection of Brent L. Kendrick.	xvi
2.1	"The Great Pine." Illustration from *Six Trees*, 1903. Image courtesy of Thompson Library Charvat American Fiction Stacks, Thompson Library Special Collections, The Ohio State University Libraries.	52
6.1	"Sylvia never turned her head." *Pembroke*, 1894. Image courtesy of Thompson Library Charvat American Fiction Stacks, Thompson Library Special Collections, The Ohio State University Libraries.	125
8.1	Child labor, making garters for Liberty Garters works. Mrs Finkelstein with Bessie, age 13, and Sophie, age 7. 127 Monroe Street, New York. Photograph by Lewis W. Hine, January 1908. Shutterstock.	159
9.1	Steen-Wilkins Block, Brattleboro, Vermont. Stereocard from the 1870s or 1880s. Collection of Brent L. Kendrick.	167
9.2	Broadside auction for Mary E. Wilkins Freeman Estate. Collection of Brent L. Kendrick.	177
10.1	"Ladies' Summer Bonnets." *Harper's Bazar*, 26 May 1883, p. 12. Image courtesy of the Home Economics Archive:	

FIGURES

	Research, Tradition, and History (HEARTH) Collection, Albert R. Mann Library, Cornell University.	186
11.1	"She told them it was Leon's, and that he had fought in it." Women at the washing line, doing the work of nationalist propaganda. *Harper's Monthly*, November 1917. Image courtesy of *Harper's Magazine*.	210
11.2	"Wake Up, America!" *America in the War*. Image courtesy of Trinity College, Connecticut.	214
11.3	Image opposite "Wake Up, America!" in *America in the War*. Courtesy of Trinity College, Connecticut.	215
12.1	Julian Alden Weir, *The Factory Village*. Superstock.	220
14.1	Front cover of *Understudies*, 1901. Image courtesy of Thompson Library Charvat American Fiction Stacks, Thompson Library Special Collections, The Ohio State University Libraries.	256
14.2	"The White Birch." *Six Trees*, 1903. Image courtesy of Thompson Library Charvat American Fiction Stacks, Thompson Library Special Collections, The Ohio State University Libraries.	263

ACKNOWLEDGMENTS

Many people and institutions helped bring this project to fruition. Monika Elbert, Debra Bernardi, and Sharon M. Harris were intrigued to hear of our ambition to establish a Mary E. Wilkins Freeman Society at the 2015 Society for the Study of American Women Writers Triennial Conference, and Alfred Bendixen and Olivia Carr Edenfield have always moved swiftly to support our American Literature Association panels. The first business meeting of the Society at the 2017 American Literature Association was attended by Leah Blatt Glasser, Sandra Zagarell, June Howard, Ellen Gruber Garvey, Dan Mrozowski, Susan Stone, Donna M. Campbell, and Paul Lauter, and they offered several ideas for steps we might take to keep Freeman's name in the critical conversation and ensure that the wider critical field understood the important developments in Freeman studies. Speakers and attendees at our Freeman panels have included many of the contributors to this volume as well as Melissa Pennell, Clare Mullaney, Austin Marie Carter, and Michèle LaRue.

When we decided to produce a new essay collection on Freeman, several prospective contributors came forward whom we had to turn down, and we appreciate their interest in Freeman and hope it continues in the future. Cécile organized a wonderful Paris Symposium to discuss drafts of the chosen papers, and the three of us, Dan Mrozowski, Justin Rogers-Cooper, Jana Tigchelaar, H. J. E. Champion, Audrey Fogels, Sandra Zagarell, Monika Elbert, and Donna M. Campbell attended on Zoom or in person or offered feedback on drafts. It was the first of many forays into Zoom for most of us. The Symposium strengthened the essay collection by determining threads that tied the essays together, and we are grateful to the participants.

We thank the Sylvia Townsend Warner Estate for permission to quote from an unpublished letter. Michelle Houston and Susannah Butler at Edinburgh University Press supported this project, and the Series Editors Andrew Taylor, Sarah R. Robbins, and Christopher Hanlon have been enthusiastic. The anonymous readers of Edinburgh University Press offered generous and incisive feedback. We appreciate the last-minute help in sourcing images of Rebecca Jewett and Martin W. Orville at Ohio State University Thompson Special Collections, along with Shane Burris at Penn State, Eve Brant at Harpers, Kelly Ashton at SuperStock, and Natasha Bishop at Cornell University, as well as Dan Mrozowski and Brent L. Kendrick. Stephanie's attendance at various conferences was supported by Nottingham Trent University. Stephanie would also like to thank Jocelyn Alford and (as ever) Fergus, Cameron, and Adrian Bolger. Cécile is grateful to her research center, LARCA UMR 8225, the center for anglophone studies at Université Paris Cité, for being receptive to the new Freeman studies and for funding the Freeman symposium in Paris as well as her own travel to various Freeman panels. Myrto would like to thank Boğaziçi University for conference travel support and the Research Fund Grant Number 15721, which provided the invaluable editorial help of Firdevs Idil Kurtulan. Warm thanks go to Stamatis, Fragkoula, and Maria Drizou for sharing in all the challenges and joys of Myrto's academic pursuits.

CONTRIBUTORS

Donna M. Campbell is Professor of English at Washington State University. She is the author of *Resisting Regionalism: Gender and Naturalism in American Fiction, 1885–1920,* and her articles on Mary E. Wilkins Freeman include "Howells's Untrustworthy Realist: Mary E. Wilkins Freeman" (*American Literary Realism*, 2006). Recent work includes *Bitter Tastes: Literary Naturalism and Early Cinema in American Women's Writing* (2016), "Edith Wharton and Transnationalism" in *The New Edith Wharton Studies*, ed. Jennifer Haytock and Laura Rattray (Cambridge UP, 2019), and "Edith Wharton and Film," *The Bloomsbury Handbook to Edith Wharton* (Bloomsbury, 2022). She is currently preparing a critical edition of Edith Wharton's *The House of Mirth* in the 30-volume *Complete Works of Edith Wharton* (Oxford UP), a series for which she is associate editor.

H. J. E. Champion received her PhD from Bordeaux Montaigne University and University of Eastern Finland. Her dissertation examines naughty nuances and searches for the sexual in the textual in short stories by nineteenth-century women writers from New England. She is the recipient of the Transatlantic Women Graduate Essay Prize (2018), the DC Watt Prize (2019) and the Elsa Nettels Award for a Beginning Scholar (2019). She has written on Ada Trevanion in *Victorian Review*, Madeline Yale Wynne for Routledge, Harriet Prescott Spofford in *EJAS*, and Edith Wharton in the *Edith Wharton Review*. In an attempt to make her research accessible, she has also self-published "Sapphists and Amazons: Lesser Known Queer Heroes" with illustrator Sofie Birkin, available in bookshops *Gay's the Word, Category Is, Lighthouse Books, Golden Hare Books,* and *Les Mots à la Bouche.*

Laura Dawkins is a Professor of English at Murray State University. Her articles on American literature have appeared in *Callaloo, South Atlantic Review, LIT: Literature Interpretation Theory,* and *49th Parallel,* among other journals, as well as in eight edited collections, including *Narrating History, Home, and Diaspora: Critical Essays on Edwidge Danticat, Modernist Women Writers and American Social Engagement,* and *Emmett Till in Literary Memory and Imagination.*

Myrto Drizou is an Assistant Professor of English at Boğaziçi University in Turkey, where she teaches American and transatlantic literature. She received her PhD in Comparative Literature from the State University of New York at Buffalo and has previously taught at Valdosta State University and the University of Illinois at Springfield in the US. She is one of the founding members of the Mary E. Wilkins Freeman Society and has contributed the Introduction to the new edition of Freeman's *The Wind in the Rose-bush and Other Stories of the Supernatural* (Hastings College P, 2015). She has published on numerous *fin de siècle* American authors, including Henry Adams, Theodore Dreiser, Frank Norris, and Edith Wharton. She is editor of the volume *Edith Wharton* for the series Critical Insights (Salem P, 2017) and serves as associate editor of the *Edith Wharton Review.* Her work on Wharton has further appeared in *The New Edith Wharton Studies* (Cambridge UP, 2019); *Gothic Landscapes: Changing Eras, Changing Cultures, Changing Anxieties* (Palgrave Macmillan, 2016); *Critical Insights: American Writers in Exile* (Salem P, 2015); and *49th Parallel: An Interdisciplinary Journal of North American Studies.* She is also editor of a special issue on the global dimensions of American literary naturalism, which appeared in the *New Centennial Review,* and is currently working on a study of the archaeological imagination of late nineteenth- and early twentieth-century American female writers.

Monika Elbert is a Professor of English at Montclair State University in New Jersey. Editor of the *Nathaniel Hawthorne Review,* Elbert has published widely on Hawthorne and on other nineteenth-century American authors, especially on Gothic writers, and on women writers (including Wharton, Freeman, Jewett, Alcott, and Margaret Fuller). Recent books include several co-edited collections: *Romantic Education in Nineteenth-Century American Literature: National and Transatlantic Contexts* (Routledge, 2014), *Anglo-American Travelers and the Hotel Experience in Nineteenth-Century Literature* (Routledge, 2017), *Haunting Realities: Naturalist Gothic and American Realism* (U of Alabama P, 2017), *American Women's Regionalist Fiction:*

Mapping the Gothic (Palgrave Macmillan, 2021), and the edited volume, *Hawthorne in Context* (Cambridge UP, 2018).

Audrey Fogels is an Associate Professor of American Literature at University of Paris 8-Saint Denis. Her scholarship focuses on nineteenth-century American women's literature and the articulation between literature and politics. She is interested in particular in the tensions at work in (re)-defining American identity in women's texts of the long nineteenth century. Her areas of interest also include the link between domestic fiction and national concerns as well as the cultural power of the Gothic tradition. She has published articles on Mary E. Wilkins Freeman, Sarah Orne Jewett, and Elizabeth B. Stoddard. Her current project is on the (de) construction of an American imagined community in Elizabeth Stoddard's *Two Men* (1865).

Brent L. Kendrick, Professor of English at Laurel Ridge Community College in Middletown, Virginia, is widely known for his scholarly work on Mary E. Wilkins Freeman and is the editor of her collected letters, *The Infant Sphinx*, praised by *The Journal of Modern Literature* as "the most complete record to date of Freeman's life as writer and woman." He is currently working on a new, two-volume update—*Dolly: Life and Letters of Mary E. Wilkins Freeman*. Vol. I: *The New England Years (1852–1901)*. Vol. II: *The New Jersey Years (1902–1930)*. He earned his PhD in American Literature from the University of South Carolina. After a 25-year career at the Library of Congress—where he received the institution's Distinguished Service Award—he relocated to the Shenandoah Valley of Virginia, where he continues to teach at Laurel Ridge Community College. He has won numerous teaching awards at the college and state levels.

Daniel Mrozowski is the Academic Director of Graduate Studies in English at Trinity College in Hartford, Connecticut. His most recent article, "Over Here: America's Great War Mobilization and Transnational Alternatives in Mary Austin and Ellen Glasgow," appeared in *CR: The New Centennial Review* in 2020, and his work on naturalism has appeared in *Studies in American Literary Naturalism*, *Haunting Realities: Naturalist Gothic and American Realism* (2017) and *American Women's Regionalist Fiction: Mapping the Gothic* (2021). He also co-edited a collection, *The Great Recession in Fiction, Film, and Television: A Busted Culture* (Lexington Books, 2013).

Stephanie Palmer is a Senior Lecturer of Nineteenth-Century American Literature at Nottingham Trent University in the United Kingdom. Her research interests include women's writing, regionalism, social class, and transatlanticism. She formerly taught at Bilkent University in Turkey. In addition to several journal articles and a co-edited special issue of *Symbiosis* on British literature and transatlanticism, she is the author of *Transatlantic Footholds: Turn-of-the-Century American Women Writers and British Reviewers* (Routledge, 2020) and *Together by Accident: American Local Color Literature and the Middle Class* (Lexington Books, 2009). Along with Myrto Drizou and Cécile Roudeau, she inaugurated the Mary E. Wilkins Freeman Society.

Aušra Paulauskienė started her academic career in the newly re-established Vytautas Magnus University in Kaunas, Lithuania in 1991. She received her Doctorate degree in English from the University of Illinois at Urbana-Champaign in 2003. In 2007, her book *Lost and Found: The Discovery of Lithuania in American Fiction* was published by Rodopi Publishers. She has been active in multiple scholarly forums, EAAS, NAAS, AJS, Nordic Summer University and ALA, and is a recipient of several fellowships, including Fulbright Visiting Scholars at UC Berkeley in 2016. Her research interests include new approaches to nineteenth-century women's literature. Her article "How Ántonia Became 'My' Ántonia: the 'New' Immigrant Woman as a Model American" was included in the collection *In the Country of Lost Borders: New Critical Essays on My Ántonia* by Presses Universitaires De Paris Nanterre (2017). She currently holds the position of a Professor at LCC International University in Klaipėda, Lithuania.

Justin Rogers-Cooper is a Professor of English at LaGuardia Community College and a faculty member in the Master's in Liberal Studies program at the CUNY Graduate Center. Through a queer Marxist approach, Rogers-Cooper's scholarship focuses on American cultural and literary studies in the long nineteenth century and the racial and gender politics of labor culture. He co-edited a special issue for *William James Studies* and has a forthcoming chapter in the book *New Directions in Print Culture Studies: Archives, Materiality, and Modern American Culture* (Bloomsbury, 2022).

Cécile Roudeau is a Professor of American Literature at Université Paris Cité. Her research focuses on the articulation between literature and politics in the long nineteenth century. Her first book, *La Nouvelle-Angleterre: Politique d'une écriture* (Sorbonne UP, 2012) read New England regionalism (Jewett and Freeman in particular) as a political attempt to repartition the sensible in the US turn to empire. Roudeau is also the author of the first translation of Jewett's *The Country of the Pointed Firs* into French (2004/2022). Her research has appeared in *ESQ*, *Leviathan*, *William James Studies*, *Revue Française d'Études Américaines*, and *European Journal of American Studies*. She is working on a book project provisionally entitled "Beyond Stateless Literature: Practices of Democratic Power in Nineteenth-Century US Literature."

CONTRIBUTORS

Susan M. Stone, recently promoted to Professor of English and Gender Studies, is the former Faculty Chairperson, Director of the Division of Language and Literature, and the O'Connor Chair of Catholic Thought at Loras College in Iowa. Her scholarly loves include literary transcendentalism, Native and Indigenous studies, ecocriticism, and nineteenth-century feminism. Recent publications appear in academic journals such as *Studies in American Fiction*, *The Concord Saunterer*, and *Teaching American Literature: Theory and Practice (TALTP)* and in edited collections, including *Navigating Women's Friendships in American Literature* (Palgrave Macmillan, 2023) and *Toward a Female Genealogy of Transcendentalism* (U of Georgia P, 2014). In addition to the above, she was the guest editor in Winter 2021 for a special issue of *TALTP* called "Teaching the West and Native American Literature."

Jana Tigchelaar is an Associate Professor and Director of Graduate Studies in the English department at Marshall University, where she teaches classes in early and nineteenth-century American literature, women's writing, literary regionalism, and textual analysis. Her current project, *Among Neighbors: Women's Regionalist Literature and the Project of Neighborly Reconciliation*, is a scholarly monograph examining the project of neighborliness, through which regionalist writers propose alternative modes of national identity and belonging. Her work has appeared most recently in *New Ohio Review*, *Legacy*, and the edited collection *Community Boundaries and Border Crossings: Critical Essays on Ethnic Women Writers* (2016).

Sandra A. Zagarell is the Emerita Donald R. Longman Professor of English and Visiting Professor at Oberlin College in Ohio. A senior editor of the *Heath Anthology of American Literature*, she has published on postbellum regionalism, on narratives of community, on the queer Americanness of Henry James's *The Portrait of a Lady*, and on the work of Mary E. Wilkins Freeman and other American writers. She is co-author, with Joanne Dobson, of "Women Writing in the Early Republic" and, with Katherine Adams, of "Recovering Alice Dunbar-Nelson for the Twenty-First Century." She is editor and author of critical introductions of *"A New England Nun," and Other Stories* by Mary E. Wilkins Freeman (Penguin, 2000), of Mary Clavers (Caroline Kirkland), *A New Home—Who'll Follow? Or, Glimpses of Western Life* (Rutgers UP, 1990) and, with Lawrence Buell, of *The Morgesons and Other Writings, Published and Unpublished, by Elizabeth Stoddard* (U of Pennsylvania P, 1984; Penguin, 1998). She is currently working on Freeman and on the Alice Dunbar-Nelson archive.

Frontispiece Mary E. Wilkins at sixteen. *The Critic*, New York, 5 March 1898, p. 156. Collection of Brent L. Kendrick.

READING FREEMAN AGAIN, ANEW

STEPHANIE PALMER, MYRTO DRIZOU, CÉCILE ROUDEAU

Mary E. Wilkins Freeman (1852–1930) is best known, read and taught today as the author of short regionalist fiction, and true enough, her literary production is largely set in rural New England, a region she depicts in its period of economic decline or marginalization after the US Civil War. A New England nun, however, she was not.[1] Reading Freeman with and against the grain implies unlearning what we think we know about her and her oeuvre. Freeman's work frustrates our attempts to situate her in clearly delineated categories because her prolific production spanned over nearly fifty years, from the early 1880s and well into the modernist era; because she experimented with a diverse array of forms and genres, writing poems and novels and sketches, children's tales, sentimental stories, and protest novels; because her biography tells us that she straddled social classes; because, and most importantly perhaps, her work ultimately resists many of the very frames that have brought her back to visibility (transcendentalism, sentimentalism, realism, naturalism). Her literary production is robust and varied enough to bear the weight of a profound critical rethinking which questions the paradigms that have obscured her work—and that of other (women) writers—from view.

An increasingly vibrant literary scholarship has already opened new critical expectations and has unsettled the conditions of normative legibility that guided the relatively cloistered readings of her work in the decades following her last publications. Some fifty years after her death, and thanks to the recovery work that brought her back from the margins of American letters in the

1980s, Mary E. Wilkins Freeman gained recognition in the US and abroad at the intersection of diverse and sometimes overlapping literary critical rubrics, including New England "local color," rebellious regionalism and female naturalism. More recently, however, Freeman studies have taken a different set of turns including Gothic, ecocritical, queer, and transnational approaches. New research on Freeman, invigorated by the foundation of the Mary E. Wilkins Freeman Society at the 2017 meeting of the ALA in Boston, has disclosed unexpected aspects of her work. This essay collection, co-edited by the three founders of the society and featuring a concluding piece by one of the most important scholars to lead the first wave of Freeman's recovery, Sandra Zagarell, aims at pushing further in this direction. It does not intend so much to *recover* Freeman as to *uncover* alternative modes of reading her work.

While the volume focuses explicitly on Freeman, it nonetheless self-consciously seeks to avoid the pitfalls that have on occasion affected projects of authorial recovery, especially the dangers of imposing self-coherence and artistic consistency. Hence, reopening the case of Freeman does not mean reverting to the trope of the writer as an exceptional figure or the myth of unified authorial intention, let alone a biographical approach that often dismisses the author's late production—in the case of Freeman, the texts that she wrote once married and "delocalized" to New Jersey. To the contrary, instead of imposing a single interpretive grid on Freeman's work, we offer a variety of authorial and critical practices, which we hope will allow future scholars to find in Freeman's texts the means to challenge previous readings, including the very categories we have chosen for analysis here. The road to at once diversifying and recovering a new set of critical readings of Freeman's oeuvre may then best begin by exploring the lesser-known history of Freeman's reception from the last decades of the nineteenth century—when she first gained fame—to today's post-recovery critical modes of approaching her oeuvre.

A New England Writer, For Better or For Worse

Mary Ella Wilkins[2] was born in 1852 in Randolph, Massachusetts, to Warren Wilkins, a carpenter and housebuilder, and his wife Eleanor (Mary changed her middle name to Eleanor to commemorate her mother, who died in 1880). Randolph's economic base of agriculture and shoe manufacturing was eroding by the time Mary was a teenager. In 1867 the family moved to the resort town of Brattleboro, Vermont, where her father set up a dry goods business, one that eventually failed. Mary was well educated, but the family was increasingly impecunious, and she taught school and gave music lessons in her youth. By the late 1870s she sent poetry and children's stories to magazines and newspapers around the country, and in 1883, she published her first story for adults, "Two Old Lovers." Soon after the publication of that story, Mary's father died, leaving her without immediate family. She, then, moved back to Randolph, where she lived for nearly twenty years with a childhood friend, Mary Wales and Wales's parents. In 1902, after a prolonged engagement, she married Dr Charles Manning Freeman and moved to his home town of Metuchen, New Jersey. The marriage seemed happy for a time, but by 1909 Charles had entered sanitariums due to excessive drinking, and the couple broke after 1919 in a formal separation. Her writing, most especially in her first two short story collections for adults, *A Humble Romance and Other Stories* (1887) and *A New England Nun and Other Stories* (1891), as well as in her novel *Pembroke* (1894), propelled her into a world of literary celebrity; she was friendly with several prominent Northeastern editors including Mary Louise Booth, Joseph Edgar Chamberlin, and Henry Alden, as well as authors like Sarah Orne Jewett, William Dean Howells, Hamlin Garland, and Rudyard Kipling. Although she earned the most royalties from her short stories, she also wrote poetry, thirteen novels, a play, work in collaboration with other writers, eight children's books, and a handful of articles.[3]

While New England made Mary E. Wilkins Freeman famous, New England also was the reason of her dismissal. Freeman, and other (female) writers of her generation, were hastily labeled "local color writers" and, as such, were excluded from the process of canon formation in the 1920s. Yet a local flavor, or a sense of rootedness, had not always rhymed with obsoleteness, or queerness. One needs only to go back to the last decades of the nineteenth century to grasp how place was *the* major paradigm in the literary reconstruction of the nation. In the 1880s, when Mary E. Wilkins entered the market of regionalist literary production, New England was no longer the "seed-bed of this great American republic, and of all that is likely to come of it," as Harriet Beecher Stowe had once claimed, and illustrated (Stowe, n.p.). New England had become a region almost like any other, a "place" with its singularity and its situatedness. William Dean Howells, a champion of "local color" in the pages of the *Atlantic Monthly* and *Harper's Magazine*, did support the New Englander Sarah Orne Jewett and Mary E. Wilkins Freeman, but he also praised Mary Noailles Murfree of Tennessee, Hart Crane of California, and Hamlin Garland of Wisconsin, with the rationale that truth, the truth of the nation most importantly, is plural, local, and always circumscribed—not indexed, that is, on the principle of generality, but contingent on the place where it was first articulated. For the dean of American letters, US literature, then, was to be as decentralized as the nation itself had become.[4] Mary E. Wilkins Freeman, as one of the particular voices of the nation, was part of this regional destiny of American literature.[5] Local as her work was, or rather because of its rootedness somewhere, it was representative of a commons that was built on differences, rather than similarities. This equivalence of local differences that Howells's influential "Editor's Studies" championed again and again was what made the nation (and national literature) again possible after the Civil War.

The cult of the local, however, did not last. When an overseas US imperialism developed at the turn of the century under the aegis of Theodore Roosevelt, the Howellsian local pluralism that had made the heyday of regionalism in American letters no longer reigned supreme. The peculiar became instead the label of an anti-Americanism. In that scheme, local color New England, being the furthest away perhaps from a mythical West where manhood could conquer and reign, featured as the true antithesis of the national mythography, and Freeman, among others, became the representative of morbid femininity and treacherous parochialism. Indeed, Roosevelt's definition of "true patriotism" left very little doubt as to who the enemies of the nation were:

> In the first place we wish to be broadly American and national, as opposed to being local or sectional. We do not wish, in politics, in literature, or in art, to develop that unwholesome parochial spirit, that over-exaltation of the little community at the expense of the great nation, which produces what has been described as the patriotism of the village, the patriotism of the belfry. (166)

The likes of the Shattuck sisters in "A Mistaken Charity" (1883), one half-deaf, the other half-blind, who braved old age and the poor house's laws, to get back "home," or the stubborn Marm Lawson in "Brakes and White Vi'lets" (1884), who kills her sickly granddaughter by keeping her in her moldy old house lest she should lose her to the city, became dissonant notes in an American clamorous symphony. Strenuous as they were, the task of being the representative, if peculiar, voices of the nation was no longer theirs—even if New England, as the former center of a national literary imaginary, kept something of its grandeur in the midst of its demise.

No wonder, then, that in his *History of American Literature since 1870* (1915), Fred Lewis Pattee, in spite of his New England origins, or rather because of them, had "the New England period" in American letters *precede* "the National period," as if New England literature could only testify to "[t]he passing of an old regime" (233). Freeman, accordingly, was classified among the "recorders of the New England decline" (Chapter XI), a declension narrative that Pattee, however, did not initiate. As Fetterley and Pryse (2003) remind us, from the turn of the century onwards, the surveys of US literature systematically categorized New England literature as passé and, as such, unfit to represent US literature. The works of Freeman, but also of Sarah Orne Jewett, Rose Terry Cooke, or Alice Brown, were spurned as delicate, or genteel at best, unless they were anathematized as deleterious reading.

Interestingly, however, at the turn of the century, Freeman did not suffer from the charge of "un-Americanness" as much as, say, Jewett, who was lastingly plagued by her genteel origins. Like her predecessor Rose Terry Cooke,

Freeman was redeemed of her New Englandness, as it were, by her social class—the modest background she grew up in. And because she wrote on what she knew—poor country people's lives, "the narrow environment of New England villages," that was hers (Pattee 236)—and did so, allegedly, by tapping in the "austere and limited" (236) schooling that she had received as a child, she was spared of the sin of bookishness or artistry. Pattee characteristically insisted that she was born a realist. "She seems to have followed no one," he wrote, "realism was a thing native to her" (236). And as a realist, she could not find the door of the pantheon of American letters entirely closed to her. In April 1926, Freeman became the first recipient of the William Dean Howells Medal for Distinction in Fiction from the American Academy of Arts and Letters—a distinction that should have sealed her fate and her fame. Not so, however.

Freeman's realism was either not enough, or too much to be true. Not grim enough for Edith Wharton, who famously reproached her for considering New England "through . . . rose-coloured spectacles," and overlooking the "outcropping granite" in favor of the "sweet-fern" and "mountain-laurel"; Freeman's stories, for Pattee, were to the contrary too stern and somber—the outcome of a Puritanism gone awry, the sickly flowering of a degenerating country.[6] "When she approached literature," he diagnosed, articulating an origin narrative that would stick to Freeman for decades,

> it was as a daughter of the Puritans, as one who had been nurtured in repression. Love in its tropical intensity, the fierce play of the passions, color, profusion, outspoken toleration, freedom—romance in its broadest connotation—of these she knew nothing. She had lived her whole life in the warping atmosphere of inherited Puritanism, of a Puritanism that had lost its earlier vitality and had become a convention and a superstition, in a social group inbred for generations and narrowly restricted to neighborhood limits. (236)

This belated, if critical, Puritanism, was to be Freeman's birthmark, both a blemish and a blessing, as well as her costly entrance fee to American letters. Three decades after Pattee, Perry D. Westbrook's influential sum, *Acres of Flint: Writers of Rural New England* (1951), made the exact same diagnosis. Intent on salvaging from oblivion those writers of rural New England that had been buried as unworthy of praise, Westbrook did so paradoxically by identifying their works as the perverted avatars of an ambivalent past. He observed in "a group of New England rural writers, most of them village-bred women," "a conscience that had been exaggerated to the point of becoming hysteria." Singling out Freeman among them as having "a morbidly sensitive conscience" (88), Westbrook read her texts as "the workings of a lopsided will," "crooked" (91) for lack of adequate objects. For Westbrook, then, one thing was certain:

the New England of cantankerous old maids and stubborn farmers could only be conjugated in the past; this literature was a morbid relic of a history that no longer holds true, and, as such, it could not be America's authoritative writing.

Myths die hard; and Freeman, labeled and advertised as "a recluse from New England," as soon as 1893, continued to feature as one vestigium of another era in the heart of Progressive America (Doyle 287). At the turn of the century, critics could wonder, without the slightest irony, at her using a typewriter (Moss). Was she supposed to wield a quill? And rare were those who tried to extricate Freeman from the enclosure of the past. When, in 1898, Joseph Edgar Chamberlin of the *Critic* tried to return her to the present, his words must have sounded like a provocation: Randolph is a suburb of Boston, he insisted, and Freeman knows and appreciates the cosmopolitan city as much as you readers. Her window overlooks electrical tracks, and her house is heated by radiators! But Chamberlin wrote against the grain; for most critics, and the readers after them, Freeman was an authentic New Englander, her prose was rooted in the granite soils of her native New England, and her gaze warped by centuries of Puritanism. New England, yet again. It may not come as a surprise, then, that New England served as the pivot of the second-wave recovery of Freeman, but this time it was as the foil against which her work was read.

In 2003, Fetterley and Pryse's *Writing Out of Place* deterritorialized Freeman's work the better to enroll her texts as regionalist critique.[7] By de-emphasizing the New England dimension of her oeuvre, they meant to counter her (and other writers') stigmatization as mere providers of quaint picturesqueness and anecdotal, if not dangerous, pre-modern peculiarity. Regionalist Freeman, they explained, has not much in common with her local color avatar, who should be regarded as an ideological fabrication serving the interests of a masculinist national hegemony. Because rootedness essentializes place and transforms it into one of the commodities produced by the nation state, it also reifies the oeuvre which, as a relic of the past, becomes yet another artefact of national production. Denaturalizing regionalism, understanding regionalism as a "discourse," instead of a "geographical manifestation," as a point of resistance in the power network that cannot be easily or exactly located, has a clear political pay-off: regionalism is thereby turned into a social or political strategy of defiance—a situated knowledge, not an essential emanation of a particular, and often marginal, place (Fetterley and Pryse 7). Accordingly, reading Freeman as partaking in regionalist critique is important: it means aligning her stories with "elements of disruption, resistance, and revolution" (125); it uncovers a "politics of resistance to the imperialism of gender, age, and class" (249); reading Freeman "out of place" allows one to read her "from inside the perspective of the queer" (332). But equally important is to understand that such radical dismissal of New England as a hermeneutic category in Freeman's work was preceded by other attempts to push beyond a reading of her work as systematically harnessed to place. Such history that unfolded from the 1970s to the 1990s is the history of Freeman's recovery.

TWISTS AND TURNS IN FREEMAN SCHOLARSHIP

Most readers who come to Freeman have been influenced by the feminist critics who prompted renewed attention to her oeuvre from the 1970s to the 1990s, a work of recovery that itself bifurcated into two main branches. On the one hand, there were those who chose to depict the predominately female world of late nineteenth-century New England that she belonged to as a nurturing, mother-centered realm (Donovan, *New England Local Color Literature*), and on the other, as early as the 1974 Feminist Press edition of Freeman's short stories by Michele Clark, and up to the 1983 Norton edition by Marjorie Pryse, there were critics who focused their commentary and story selection on tales of defiance featuring characters (mostly female) who rebelled against the gender and class conventions of their time. Writes Pryse, "For the first time in American peacetime history, the women of an entire region were left in a world transformed into a quasimatriarchal one both by the casualties of the Civil War and by the departure of a substantial proportion of the region's remaining young healthy male population." And she adds, more specifically about Freeman: "Throughout her career, whenever she addressed the themes of rebellion and revolt, in the village fiction that focuses primarily on women, she wrote her most successful work" (viii, xii). The boundaries between the two readings were not as clear-cut as it may seem. But suffice it to say that, coming out of the works of philosophers, psychologists, or historians as diverse as Hélène Cixous, Lillian Faderman, Nancy Chodorow, Carol Gilligan, or Carroll Smith-Rosenberg, some feminist critics insisted on women's ethic of care, and their willingness to cultivate and maintain mutual bonds, particularly with other women, while others emphasized instead women's resistance and direct confrontation to patriarchy. Because there was in both cases a potential for essentialist application, much of this scholarship has been contested over the years, sometimes by the very critics that had initiated it. Yet its central premise, more carefully historicized and somehow nuanced, has remained a pivot of later criticism—that women of a certain class and ethnicity have drawn sustenance from each other rather than from the men around them.

Between the two, Freeman's fiction has largely fallen on the side of rebellion and resistance, as chafing against the directive of the female ethic of care. Michelle Clark (1974) wrote that Freeman characters' dependence on each other economically and socially leads them to "fight, envy, disagree, compete, bicker, and manipulate" even though they are often usually intensely loyal in the end (195). Josephine Donovan details a shift in the 1870s and 1880s toward female education and work outside the home, causing a rift between mothers and daughters in fiction by Jewett and Freeman. Whereas

Jewett chooses the mother's matriarchal realm, Donovan proposes, Freeman chooses the daughter's longing to escape ("Silence or Capitulation"). Similarly, Pryse associates Jewett with a "reunion with mother" and Freeman with a "revolt of the mother" (ix). Most notably, Mary R. Reichardt's work recovering Freeman's short fiction across her long career argues that Freeman's fiction only partially corroborates the findings of feminist researchers into women's lives: "Rather, the emotional and mutually dependent bonds women form with other women in Freeman's New England more often than not take on a disturbingly threatening or ominous tone" (104). Indeed, for every early Freeman story that celebrates a women's special brand of strength—"The Revolt of 'Mother'" (1890), "Louisa" (1890), "A Church Mouse" (1889), and "A Poetess" (1890)—there are later stories in which caring and nurturing resemble smothering or disciplining—"Old Woman Magoun" (1905), "The Reign of the Doll" (1904), "The Lost Ghost" (1903), or "The Selfishness of Amelia Lamkin" (1908). More than other female writers of her generation, then, Freeman has gained prominence as "dark Freeman," away from the matriarchal utopias of Jewett's stories or the "rose-and-lavender" palette that Wharton had tried to attach to her name (*A Backward Glance* 294). Freeman thus complicates an abstract sense of quasimatriarchal realms and the female ethic of care by showing that women's power involves the same contradictions, difficult choices, and abuse of boundaries that any kind of power inherently entails. Rather than romanticizing an idealized view of women's nurturing lives, Freeman adopts a decidedly more modern stance that anticipates the expansion of power that women have gradually, albeit not unconditionally, enjoyed. With sobriety and compassion, she looks into particular instances where women's power takes the edge of abuse. From our vantage point of the twenty-first century, we are more prepared to discuss these aspects of her work.

Freeman scholars are indebted to Leah Blatt Glasser's critical biography of Freeman *In a Closet Hidden* (1996), which was among the first works to unlock Freeman's complex identity as a woman and an author. Glasser meticulously analyzed Freeman's "psychology of self-division" (xviii) that would find expression in thematic and narrative motifs, such as character doubles and mirror scenes, which convey Freeman's own ambiguity about rebellion. Glasser's research into Freeman's letters and manuscripts was paved by Brent Kendrick's collection of Freeman's letters *The Infant Sphinx* (1985), another seminal book that was based on archival research. Considering Freeman's long life, the scarcity of her archives bears further question. The Mary Wilkins Freeman Collection #7407 at the Clifton Waller Barrett Library, Special Collections Department, University of Virginia, houses her books, a few of her story manuscripts, and several letters which have already been published in *Infant Sphinx*. New letters will appear in Brent Kendrick's forthcoming edited collection of her letters. Additionally, Glasser cites a collection of three letters at the Alfred Williams

Anthony Collection, Rare Books and Manuscripts Division, New York Public Library, and reminiscences of Freeman's time at Holyoke in the Mary E. Wilkins Freeman folder at Mount Holyoke College Archives. As we are uncovering new directions in Freeman studies, her correspondence may contain formerly ignored evidence that would buttress the hypotheses put forward in this collection. Going back to the archives may indeed flesh out what we perceive makes Freeman interesting today: the vibrant productivity of her later years; the move towards the non-human and non-normative forms of kinship with trees or non-human animals; the ongoing tensions of her oeuvre between writing to formula and experimentation with genres, between a complicity with certain forms of capitalism and a courageous resistance to the exploitation of labor, between her queer leanings and the necessity of female solidarity *malgré tout*.

Readers and scholars will likely continue to be drawn to Freeman for her depictions of female rebellion and defiance, yet recent work carries this line of inquiry into new directions: the fetish, the Gothic, and what Donna M. Campbell in this volume calls "the criminal."[8] Taking up Westbrook's argument, yet reinscribing Freeman in her time and age, that of turn-of-the century consumerism, Monika Elbert argues forcefully that her characters' sense of frustration with their narrow lives "leads to an excess of senseless and compulsive behavior reflected in frenzied and repeated activities, such as spending money, sewing incessantly, or collecting useless knick-knacks" (192). Such characters are fetishists rather than benign objects of cosmopolitan readers' sympathy. Jennifer Fleissner similarly argues that Louisa Ellis and other famous Freeman characters suffer from what is now called obsessive compulsive disorder (111–22), while Linda M. Grasso, reading Freeman's "Old Woman Magoun" alongside Sui Sin Far's "The Wisdom of the New," understands these desperate matricides as "symbolically encapsulat [ing] the writers' frustration, rage, and despair about their status as artists in a 'young' America that refuses to allow them to nurture their talent" (19). Rather than frightening and unproductive violence, these stories, Grasso concludes, produce "righteous anger" that "demands social justice" and "has the potential to create community" (19).

The political and social work of Freeman's communities of angry women and downtrodden men is probably most visible in her Gothic short fiction. Beth Wynne Fisken argues that ghosts in Freeman's stories record anxiety and ambivalence about childrearing. Roxanne Harde treats Freeman's child ghost in "The Little Maid at the Door" (1891) as one of several Victorian British or American child ghosts that indict society's practice of allowing children to suffer, particularly if they are involuntarily associated with erring and disgraced parents. Gothic short fiction has become a popular topic among Freeman critics in recent years, with new analyses by Dara Downey, Nicole Diederich, Daniel Mrozowski, Melissa Pennell, and Jennifer Bann among others, which mostly corroborate Fisken's sense that there is something disturbing about Freeman's reading of mothers and children. In that sense, Freeman's Gothic was not only a belated reworking of the genre, but it also partook of a larger denunciation of the world in which she lived. A new edition of *The Wind in the Rose-Bush and Other Stories of the Supernatural* edited by Myrto Drizou, points to the importance of this later collection in which "Freeman's Gothic challenges not only traditional gender stereotypes but also conventional representations of home" (xiv) and mother-daughter relationships in a changing world. Indeed, what remains thought-provoking about Freeman's work is how much she rebelled against the social wrongs of the turn-of-the-century US while simultaneously embracing some of the premises of a cosmopolitan, urban, and consumerist society (Elbert); how she was both fascinated by modernity and wary of a "progress" that brought its lots of social and economic problems to the US countryside.

As Sandra Zagarell reminds us in her introduction to the Penguin Classics edition of Freeman's stories, Freeman's first published short story, "Two Old Lovers" (1883), as well as "A Wayfaring Couple" (1885) are set in factory towns, as is *The Portion of Labor* (1901). Mostly because of the predominating sense that regionalism was a form of the pastoral, or because it was associated with the tradition of female benevolence literature, labor-capital relations have never been a major strand in Freeman criticism. But here again we may well have been blinded by persisting critical a-prioris concerning female "regionalists." Debra Bernardi, for one, has read Freeman out of the tradition of female benevolence, and shown how Freeman's characters in her short stories rebel against scientific charity as bungled by ministers and middle-class female neighbors. Focusing on *The Portion of Labor* (1901), a novel about a shoe factory strike, Mary Marchand and Dorothy Berkson, on the other hand, have read it as a failed attempt to update a nineteenth-century tradition of benevolence literature, in which middle-class white women—drawing on their uniquely feminine powers of sympathy—descend upon a multi-ethnic working class. However, focusing on the childlike, unreasoning qualities of Freeman's heroine, Ellen Brewster, they disregard Ellen's acumen at public speaking, or Freeman's talent at reproducing the sordid self-respect of the working-class families that surround her main character. The novel does not sit neatly in a feminist tradition of middle-class heroines who enter the public sphere through their reform work, because it focalizes factory conditions through the workers. Two essays in this volume revisit *The Portion of Labor*, a novel not reprinted since 1967, so as to draw attention to one neglected facet of Freeman's work, her social awareness and stubborn reformism.

Freeman's social reformism should not however be too quickly dissociated from her vision of racial relations. Freeman critics have begun to investigate the presence of racial anxiety in her work. In the introduction to the 1991 *Critical Essays on Mary Wilkins Freeman*, Shirley Marchalonis makes it clear that Freeman partook of the race theories of her day, using the language of bloodlines in her fiction and nonfiction, highlighting the Puritan ancestry of her characters, and contrasting that lineage to the more exotic, passionate, or violent French, Native American, and African American characters. Stephanie Palmer's work (2020) further addresses how Freeman's fictions were championed by contemporary critics as fine products of an Anglo-Saxon bloodline, but the wayward, nonconforming nature of Freeman's eccentrics, Palmer argues, ultimately troubled critics intent on upholding an image of the United States as a modern nation.

Many of the essays in this volume investigate the racial significations of Freeman's fiction and resist a "Freeman so white" reading of her oeuvre. Fogels's chapter, for instance, complicates what may first appear as the monolithic whiteness of Freeman's texts. Whiteness, as Hannah Lauren Murray has recently shown in her study of early US fiction, was less an essence than a status bestowed on those who exhibited certain traits, including respectability, industry, and sociality (4). The Shattuck sisters of "A Mistaken Charity," Fogels's chapter shows, fail to exhibit these typical traits by sliding into poverty and not caring that their roof is full of chinks or their chins full of hairs. Their refusal to accept charity raises questions about the instability of whiteness for poor women, the way that whiteness can be bestowed or lost in a liminal process involving "precarity and demotion" (Murray 6). Whereas many writers viewed the loss of white privilege as anxiety provoking, for Freeman, it could be humorous or even joyful. Monolithic whiteness is also unsettled by Freeman's complex handling of ethnicity. In *The Portion of Labor*, as shown in Rogers-Cooper's chapter, the intersection of gender, class, and ethnic identity questions working-class forms of resistance as found in naturalist novels of the time. While Ellen, Freeman's main character, is exceptionally beautiful, intelligent, and charismatic, she is also ableist and racialized as belonging to an Irish American culture—which turns the text into an exemplar of what Zagarell might call Freeman's, and the era's, ideological "cross-currents" (Zagarell, "Cross-Currents"). We tend to forget that power, and the power of women especially, can be racialized in Freeman. Campbell offers a rare reading of Freeman's disturbing novel *Madelon* (1896) which features a mixed-race heroine. The eponymous character, with French and Native bloodlines that are implicated in her stubborn self-reliance, is one of Freeman's strongest women, and her capacity for violence is rarely dealt with in feminist readings.

Acknowledging the series of interlinked turns that criticism on Freeman has undergone since the 1970s, and more specifically in the three decades since *Critical Essays on Mary Wilkins Freeman* appeared (Marchalonis 1991), this volume, then, intends to push beyond critical regionalism (Zagarell, "Introduction" xviii), or rather, push critical regionalism into new directions. Cutting across the emphasis on both a Foucauldian discourse of heterotopia and a Deleuzian deterritorializing impulse that tended to erase the material and historical presence of New England (Fetterley and Pryse 2003), we believe that it is possible to evade the pitfalls of essentialism without throwing away place with the bathwater of antiquarianism or the logic of regional commodification. In the 2000s and 2010s, critics did recover New England yet not the New England of Pattee, Westbrook, or, for that matter, Richard Brodhead.[9] Cécile Roudeau's *La Nouvelle-Angleterre: Politique d'une écriture* (2012) argues that erasing New England amounts to disallowing the tension between center and periphery that haunts Freeman's regionalism. If New England shapes Freeman's critical regionalism, she argues, it is because Freeman's New England, as both (ex-)center and periphery, is always critical of itself. For J. Samaine Lockwood, this self-criticism is related to a queer historicism practiced by Freeman and other women archivists, who returned to history with a difference, by placing the unmarried New England daughter at the heart of their endeavor.

On the other hand, if differently, ecocriticism also reiterates that Freeman really *is* writing about New England, with its flowers, trees, animals, mountains, rivers, bridges, gardens, and crops, as well as, but not predominantly, the humans that dwell within it. Terrell F. Dixon shows how Freeman's *Understudies* (1901) and *Six Trees* (1903), later collections that have not yet received the attention they deserve, "present an expansive, evolving ecofeminist vision— one that avoids essentialism and that creates green women and green men who love and defend nature while engaged in ordinary life" (173). While it is useful to draw links between Freeman and the earlier New England transcendentalists—and Dixon, Alaimo, and Stone have done so—these critics also identify differences, in that Freeman critiques traditional gender relations (Alaimo 60) to the point of proposing her own kind of queer regionalism or queer ecology. Freeman's intimate relationships between women and women,[10] humans and trees, or women and objects, are not just sisterly, empathetic, or fetishistic. "(B)ecause of the non-normative formulation of kinship and domesticity that emerged out of them but also because of the ways in which they embody experiences of alienation from forms of biological, social, and economic reproduction involved in heterosexual domesticity" (Ansley 434–5), these alliances offer a queer form of resistance to hegemonic discourses and categories, something that has been increasingly brought to the fore as critics read more of Freeman's oeuvre, moving beyond her two canonical collections.

With the emergence of digitized newspaper databases, more and more Freeman stories are being discovered that were not reprinted in her story collections or listed in Freeman bibliographies. One of these newly discovered stories is the fascinating "An Idyl of a Berry Pasture," which was published in *Once a Week* (Aydelott and Wilkins). It is becoming evident, then, that Freeman has not said her last word. These discoveries significantly undermine lingering suspicions that she was just a cog in the wheel of the Harper's publishing house, and that her regionalism was but a fashionable way for readers of the national literary monthlies to consume rural otherness. Freeman was a writer of her time, and her tales were tales of New England; she did write some of her stories to formula—the result, perhaps, of the precariousness of her family finances—and resolved plots with marriages or lovers' reunions. But if she catered to the late nineteenth-century metropolitan tastes for tales of life in the backward but virtuous countryside, she also wrote—against them—texts that still unsettle our appreciation of her today. Against the Freeman that we know, this volume wants to go one dig into the Freeman that we don't quite know yet. Doing so requires that we do not stop at her two early collections, but that we read her *against* the periodization that has relegated late (married) Freeman to oblivion and beyond the local and national scale that has traditionally been hers. In brief, and most importantly, it demands that we leave aside our assumptions about how a middle-class white female writer of turn-of-the-century New England *should* write and accept, instead, a rare, if unexpected, complexity that requests patient unravelling once again.

Collection Overview

The chapters in the volume are organized into four sections that conclude with an afterword by Sandra Zagarell. The sections collectively explore how Freeman pushes against dominant critical perspectives and question our own assumptions about major epistemological rubrics, including genre and periodization, as well as normative structures such as local and national belonging, class, age, and gender affiliation. Reading Freeman with and against the grain, the following chapters engage with her diverse literary production—not her canonical stories only, but also her lesser-known novels—so as to let her texts speak back to us in new and unpredictable voices.

The first section, "Kinship Outside of Normative Structures," uncovers alternative modes of communality in Freeman's fiction. In the chapter "Mary E. Wilkins Freeman's Neighborly Encounters and the Project of Neighborliness," Jana Tigchelaar introduces the concept of "neighborliness" to describe Freeman's complex representation of kinship bonds beyond normative constructs. Looking at a wide range of Freeman's short stories—from staples, such as "Christmas Jenny" and "A Village Singer," to less widely discussed stories in the volume *Understudies*—Tigchelaar argues that Freeman's neighborly encounters occur at liminal spaces that imagine new forms of belonging within (and across) regional hierarchies of class, age, gender, and ability. In the next chapter, "'Her Own Creed of Bloom': The Transcendental Ecofeminism of Mary E. Wilkins Freeman," Susan M. Stone reads some of the stories discussed by Tigchelaar—including "Christmas Jenny" and "The Great Pine"—yet from a different perspective. Stone argues that Freeman's fiction acts as a bridge between first-wave transcendentalism and ecofeminism insofar as it centers on ecological stewardship to rethink boundaries between nature and the human, "providing readers with option-filled alternatives to socially prescriptive (and restrictive) domesticity and gender conventions" (44). As a sustained expression of ecofeminist views, Freeman's work inflects key transcendental concepts to envision new forms of companionship, responsibility, and belonging. Freeman's search for new modes of belonging is also the focus of the following chapter, "'Preposterous Fancies' or a 'Plain, Common World'? Queer World-Making in Mary E. Wilkins Freeman's 'The Prism' (1901)," in which H. J. E. Champion explores Freeman's representation of queer children. Through a close reading of "The Prism," a rarely anthologized story, Champion analyzes the protagonist's eccentric sense of autonomy that borders on autosexuality, resisting normative projections of linearity in terms of age, domesticity, and marriage. Although the plot concludes with marriage, Champion contends, it suggests the possibility of imagined queer futures.

The second section, "Violent, Criminal, and Infanticidal Womanhood," continues the examination of deviant female characters throughout Freeman's fiction. In "The Reign of the Dolls: Violence and the Nonhuman in Mary E. Wilkins Freeman," Donna M. Campbell addresses criminal acts of violence, in which women are not just victims but also perpetrators and aggressors. Freeman's representations of child kidnapping, fatal neglect, and murder rely on nonhuman surrogates such as dolls and animals. Through their power to signify suffering, desire, and trauma, Campbell argues, these surrogates not only embody but also catalyze the disruption of power structures, including the market economy, racial discrimination, gender inequality, and colonial history. The next two chapters explore Freeman's eccentric and violent heroines from a transatlantic scope, placing Freeman in new cross-cultural contexts. In her chapter, "Transatlantic Lloronas: Infanticide and Gender in Mary E. Wilkins Freeman and Alexandros Papadiamantis," Myrto Drizou argues that the depiction of child murder, which she interprets as infanticide, in "Old Woman Magoun" evokes a transatlantic mythology of deviant maternal figures epitomized by La Llorona, the Wailing or Weeping Woman in Meso-American mythology that is also central to Alexandros Papadiamantis's 1903 Greek novella, *The Murderess*. In the following chapter, Aušra Paulauskienė argues that Freeman's deviant women—both in well-read stories, such "A New England Nun" and "Louisa," and lesser studied novels—evoke Catholic tropes to criticize old-dogma Puritanism. These tropes, including religious ritual, cloister motifs, and the representation of motherhood as the stronghold of outdated religion, bring Freeman closer to Irish American fiction, a new context for reading her work. As Paulauskienė concludes, such connections to Irish American texts draw out the powerful entanglement of social, religious, and political systems of belief in the increasingly multi-ethnic nation.

The third section, entitled "Women's Work: Capital, Business, Labor," situates Freeman within a range of turn-of-the-century economic discourses, such as the literary market, social class, and labor reform. The first two chapters place Freeman's neglected novel *The Portion of Labor* in the vexed terrain between a sentimental tradition of protest novels à la Stowe and the early twentieth-century realist and naturalist reform fiction with which Freeman has rarely been associated. Justin Rogers-Cooper argues that it is the novel's "feminist labor solidarities" that engender the conditions for working-class forms of resistance such as strikes. In Freeman's text, the performance of queer intimacy and desire are recast as a political tool for social reform. Laura Dawkins, on the other hand, analyzes the thorny issue of child labor, as represented in the novel. Freeman, Dawkins argues, turns the "cult of childhood" into the "theft of childhood" in the context of a family wage economy that forces tough decisions on both parents and children. Freeman's conflicted adherence to reform should not, however, be dissociated from her own multifaceted relation to labor and capital as a writer. Brent L. Kendrick sheds light on one of the lesser-known aspects of Freeman's literary career, namely, her financial competence and business acumen. Taking Freeman as a prime example of a highly successful "literary businesswoman," Kendrick examines her business decisions, publishing strategies, and various dealings with cash, property, and investment. Given her successful navigation of the literary market, Kendrick suggests, Freeman deserves to be noted not only for her prolific output but also for her economic skill. This section concludes with Audrey Fogels's chapter "Deconstructing Upper Middle-Class Rites and Rituals: Reading Mary E. Wilkins Freeman's Stories Alongside Mary Louise Booth's *Harper's Bazar*." Fogels argues that Freeman's archaic New England settings and quaint lower-middle-class characters function as ironic mirrors to the world of *Harper's Bazar* and the privileges of upper-middle-class membership. Fogels's analysis of well-known stories, such as "A Mistaken Charity" and "Sister Liddy," and rarely discussed ones, such as "A Modern Dragon," draws on textual and visual evidence to suggest that Freeman's portrayal of consumer culture, financial hardship, and women's competition underwrites the *Bazar's* covert yet complex commitment to feminist concerns.

The final section, "Periodization Reconsidered," addresses how Freeman's work extends beyond conventional period markers and established literary histories. Daniel Mrozowski examines Freeman's late collection of stories that has received scant scholarly attention. Mrozowski points out that Freeman's portrayal of war mobilization in the home front challenges traditional modes of representing the war, as it combines mundane choices and reversals of fate with larger questions of pacifism and internationalism. What is more, Freeman's response to the Great War questions our own response to "realist" writers at the close of their careers, especially when they continue to write well into the period we tend to define as "modernism." Monika Elbert's essay, "A Cacophony of Voices: Freeman's Modernism," further elaborates on Freeman's engagement with modernist anxieties and concerns in the context of an increasingly industrialized New England. Elbert suggests that Freeman represents her home not as a pastoral rural space but as a site of alienation, consumerism, and capitalism, connected to global problems such as World Wars. Freeman's early twentieth-century stories, in particular, feature false relationships, disenchantment with objects of prestige, and struggles of self-actualization in a disintegrating world, all of which bring Freeman closer to themes of modernist fragmentation and disenchantment than regionalist wistfulness and nostalgia. The following chapter, "Underground Influence: Sylvia Townsend Warner's Pastiche of Mary E. Wilkins Freeman," argues that Freeman's work lived on into the 1920s through the 60s, even after Freeman lost her main audience. Stephanie Palmer explores Freeman's transatlantic influence on the twentieth-century British writer Sylvia Townsend Warner. Palmer identifies a "progressive female-to-female influence" that is structured differently than the Bloomian model of influence, featuring a broader array of emotions including but *not only* about anxiety. The final chapter of the volume, entitled "Untimely Freeman," sheds new light on Freeman's "understudies" from the deliberately anachronistic perspective of a twenty-first-century reader. Part of the "late Freeman" corpus, *Understudies* has been recently recovered as her "first volume of ecofiction," yet has remained, perhaps in accordance with its title, somewhat obscure. Reading *Understudies* from the perspective of recent scientific hypotheses and philosophical developments about the animal and the vegetal world as a world of relations in which the human no longer abides as center, does not imply de-historicizing her, Roudeau argues; it rather requires historicizing both her writing and our reception in order to engage with the non-coincidence between the two as an opportunity to be seized, not a discontinuity to be lamented.

Sandra Zagarell, in her "Afterword," brings these voices together and offers an incisive assessment of Freeman's resonance with the twenty-first-century reader and critic. As each contributor to this volume shows, Freeman's texts continue to yield fresh insight, especially in the context of new critical approaches to gender, race, age, and class. This insight is never unidirectional, however. Freeman's work speaks back to contemporary critics insofar as it illuminates the fault lines of current social and political debates and, in doing so, opens the space for further conversations that help us navigate the complexities of our own time and age. In a world where modes of connection have been largely restructured by the global pandemic, in which the climate crisis, the fear of massive deforestation and species extinction demand both a planetary response and practical changes within our most quotidian practices, Freeman's fiction seems all too familiar, as her plots place the minute, the domestic, and the monotonously mundane at the core of narratives that echo forward to our carefully sheltered lives. This deep-rooted desire for connection is both soothing and unsettling. Some may choose to spend their lives "in a closet hidden," after all, a phrase that perhaps echoes differently in pandemic times, when unable or unwilling to confront the world, we remain wary of contact, and contagion, ready to invent or reactivate new forms of (remote) sociability. The spectral, the ghostly, are forms of correspondence that we have reconfigured to experience and learned to newly appreciate.

But Freeman's way of releasing the unsettling power of connectiveness is also instructive insofar as it embraces and reaches beyond the orbit of individual existence, combining examples of subtle, everyday revolt and larger-scale examinations of organized movements, as in *The Portion of Labor*. The global crises we have experienced in the 2020s, pandemic- or climate-related, and evidenced in the migrant crises and a global political and social unrest, have revealed that class, race, and gender inequalities persist amidst radical change; indeed, they necessitate new modes of struggle beyond conventional paradigms of connection and outside conventional alliances. Freeman's shifts between forbearance and defiance continue to comfort and inspire new readers, who may be more ready than they were in the 1990s, during the heyday of Freeman's recovery, to commit themselves, individually or collectively, at the level of their local community or more broadly, to activist action and a new language of hope.

Works Cited

Alaimo, Stacy. *Undomesticated Ground: Recasting Nature as Feminist Space*. Cornell, 2000.

Ansley, Jennifer. "Geographies of Intimacy in Mary Wilkins Freeman's Short Fiction." *New England Quarterly*, vol. 87, no. 3, 2014, pp. 434–63.

Aydelott, Kathrine C., and Mary E. Wilkins, "'An Idyl of a Berry Pasture': A Rediscovered Mary Wilkins Freeman Story." *Resources for American Literary Study*, vol. 38, 2015, pp. 65–93.

Bann, Jennifer. "Ghostly Hands and Ghostly Agency: The Changing Figure of the Nineteenth-Century Specter." *Victorian Studies*, vol. 51, no. 4, Summer 2009, pp. 663–85.

Berkson, Dorothy. "'A Goddess Behind a Sordid Veil': The Domestic Heroine Meets the Labor Novel in Mary E. Wilkins Freeman's *The Portion of Labor*." *Redefining the Political Novel: American Women Writers, 1797–1901*, edited by Sharon M. Harris, U of Tennessee P, pp. 149–68.

Bernardi, Debra. "'The Right to be Let Alone': Mary Wilkins Freeman and the Right to a 'Private Share.'" *Our Sisters' Keepers: Nineteenth-Century Benevolence Literature by American Women*, edited by Jill Bergman and Debra Bernardi, U of Alabama P, 2005, pp. 135–56.

Brodhead, Richard. *Cultures of Letters: Scenes of Reading and Writing in Nineteenth-Century America*. U of Chicago P, 1993.

Campbell, Donna M. "Mary Wilkins Freeman: Shapeshifter." American Literature Association Conference, Boston, May, 2017.

Chamberlin, Joseph E. "Authors at home." *Critic*, vol. 29, no. 837, 5 March 1898, pp. 155–6.
Chodorow, Nancy. *The Reproduction of Mothering: Psychoanalysis and the Sociology of Gender*. U of California P, 1978.
Cixous, Hélène. "Castration or Decapitation?" Translated by Annette Kuhn. *Signs*, vol. 7, Autumn 1981, pp. 41–55.
Clark, Michele. "Afterword." *The Revolt of Mother and Other Stories*, by Mary E. Wilkins Freeman, Feminist P, 1974, pp. 165–201.
Diederich, Nicole A. "The Gothic as Semiotic Disruption: Layers and Levels of Terror and the Abject in Mary Wilkins Freeman's 'The Wind in the Rose-Bush.'" *Journal of the Midwest Modern Language Association*, vol. 44, no. 2, Fall 2011, pp. 21–41.
Dixon, Terrell F. "Nature, Gender, and Community: Mary Wilkins Freeman's Ecofiction." *Beyond Nature Writing: Expanding the Boundaries of Ecocriticism*, edited by Karla Armbruster and Kathleen R. Wallace, UP of Virginia, 2001, pp. 162–76.
Donovan, Josephine. *New England Local Color Literature: A Woman's Tradition*. F. Ungar Publishing Company, 1983.
—. "Silence or Capitulation: Prepatriarchal 'Mothers' Gardens' in Jewett and Freeman." *Studies in Short Fiction*, vol. 23, no. 1, Winter 1986, pp. 43–8.
Downey, Dara. "Dangerous Houses in the Uncanny Tales of Charlotte Perkins Gilman and Mary E. Wilkins Freeman." *Haunting Realities: Naturalist Gothic and American Realism*, edited by Monika Elbert and Wendy Ryden, U of Alabama P, 2017, pp. 119–31.
Doyle, Albert. "A New England Recluse." *Donahoe's Magazine*, March 1896, p. 287.
Eaton, Edith Maude/Sui Sin Far. "The Wisdom of the New." *Mrs. Spring Fragrance*, edited by Hsuan L. Hsu, Broadview Editions, 2011, pp. 61–79.
Elbert, Monika M. "The Displacement of Desire: Consumerism and Fetishism in Mary Wilkins Freeman's Fiction." *Legacy*, vol. 19, no. 2, December 2002, pp. 192–215.
Faderman, Lillian. *Surpassing the Love of Men: Romantic Friendship and Love Between Women from the Renaissance to the Present*. Women's P, 1981.
Fetterley, Judith, and Marjorie Pryse. *Writing Out of Place: Regionalism, Women, and American Literary Culture*. U of Illinois P, 2003.
Fisken, Beth Wynne. "The 'Faces of Children That Had Never Been': Ghost Stories by Mary Wilkins Freeman." *Haunting the House of Fiction: Feminist Perspectives on Ghost Stories by American Women*, edited by Lynette Carpenter and Wendy K. Kolmar, U of Tennessee P, 1991, pp. 41–63.
Fleissner, Jennifer L. *Women, Compulsion, Modernity: The Moment of American Naturalism*. U of Chicago P, 2004.
Freeman, Mary Wilkins. "Brakes and White Vi'lets." *A Humble Romance and Other Stories*. Harper & Brothers, 1887, pp. 107–17.
—. "A Church Mouse." *A Mary Wilkins Reader*, edited and introduced by Mary R. Reichardt, Nebraska UP, 1997, pp. 93–106.
—. "The Little Maid at the Door." *Silence and Other Stories*. Harper & Brothers, 1898, pp. 225–54.
—. "The Lost Ghost." Reichardt, ed., pp. 261–78.
—. "Louisa." *A New England Nun and Other Stories*, edited and introduced by Sandra A. Zagarell, Penguin, 2000, pp. 48–63.

—. "A Mistaken Charity." Zagarell, ed., pp. 11–21.
—. "A Modern Dragon." *A Humble Romance and Other Stories*, pp. 60–77.
—. "A New England Nun." Zagarell, ed., pp. 22–33.
—. "Old Woman Magoun." Zagarell, ed., pp. 218–34.
—. "A Poetess." Zagarell, ed., pp. 34–47.
—. *The Portion of Labor*. Harper & Brothers, 1901.
—. "The Reign of the Doll." Reichardt, ed., pp. 317–32.
—. "The Revolt of 'Mother.'" Zagarell, ed., pp. 64–78.
—. "The Selfishness of Amelia Lamkin." *The Revolt of "Mother" and Other Stories*, Dover Thrift Editions, 1998, pp. 98–118.
—. "Sister Liddy." *A New England Nun and Other Stories*. Harper & Brothers, 1891, pp. 81–98.
—. "Two Old Lovers." *A Humble Romance and Other Stories*. Harper & Brothers, 1887, pp. 15–36.
—. "A Wayfaring Couple." *A New England Nun and Other Stories*. Harper & Brothers, 1891, pp. 121–39.
—. *The Wind in the Rose-Bush and Other Stories of the Supernatural*, edited and introduced by Myrto Drizou, Hastings College P, 2015.
Gilligan, Carol. *In a Different Voice: Psychological Theory and Women's Development*. Harvard UP, 1982.
Glasser, Leah Blatt. *In a Closet Hidden: The Life and Work of Mary E. Wilkins Freeman*. U of Massachusetts P, 1996.
Grasso, Linda M. "Inventive Desperation: Anger, Violence, and Belonging in Mary Wilkins Freeman's and Sui Sin Far's Murderous Mother Stories." *American Literary Realism*, vol. 38, no. 1, Fall 2005, pp. 18–31.
Harde, Roxanne. "'At Rest Now': Child Ghosts and Social Justice in Nineteenth-Century Women's Writing." *Transnational Gothic: Literary and Social Exchanges in the Long Nineteenth Century*, edited by Monika Elbert and Bridget M. Marshall, Ashgate, 2013, pp. 189–200.
Holbo, Christine. "Hamlin Garland's 'Modernism.'" *ELH*, vol. 80, no. 4, December 2013, pp. 1205–36.
Howard, June. *The Center of the World: Regional Writing and the Puzzles of Place-Time*. Oxford UP, 2018.
Howells, W. D. "Editor's Study." *Harper's New Monthly Magazine*, September 1887, pp. 638–42.
Koppelman, Susan, ed. *Two Friends and Other Nineteenth-Century Lesbian Stories by American Women Writers*. Meridian, 1994.
Lockwood, J. Samaine. *Archives of Desire: The Queer Historical Work of New England Regionalism*. U of North Carolina P, 2015.
Lutz, Tom. *Cosmopolitan Vistas: American Regionalism and Literary Value*. Cornell UP, 2004.
Marchalonis, Shirley, ed. *Critical Essays on Mary Wilkins Freeman*. G. K. Hall, 1991.
Marchand, Mary V. "Death to Lady Bountiful: Women and Reform in Edith Wharton's *The Fruit of the Tree*." *Legacy*, vol. 18, no. 1, April 2001, pp. 65–78.
Moss, Mary. "Some Representative American Story Tellers." *Himan*, September 1906, pp. 21–9.

Mrozowski, Daniel. "Hallowed Ground: The Gothic New England of Sarah Orne Jewett and Mary Wilkins Freeman." *American Women's Regionalist Fiction: Mapping the Gothic*, edited by Monika Elbert and Rita Bode, Palgrave Macmillan, 2021, pp. 97–113.

Murray, Hannah Lauren. *Liminal Whiteness in Early US Fiction*. Edinburgh UP, 2021.

Palmer, Stephanie. *Transatlantic Footholds: Turn-of-the-Century American Women Writers and British Reviewers*. Routledge, 2020.

Pattee, Fred Lewis. *A History of American Literature Since 1870*. D. Appleton-Century Company, 1915.

Pennell, Melissa. "New England Gothic/ New England Guilt: Mary Wilkins Freeman and the Salem Witchcraft Episode." *American Women's Regionalist Fiction: Mapping the Gothic*, edited by Monika Elbert and Rita Bode, Palgrave Macmillan, 2021, pp. 39–56.

Pryse, Marjorie. Introduction and Afterword. *Selected Stories of Mary E. Wilkins Freeman*, by Mary E. Wilkins Freeman. Norton, 1983, pp. vii–xix, pp. 315–42.

Reichardt, Mary R. *A Web of Relationship: Women in the Short Fiction of Mary Wilkins Freeman*. UP of Mississippi, 1992.

Roosevelt, Theodore. "True Americanism." *Theodore Roosevelt: An American Mind. Selected Writings*, edited by Mario R. Di Nunzio, Penguin Books, 1994, pp. 165–72. Originally published in *Forum*, April 1894.

Roudeau, Cécile. *La Nouvelle-Angleterre: Politique d'une Écriture. Récits, Genre, Lieu*. Presses Universitaires Paris Sorbonne, 2012.

Smith-Rosenberg, Carroll. *Disorderly Conduct: Visions of Gender in Victorian America*. Alfred A. Knopf, 1985.

Stone, Susan M. "'A Woman's Place': The Transcendental Realism of Mary Wilkins Freeman." *Toward a Female Genealogy of Transcendentalism*, edited by Jana L. Argersinger and Phyllis Cole, U of Georgia P, 2014, pp. 377–98.

Stowe, Harriet Beecher. Preface. *Oldtown Folks*, by Harriet Beecher Stowe. Fields, Osgood, & Co., 1869, n.p.

Westbrook, Perry D. *Acres of Flint: Writers of Rural New England*. Scarecrow Press, 1951.

—. *Mary Wilkins Freeman*. Revised edition, Twayne Publishers, 1988.

Wharton, Edith. *A Backward Glance*. D. Appelton-Century and Company, 1934.

—. "Introduction." *Ethan Frome*. Penguin Classics, 1987, pp. iii–xxv.

Zagarell, Sandra A. "Crosscurrents: Registers of Nordicism, Community, and Culture in Jewett's *Country of the Pointed Firs*." *Yale Journal of Criticism*, vol. 10, no. 2, 1997, pp. 355–70.

—. "Introduction." *A New England Nun and Other Stories*, by Mary E. Wilkins Freeman, Penguin, 2000, pp. ix–xxvii.

Notes

1. Freeman published her story "A New England Nun" in *A New England Nun and Other* Stories (Harper & Brothers, 1891), and it remains one of her most famous stories.
2. Throughout this collection, we generally use Freeman's married name—the one that editors and anthologists have preferred.

3. The most recent biography is Leah Blatt Glasser, *In a Closet Hidden: The Life and Works of Mary E. Wilkins Freeman*. Many of her stories are in print; Jeff Kaylin's website reprints the serialised version of much of her writing, <http://wilkinsfreeman.info/> (last accessed 1 June 2022) and can serve as a resource for readers of this volume.
4. "It is true that no one writer, no one book, represents it, for that is not possible; our social and political decentralization forbids this, and may for ever forbid it" (Howells 641).
5. "[We] should call the present American work, North and South, thorough, rather than narrow. In one sense it is as broad as life, for each man is a microcosm, and the writer who is able to acquaint us intimately with half a dozen people, or the conditions of a neighborhood or a class, has done something which cannot in any bad sense be called narrow," Howells writes, before enrolling Freeman's first collection of New England stories in this national scope (640).
6. "[I wanted] to draw life as it really was in the derelict mountain villages of New England, a life . . . utterly unlike that seen through the rose-coloured spectacles of my predecessors, Mary Wilkins and Sarah Orne Jewett" (Wharton, *A Backward Glance* 293). "I had had an uneasy sense that the New England of fiction bore little—except a vague botanical and dialectical—resemblance to the harsh and beautiful land as I had seen it. Even the abundant enumeration of sweet-fern, asters and mountain-laurel, and the conscientious reproduction of the vernacular, left me with the feeling that the outcropping granite had . . . been overlooked" (Wharton, "Introduction," *Ethan Frome* xvii).
7. The feminist perspective on regionalism is multifaceted, as the bibliography of this essay attests, but Judith Fetterley and Marjorie Pryse have been the most prolific and influential at lifting the notion of reading regionalism for feminist critique into the realm of theory. See *Writing Out of Place*.
8. Our thinking on this particular turn in Freeman scholarship is indebted to Campbell, "Shapeshifter."
9. The most influential reading of regionalism as a form of consumption for urban audiences is Richard Brodhead's *Cultures of Letters*. Scholars have long sought to build bridges between the feminist and the historicist ways of reading regionalism, including June Howard, Tom Lutz, and Christine Holbo.
10. Given the warmth of Freeman's letters about Mary Wales, contrasted with the wryness with which she dismissed Charles in some late correspondence, scholars including Koppelman (124–7) and Reichardt (105) have wondered whether her relationships with Wales and other women were on the lesbian continuum. Nearly all scholars tend to agree that what she wrote after her wedding in 1902 was of lesser interest.

PART I

KINSHIP OUTSIDE OF NORMATIVE STRUCTURES

MARY E. WILKINS FREEMAN'S NEIGHBORLY ENCOUNTERS AND THE PROJECT OF NEIGHBORLINESS

JANA TIGCHELAAR

Against a familiar backdrop of economic recession, industrial innovation, and a shifting social landscape, Mary E. Wilkins Freeman wrote the short fiction she is best known for—scenes of New England village life that depict with clarity, insight, and humor the daily dramas of courtship and marriage, family life, religious faith, and domestic spaces. Freeman also wrote poetry and novels, as well as short fiction in innumerable other veins, including dozens of stories for children, supernatural tales, and series of fiction focused on animals, flowers, and trees. And yet Freeman's fame rested on her depictions of villages and their seemingly anachronistic inhabitants. This fame was a double-edged sword—Freeman's skill in depicting regional locales and residents cemented her status as a regionalist writer during a time when even regionalism's most vocal supporters voiced their defense of the movement in limiting terms. In an 1891 "The Editor's Study," for example, William Dean Howells describes Freeman's stories as "miniatures" that record "narrowly" lived lives (20). Freeman and other local colorist or regionalist authors were frequently seen by their contemporaries as merely chronicling a fast-disappearing rural reality. Even when acknowledging the artistry of regionalist authors, critics emphasized their work as secondary or marginal; for example, in an 1895 article examining Boston's literary history since the Civil War, Howells writes that while he does not "forget the exquisitely realistic art of Miss Jewett or Miss Freeman," their stories "[have] hardly the novelist's scope" (868).

However, as the work of recovery over the past few decades has turned critical attention to literary regionalism, this narrow conception of the genre's scope has been scrutinized. The first work of feminist critics, including Judith Fetterley, Marjorie Pryse, and Sandra Zagarell, was to read the female-centered imaginaries of much regionalist fiction in the context of the patriarchal systems and structures of the late nineteenth century. Their oppositional reading has often situated appraisals of Freeman alongside other recovered regional writers, arguing that Freeman's regional stories oppose national narratives, her female characters resist patriarchal control, and her domestic spaces counter the public sphere. Further work in reading regionalism's complex relationship with the larger social, cultural, political, and commercial forces shaping not just local but national and global power relations during the late nineteenth and early twentieth centuries has emerged from critics including Stephanie Foote, June Howard, Hsuan L. Hsu, Tom Lutz, Mark Storey, and Edward Watts.[1] Hsu contextualizes even the most nostalgic portrayals of seemingly pre-industrial regionals as subject to the global or national forces their regions imagine to escape, and that their regional productions "[occur] in relation to large-scale phenomena such as migrant flows, transportation networks, and international commerce" (Hsu 164). Like Hsu, other critics see regionalist writers as deeply entangled (whether deliberately or inadvertently) in issues of national and global significance. Howard, for example, notes the recent trend in "relational" studies of concepts including regionalism, pointing toward the way social sciences and policy studies position region in terms of the "interdependence of neighboring states" and often focus "on how economic, political, and cultural connections mesh" (*Center* 3). Storey states that the literature characterized as regional reveals "the hidden and encoded traces of social and cultural change on a level that is shared and transregional," a depiction that is always in dialogue with "the geographically indiscrete experience of modernity" (205).

Following Howard's advice as she encourages reading regionalism "in relation to a form or practice that illuminates" both individual texts and cultural and historical context ("Circuits" 123), this essay suggests another form for reading Freeman's regionalist stories that clearly indicates the genre's imbrication in the intricate web of power relations that structured the late nineteenth and early twentieth centuries: what I am calling Freeman's project of neighborliness. By neighborliness, I mean the recurrent formations of kinship bonds outside of normative structures that appear with regularity in her short fiction.[2] These bonds do not merely oppose these structures, but actively work to enact structural transformation, reimagining the closed space of the domestic family, the restricted Calvinist environment of the village church, or the hierarchical social structure of the regional community. Central to the project of neighborliness is the neighborly encounter, a liminal, transformative meeting that instigates the reimagining of a community's power and structure along neighborly lines. Freeman's neighborly encounters promote neighborliness by proposing a modified network of meaning and belonging in her regional communities.

Reading Freeman's regional fiction in light of neighborly encounters illuminates another purpose behind the project of neighborliness: it also serves as the means by which Freeman attempts to make legible to her largely urban readership the proper mode for consuming these stories and the regional inhabitants they represent. In this, the neighborly encounter serves as an alternative mode of reading regionalist texts, in contrast to the hierarchical mode suggested by the figure of the urban observer/narrator apparent in much regional literature. The success of the neighborly encounter in transforming culture and community rests on collaborative efforts that cross boundaries of class, age, gender, and ability. The community transformation that results from these neighborly encounters serves by extension as a model for the reconciliation of the regional "other" in configurations of national identity. Freeman's empathetic portrayal of socially sidelined individuals whose marginalization is compounded by the perception of their communities as peripheral reveals the potential for social transformation via neighborly encounters. Neighborliness as dramatized by Freeman in these stories also suggests a privileging of communitarian values over individualism—a revaluation that resonates today. By staging neighborly encounters in liminal spaces and states, Freeman's regional texts work to transform relationships both within the text and within the nation, reframing the modes by which her readers would recognize themselves and others.

"Christmas Jenny" and the Neighborly Encounter

In order to define what I mean by neighborliness and what I am describing as the neighborly encounter, I turn to Freeman's story "Christmas Jenny," originally published in *Harper's Bazar* in December 1888 and collected in *A New England Nun and Other Stories* in 1891. "Christmas Jenny" tells the story of an elderly couple, Jonas and Betsey Carey, and their neighbor, Jenny Wrayne, who is known as "Christmas Jenny" for the handmade wreaths and seasonal greenery she sells in the village around Christmastime. Jonas is prone to "tantrums" when things don't go his way, and Jenny rescues Betsey during two of these tantrums (offering the advice that parents of toddlers have known for decades: ignore him and he'll get over it on his own). These acts of neighborly kindness bookend the story, and in-between plays out the other central drama: the village's judgment of Jenny, whom they perceive to be unusual, perhaps a witch, and in need of the intervention of the community. When the minister and church deacon pay Jenny an unannounced visit to confirm for themselves the charges that she is abusing the sick and injured animals she has rescued and the young disabled child she has adopted, Betsey intervenes to speak on behalf of the absent Jenny. The men are convinced by Betsey and moved to generosity, sending Jenny a Christmas turkey, gifts for Willy, her ward, and a new calico dress. The story ends with a feast Jenny shares with the Careys and the light from Jenny's Christmas candle shining down on the village, an emblem for the general blessing of neighborly kindness.

"Christmas Jenny" illustrates a number of key characteristics of the neighborly encounter, specifically in the meeting between Betsey Carey and the visiting minister and deacon. Neighborly encounters often occur in liminal or interstitial spaces, settings which facilitate the transformative nature of the encounters. Liminality, a term I am reading in light of Victor Turner's notion of the liminal state as the middle stage of the ritual process by which social order may be transformed, appears as a setting or as a condition in many of Freeman's stories.[3] In "Christmas Jenny," Betsey encounters the minister and deacon in the liminal space of Jenny's home, which is described as being neither fully domestic nor out of doors, but mingling the two. The liminality of neighborly encounters enables the inversion or questioning of hierarchical power arrangements, as is the case in the meeting between Betsey, who is an elderly female parishioner, and the minister and Deacon Little, who hold positions of power in their New England village. Challenging social structures, the liminal figure in the neighborly encounter often experiences a transcendent, empowered state which temporarily inverts power structures and has the potential to enact long-term community change. In "Christmas Jenny," Betsey's liminal empowerment persuades the two men of the importance of neighborly values, which in turn blesses the entire community.

The neighborly encounter, then, is a transformative meeting, often in a liminal space or setting, between "neighbors," people who are united by geographic proximity but often separated within their communities by reasons of social station, age, ability, behavior, or gender. The encounter serves the purpose of promoting neighborly values such as radical generosity and hospitality and moves the participants to prioritize their neighborly relationships. While neighborliness is in a sense a tenet of Christianity and village life (recount the New Testament story of the Good Samaritan, where Jesus answers the question "who is my neighbor," intended by the "expert in the law" who asked the question to narrow his range of obligation to others, with a parable about radical hospitality), Freeman's neighborliness reveals the ways in which patriarchal theology and civic structures have restricted the range of care and responsibility toward others. Frequently the neighborly encounter illuminates the failures of traditional Christian benevolence and civic charity to truly address the needs of all neighbors. Freeman's neighborliness therefore works to address internally a social wrong in the community, and as such functions as a community corrective that brings with it the additional benefit of the general promotion of community-kinship bonds that extend beyond normative structures like the domestic family unit and the village church. In promoting the project of neighborliness, these stories reveal the ways in which Freeman is speaking to larger questions of identity and belonging beyond her regional communities.

In focusing on belonging and on individual and collective identity, Foote argues that "neighborliness gives us a way to imagine the social work of regional fiction outside the conventional models of family or nation" ("Neighborliness").[4] In this, neighborliness bears similarities to a few other approaches to reading regionalist literature. Jennifer Ansley's "Geographies of Intimacy in Mary Wilkins Freeman's Short Fiction" proposes reading "female-centered communal imaginaries," which she describes as queer due to their "non-normative formulations of kinship and domesticity," as one of Freeman's narrative strategies for navigating the economic impact of industrialization and the concurrent changes to normative domesticity in New England communities (434). Ansley's queer imaginaries can be read alongside Zagarell's narratives of community as describing the social work of regionalist texts in relationship to formations of community. Zagarell's concluding essay to *Narratives of Community: Women's Short Story Sequences* complicates her initial discussion of community-based narratives by examining Freeman's *The Jamesons*, a text she sees as in direct communication with (and critique of) the foundational regional text, Jewett's *The Country of the Pointed Firs*.[5] While Zagarell states that her 1988 definition of the genre of narratives of community "idealized it as a fully positive form of social organization," her 2007 essay recognizes that representations of community can be "limiting" and "destructive," and that all readings of narratives of community should be contingent upon the social and historical contexts of their production and reception (434). Zagarell's particular project here, reading *The Jamesons* in the context of Jewett's *Country* (and particularly *Country*'s urban narrator, who sees Dunnet Landing through a nostalgic lens) as well as in light of *The Ladies' Home Journal*'s narrow notion of commercialized domesticity, offers one such contingent reading.

Similarly, in *Regional Fictions*, Foote takes up the idea of community formation, identity, and citizenship in Jewett's *Country*, and like Zagarell notes that *Country* promotes a sense of regional unity on the foundation of "suppressed relationships between natives and strangers," relationships which "are themselves modulated interventions in a more general concern over origins and nativity" (18). Much of Jewett's *Country* is concerned with the urban narrator's anxiety over her own belonging to the idealized community of Dunnet Landing, and this anxiety, Foote argues, is embedded in the eventual revelation that regional identity is not homogenous but is in fact paradoxically reliant upon the shifting notions of "foreign" and "strange" which are used to define who is a native insider. Although Foote's focus is Jewett's *Country*, which she uses "to show that the foreign constitutes what seems most comfortably homelike in the region," she also notes that "the problems of citizenship in the supposedly homogeneous region" extends to other New England women's regionalism as well, including Freeman, whose short stories "[reveal] her belief in the necessity of community and also the variation in many characters' local or individual relations with a normative community" (37). Withdrawal from community, as seen with Louisa Ellis of "A New England Nun," is one such variation, Foote notes.

In their discussions of community formations in regional texts, Foote and Zagarell both identify the meeting between the urban observer narrator and the regional resident as essential to the mediation of community identity and membership in regional fiction. Zagarell reveals that *The Jamesons'* narrative of community differs from *Country*'s in that what threatens the village of Linnville's integrity is not modernization, but nostalgic, urban interlopers—the Jameson family of New York City, who summer in Linnville, to be specific.[6] Foote, too, focuses on the unnamed narrator of Jewett's *Country* whose own subject position as insider or outsider (and simultaneously as a privileged authority figure) in Dunnet Landing is in constant flux. In this, Zagarell and Foote join many other critics of regionalist fiction, including Judith Fetterley and Marjorie Pryse, in identifying the significant narrative role played by the urban visitor in regionalist fiction. However, in my discussion of neighborliness in Freeman's fiction, I identify another stage on which the negotiations of community identity and belonging take place. Neighborly encounters resemble the meetings between metropolitan visitor and rural resident that animate much regional fiction; however, in Freeman's neighborly encounters, participants are members of the same community who are working within their communities to take up similar questions about community belonging and regional identity. By dramatizing meetings that encourage seeing liminal regional inhabitants as "neighbors," the neighborly encounter serves as an alternative way of reconciling outsiders within the social fabric of the regional community, one which attempts to avoid the fetishization of regionalist literature and its regional residents that the outsider narrator often enables.

Interstitial Spaces, Liminal Encounters

The neighborly encounter is characterized by a "betweenness," which implies both literal and figurative notions of thresholds, doorways, and margins and instigates the blurring of arbitrary boundaries between identity categories. As Turner discusses in *The Forest of Symbols*, while this liminal stage suggests alienation, it also carries with it the possibility of transformation (236). Key to the neighborly encounter is the collective outcome of neighborliness; the liminal figure does not experience transformation alone, but instead in her reintegration into society brings new knowledge to her place in a typically hierarchal structure. The liminal process is, therefore, central to social change, given its capacity to generate new, communitarian social arrangements.[7] In many of

Freeman's stories, the liminality of the neighborly encounter manifests spatially in interstitial zones such as front steps, doorways, or thresholds, spaces whose "betweenness" mediates public and private, inside and outside. These border spaces symbolically stand for the liminal person's status as both temporarily outside of social boundaries and working to promote neighborliness within the freedom from social constraints that outsider status offers. These liminal spaces, already located in-between categories of identification and setting, are particularly apt stages for neighborly encounters. Examples of these interstitial spaces abound in Freeman's regional fiction. In stories like "A Conflict Ended," in which a man spends every Sunday for years sitting on the church steps in protest of a minister's doctrinal interpretation, or in "The Outside of the House," in which an elderly couple take up residence on the porch of a seaside mansion when their wealthy neighbors who own the house are away, Freeman explores the way interstitial spaces like front porches, doorways, and yards can be used to negotiate not just individual but collective identity.

For example, Freeman's "Peony," one of her stories in *Understudies* that draw on flowers and animals for their central metaphors, offers a clear depiction of threshold liminality in the service of neighborliness. As Mary Reichardt has observed, the central metaphors in *Understudies* explore the Emersonian idea that "all elements of the natural world bear correspondence to each other" (*Study* 76). For Arabella Lambert, her corresponding natural element is the peony, described as coarser than the more refined rose—an ironic description, since Freeman offsets Arabella's supposed coarseness with an excessive empathy and abundant generosity toward her neighbors. Arabella's niece, Sarah, condemns her generosity, telling her aunt that "The door of your heart is always open, and [neighbors] walk in and take advantage of it" (199). The story's neighborly encounter occurs after Arabella has given away much of the home's furnishings to a couple who lost their savings in a bank collapse. She blocks the doorway to her house, refusing her niece entry until she accepts the latest in her aunt's series of acts of radical generosity. The central metaphor is underlined during this scene: as Arabella stands in the doorway, unmoving and unspeaking, she fixes her gaze on her peonies, vowing to continue to "yield unstintingly all her largess of life to whomsoever crossed her path with a heart or hand of need for it" (213).

Arabella's immovable doorway meeting with her niece is one of Freeman's more obvious instances of a threshold encounter in service of neighborliness, but the liminal threshold space appears in many other stories, as well. In addition to these literal thresholds, Freeman grapples with the hierarchies of power in regional communities in her depictions of encounters in public gathering places like meeting houses, churches, schools, and village squares. These more traditional public spaces intended for social interaction are ostensibly held in common but are in practice often male-controlled and dominated by normative narratives and ideals. These spaces become liminal stages for neighborly encounters when they are "misused" according to social norms. One type of misuse has to do with a liminal blurring of boundaries in these public spaces—boundaries between domestic and public, between inside and outside, as in the case of Betsey's neighborly encounter in the liminal space of Jenny's house.

This is true of the liminality in a number of well-known stories, like "A Church Mouse," in which Hetty Fifield sets the stage for the neighborly encounter that marks the story's climax through her transformation of the village church into a domestic space. Hetty decorates the meeting house with "treasures of worsted-work," hangs a "gay sunflower quilt" to curtain off a living area for herself, and cooks strong-smelling food for herself in the building (98–100). Similarly, in "The Revolt of 'Mother'," the appropriated space is Adoniram Penn's new barn, which he has built instead of the new home he has been promising his wife, Sarah, for decades. Sarah's interstitial misuse of the barn, a space meant to mark her husband's commercial success, brings about a personal and familial transformation. The liminal settings of neighborly encounters demonstrated in these two stories are echoed throughout other of Freeman's stories that feature interstitial spaces. For example, in "A Village Singer," Candace Whitcomb, the former leading soprano in the church choir, has been forced out due to her "cracked and uncertain" aging voice and replaced by the younger Alma Way (80). To protest her removal, Candace, whose house is next door to the church, plays her own parlor organ and sings loudly over Alma's vocal performances. Like Hetty's experience in "A Church Mouse," this interstitial encounter emphasizes the blurred boundaries between the domestic space of Candace's home and the public, patriarchal space of the church.

Whether taking place in misused, appropriated public spaces or in interstitial zones, neighborly encounters work to disrupt the narrative and structure of authority. At times in these stories, marginalized characters' mere existence is enough to illuminate arbitrary and oppressive hierarchical structures. This is the case in "A Church Mouse," where Hetty's plight comes about because the village's twin structural pillars of the church and the domestic family unit neglect the neighborly values of charity, hospitality, and generosity toward those who don't fit into either of those normative structures. Hetty's village is filled with families who keep to their own "company," a network of relatives and in-laws. Within this private, domestic framework and without the benefit of charitable organizations, the village has no place for someone in Hetty's position. In addition, the resistance of church authorities to Hetty serving as the church sexton, a job typically done by a younger male villager, reveals the gendered, ageist, and ableist hierarchy of the church that defines the social fabric of the village. By challenging the village's social order, Hetty draws attention to the need for neighborliness and the negative repercussions that patriarchal social structures and gaps in social services have caused in regional settings. Candace's situation in "A Village Singer" is similarly gendered; Candace points out to the visiting minister that the leading tenor, who is three years her senior, was not given the same treatment as she was. Candace's interstitial actions initiate an encounter that challenges the hypocrisy of the congregation and the patriarchal authority of the church. While she has not succeeded in transforming her village, she has stepped outside of the bounds of propriety, demonstrating how marginalized people can harness the implicit power of liminality to resist absorption into dominant ideology.[8]

"Strange" Deviance and Community Transformation

In the interstitial spaces and liminal situations of the neighborly encounter, Freeman's marginalized characters use their position from outside of the social order to both reimagine their communities and to revise their own subject positions within their communities. Part of this reimagining comes from a deviation from conforming to social norms, a deviation that can be temporary (as in Candace's protest singing) or enduring (such as Hetty's move into the church). A number of stories focus on characters whose promotion of the values of neighborliness comes at the price of their role within the social order. Esther Gay of "An Independent Thinker," who is hard of hearing, is ostracized for not attending church services she cannot hear; however, she occupies the hours she would spend at church meetings knitting to earn income which she gives anonymously to help her impoverished neighbors. In "Life-Everlastin'," Luella Norcross offers sustenance and care to many of the community's marginalized, poor, and transient figures, but refuses to attend church due to unbelief. Here as elsewhere, Freeman aligns blind adherence to church doctrine or other social norms with unthinking conformity—Luella's sister's frustration that Luella will not attend church meetings does not come out of any concern for her mortal soul, but because she wants her to behave (and dress) "like other folks" (67). In "A Church Mouse," Hetty's "reputation of always taking her own way, and never heeding the voice of authority" has given her an "unfortunate name" in her village (99). Consequently, Hetty is imagined by the villagers as a "brier among the beanpoles, or a fierce little animal with claws and teeth bared" (99); described as a weed or an animal, Hetty's strong will and eccentricity lead to her dehumanization. Similarly, Jenny is considered "somewhat fantastic" as a result of a failed love affair that has rendered her "love-cracked," according to the villagers (54); her "eccentricity," which the church authorities believe is a "possibly uncanny deviation from the ordinary ways of life," leads to the "witch-hunt" that Betsey thwarts (59). Jenny's outsider status has "tinctured her whole life with an alien element" (54); Freeman's use of the term alien here suggests both foreign and nonhuman.[9]

Beyond these strange characters who are othered due to their eccentric natures, Freeman also aligns othering with the experience of otherwise normative characters who are situationally marginalized during neighborly encounters. While Sarah, Candace, and Betsey are not initially considered odd in the way Jenny and Hetty are, each of them comes to be seen as strange by the authority figure with whom she clashes in their encounter. The minister in "The Revolt of 'Mother'" finds Sarah to be "beyond him," noting that "[he] could deal with primal cases, but parallel ones worsted him" (133). Following one of her interstitial performances in "A Village Singer," Candace is accused by her nephew of being "crazy," and the visiting minister too "could not account for such violence, such extremes, except in a loss of reason" (88, 87). The deacon and minister who encounter Betsey in "Christmas Jenny" describe her as transformed and frightening: "They were thankful to leave that small, vociferous old woman, who seemed to be pulling herself up by her enthusiasm until she reached the air over their heads, and became so abnormal she was frightful" (59). In their deviation from the restrictive, normative behavior in their regional communities, Sarah, Candace, and Betsey, too, become strange.[10]

But strangeness alone is insufficient to enact social change in the service of neighborliness in Freeman's stories; it is in the interaction between the marginalized, liminal figures and those in positions of authority that the transformative potential of the neighborly encounter is realized. The encounters themselves are characterized by the temporary inversion of power Turner describes as central to the liminal phase. In "The Revolt of 'Mother'," for example, Sarah speaks in language and is described in terms that highlight her power and authority in her confrontation with the minister. Sarah "returned [the minister's] salutation with dignity" before defending herself with a spirit previously hidden by a "meek front" (132). Sarah asserts that she has "[her] own mind an' [her] own feet" and needs only consult with God about her decisions, arguing for her full humanity as a Christian with direct access to God, rather than a wife who is subservient to her husband's control and divine intervention (133). Similarly, in "Life-Everlastin'" Luella is described as having an almost extrasensory perception during her conversation with the visiting minister: "Luella . . . looked at the minister. Her deep-set blue eyes seemed to see every atom of him; her noble forehead . . . seemed to front him with a kind of visual power of its own" (71).

This combination of unexpected physical and verbal power can be seen throughout Freeman's neighborly encounters. In "A Village Singer," when Reverend Pollard calls on Candace with the aim of gently reprimanding her, Candace speaks forcibly and effectively, highlighting the hypocrisy of the church and the social fabric of the village. Rather than acceding to the clergyman's admonishments, Candace defiantly defends her disruptive singing, strategically pointing out the congregation's un-Christian duplicity: when Pollard suggests they "kneel and ask the guidance of the Lord in the matter," Candace refuses, noting that it wasn't the Lord who created this situation, but rather status-conscious people "'gettin' as high-steppin' an' fussy in a meetin'-house as they are in a tavern, nowadays'" (86, 85). Candace's strategies here resemble Betsey's emotional defense of her neighbor in "Christmas Jenny," as both women point out the Christian hypocrisy at work in their subjugation. Betsey argues, in fact, that Jenny's care for wounded or sick animals and a young disabled child "'mounts to jest about as much as sendin' money to missionaries'," elevating her strange neighbor's behavior from eccentric to Christ-like (58). Candace, too, uses native logic and the assertion of her own authority to engage in discursive cultural criticism; her dying words, a negative commentary on Alma's singing, reassert herself as the authority on quality singing from outside of the bounds of both the church building and patriarchal authority.

The inversion of social hierarchies during the neighborly encounter does not just empower the marginalized; during these encounters, characters who hold positions of power within the normative structures of the community are described in terms that highlight their loss of mastery as they meet these marginalized figures. In "The Revolt of 'Mother'," the minister "stood awkwardly," spoke "helplessly," and uttered "perplexed apologetic remarks" during his encounter with Sarah, while Adoniram similarly loses the power of speech (132–3, 134). In "A Church Mouse," Deacon Gale and two other church authorities stand before Hetty "stiff and irresponsive," speaking hesitantly and "feebly" to the stubborn woman (101–2). In "Life-Everlastin'," Reverend Sand is "filled . . . with amazement and terror" as he confronts the agnostic Luella (72). So, too, does Reverend Pollard encounter Candace's defense of her singing protest in "The Village Singer"—never imagining that a quiet New England woman could engage in "such violence, such extremes," which he likens to "the elements of revolution" (87) and does not feel competent to address.

In these encounters that promote neighborly values, Freeman repeatedly re-creates alternative strategies of representation that resist normative structures. While these neighborly encounters most obviously promote neighborliness within the regional communities Freeman depicts in her stories, they also serve a larger purpose: as a culturally resonant image of the proper mode by which regionalism's urban audience should approach a region's "strange" inhabitants. As many critics have noted, in dramatizing the encounter between "native" and "stranger," regional literature frequently functioned as a seemingly fixed point of reference against which to define normative national identity. In my examination of neighborliness, the dramatized encounter is intraregional, further unsettling the supposed fixed categories of identification. While these characters are indeed strange, the function of their strangeness isn't to reinforce others' normalcy, but to call into question these fixed categories of identity on multiple scales. While Freeman's ministers, husbands, socially conscious housewives, and other characters who have embraced their positions within the normative structures of their communities do initially define themselves against deviant characters' strangeness, the project of neighborliness refuses to allow these figures to reaffirm their own normalcy by these means.

This is because the recognition of common humanity that is key to the project of neighborliness demonstrates that transformation is communal, not just individual. The power liminal figures gain during neighborly encounters translates into social restructuring on multiple scales. For example, "The Revolt of 'Mother'" transforms Sarah's social standing, both within her family and in the eyes of the community: Sarah's rebellion inspires an "inborn confidence" in her children for their mother, who anticipate the encounter between their parents in the new house with "pleasant excitement" (133), and the townspeople who learn of Sarah's revolt are similarly captivated, "[pausing] to look at the staid, independent figure on the side track" (132). Similarly, in "Christmas Jenny," the minister and Deacon Little begin their patriarchal survey of Jenny's house "remorselessly," but following their encounter with Betsey, they speak "apologetically," and vow to support Jenny rather than condemn her (56, 59). The collective nature of neighborly transformations is even more apparent in "A Church Mouse," in which it is the support of other women, who combine efforts with Hetty and against the male church officials, that enables a communitarian compromise. In addition, following the dramatic encounter between Hetty, the male church authorities, and the women who come to her aid, Hetty takes further steps toward promoting neighborliness: Hetty's act of bell-ringing to "awaken" the town on Christmas Day solidifies her authority as sexton while also supporting a relatively new tradition (keeping Christmas, which, when Hetty was young, was not common in the village), one that unites the townspeople and breaks from strict Congregationalism. Freeman's use of the word "awakened" in this context is intriguing, considering the religious overtones the word carries—Hetty is the instigator of the awakening, and it is an act that unifies the community along neighborly rather than traditional domestic or civic lines. In this, "A Church Mouse" resembles the conclusion of "Christmas Jenny," where Jenny's Christmas candle serves as a symbol for the community's privileging of neighborly values.

The collective efforts of Hetty and the women of her village, Jenny's communally enjoyed candle, Arabella and Luella's excessive generosity toward their neighbors, and the many other encounters between liminal and normative figures in Freeman's stories reveal a thematic pattern of disruption and transformation in the service of neighborliness, or the elevation of non-domestic bonds of neighborly kinship within a community. The project of neighborly reconciliation in Freeman's fiction, which illuminates the oppressive nature of normative structures, pivots on acts of generosity and hospitality for outsiders. This radical hospitality is illustrated in stories like "The Great Pine," in which a man named Dick, having returned home from a lengthy sojourn at sea, discovers that during his absence his wife married a neighbor man, had a child with him, and died. The baby and the new husband, who is bedridden by illness, are being cared for by Dick's daughter. In this unusual domestic setting, Dick both gives and receives hospitality as he is welcomed by his replacement and as he chooses to become caretaker to the motley assortment. As in the other stories collected in *Six Trees*, "The Great Pine" builds on a central metaphor—in this case, the pine tree of the story's title represents the paradoxical binary of solitude and fellowship, polarities with which Dick wars. Freeman's narrator muses about the "intimate connection and reciprocal influence" among "all forms of visible creation"—initially illustrated with the care Dick eventually shows to the tree, but ultimately embodied in the radical neighborliness Dick extends to his wife's second husband and family (241). Dick's conversion to neighborliness by the story's end is echoed when the great pine falls: "He was no more to be seen dominating the other trees, standing out in solitary majesty among his kind" (247). Dick's transformation, like that of the forest, illustrates the collective purpose of neighborliness, opposing the "solitary majesty" and individual domination typical of normative, hierarchical structures.

"Among New England Neighbors"

In a letter to her friend and editor Mary Louise Booth on 15 March 1887, Freeman expresses distress with the proposed title for her first story collection for adults and wonders "if Among New England Neighbors would have been any better" (Kendrick 79).[11] Freeman's use of the word "neighbors" here is intriguing, but even more telling in the context of the project of neighborliness is her use of the preposition "among," a term which suggests not only being surrounded by something, but being a member of that something. In contrast to local color and regionalist fiction that dramatizes the encounter between native and stranger in order to both reaffirm the superiority of the urban perspective and infuse regional settings and people with a nostalgic authenticity against which and in the context of which to define modern advancement, the stories in Freeman's *A Humble Romance and Other Stories* and the many stories that followed dramatize a different encounter, one that places the reader "among" their regional "neighbors."

The neighborly encounter's empowerment of the marginalized within the community alongside the transformation of their communities into places that value even the strangest among them is a strategy of representation intended to reimagine the encounters between the urban readers who consume the stories and the regional residents represented by the stories. In this way, Freeman's stories don't just depict encounters between the socially unequal residents of regional communities but work through these literary encounters to display to the consumers of regional literature the proper attitude they should adopt toward both the genre of regionalism and regional residents. As such, Freeman simultaneously employs and exploits the reader's expectations for regional literature's settings and characters, producing scenes of community reconciliation in which categories of normalcy and deviation are unsettled. While Zagarell notes that in some cases, a community's coherence "may be grounded in categorizing certain people as outliers, outcasts, deviants" ("Reflections" 434), the neighborly encounter empowers those who are categorized as outsiders within their own communities to communicate a transformed vision of coherence and unity. By encouraging readers to recognize these outsiders as "neighbors," Freeman's fiction proposes an alternative mode by which outsiders can be assimilated—both into the social fabric of the village and into the broader narrative of national identity.

This assimilation is not without its limitations or its areas of concern, however. If, following Zagarell, we recognize that narratives of community reflect not a purely positive or even benign mode of belonging to communities, then the emphasis in Freeman's neighborly encounters on the collective benefit of neighborliness should be read with caution. Neighborliness is the means by which one's obligation to others—especially to others who exist outside of the closed systems that structure the community—is defined and reinforced. For Freeman, neighborliness bridges the gaps that outsiders—those marginalized within their communities due to reasons of age, solitude, ability, poverty, nonconformity, and gender—have fallen through. But here it is important to note the significance of the community blessing at the end of "Christmas Jenny" and other stories featuring neighborly encounters. As an outcome of the neighborly encounter, the broader benefit to the collective makes the excesses of neighborliness more palatable, particularly when neighborliness is seen as a culturally resonant metaphor for the reception of regional texts and people. In emphasizing the collective benefit resulting from the neighborly encounter, Freeman paradoxically demonstrates that individual empowerment alone is an insufficient cause for the extravagance of neighborliness.

While Freeman's project of neighborly reconciliation offers tantalizing possibilities for reimagining the modes of belonging to regional and national imagined communities, the limitations of neighborliness leave many questions unanswered. Is the transformative insight gained and communicated by marginalized figures during their liminal encounters lost in their reintegration into their communities, or are their communities truly transformed? Freeman's tendency at the end of her stories featuring neighborly encounters to broaden her focus, shifting from scenes centering her "strange" outsiders to a more wide-angle perspective on the entire village, offers an intriguing entry point at which to probe this question. Is Freeman limiting the transformative power of neighborliness by encouraging her readers to focus ultimately on the benefit of collective transformation that reintegrates deviant characters into the fabric of the community?

Freeman's neighborly project is also limited in a more apparent way: her vision of neighborliness asks readers to imagine kinship with marginalized figures who fall outside of normative domestic and civic structures for reasons of age, class, ability, and gender. Absent from this list are those marginalized due to race or ethnicity. Whiteness is presumed in all of these encounters, spotlighting the structural inequalities that are intrinsic to regionalism's vision of community. The inherent whiteness of Freeman's neighbors is perhaps the most obvious limitation of the project of neighborliness, but the role neighborliness plays in service to community reintegration suggests that Freeman's larger message to her urban readers is perhaps not so revolutionary as one might hope. While the metric of neighborliness enables a vision of community formation that exceeds the boundaries of the domestic family and normative religious and civic structures, the regional "other" who is reintegrated into her community is ultimately a relatively safe and familiar outsider, particularly at a time when questions of racial and ethnic difference and nativist notions of national identity were rife. Ultimately, the neighborly encounter is the means by which Freeman's communities move toward a transformed coherence—one that in opposing normative structures and working to redistribute power among the marginalized of the community paradoxically demonstrates that such transformation requires the participation of those in power to truly effect change.

Works Cited

Ansley, Jennifer. "Geographies of Intimacy in Mary Wilkins Freeman's Short Fiction." *The New England Quarterly*, vol. 87, no. 3, September 2014, pp. 434–63.

Fetterley, Judith and Marjorie Pryse. *Writing out of Place: Regionalism, Women, and American Literary Culture*. U of Illinois P, 2003.

Foote, Stephanie. "Neighborliness, Race, and Nineteenth-Century Regional Fiction." *Cambridge Companion to Race and American Literature*. Cambridge UP, forthcoming, n.p.

—. *Regional Fictions: Culture and Identity in Nineteenth-Century American Literature*. U Wisconsin P, 2001.

Freeman, Mary E. Wilkins. "Christmas Jenny." *A Mary Wilkins Freeman Reader*, edited by Mary R. Reichardt, U of Nebraska P, 1997, pp. 50–62.

—. "A Church Mouse." Reichardt, pp. 93–106.

—. "A Conflict Ended." Reichardt, pp. 13–24.

—. "The Great Pine." Reichardt, pp. 238–47.

—. "An Independent Thinker." Reichardt, pp. 25–38.

—. "Life-Everlastin'." Reichardt, pp. 63–79.

—. "The Outside of the House." Reichardt, pp. 414–28.

—. "Peony." *Understudies*, Harper & Bros, 1901, pp. 193–213.

—. "A Poetess." Reichardt, pp. 107–20.

—. "The Revolt of 'Mother'." Reichardt, pp. 121–35.

—. "A Village Singer." Reichardt, pp. 80–92.

Howard, June. "American Regionalism: Local Color, National Literature, Global Circuits." *A Companion to American Fiction, 1865–1914*. Edited by Robert Paul Lamb and G. R. Thompson, Blackwell, 2005, pp. 119–39.

—. *The Center of the World: Regional Writing and the Puzzles of Place-Time*. Oxford UP, 2018.
Howells, William Dean. "The Editor's Study, June 1891." *Critical Essays on Mary Wilkins Freeman*, edited by Shirley Marchalonis, G. K. Hall, 1991, pp. 19–21.
—. "Literary Boston Thirty Years Ago." *Harper's New Monthly Magazine*, vol. 91, no. 546, November 1895, pp. 865–79.
Hsu, Hsuan L. "Literature and Regional Production." *American Literary History*, vol. 17, no. 1, Spring 2005, pp. 36–69.
Kendrick, Brent L., ed. *The Infant Sphinx: Collected Letters of Mary E. Wilkins Freeman*. Scarecrow Press, 1985.
Lutz, Tom. *Cosmopolitan Vistas: American Regionalism and Literary Value*. Cornell UP, 2004.
Reichardt, Mary R. *Mary Wilkins Freeman: A Study of the Short Fiction*. Twayne Publishers, 1997.
Rosenblum, Nancy L. *Good Neighbors: The Democracy of Everyday Life in America*. Princeton UP, 2016.
Storey, Mark. "Country Matters: Rural Fiction, Urban Modernity, and the Problem of American Regionalism." *Nineteenth-Century Literature*, vol. 65, no. 2, 2010, pp. 192–213.
Turner, Victor. *Dramas, Fields, and Metaphors: Symbolic Action in Human Society*. Cornell UP, 1974.
—. *The Forest of Symbols*. Cornell UP, 1967.
—. *The Ritual Process*. Penguin, 1969.
Watts, Edward. "The Midwest as a Colony: Transnational Regionalism." *Regionalism and the Humanities*. Edited by Timothy R. Mahoney and Wendy J. Katz, U of Nebraska P, 2008, pp. 166–89.
Zagarell, Sandra A. "Narrative of Community: The Identification of a Genre." *Signs*, vol. 13, no. 3, Spring 1988, pp. 498–527.
—. "Reflections: Community, Narrative of Community, Mary E. Wilkins Freeman's *The Jamesons*." *Narratives of Community: Women's Short Story Sequences*. Edited by Roxanne Harde, Cambridge Scholars Publishing, 2007, pp. 433–48.

Notes

1. For example, Foote describes the project of regionalism not as "representing a common national past" but characterizing in its diverse communities the conflicts over immigration, industrialization, and modernization that were plaguing the nation (*Regional Fictions* 13). Lutz also defines regionalist literature as exemplified not by nostalgic consistency, but as "dramatiz[ing] the differences between and within classes, regions, sexes, and communities," seeking not resolution but "an oscillation between the sides" (28). Watts similarly focuses on regionalism's "moments of interregional exchange," which are characterized by "continual tension" between loyalty to the region or the nation (178).
2. In this, Freeman's neighborliness resembles historian Nancy L. Rosenblum's discussion of the figure of the "good neighbor" as central to the "democracy of everyday life" which shapes our expectations in our daily encounters (7).

3. During the liminal phase, participants are necessarily outside of ordinary grouping systems; they are, as Turner says, "betwixt and between the positions assigned and arrayed by law, custom, conventions, and ceremonial" (*Ritual Process* 95).
4. Foote takes up the topic of neighborliness in a forthcoming essay that comes to some similar conclusions as I do here, although Foote's overall project has a different aim from mine. For example, she defines neighborliness as a "social interaction generated by the accident of physical proximity" that "provides a more nuanced way than community to look at the dialectics between strangers and natives, and at the unspoken but customary obligations people owe to one another." However, Foote's essay differs from mine in some key ways. One of these is that she describes Freeman's neighborliness as "almost always [having] an expressly legislative function," chief among which is "help[ing] to draw boundaries between different social actors" (5). While I also read Freeman's neighborliness as exploring the limitations of traditional conceptions of community within normative structures (Foote specifically discusses the structural forces of the domestic sphere and US imperialism), my examination ties neighborliness to liminal encounters that work to erase boundaries rather than further reinscribe them. I am grateful to Stephanie Foote for generously sharing this essay with me in draft form, and I look forward to engaging with her ideas more when the essay is published in the forthcoming *Cambridge Companion to Race and American Literature*.
5. In the case of *The Jamesons*, Zagarell argues, Freeman offers a "canny critique" of the regionalist narrative of community, turning "the genre into a satire of *Country* and other regionalist works for their unquestioned metropolitanism and proffers a community that differs" from other regionalist communities (such as Jewett's Dunnet Landing) which are steeped in tradition (440).
6. Zagarell notes that Freeman's *The Jamesons* "might be called a narrative of community preservation, for its six sketches focus on Mrs Jameson's assaults on community life and the community's deepening skill in withstanding her" (441).
7. Turner calls the more direct and egalitarian exchanges that grow out of the ambiguity in social relations created by liminality "communitas." While Turner describes these exchanges as "essentially opposed to structure," he also notes that communitas is simultaneously invested in remaking social structures from within (*Dramas, Fields, and Metaphors* 243).
8. This is similar to the conclusion of another of Freeman's stories of frustrated women artists, "A Poetess" (1890). What seems like a spiteful act at the story's end (Betsey Dole's request that the minister who unknowingly destroyed her dreams of writing poetry bury her with the ashes of her burned poems) is in a sense a criticism of the confining structure of the church, which, rather than offering true Christ-like welcome to someone like Betsey, instead replicates social hierarchies.
9. The "strangeness" I discuss here has been read by Ansley as "queer" ways of identifying. Ansley also argues that disability, poverty, and non-reproductivity are seen as deviant because they don't contribute to (or produce workers for) the capitalist system. In many of Freeman's stories, Ansley notes, "characters' orientation to space is 'queer' insofar as their perceived relationship to their environment is shaped by their disaffection from the demands of capitalism as it pulls them toward normative spaces of capital, biological, and social reproduction" (452–3).

10. Foote notes that regionalism "both displaces cultural anxiety about strangers, as well as paradoxically registering the fact that anyone may become an alien, an exotic fetish," a phenomenon she reads as a result of "the smooth function of commodity culture" (*Regional Fictions* 57); here, the "alienation" of Freeman's characters is certainly related to commodity culture, which I see as one component of the hierarchies of power Freeman examines in her stories.
11. Booth apparently suggests a geographically based name ("Green Mountain Stories"), which was used in advertising the stories, although the publisher's original title, *A Humble Romance and Other Stories*, was ultimately the final title, as Brent L. Kendrick notes (448).

2

"HER OWN CREED OF BLOOM": THE TRANSCENDENTAL ECOFEMINISM OF MARY E. WILKINS FREEMAN

SUSAN M. STONE

Although not a nature writer in the traditional sense, many of Mary E. Wilkins Freeman's works explore intriguing relationships between human characters and the natural world.[1] For Freeman, nature is more than mere backdrop; it is front and center, personified, glorified, liberating, mysterious, and transformative. A literary innovator and an early ecofeminist,[2] Freeman frequently drew from the ideas proposed by the antebellum, essay-writing transcendentalists[3] by reinventing the boundary between human and nonhuman. Moreover, Freeman's numerous short stories, novels, and critical pieces[4]—as well as her involvements with Annie Fields's literary salon,[5] the New England Women's Club,[6] and the Quiet Hour Club[7]— realize Margaret Fuller's vision for a true, *female* author of American literature,[8] a "second-wave" transcendental realist[9] who believes that the inner worlds of the soul and intellect correspond to the outer world of "Mother" Nature.[10] Like many of her transcendentalist predecessors, Freeman utilized her writing to promote key goals: social reform, respect for the individual and self-culture, and the study of one's corresponding relationship to environment. However, Freeman's efforts and influence go beyond the eco-critical aims of the earlier writers by showcasing forward-moving, influential fictional protagonists who actually achieve and reflect on these lofty aspirations. At the center of Freeman's stories "Christmas Jenny" (1888), "Arethusa" (1901), "The Great Pine" (1903), and "The Apple-Tree" (1903), characters educate and improve themselves and their worlds. They challenge and change restrictive views on gender, not only prioritizing and appreciating the spiritual beauty and companionship of the natural world—as did the first-wave transcendentalists—but also protecting it, confronting and transforming environmental irresponsibility and the patriarchal institutions who seek to perpetuate nature's destruction for profit.[11]

Ecofeminism emphasizes "the ways in which both nature and women are [mis]treated by men and patriarchal society," calling for "an egalitarian, collaborative society in which there is no dominant group" (MacGregor 286; Merchant 193). Since Françoise d'Eaubonne's 1974 introduction of the term,[12] several offshoots have emerged, yet most ecofeminists seek to end social injustice and oppression through nonviolent action and respect, advocating the protection and conservation of wildlife and natural resources. For some, ecofeminism is spiritual in its recognition that "the Earth is alive" and humans are linked to it in both knowable and unfathomable ways (Starhawk 73–86). For others, ecofeminism "argues that both nature and women be respected" (Spretnak 3). It is inclusive, redemptive, empowering, and often gynocentric. Freeman, writing a half century after the transcendentalists and half a century before d'Eaubonne, embraced these ideals in her fiction, a genre that afforded her opportunities the nonfiction-writing transcendentalists (or even modern ecocritics) did not have. Freeman's characters do not merely ask questions and philosophize about the world around them; they also actively explore and respond to those queries and environments. This essay argues that Freeman is the bridge between first-wave transcendentalism and ecofeminism, her stories the ties that bind. She presses the reader to consider the varied relationships her characters have not only with flora and fauna, but also with place, landscape, and each other in a rapidly shrinking natural world[13] (Spretnak 3). Like her contemporary and friend Sarah Orne Jewett, Freeman "uproot[s] rigid notions of gender," examining the impacts of patriarchy and industrialization on women, children, and the environment and creating complex "hybrid" New England landscapes (Alaimo 16). Resisting "environmental degradation," Freeman foregrounds the need for diverse, balanced ecosystems containing both human and nonhuman inhabitants (Gaard and Murphy 2). She questions and reimagines power dynamics and emphasizes ecological stewardship, blurring boundaries, inviting the outside in, and providing readers with option-filled alternatives to socially prescriptive (and restrictive) domesticity and gender conventions.

Although Freeman's early ecofeminist views are possibly the first to appear consistently in American fiction, sociologist Susan Mann notes that "from the late-nineteenth through the early decades of the twentieth century, women in the United States played important roles in the conservation and preservation of wildlife, as well as in environmental activism" (26). These individuals, including Freeman, were "both women's rights activists and environmental activists as precursors to ecofeminism" (Mann 26). Moreover, Freeman and fellow author and literary salon member Sarah Orne Jewett,[14] expanded upon the ideas of transcendentalist Margaret Fuller, who "laid important ground work for ecofeminist theorizing" in *Summer on the Lakes, In 1843* (Forbes and Jermier 322). In this work's "nascent critique of the ideologies of imperialism, sexism, and racism," Fuller "foresaw how masculine hegemony bound together land, women, and minorities" as "exploitable commodities" (Steele xi–xlix). Indeed, Sanjay D. Palwekar asserts that Fuller's entire journey West was "a reaction against the maternal and industrial development that was taking place in America in general, and around New England in particular," one in which she "appreciates all aspects of nature and grieves for degradation of human existence due to patriarchal development projects" (165). From Fuller, Freeman inherits the recognition that the "fate of nature is linked to the fate of women" (Palwekar 164).

Freeman's nature educates, transforms, democratizes, and often appears distinctly female and matriarchal. In her holiday tale "Christmas Jenny," Jenny Wrayne—a self-fulfilled, middle-aged artist and independent thinker whose surname calls to mind the obvious natural homonym of "rain"—dwells on the side of a mountain. A "model for female insurgency," Jenny introduces the wild into her woodsy domicile by creating an early animal sanctuary for creatures harmed by man; she offers the reader "feminist possibilities for inhabiting spaces in which human and animal, nature and the domestic, merge and collide" (Alaimo 16, 41). In sync with her environment, Jenny appears as "a broad green moving bush," a "green woman" who "love[s] and defend[s] nature while engaged in ordinary life" ("Christmas Jenny" 52; Dixon 162–3). She not only utilizes the pine trees' cast-off cones and boughs for creating magnificent holiday art and an income, but she also "melts" into the trees, literally becoming one with the forest.

As Leah Blatt Glasser notes, Freeman frequently "defines herself against rather than within the context of male values" (80). As happy in her hermitage as Thoreau was in his cabin by the pond, Jenny interacts regularly with only two humans: her young, adopted son—an effeminate, pinafore-wearing, "deaf-and-dumb" child rejected by society—and her timid neighbor Betsey Carey, whose stubborn, abusive spouse Jonas throws "temper tantrums" ("Christmas Jenny" 51). Only "caring" about himself and dominating his wife and surroundings, mulish Jonas resents and fears nature—and sylvan Jenny—because he gets lost in the woods and cannot navigate the ice to fetch a pail of water. Embodying Freeman's critique of destructive masculinity, Jonas aggressively fights nature and is satisfyingly thwarted by it. Creative and maternal Jenny, on the other hand, appreciates nature's beauty, respects its functionality, and successfully traverses the rugged terrain to help Betsey when Jonas cannot. Jenny's easy connection to nature simultaneously emasculates Jonas and empowers her.

Although Jonas and the community's patriarchs try to marginalize and oppress Jenny, she doesn't let them. Much to the collective male consternation of the townsmen—and to the confusion of the brainwashed townswomen who unquestioningly adhere to the rules of the cult of domesticity and who have been taught to fear the forest—this able artist-woman leads a happy life, calling to mind both Hawthorne's Hester Prynne and a grown-up version of Sylvia, from Freeman's favorite Jewett story, "A White Heron." Jonas, the minister, and the deacon judge Jenny as lonely, "fantastic," and "love-cracked" because she isn't married, yet Jenny loves and is loved. Although she shuns "the reg'lar road of lovin'," Jenny is an early example of cultural ecofeminism,[15] an "Earth-mother" who challenges and intimidates the patriarchal order. She is self-sufficient, moves freely up and down the mountain, and spends her earnings nurturing her child and hungry, injured blue-jays, rather than donating to the church or buying man-made trinkets (58). The xenophobic villagers misunderstand Jenny. She is their urban legend—a mystical (m)Other. And, when the church leaders seek to confront Jenny at her "curious sylvan" home, she is—naturally—out in the woods (55). Justifying their breaking and entering by claiming their own righteousness, the minister and deacon are immediately unsettled by the unconventional deaf-and-dumb youth, "who looked up in their faces with an expression of delicate wonder and amusement" (55). The gender-nonconforming child cannot—or will not—talk to the townsmen, and they do not understand the room full of "wild and inarticulate" creatures Jenny is nursing back to health, whose chatter "seemed to have a meaning of its own" (56-7). The men are flummoxed, out of their element. As they contemplate the cacophonous scene, which they believe to be evidence of Jenny's cruelty and witchcraft, Betsey bursts in, declaring "fiercely" and "like a ruffled and defiant bird" that she "ain't goin' to have [them] comin' up here to spy on Jenny, an' nobody to home that's got any tongue to speak for her" (58). One of Jenny's beloved loyal "flock," Betsey returns the protection and affection Jenny has given by adding her new-found voice—a mediating, clarifying one—to the unclear but "eloquent appeal" begun by the boy and the beasts (55). When the men ask what "mischief" Jenny is up to, Betsey proudly tells them that Jenny rescues creatures injured by men and "lets 'em go again" when they "git well" (58). Full of fire—and before the interlopers can get in a word—Betsey chastises the duo, asserting that they, like all men, are unwanted trespassers, exploiters, and sadistic bullies. They destroy nature, while Jenny "ministers" to its needs, and they need to change their ways, not Jenny.

As Barbara Johns suggests, Jenny is "a mystic," a spinster "so misunderstood by her society that she is considered strange, yet so united with the universe that she is capable of profoundly influencing two of society's most unyielding institutions, marriage and the church" (11). Through her, Freeman shows that "spirituality and feminism are deeply intertwined, and neither can be separated from her environmentalism" (Coturri 61). In Betsey's eyes, Jenny is a "missionary," a better Christian than the male leaders of the church, who jealously judge and seek to eradicate Jenny's sacred space. Jenny cares for the sick, dotes upon the child that society and the church rejected for being "odd," and inspires Betsey to stand up for her beliefs, to act as Jenny's *in absentia* representative—even if she goes against society and her spouse's expectations. Indeed, Jenny's ecofeminist example empowers Betsey to challenge her abusive husband, who would have her home-bound and silent, and impelling her to speak "in poetry full of fire" about the sacrosanctity of Jenny's woodsy animal sanctuary (58–9). Moreover, Betsey's passion so shakes the encroaching men—who reluctantly admit that they were "on a witch-hunt" because of Jenny's "eccentricity"—that they retreat, mumbling that, "they were thankful to leave" Betsey, "who seemed to be pulling herself up by her enthusiasm until she reached the air over their heads, and became so abnormal that she was frightful" (59). Betsey evolves from victimhood and needing Jenny's charity to being "a veritable enthusiast" and Jenny's champion. Their mutually reciprocal relationship exemplifies the positive ways that Freeman believes women can—and should—support each other, even if they make different life choices. It also suggests that, while Jenny prefers blending into and caring for her environment and avoiding the town and its men, Betsey decides to be no longer invisible to the male members of the community. She feels compelled to be active in influencing and changing them, rather than being submissive and quiet.

Although Freeman's ecofeminist views in the first half of "Christmas Jenny" are clear, she offers two additional, illuminating scenes on Christmas. First, as the Careys approach Jenny's door, Jonas stops in his tracks and refuses to move, recalling Marcus Woodman in Freeman's "A Conflict Ended." At Jenny's urging, Betsey finally puts her own needs first, leaves Jonas to his fit, and enters Jenny's safe space. There, an abundant dinner, courtesy of the now-contrite and converted minister, roasts aromatically, and Jenny's new earth-brown dress—a gift from Deacon Little and "that color she's always liked"—is laid out for the women to admire (61). Seemingly repentant in the face of true charity and missionary work—and perhaps feeling a bit guilty about their own sins—the villagers have also sent Jenny's child pretty "picture-books and cards, and boxes of candy, and oranges," which the rapt youth giggled over and clutched "all tightly gathered into his pinafore" (61). Here, Freeman utilizes loving, decidedly feminine descriptions of the happy child as one who is "delicate" and "full of wonder" in "pink and white" ("Christmas Jenny" 61). In doing so, Freeman promotes Fuller's assertion that there is "no wholly masculine man, nor wholly feminine woman," nor should there be (Chevigny 263). By repeatedly using traditionally girlish descriptors for Jenny's ward—"dressed like a girl," wearing a "gingham pinafore," with "pretty, soft, fair hair" in a "smooth scallop over his full white forehead"—Freeman blurs gender identity (56). With a nod to Fuller's use of appearance and "dress code as another index for rebellion," Freeman implies that Jenny's child possesses an admirable adaptability, a creative, hopeful femininity that thrives in the freedom of the forest—a versatility she far prefers to ignorant, toxic masculinity. And, rather than continuing attempts to remake Jenny into the submissive, married image of what they believe women should be, and rather than shunning her as a witch or pariah, the townsmen have sent her a peace-offering dress the color of "earth," of nature itself.

Together, Jenny and Betsey "confront male institutions and transcend the witch-hunt," protecting the natural world and their relationship while eliciting change (Glasser 83). With "Christmas Jenny's" conclusion, Freeman considers the ways in which nature and women's abilities facilitate individual, spiritual, and social reform. When Jonas refuses to enter, Jenny treats him as one might a stubborn or skittish woodland creature: she ignores him. And, when she does, Jonas's gaze shifts to the wintery wonderland, with its language of animal tracks and soft, glittering snowflakes. With no one to yell at, he has to listen. In that moment, Jonas experiences an Emersonian epiphany; standing "on bare ground . . . uplifted into infinite spaces," Jonas's "egotism vanishes" (*Nature* 144). Alone in nature on Christmas Day, his perspective shifts, and he discovers its beautiful divinity, changing for the better. He is spiritually awakened in and redeemed by nature—and Jenny. Aware for the first time that he is "part and parcel of God," Jonas voluntarily enters Jenny's abode, which is described as a sort of natural chapel (*Nature* 144). There, he "sits with sober dignity" and smiles for the first time at her unconventional ward, who knowingly returns his grin ("Christmas Jenny" 62). With both her internal light and the physical candle she gives him for the dark journey home, Jenny helps Jonas see his path and understand how he is connected to everything and everyone around him. She shows him that "disconnecting from the natural environment impacts humans negatively" (Coturri 53). Together, Jenny and Betsey rescue Jonas from rigid, patriarchal ideas about gender, the environment, and marriage. They open his eyes to nature's power and teach him to compromise with his wife and appreciate difference. Jonas realizes that "Christmas Jenny's candle was something more . . . its own poem," a gift that warms Jonas and illuminates both his path home—and to truth (52). Like Fuller, Freeman knows that, "if you have knowledge," it is imperative to "let others light their candles in it." Because of Jenny's example, Jonas and the churchmen become more open-minded and less oppressive. They finally understand Fuller's idea that one must "enter into the nature of another being and judge" by "its own law" ("Essay on Critics" 6–7). They grow.

Freeman's thought-provoking ecofeminism and preoccupation with the transcendental powers of nature peak in *Understudies* (1901) and *Six Trees* (1903), as she challenges the narcissistic, masculine notion that humanity is somehow the major player while plants and animals are merely understudies. Written in a time of increasing incursions on and destruction of nature, including trees, these stories offer a "natural item employed as metaphor," one with "potentially transforming powers" (Reichardt, *SSF* 77). In *Understudies*, Freeman offers a dozen profiles of plant- and animal-characters —all of whom she assigns distinct personalities and recognizable souls, and each of whom interacts with a human protagonist with whom they co-occupy center stage. In "Arethusa," a story of kinship and correspondence, the maturation of the titular plant parallels and informs the development of a young woman appropriately named Lucy Greenleaf. Nymph-like, Freeman's human protagonist—another of her "green women"—feels more at home in nature than in the man-made and dominated town built from deforestation. She finds it easier to love the sweet-smelling Arethusa, a type of pink swamp orchid, than the boy next door. Unlike Freeman's early flower lovers,[16] Lucy does not want to domesticate the Arethusa, which reveals to her the "poetical and ultra-imaginative" (161). Nor does *she* wish to be domesticated. The plant is Lucy's antidote to the confines of "True Womanhood" and her old-fashioned, tellingly unnamed mother, who thinks Lucy a "queer child" and unrelentingly pushes her to marry Edson Abbot, a man who both "treat[s] the tillage of the earth from a scientific standpoint" and sees nature as a problem to be solved, an enemy to be conquered for personal gain (151, 154). When her mother advocates matrimony, Lucy resists, wanting only to coexist in reciprocity with nature, to protect and preserve the rare, inspirational Arethusa. She cries, "Oh, mother, I don't want to. I don't want to marry anybody. I don't like men. I am afraid of them" (155). Like a woodland creature hunted, Lucy always has the "impulse of flight in her eyes, like a rabbit or a bird" when Edson comes calling. He wants to domesticate her, to "demand . . . her obedience," but Lucy enjoys her "wild impulses" (157). When she reluctantly agrees to wed, mostly to please her mother, Lucy almost immediately regrets the decision. Here, Freeman's early ecofeminism waxes biographical, as she criticizes the submissiveness that society, including other females, expected women to show their spouses.[17] Again, Freeman makes critical connections between men's exploitation of nature and their domination over women, lamenting women's oppression of one another and all things wild and free in order to uphold "True Womanhood."

When Lucy hesitantly confides to Edson that her beloved Arethusa is in bloom, any possibility for a deeper, meaningful connection between the two humans disappears. Rather than suggesting that they enjoy viewing it together—alive and gloriously thriving in its wild habitat—Edson declares that he will pluck all the blooms for Lucy to enjoy at home, as a passive, domesticated recipient of his destructive, short-sighted gift. His commodification of the sublime and lack of respect for the value of the living flower recalls a disturbing memory Fuller shared in *Summer on the Lakes, in 1843* about her first awe-inspiring view of Niagara Falls. As Fuller stood transfixed by nature's strength and glory, a man "walked close up to the fall, and, after looking at it a moment, with an air as if thinking how he could best appropriate it to his own use, he spat into it" (*Summer* 15). This moment revealed to Fuller that men "have a clash of material interests" and "would do well to harmonize themselves with nature's simultaneously physical and moral truths" (Palwekar 171). Likewise, almost a death blow to his relationship with Lucy, Edson's declaration marks a critical turning point in the relationship and Lucy's understanding. With his comment as her bargaining chip, Lucy fiercely threatens, "If—if you do that, if you pick that flower, I—I will never marry you" (161). Edson relents.

On the evening of the nuptials, Lucy goes missing. Resplendent in her flowery wedding finery, she is a runaway bride. Rather than completely acquiescing to Edson's—and her mother's and society's—restricting terms for marriage and the submission of her will to a man's, Lucy "set herself against him in a last assertion of her maiden freedom" (165). Rebelling, she journeys to the swamp to visit her "sister," returning late and under her own conditions. This powerful reversal of the male idea of journeying in nature for the purpose of conquest to a female quest for inspiration shapes the rest of Lucy's and Edson's lives. Recalling Edna Pontellier in Kate Chopin's *Awakening*, married-Lucy—still referred to as "Lucy Greenleaf"—comes "to an awakening either of latent cleverness or inherited instincts" (163). Like Fuller and the twentieth-century cultural ecofeminists she predates, Lucy believes that "if there is any hope of transcending the crude utilitarianism of America of her time," it will be by harmonizing herself with the multiple truths of the natural world (Palwekar 171). She often visits the Arethusa but "never allow[s] her children to follow her," seeking "the fair neutral ground of the flower kingdom as a refuge from the exigency of life" (168–9). Here, Freeman explores what Glasser calls "the geography of gender" (215–16). For Lucy, nature is female and provides a "safe space" away from the harmful forces of men. It is an antidote to their oppression. If the lovely-but-fragile sister-flower can bloom amid the slime, she too can reach her own potential, despite the gendered limits placed upon her. Lucy and her sister-Arethusa perfectly illustrate Fuller's assertion that "plants of great vigor will almost always struggle into blossom, despite impediments" (*Woman* 49).[18] The Arethusa helps Lucy prioritize and force compromise, and Lucy morphs into another of Freeman's ecofeminist "green women," adaptable beings who thrive in the sunlight but are able to maintain their selfhood even in shade. Although she marries Edson, Lucy retains a separate identity and her name. Yet, her feet and thoughts often travel beyond the domestic, prescriptive roles of wife and mother. When the Arethusa blooms, Lucy visits, adding another stanza to her life. The Arethusa adds "a fair rhyme to her little halting verse" ("Arethusa" 161), thus providing a "symbolic landscape whose moral events signif[y] the state of women entering the twentieth century" (Donovan 119). Moreover, as Lucy's interactions with the Arethusa lead to clarity and she grows increasingly cognizant of her need to keep some things to and for herself, her spouse becomes less aware, less authoritarian, and less masculine. He thinks, in warlike terms, that he has "won" her over; however, "in his full tide of triumphant possession, he was as far from the realization of the truth as was Alpheus, the fabled river god, after he had overtaken the nymph Arethusa" (169). Edson "never knew that, while forever his . . . she was forever her own" (169). A wonderfully open-ended text, "Arethusa" invites the reader "to consider what the dreamy and sensitive 'flower' of a girl gains or loses by marrying the worldly, forceful, impatient man," and vice versa (Reichardt, *SSF* 83).

In the critically well-received *Six Trees*, Freeman poses prescient questions that foreshadow modern conservationists' concerns. She asks:

> "Who shall determine the limit at which the intimate connection and reciprocal influence of all forms of visible creation upon one another may stop? A man may cut down a tree and plant one. Who knows what effect the tree may have upon that man, to his raising or undoing?" ("Great Pine" 79–80)

With half as many stories as *Understudies*, this slim volume—Freeman's favorite—expands upon her growing anxiety about the commodification of nature and humanity's need for balance. Each story argues that trees are "something akin to a testimony of God"; not only are they divine and better companions to people than their human counterparts, but "one cannot exist without the other" ("Elm Tree" 5; "Balsam Fir" 126). Together, they "constitute a small Emersonian forest amid the terrain of Freeman's landscape" (Luscher 365). "Nowhere" in American literature, Perry Westbrook asserts, is "Emersonian doctrine, the touchstone of transcendentalism" incorporated "so consciously and so successfully" (112).[19]

In "The Great Pine," Freeman traces the "mystical, intimate connection" of the natural world to the human spirit (Reichardt, *SSF* 85). The reader first meets the "majestic" Pine-protagonist, then encounters the restless human traveler, a former sailor-soldier who wanders lost in ever-expanding circles around the compelling Pine. One of Freeman's most intricate and evocative ecofeminist explorations, this work recalls both Emerson's "Circles" and *Nature*, suggesting that the "moral influence of nature upon every individual is that amount of truth which it illustrates to him" (*Nature* 39). While under the regal Pine, the nameless traveler—who, like Adam in "The Slip of the Leash" and Hawthorne's wayward Wakefield, has abandoned his wife and children in search of something more—develops direction and purpose ("Great Pine" 79). Yet his quest for knowledge is not without price. When the phallic Pine seems to mock his lack of masculinity and internalized feelings of inferiority, the insecure man attempts to eliminate the tree's "whispering voice" by setting fire to it. The only form of change he can imagine is destruction. Yet, before the flames catch,

Figure 2.1 "The Great Pine." Illustration from *Six Trees*, 1903. Image courtesy of Thompson Library Charvat American Fiction Stacks, Thompson Library Special Collections, The Ohio State University Libraries.

the traveler hears a "divine" utterance urging him to take responsibility and become a good man, to alter himself rather than his surroundings. Viewing the tree as "a prophet with solemnly waving arms of benediction," he instantly repents and fights the fire with body and soul (78–9). In some "unknown fashion this seemingly trivial happening . . . tune[s] him into a higher place in the scale of things than he ha[s] ever held," and "for the first time in his history," the outcast "rose superior to his own life" (79). "Through saving the tree from himself," he "gain[s] a greater spiritual growth than the tree had gained in height since it first quickened with life" (79). This scene is pivotal. After receiving the Pine's grace, the man evolves from lost soul to pilgrim to disciple. Like Jonas Carey, he simultaneously undergoes a *bildungsroman* and a spiritual awakening at the hands of nature. Becoming a conservationist—a late-to-the-table advocate for preserving and protecting the environment—the wanderer transitions instantly from ignorance to insight, from destruction to protection, from anger to joy, and from insensitivity to that which is beyond the senses—all because of a tree. As Matthiessen notes, "the parts of [Freeman's] stories one remembers are these flashes of illumination" (100).

Freeman does not merely personify nature; she also naturalizes humanity. After rescuing the Great Pine, now described as both masculine and maternal, the lonely man miraculously gains a sense of direction and a name: Dick. He stops walking in circles and starts questioning not only his place in the world, but also the significance of all of God's creations, discerning "the miraculous in the common" (*Nature* 55). As Dick waxes transcendental about "his own smallness and the largeness of nature which seem[s] about to fall on him," he ponders his mortality and duty to his human kin (80–1). In a Darwinian twist, Dick returns home humbled and ready to beg forgiveness for abandoning his family, accept responsibility, and embrace his family only to discover his wife dead, his house ice-cold and empty, and his children living with a deathly ill man, presumably his deceased wife's lover. Rather than fleeing his responsibilities or seeking to dominate the fellow, Dick compassionately nurses him and cares not only for his own children, but also the other man's. In addition, Dick willingly assumes traditionally feminine, domestic tasks, "wash[ing] and iron[ing] like a woman" (96). Moving back and forth across the line between the wild and civilization, Dick sheds both the influence of his regimented, destructive occupation and civilization's gendered pressures upon men to be hands-off parents and unemotional economic providers. Nature impacts Dick on an intimate level, once he is finally able to be open to its teachings. By embracing his interconnectedness to those living and lost, "the whole establishment was transformed" (96). Again, Freeman's hybrid landscape breaks down gender roles, suggesting that, in nature, "the male characters [become] more 'feminine' and the female more 'masculine'" (Alaimo 58).

With her "power of vivid and delicate description," Freeman sees nature "in its relation to human passion. It is what the tree [symbolizes] that appeals to her imagination" (Tutwiler 91). In "The Apple-Tree," Sam Maddox and his impoverished, proto-hippie family "had become in a certain sense, a part of the soil, as much the weeds and flowers of the spring" (175). Like the tree's roots, the Maddox clan's "bare toes clung to the warm, kindly earth with caressing instinct" (175). The happy, well-behaved children play like docile squirrels, as they "grubbed in [the soil] tenderly with little, clinging hands" and "burrowed in soft sunny nests" (175). Although their fastidious neighbors, the Blakes, think them poor and uncivilized, the Maddoxes' nature-loving simplicity renders them rich. The sustainability-driven tree-lovers wonderfully illustrate Thoreau's 1856 journal comment, "that man who is richest whose pleasures are cheapest" (*Early Spring* 115). For Sam, the world is "dreadful pretty" ("The Apple-Tree" 207). He likes the disarray and originality of the wild, its Emersonian "unity in variety," and he thinks the divine way of ordering or situating the world superior to the resource draining ways of patriarchal society ("The Poet" 164). Although the Blakes pity the Maddoxes, the reader pities the Blakes, who sweep the dirt like an enemy from their floors and box in their tiny yard with a tall fence. They are trapped in meaningless lives, unable—or unwilling—to connect to nature and humanity in any productive way. They want to cut the branches of the Apple-Tree that hang over their wall, to throw away the rotten fruit and sell or eat the remaining, as a fee for the tree's encroachment upon what is perceived as theirs. Sadly, they see nature solely as "a commodity to be transformed rather than as beauty to be appreciated" (Luscher 377).

This blatant contrast of views seems to be Freeman's response to Emerson's query: "To what end is nature?" (*Nature* 27). If the Blakes are to be scolded, Freeman only praises the Maddoxes, a family of literal tree huggers who reflect a pre-fall Edenic simplicity and an honest acceptance of (and appreciation for) nature, one not tainted by their eating of the tree's fruit. Unlike the Blakes, the Maddoxes do not wish for more than they have; they appreciate all that life offers. And, whereas "eating the Edenic apple resulted in a more rigid distinction between the sexes," the Maddox offspring who dwell under the Apple-Tree "are unmarked by gender and nearly indistinguishable from their environment" (Alaimo 61). Like the child in "Christmas Jenny," they become gender-fluid "green children," the apples of their parents' eyes. The Maddoxes and Freeman's other "green" characters, not content to lead what Thoreau would call "lives of quiet desperation," embrace nature as companion and mentor, as a source of solace and a place where they can throw off rigid gender restrictions (Walden 3). They appreciate and protect it. As it was for Fuller, the "earth is [their] school," and they are free of capitalist trappings (*WNC* 112). Sam rejects Sarah Blake's money and her philosophy that one must always work harder, earn more, and buy unnecessary things. A pacifist who shares household duties equally with his wife and rejects gendered social expectations, Sam coexists harmoniously with his family and the "Apple-Tree." Under its nurturing, protective branches, his children grow strong beyond the dangers of commodity-driven, patriarchal society. And, away from the sins of the city, the family approaches an insightful awareness, embracing the "essential facts of life" and constantly striving to live as "simply" and "deliberately as nature" (Thoreau, *Walden* 69).

Mary E. Wilkins Freeman's early ecofeminist fiction seems particularly prescient, given both current environmental concerns and contemporary global conversations about gender identity, equity, and women's empowerment. Her fiction rejects restricting stereotypes, challenges social norms, and promotes self-knowledge through the transcendental understanding that "the Supreme Being" "does not build up nature around us, but puts it forth through us, as the life of a tree puts forth new branches" (*Nature* 38). In "Christmas Jenny" and the works of *Six Trees* and *Understudies*, boundaries blur and characters bloom, as "every object [in nature] rightly seen, unlocks a new faculty of the soul" (*Nature* 23). For Freeman's non-conforming characters, all roads lead to self-discovery, growth, and change, often via unexpected and unconventional means. Freeman breaks down rigid definitions of gender, and she shows nature is worth fighting for and speaking up about. A champion of social and environmental justice, Freeman argues that the natural world not only provides for those who have been denied—or who have been afraid to claim—a voice or a viable place of their own in society, but it also fosters a non-violent yet passionate will to action and advocacy, a philosophy similar to the powerful activism of the #MeToo movement a century later. In her own era, one defined by domestic ritual, industrialization, declining agrarianism, and "True Womanhood," Freeman boldly explores what might happen if one were to follow their "own creed of bloom," to live "beyond the household garden" and "civilization" in reciprocity with wild and untamed nature and without being "defined by others' labels" ("Bouncing Bet" 100; "Lombardy Poplar" 149).

Yet, her ideas are far from outdated. For those of us living a century later in a world filled with ever-growing and complex concerns about gender identity and parity, sexual harassment, sustainability, public environmental policy, and deforestation, Freeman's works are transformative; they place gender at the center of the analysis of—and solutions for—environmental problems, and they argue that the natural world and our relationships with it and each other are at the core of overcoming discrimination and effecting both personal and social progress.

Works Cited

Alaimo, Stacy. *Undomesticated Ground: Recasting Nature as Feminist Space*. Cornell UP, 2000.

Chevigny, Bell Gale, ed. *The Woman and the Myth: Margaret Fuller's Life and Writings*. Northeastern UP, 1994.

Coturri, Giana Maria. "Fled for Shelter to a Heart of Nature: Gender and the Environment in Mary Wilkins Freeman's *Six Trees*." MA Thesis, UNC Greensboro, 2015.

D'Eaubonne, Françoise. *Le Féminisme ou la Mort*. P. Horay, 1974.

Dixon, Terrell F. "Nature, Gender, and Community: Mary Wilkin's Freeman's Ecofiction." *Beyond Nature Writing: Expanding the Boundaries of Ecocriticism*, edited by Karla Armbruster and Kathleen R. Wallace, UVA Press, 2001, pp. 162–76.

Donovan, Josephine. "Mary E. Wilkins Freeman and the Tree of Knowledge." *New England Local Color Literature: A Women's Tradition*. Frederick Ungar, 1983, pp. 119–51.

Emerson, Edward, ed. *The Complete Works of Ralph Waldo Emerson, Volume I*. Houghton Mifflin, 1903.

Emerson, Ralph Waldo. "Circles." *Essays and Poems*. Library of America, 1996.

—. *Nature*. James Munroe & Co., 1836.

—. "The Poet." *Selected Writings of Ralph Waldo Emerson*. Signet, 1965.

Evans, Deborah M., with the assistance of Heidi L. M. Jacobs Editorial Assistant, and Jennifer Putzi Editorial Assistant. "Annie Adams Fields." *American Women Prose Writers, 1870–1920. Dictionary of Literary Biography, Vol. 221*. Edited by Sharon M. Harris, Heidi L. M. Jacobs, and Jennifer Putzi, Gale Group, 2000, pp. 120–7.

Fisken, Beth Wynne. "'Unusual' People in a 'Usual Place': 'The Balking of Christopher' by Mary Wilkins Freeman." *Colby Library Quarterly*, vol. 21, no. 2, June 1985, pp. 99–103.

Forbes, Linda C., and John M. Jermier. "Experiencing Niagara Falls from the Perspective of an Early Ecofeminist: An Introduction to *Margaret Fuller's Summer on the Lakes, in 1843*." *Organization & Environment*, vol. 13, no. 3, September 2000, pp. 322–7.

Freeman, Mary Wilkins. "The Apple-Tree." *Six Trees*. Harper & Brothers, 1903, pp. 171–207.

—. "Arethusa." *Understudies*. Harper & Brothers, 1901, pp. 151–72.

—. "The Balsam Fir." *Six Trees*. Harper & Brothers, 1903, pp. 100–28.

—. "Bouncing Bet." *Understudies*. Harper & Brothers, 1901, pp. 99–119.

—. "Christmas Jenny." *A New England Nun and Other Stories*, 1888. Rpt. in *Mary E. Wilkins Reader*, edited by Mary Reichardt, U Nebraska P, 1997, pp. 50–62.

—. "The Great Pine." *Six Trees*. Harper & Brothers, 1903, pp. 67–99.

—. "Lombardy Poplar." *Six Trees*. Harper & Brothers, 1903, pp. 129–68.

Fuller, Sarah Margaret. "A Short Essay on Critics." *Papers on Literature and Art, Part 1*. Wiley & Putnam, 1846, pp. 1–8.

—. *Summer on the Lakes, in 1843*. Charles S. Francis & Co., 1844.

—. *Woman in the Nineteenth Century and Other Writings*, 1845. Edited and introduced by Donna Dickenson. Oxford UP, 1994.

Gaard, Greta, and Patrick D. Murphy, eds. *Ecofeminist Literary Criticism: Theory, Interpretation, Pedagogy*. U of Illinois P, 1998.

Glasser, Leah Blatt. *In a Closet Hidden: The Life and Work of Mary E. Wilkins Freeman*. U of Massachusetts P, 1996.

Johns, Barbara. "Love-Cracked: Spinsters as Subversives in 'Anna Malann,' 'Christmas Jenny,' and 'An Object of Love'." *Colby Library Quarterly*, vol. 23, 1987, pp. 4–15.

Kendrick, Brent L., ed. *The Infant Sphinx: Collected Letters of Mary E. Wilkins Freeman*. Scarecrow, 1985.

Klawunn, Margaret. "The 'New Women' of Suburbia; A Study of the Quiet Hour Club of Metuchen, New Jersey." *Journal of Rutgers University Library*, vol. 46, 1984, pp. 91–100.

Luscher, Robert M. "Seeing the Forest for the Trees: The 'Intimate Connection' of Mary Wilkins Freemans's *Six Trees*." *ATQ*, vol. 3, 1989, pp. 363–81.

MacGregor, Sherilyn. *Beyond Mothering Earth: Ecological Citizenship and the Politics of Care*. UBC Press, 2006.

Mann, Susan Garland. "Gardening as 'Women's Culture' in Mary E. Wilkins Freeman's Short Fiction." *New England Quarterly*, vol. 1, no. 1, 1998, pp. 33–54.

Marchalonis, Shirley. "Another Mary Wilkins Freeman: *Understudies* and *Six Trees*." *ATQ*, vol 9, no. 2, 1995, pp. 89–101.

Matthiessen, F. O. "New England Stories." Rpt. in *Critical Essays on Mary Wilkins Freeman*. Edited by Shirley Marchalonis. G. K. Hall & Co., 1991, pp. 95–105.

Merchant, Carolyn. *Radical Ecology: The Search for a Livable World*. Routledge, 1992.

Palwekar, Sanjay D. "Ecofeminist Study of Margaret Fuller's *Summer on the Lakes in 1843*." Universitatea de Vest din Timisoara, supplement, November 2012, pp. 163–73.

Reichardt, Mary R., ed. *Mary Wilkins Freeman: A Study of the Short Fiction*. Twayne, 1997.

Smith, Rosamund. "The Celebration of Self-Reliance in the Fiction of Mary Wilkins Freeman" (unpublished diss., U Alberta, 1975).

Sprague, Julia. *History of the New England Women's Club, from 1868 to 1893.* Lee & Shepard, 1894.

Spretnak, Charlene. "Ecofeminism: Our Roots and Flowering." *Reweaving the World: The Emergence of Feminism*, edited by Irene Diamond and Gloria Orenstein, Sierra Club Books, 1990, pp. 3–14.

Starhawk. "Power, Authority, and Mystery: Ecofeminism and Earth-based Spirituality." *Reweaving the World: The Emergence of Feminism*, edited by Irene Diamond and Gloria Orenstein, Sierra Club Books, 1990, pp. 73–86.

Steele, Jeffrey. *Transfiguring America: Myth, Ideology, and Mourning in Margaret Fuller's Writing.* U of Missouri P, 2001.

Stone, Susan M. "A Woman's Place: The Transcendental Realism of Mary Wilkins Freeman." *Towards a Female Genealogy of Transcendentalism*, edited by Jana L. Argersinger and Phyllis Cole, UGA Press, 2014, pp. 377–95.

—. "Transcendental Realism: The Thoreauvian Presence in Howells' *A Modern Instance.*" *Studies in American Fiction*, vol. 27, no. 2, 1999, pp. 149–57.

Thoreau, Henry David. *Early Spring in Massachusetts. From the Journal of Henry D. Thoreau.* Houghton Mifflin and Company, 1881.

—. *Walden; or, Life in the Woods*, 1854. Edited by J. Lyndon Shanley. Introduction by Joyce Carol Oates. Princeton, 1989.

Tutwiler, Julia R. "Two New England Writers—In Relation to Their Art and to Each Other." *Critical Essays on Mary Wilkins Freeman*, edited by Shirley Marchalonis, G. K. Hall & Co., 1991, pp. 90–4.

Westbrook, Perry D. *Mary Wilkins Freeman.* Revised edition. Twayne Publishers, 1988.

Notes

1. Others who have started working on these questions include Stacy Alaimo, Josephine Donovan, Terrell F. Dixon, and Shirley Marchalonis.
2. Here, "ecofeminism" is used not as a "single master theory," but rather a type of literary criticism that illustrates and questions relationships between human and nonhuman nature; views nature as diverse, transformative, and sacred; suggests forms of ecocentric egalitarianism; and recognizes "connections between the exploitation of nature" and the oppression of minorities, including women and children (Gaard and Murphy 3–5).
3. Freeman called Emerson her "spiritual father." For more connections to Emerson, see Leah Blatt Glasser, Rosamond Smith, and Beth Wynne Fisken.
4. Freeman penned over 250 short stories for children and adults, 17 novels, and dozens of poems, critical essays, and letters between 1886 and 1918, many of which appeared or were reviewed in respected venues, including *Harper's*, *Ladies' Home Journal*, *The Saturday Evening Post*, and the *Atlantic Monthly*.
5. For a discussion of this intriguing group, consider Deborah Evans, who suggests "Fields was a bridge between the two ages" of female writers and reformers. Evans also mentions that Fields was a memoirist of Emerson and Stowe, a regular participant and lecturer at the New England Women's Club, and a literary critic (123).
6. For more on the New England Women's Club and Fields's salon, see Julia Sprague, who notes that Emerson and Thomas Wentworth Higginson, Margaret Fuller's biographer, visited both Fields's home and participated in occasional NEWC meetings.

Although nothing exists to confirm Freeman's official membership, Sprague establishes that Freeman had several connections to it and Fuller's legacy through its members, including Elizabeth Palmer Peabody, Ednah Dow Cheney, Louisa May Alcott, and other known friends and students of Fuller.

7. The Quiet Hour Club was a women's group that held bi-monthly conversations on topics ranging from Emerson's "Self-Reliance" to suffrage. Participants had both textual and personal connections to Fuller and other activists from her generation through Susan B. Anthony, Harriet Beecher Stowe, and the club's founder Hester Poole. Freeman was actively involved with the group and friends with Poole, also a well-known writer, founder of the International Council of Women, and a member of Sorosis, "the best known of the pioneer women's clubs of the nineteenth century" (Klawunn 92).
8. See Fuller's "A Short Essay on Critics" (1–8).
9. Transcendental Realism considers turn-of-the-twentieth-century works of fiction as responses to "a transcendental call or ethos." It acknowledges the genre-crossing legacies of first-wave transcendentalists Emerson, Thoreau, and Fuller via half a dozen common thematic connections and literary aims shared by later writers and activists, making it clear that subsequent writers also consciously grapple, albeit in different economic, social, and cultural contexts and via fiction rather than nonfiction, with six central concerns: (1) truth and accuracy of vision; (2) the use of literature to reform society and champion equality; (3) the promotion of individual and self-culture; (4) the exploration and exaltation of the beauty of the real and commonplace; (5) inspiration and interpretation of intuited divinity; and (6) the study of one's corresponding relationship to the environment. See "Transcendental Realism" (149–57).
10. For more about Freeman's feminism and embrace of Fuller, see Susan M. Stone, "A Woman's Place: The Transcendental Realism of Mary Wilkins Freeman" (392).
11. Other nature-centered stories include "Evelina's Garden, "A Gatherer of Simples," and "A Lover of Flowers." Freeman sometimes signed letters as "Pussy Willow" and often wrote about animals, trees, and her garden.
12. The term "ecofeminism" originated in French feminist Françoise d'Eaubonne's seminal text *Le Féminisme ou la Mort*.
13. This is reminiscent of Emersonian "correspondence," which asserts that, since humanity and nature were both made by the divine "Over Soul," they necessarily are connected. See Edward Emerson (25–60).
14. At Fields's famous Boston literary salon, Freeman and Jewett met, socialized, and compared ideas. They also corresponded, with Jewett praising Freeman's short stories and offering her advice. Jewett, by way of relationships with Stowe and Fields, was quite familiar with and fond of Fuller.
15. Cultural ecofeminism contends that women biologically and instinctively have an inherently closer and more spiritual and intimate relationship with nature than men. For more on this, see Carolyn Merchant.
16. See Susan Garland Mann for a fascinating discussion of gardening as "domestic ritual" (33–54).
17. Glasser and Reichardt speculate that "Arethusa" reflects Freeman's swelling anxiety about the possibility of losing her independence in her upcoming marriage to Dr Charles Freeman (Glasser 76; Reichardt, *SSF* 83).

18. In journal entries, *Summer on the Lakes, In 1843*, and *Dial* essays, Fuller wrote about and personified flowers and trees, including roses, pine trees, and the *yucca filamentosa*.
19. Brent Kendrick compares *Understudies* and *Six Trees* to Emerson because of Freeman's "use of the outer world to illuminate the inner man [or woman]" (201).

3

"PREPOSTEROUS FANCIES" OR A "PLAIN, COMMON WORLD"? QUEER WORLD-MAKING IN MARY E. WILKINS FREEMAN'S "THE PRISM" (1901)

H. J. E. CHAMPION

The short stories of Mary Eleanor Wilkins Freeman hum with the whispered secrets of the young girls who hop, skip and jump across her pages, sniffing flowers, clutching dolls, and fiddling with patchwork. Freeman wrote for and about young girls: her first publication was a collection of children's poetry and she remained a prolific writer of juvenile literature throughout her career.[1] Yet Freeman's more adult fiction also regularly evoked the figure of the child, with childhood often portrayed as a site of liberated imagination; child's play a state of possibility and the child a figure of queer potential.

The term "queer" is—by its very nature—hard to define. Its general use in the nineteenth century implied a strangeness, a deviation from what was considered to be "normal." Freeman repeatedly uses "queer," alongside its synonyms "peculiar," "odd," "strange," and "unusual," when describing particular girls in her writing, her use of the word during non-heteronormative situations of ambiguous sexuality or gender confusion foreshadowing its later signification. By 1913 Merriam-Webster had defined the term as "[a]t variance with what is usual or normal; differing in some odd way from what is ordinary; odd; singular; strange; whimsical; as, a queer story or act" as well as "[m]ysterious; suspicious [and] questionable" and "homosexual." Such definitions can easily be aligned with the utilization of the term in contemporary queer theory. David Halperin, for example, states that "[q]ueer is by definition whatever is at odds with the normal, the legitimate, the dominant . . . 'Queer,' then, demarcates not a positivity but a positionality vis-à-vis the normative" (62). Likewise, Michael Warner defines queerness as a "thorough resistance to regimes of the normal" (xxvi) and Annamarie Jagose writes that the term is "necessarily relational rather than oppositional," and that by "refusing to crystallize in any specific form, queer maintains a relation of resistance to whatever constitutes the normal" (98, 99).

Such "regimes of the normal," this essay argues, are put to task in Freeman's depiction of childhood. While her fiction charts the lives and labor of young girls who grow up toward domestic womanhood, Freeman also emphasizes the "uncommon" nature of those who resist such growing up. As such it counters the ways in which childhood is framed as a period of time through which not-yet-grown children pass in a linear fashion towards an acceptable heteronormative outcome. Critic Kathryn Bond Stockton writes how "the child, from the standpoint of 'normal' adults, is always queer: either 'homosexual' . . . or 'not yet-straight,' merely approaching the official destination of straight couplehood" (283). Richard Dyer underlines the uncertainty of youth, calling it a "period of transition, of uncertain narrative outcome" (128). The fact that nineteenth-century literature (including Freeman) typically contained narratives that concluded with the neat and tidy certitude of a happy-ever-after heterosexual marriage, gives special importance to those literary children who resist heteronormative adulthood and bring about an "uncertain narrative outcome." Indeed, while many of Freeman's literary girls grow up, get married, and have little girls of their own, for some this potential future of heterosexual domesticity is deemed particularly threatening. They are doubtful about moving toward what Stockton calls an "official destination," defying social and familial expectations in their hesitation to become married women, a social "stalling" that suggests their particular queerness. A young girl that engages in such non-normative reluctance therefore might easily fit Steven Bruhm and Natasha Hurley's definition of the queer child as one "which doesn't quite conform to the wished-for way that children are supposed to be in terms of gender and sexual roles" (x).

Scholarship on queerness in Freeman's fiction is most often concentrated on adult characters. Critics have proposed several of Freeman's tales as sites of same-sex or "lesbian" subtexts—most notably "Two Friends" (1887) and "The Long Arm" (1895) as well as the novel *The Portion of Labor* (1901). Judith Fetterley and Marjorie Pryse move away from such terminology, stating instead that Freeman "writes from inside the perspective of the queer" (332). For Fetterley and Pryse, regionalist fiction, of which Freeman is an example, is a genre that "self-identifies as non-heteronormative and as resisting regimes of the normal that include regimes of sexuality" (317). They go on to identify queerness in the autoeroticism of "A New England Nun," the oddness of "A Christmas Jenny" and "Sister Liddy," and the underlying homoeroticism of "Up Primrose Hill" (all 1891).[2] Critic Jennifer Ansley locates the queerness in Freeman's characters in their "alienation from forms of biological, social, economic reproduction involved in heterosexual domesticity" (434–5). Such an understanding of queerness allows Ansley to expand the field further, including short stories such as "A Mistaken Charity" and "A Humble Romance" (both 1887), and "An Honest Soul," "A Taste of Honey," and "A Symphony in Lavender" (all 1899) in their analysis.

The following close reading of Freeman's 1901 short story "The Prism" will adhere to a similar line of questioning, with the understanding that heteronormative domesticity within a heterosexual marriage upholds "regimes of the normal." The chapter will first focus on Freeman's protagonist Diantha Fielding's resistance to a traditionally expected linear movement toward marriage, children, and domesticity. Diantha's autonomous pleasure-taking, I propose, borders on autosexuality as suggested through the unruly tangle of the garden as well as metaphorically through the queer world she is able to conjure up with her prism. Finally, the ambiguous ending of the short story begs the question of why Freeman complicates the heteronormative teleology of Diantha before seeming to restore her back to appropriate social kinships through heterosexual marriage. All might not be as it seems, however. The story's inconclusiveness allows for a reading of "The Prism" that suggests the possibility of an imagined queer futurity and urges us to ruminate on the ways in which that futurity may be comprised.

Ignoring the Supper Bell: Diantha Disrupting Domestic Time

Upon first reading, "The Prism" is the story of a young girl growing up and deciding to leave behind her childhood imaginings in order to get married. Yet right from the beginning of the short story, protagonist Diantha Fielding is clearly situated outside of family life, as well as social and gender norms. An understanding of queerness as juxtaposed to heteronormative domesticity allows one to understand Diantha's positioning as a "queer" child. To use Freeman's own synonym, she is clearly in a "curious position" (57), both figuratively and literally, with the reader first introduced to Diantha as she lazes peaceably in her concealed hiding place in the overgrown wilderness of the garden (55). Her position outside the stone wall that marks the boundary of the pasture and the way in which she obstinately ignores the clang of the supper bell situate Diantha outside domestic space, as clearly as the stone wall marks out her stepfather's field.

Diantha's refusal of normative household rhythms—what Elizabeth Freeman has called "domestic-sentimental chrononormativities," or, "the synchronic, synchronized time of middle-class domesticity" (95, 59)—is underlined by her refusal to conform to this marker of domestic time (the bell). In *Time Binds* (2010), Elizabeth Freeman outlines how nineteenth-century domestic space in women's writing was controlled by a "particularly heterogendered and class-inflected chrononormativity, an enforced synchronicity that seems at once to suffocate their female characters and to offer queer possibilities" (39). This heteronormative timekeeping engendered an understanding of time as "seamless, unified, and forward moving" while queer temporalities forge "points of resistance to this temporal order" (xxii). Diantha's refusal to engage in domestic time, symbolized by her disregard for the ringing of the supper bell, therefore underlines her own "point of resistance." To use Elizabeth Freeman's understanding of nineteenth-century literature, Diantha's own narrative outcome swings between potential domestic suffocation and queer possibility, much like the clapper of the bell.

This resistance is further emphasized by Diantha's marked difference from other children; from her stepmother's grandchildren, described as "two little girls in pink frocks" and who have "girlish dreams" of getting married; as well as from her "little step second cousin" Libby, a hyper-feminized child with a "thin, sweet voice" who steps "very cautiously and daintily; for she wore slippers of her mother's, which hung from her small heels" (56, 63, 57, 58, 57). The children's performed feminine gestures show how they are (potentially unwittingly) preparing for their future as conforming women—a future that is itself foreshadowed by the adult female characters surrounding Diantha. These women are normal-because-feminine, as well as normal-because-domestic, with Diantha's stepmother busily washing dishes in the kitchen while her daughter sings a lullaby to her children in "a high sweet voice" (59). Diantha, who can instead be found lazing outside, thus clearly signifies difference from such heteronormative characterization, a queerly incomprehensible figure when compared to those around her.

Ellis Hanson uses Foucauldian language to describe the subjection of queer children to "an unusually intense normalizing surveillance, discipline, and repression of the sort familiar to any oppressed sexual minority" (134–5, 110). Diantha is certainly scrutinized by those around her. Cousin Libby stares at Diantha with "unimaginative wonder," unable to comprehend her strange undomesticated behavior: "she could not understand this other child, who was a law unto herself" (58). Presumably sent by their grandmother to look for Diantha, the two girls in pink frocks are described as "little ferrets" and Diantha is determined not to be sniffed out by them (56). When she eventually slopes into the house much later in the evening, her stepmother gives her a long look: "it was simply the gaze of one on a firm standpoint of existence upon another swaying on a precarious balance" (59–60).[3] Diantha is, to her stepmother, an unfixed, destabilized, and incomprehensible threat to the domesticated order of the house. Her very presence (after lying in the earth) threatens to sully the domestic ideal realized by her stepmother, who "polish[es] the tumblers . . . in ammonia water" and cleans so that "not a speck of dust" remains (60). Her peculiar difference is made obvious to the reader through the "normalizing surveillance" of her stepmother's cold gaze and Libby's perplexed one, Diantha's stepmother embodying the role of agent of repression as she declares bluntly "The supper-table is cleared away" (60). This typical childhood punishment simultaneously denies Diantha access to the domestic space and underlines her unstable relationship to the maternal figure in her home who refuses to nourish her.

Ansley makes a point of the "non-normative formulations of kinship and domesticity" in Freeman's writing, and indeed all notions of traditional family networks are unstable in "The Prism" (434). Diantha's family line is curiously complicated:

> Diantha Fielding, as far as relatives went, was in a curious position. First her mother died when she was very young, only a few months old; then her father had married again, giving her a stepmother; then her father had died two years later, and her stepmother had married again, giving her a stepfather. Since then the stepmother had died, and the stepfather had married a widow with a married daughter, whose two children had raced down the road behind the cows. Diantha often felt in a sore bewilderment of relationships. (57)

Diantha is not alone in her "sore bewilderment" at this complicated web of kinship that Freeman has spun. Indeed, the reader might need to read this explanation several times before becoming more familiar with exactly how Diantha belongs to this family. Diantha's "curious position" is thus derived from her unstable placement in familial structures, her existence a hiccup in a generationally diachronic timeline, uprooted from the traditional kinship diagram of the family tree.

This confused generational timeline is one that Diantha does not seem to want to stabilize, however. Nonchalant in the face of marriage, as expressed by her later admission that she had "never thought much about getting married," Diantha is similarly unimpressed by the notion of children (56). As she lies in the undergrowth listening to the "soft padding of many hoofs," which indicate the hired man driving a herd of cows home for the evening, she can smell "the fragrance of milk-dripping udders," which leak into the "heavy dust of the road" (56). The wasted milk positions Diantha further outside the realm of motherhood, and indeed (unlike her singing stepsister), she "did not like children very well under any circumstances. To her they seemed always out of tune; the jar of heredity was in them, and she felt it, although she did not know enough to realize what she felt" (56). Her denial of the teleological regimes of marriage and reproduction needed for social continuity and her dislike of children due to their "heredity," complicates even further the genealogical linearity of her family tree.

This is illustrated figuratively when, unlike the family tree, strongly rooted and growing upwards, Diantha is shown instead to embody a veritable "curious position," lying "flat on her back" in the undergrowth (57, 55). Diantha's lateral posture mirrors Elizabeth Freeman's understanding of queerness, as an implication of "living aslant to dominant forms" (E. Freeman xv). I read this "aslant-ness" as a metaphorical embodiment of "delay" (Stockton), a disruption of heterotemporal linearities that lead to normative adulthood (304). Unlike Libby, who "married before Diantha, before Diantha had a lover even" (62), Diantha "delays" having a lover, getting married, and having children just as she "delays" answering the supper bell. For Stockton, "delay" is an "ultimately anti-generational" nonnormative growth direction signifying queerness, with queer children "growing sideways" instead of "growing *up*" (281, 279, emphasis in the original). Yet Diantha's alternative "time zone," or "sideways space," i.e. the garden, is not only queered by its function as a delay of her growth towards heteronormative adulthood, it is also queered through the sensual symbolism and the suggestion of deviant desires and pleasures enabled by it. "For everyone," Giorgio Agamben writes, "there is an immediate and available experience on which a new concept of time could be founded . . . it is pleasure." He goes on to underline how the "lack of correspondence between pleasure and quantified time" upheld the "Edenic project of a perfect pleasure [*fin'amors, joi*] outside any measurable duration" (104, qtd in E. Freeman 118). Diantha hiding in the bushes may indeed illustrate such "Edenic project" of pleasurable space in alternative time.

Deviant Desires, Divine Flowers: Diantha's Sideways Space of Sexuality

Let's crawl back into the undergrowth where Diantha hides at the beginning of the short story. It's a hot summer day and Diantha reclines in the lush, "jungle" space, basking in the heat all afternoon (55). There is an air of delicious sensuality in the description of Diantha as she "stretche[s] her slender length luxuriously" amongst fertile, pungent bushes, breathing in the smell of pine, wild grapes, and blackberry-vines (56). Ansley notes the queer "relational quality that exists between Freeman's characters and in their felt relationships to [space]," and remarks that "queer" space is often "invaded by plants and mosses" (452). In "The Prism" Diantha is herself "invaded" by flourishing vegetation to the point that she *becomes* flora. Her first name (of Greek origin) means "divine flower," while her surname "Fielding" reflects the surrounding landscape. In her hiding place amongst the undergrowth Diantha is not only encircled by vines, she *becomes* "as irresponsive as the blackberry-vine" when she is trying to avoid her stepsister's children, and the winding form of the vines is further suggested by her tightly braided hair (56). She is, in a sense, "Field*ing*," in an active engagement with the landscape; she is "almost wild," becoming, that is, part of the wilderness—divine, a vine, a flower, a field.

Diantha is a young girl on the cusp of womanhood—"twelve years old, a child still, though tall for her age"—experiencing the onset of puberty and a stirring sexual curiosity (56), the "reluctantly ripening" wild grapes a bitter metaphor for her own hesitant entry into adulthood (59, 55). Bruhm and Hurley observe that "people mark sexual awakening by a person's ability to reproduce—a stunning index of the heteronormativity that infuses theories of human development (operating with a fairy-tale logic of Sleeping Beauties with pricked fingers)" (xxv). Apart from the fact that Diantha seems entirely uninterested in reproduction, she is also, like Little Briar Rose, enwreathed in a fortress of protective vines. This encircling of creepers suggests that she is at danger of being "pricked" all over (with thorns replacing the spindle). Death surrounds her, and her thrill of "indolent fascination at the virile sprays of poison-ivy" beckons to her as she morbidly dares to touch them: "It was like innocence surveying sin, and wondering what it was like" (55). Diantha is a traditional Eve in Eden, poised on the edge of sexual deviance.

Diantha is surrounded by a queer intermingling of metaphorical signification of deviance, fertility, and Christian sacrifice, leaving the question of her "nature" open to interpretation. Freeman's language here is soaked in biblical imagery, the blackberry runners standing in for the crown of thorns and the deep hue of the berries symbolizing the spilt blood, which might be a subtle recognition of Diantha's puberty and the resulting menstrual stain. A reference to menstrual cycles might be suggested again later in the story when Diantha is alone in her room, bathed in the light of the moon, her head cupped in her hands in a vulvic shape (472). The moon (and Diantha's name) evoke Diana, the goddess of the moon and fertility.[4] The "ripening" grapes represent both fertility and salvation in their link to the blood of Christ, as well as the debauchery of Bacchus rites. As does the ivy, also a sign of fertility and emblem of Bacchus. But Diantha is also described as snakelike—she "loved the heat" (55) and lies "as irresponsive as the blackberry-vine which trailed beside her like a snake" (56)—even though Freeman writes that Diantha enjoys "the gentle languor which is [the heat's] best effect, instead of the fierce unrest and irritation which is its worst. She left that to rattle-snakes and nervous women" (55). By shrugging off clearly defined binary categories or symbols that typically figure the sinful, sexual, and deviant female, Freeman allows Diantha to potentially reclaim her own sense of intimate, autonomous, and pleasurable sensuality. Diantha is a Briar Rose who does not wait passively for her male suitor to arrive but who chooses instead to find sensual pleasure for herself.

The "almost tropical" (read, wet) thicket that grows around her body reflects Diantha's blossoming desires (55). The "gentle languor" she feels in the heat, the references to her shifting body and the sensual imagery of the scene build to a climax—"times of extreme heat," in which Diantha "hung over life with tremulous flutters, like a butterfly over a rose" "realizing to the full the sweetness of all about her" (55). The quivering Diantha again seems to be within moments of death, the orgasmic quality of the writing suggesting that this death could be a *petite* one.[5] Fetterley and Pryse outline the queer nature of sexual autonomy, claiming that Freeman's writing "destabilizes the supposedly stable relations of sex, gender, and desire, raising the profoundly provocative and deeply disturbing possibility that any woman who retains the birthright of self-love may indeed be labeled sexually 'queer'" (317).[6] Diantha can thus be labeled queer through her desire to take pleasure from her own body, the "tremulous fluttering" she feels climaxing in a feeling of intense "sweetness." Hidden in the bushes in a "curious position" of sexual curiosity, outside domestic space and chrononormative time, Diantha is in a pleasurable Edenic bliss in which her masturbatory desires—much like the blackberry vines—are left to grow (sideways). She exists in a "new concept of time," to take up Agamben's proposition, one of pleasure, just for herself.

Nature is thus a metaphor for Diantha's "naturally" blossoming autosexuality, with "nature" tied into her "*nature*" (one which is deemed "unnatural" by society). Bruhm and Hurley write: "If there is anything 'natural' about children it is their curiosity about bodies and pleasure," and indeed, Diantha's curious pleasures are extended by what she imagines through using her prism, the most potent metaphor of the short story.

Fairy Figments and Prismatic Pleasuring: Creating Queer Colors

The metaphorical possibilities created by the prism allow us to develop Stockton's theory of "sideways growth" even further. For Stockton, "meaning is moving and growing in a metaphor even while time almost seems to hang suspended." Much like the prism that hangs in the air (or indeed the butterfly that hangs "over a rose") Diantha's pleasurable "delay" suspends her in time (280). Pointing out the importance of metaphor in our understanding of sideways growth, Stockton uses the metaphor of the dog as a body that represents the lateral movement of growing sideways. While Diantha is visited by an exuberant dog in her hiding place (described as "a friend," 56), this is not the metaphor that is most interesting to explore in "The Prism." Rather, a deconstruction of the eponymous prism itself, will allow the reader to explore the nature of the queer spatiality created by Diantha.

Diantha keeps the small drop of glass hidden under her dress (and over her heart/between her developing breasts) like a pendant, pulling it out when she is alone in order to catch the light and thus envelop herself in rainbow colors, with "wonderful lights of red and blue and violet and green and orange" appearing "before her delighted eyes" (57).[7] When Libby finds her in the undergrowth playing with her prism Diantha decides to confide in her step-cousin, telling her that she has stolen a crystal prism from the best-parlor lamp. Libby is bewildered at the theft but Diantha adamantly replies: "I took it . . . I had a right to it" (58). The fact that this lamp was bought by her (biological) mother with wages earned before she was married situates the prism as a symbol of unmarried autonomy for Diantha, and further underlines its potential to deconstruct domesticity.

Diantha flashes the prism for Libby, asking her what she can see in the colors, but is unsatisfied by her response of "grass and things" (58). It seems that Libby, described by the narrator as "unimaginative" and with "no speculation in her face," is unable to see what excites Diantha (58). The reader, too, is left in the dark for now. It is only later in the story that the true depth of the secret is revealed, that (psst!) Diantha can see fairies dancing in this space of rainbows. One might consider the connection of fairies and rainbows to queerness as fairly modern, yet both have a queer historical signification that should not be overlooked. Indeed, much like the word "queer," the word "fairy" was used to describe camp effeminacy from the 1890s onwards. The *Oxford English Dictionary* references an extract from the 1895 *American Journal of Psychology* VII, which wrote of the "peculiar societies of inverts" who enjoyed parties "where the members dress themselves with aprons, etc., and knit, gossip and crotchet; balls, where men adopt the ladies' evening dress, are well known in Europe. 'The Fairies' of New York are said to be a similar secret organization" (qtd in Scott 216). For illustrator Palmer Cox the words "queer" and "fairy" functioned interchangeably, with his *Brownies* series containing books such as *Queer People with Paws and Claws* and *Queerie Queers with Hands Wings and Claws*. Similarly, E. H. Knatchbull-Hugessen's *Queer Folk: Seven Stories* (1874) depicts fairies and other such magical entities.

The rainbow, now the most recognizable symbol of the LGBTQ+ community (post-Gilbert Baker flag, created in 1978), is much trickier to pin down historically. While it would naturally be anachronistic to assume that a rainbow would have been read by Freeman's readers as queer in the contemporary sense of the word, it is worth considering the signification of the accentuated *difference* found in its shifting colors. The emphasis on the variation of rainbow colors may be said to be in itself a critique of the binaries of black/white, or even of essentialism (with white itself a combination of colors). Likewise, its symbolism as a biblical promise for a better world underlines Diantha's creation of her fairy rainbow world and its potential for autonomous escape from heteronormative expectations.

Andrew Scahill considers *queer* children to be "growing—but not growing up—in a land of never-never . . . a state of permanent impermanence" (5). Diantha's imagined world evokes Scahill's "land of never-never," the prism a metaphor for Diantha's nonnormative sexuality and the key that enables her to "actively [imagine] a necessarily and desirably queer world," as defined by Warner (xvi). Freeman's writing becomes increasingly orgasmic when referencing the prism and creates a prismatic world of autosexual pleasure. Concealed inside her dress, Diantha's treasure seems to arouse her as she pulls it out and "dangle[s] the prism in the rays of the setting sun," her face "flushed, eager to enthusiasm, almost wild, with a light in her blue eyes which did not belong there, according to the traditions concerning little New England maidens" (59).

She has "a feverish rose on her cheeks, which *should have been* cool and pale" (59, my emphasis). Here the transgressive nature of Diantha's (metaphorically clitoral) prism is made evident. By playing with the prism (read, enjoying self-pleasuring/imagining a queer world) Diantha is not doing what she "should have been" doing, nor is she acting "according to the traditions concerning little New England maidens," but rather does not "belong there." The prism thus others her from society, marking her difference from New England heteronormative "traditions."

Jack Halberstam writes how a sense of "*unbelonging* characterizes a queer girl identity" and that "while childhood in general may qualify as a period of 'unbelonging,' for the boyish girl arriving on the doorstep of womanhood, her status as 'unjoined' marks her out for all manner of social violence and opprobrium" (196, my emphasis, 195). While Halberstam links "unbelonging" to gender, it is also Diantha's childlike *curiosity* that marks her out as *curious*, and thus a target for "social violence." As Diantha gazes at her prismatic world, where fairies dance between rainbow colors, there is a "curious expression of daring, of exultation, of fear . . . in her face" (56). Diantha's underlying fear foregrounds her knowledge of the queer nature of her emotional connection to her fairy realm, and foreshadows the social response to such imaginative "delay" as she grows older. Furthermore, the clear juxtaposition of Diantha and Libby and their differing ability to *see* and *believe in* the fairies dancing in the colors underlines their differing "growth." While both girls are growing older, Libby's incuriosity in relation to Diantha's curiosity, or indeed *indifference* as compared to *difference*, clearly queers the latter. Diantha's "curious position" is so peculiar in fact that Libby continues to keep the secret of the prism "all to herself," in an acknowledgement that Diantha's indiscernible nature renders her dangerous and to be avoided (57, 62).

As Diantha grows *older* she resists growing *up* and her difference from those around her becomes increasingly apparent. While Libby is suitably "married before Diantha, before Diantha had a lover even," Diantha remains unintelligible to potential suitors and has thus far been avoided when it comes to the social customs of courtship and marriage (62). The young men in her village are, "for some reason, . . . rather shy" of her, yet this "reason" is never made explicit, explained instead as a result of her "curious impression of mystery" (62). "But," to use Freeman's forbidding words, "her turn came" (62) and Diantha falls into an engagement with the local teacher: Robert Black.

Between Commonsense and Nonsense: Queer Death and Questions of Queer Futurity

It is not long before the ever-pragmatic scholar is compelled to "struggle against" his feelings for the peculiar Diantha (62). Robert begins to reason that she is clearly unsuited to domestic hardship: "He said to himself that she was too delicate, . . . that he ought to have a more robust wife, who would stand a better chance of discharging her domestic and maternal duties without a breakdown" (62). They are, of course, wholly unsuited: unlike Diantha, who derives great pleasure from her imaginary world, Robert is described as a man of "reason and judgment" (62) and while Diantha's prism detracts white light into a multiplicity of colors, Robert *Black* is named after the very absence of color. His name might imply his lack of imagination just as it may also suggest that he is left in the dark as he, like Libby, seems unable to "see" what Diantha is able to. Robert also seems unable, or unwilling, to truly *hear* her. When Diantha repeats twice after his proposal that she "never thought much about getting married," he takes this for a yes, "[catching] her in his arms," and "[laughing] a great triumphant laugh" (62). And thus they are engaged.

As Bruhm and Hurley note, one effect of "projecting the child into a heteronormative future" is that "we accept the teleology of the child (and narrative itself) as heterosexually determined," which results in "narrative pressure on producing the proper ending of the story (the heterosexual adult)" and a "moment of ascension into that heterosexual future" (xiv). For most of the story Diantha manages to avoid this "ascension." Yet her double nature, perhaps emphasized by the "di" in Diantha, not only evokes her underlying (undergrowth) "nature," it may also suggest the inevitable choice she must make: in which direction to *grow*. Not only does Robert, in his assumption of her compliance, take away the choice from Diantha, he also threatens her sideways growth through his obvious disinterest in her queer world.

Unsurprisingly, when Diantha shares her secret and shows her betrothed the prism, Robert laughs it off as merely a childhood toy: "He looked astonished, even annoyed; then he laughed aloud with a sort of tender scorn. 'What a child you are, dear!' he said" (63). Yet when Diantha persists and Robert realizes the depth of her continued emotional connection to this rainbow world, his tenderness dissipates. Robert is unable to see the dancing fairies when Diantha flashes the prism, so she very solemnly "comes out" to him with a "confession of an alien faith" (64). This otherworldly revelation strikes visible fear into her lover, who turns pale and "brutally" declares: "For heaven's sake, put up that thing, and don't talk such nonsense Diantha!" repeating "Don't talk such nonsense. I thought you were a sensible girl" (64). A modern reading of the phrase "coming out" aside, the contrast of "sense" and "nonsense" outlines how childhood imagination is queered when expressed in lived adulthood, to the point of a potential indication of insanity.

Robert panics when he realizes that the childhood notion of fairies still has a place in Diantha's adult present, terrified to see that "there was in her eyes a light not of her day and generation, maybe inherited from some far-off Celtic ancestor—a strain of imagination which had survived the glaring light of latter days of commonness" (63). Here "commonness" is juxtaposed to "queerness,"

Diantha's nonsense situating her in some form of alternative time, a strain of the Celtic in a Puritan New England. For Robert, who sees only "prismatic colors" (a man of his—scientific—time), the fear of Diantha having a "breakdown" (62) has become a real possibility. Robert sees Diantha's fairy world as merely "preposterous fancies" and worries that she may not be "right in her mind" (64). Freeman threads in metaphorical hints as to her protagonist's sanity throughout the story, with Diantha treated with suspicion by both her family and the people in the village from a young age. Her connection to a "Celtic ancestor," her summoning of the fairies, and her subsequent ostracism lends itself to a reading of Diantha as "witched," emphasized by the light of the full moon as it illuminates the moment she dreams in her bedroom window (61).[8] The shift from lunar light to *lunacy* is significant to a story that contrasts common sense and *non*sense. Robert Black, fearful for her sanity, steps back from courting Diantha.

It seems that Diantha must choose between her autonomously queer space of rainbows and the "common" world of heterosexual marriage with Robert. She chooses the latter, and he eventually accepts her apology, emphasizing her infantilism and unreasonable nature in the process: "'It's all right, little girl,' he replied; 'but don't let such fancies dwell in your brain. This is a plain, common world, and it won't do.'" Diantha replies docilely: "I saw nothing; it was only my imagination" (65). Chastened, Diantha goes through the motions of becoming "common," through stepping back into a linear teleological social time and learning to "unsee." Such a sacrifice of her own pleasures results in death, albeit a metaphorical one, as she decides to win Robert back by disposing of her prism and burying it in "a little grave . . . out of sight" (65). Interring the prism transforms it into a common object: a grimy piece of glass rather than a portal to the fairies. Diantha in turn becomes common, washing and drying her hands of the "oozy soil" and repeating to her future husband: "I have put it away, Robert . . . I saw nothing; it must have been my imagination" (65). Thus, in exchange for life as a common woman in a heterosexual marriage, Diantha's "uncommon" imagination and autosexual desire must be both literally and figuratively submerged. Diantha therefore conceals her secret deep in the earth, away from the sun where it can no longer cast prismatic light and thus consumed by the darkness that Robert Black represents. She washes her hands clean of her*self*, having learned that her prism and all it signifies must remain hidden if she is going to be socially accepted as Robert's wife.

"The Prism" seems to imply that playful spaces of imagination must be ignored and childish "preposterous fancies" must be deeply buried in order to comply with the "plain, common world" of regulated heterosexual adulthood. Certainly, after she becomes Robert's wife, Diantha is described by the narrator as "improved," "a fine housekeeper" with "common sense" and a "fitting mate for her husband, whom she adored" (65). She is "very happy" and indeed "[f]or the time being at least all the mysticism in her face had given place to an utter revelation of earthly bliss" (65). So far, so traditionally normal, yet Freeman also leaves a small clue for the reader as to the potential for future resistance. Indeed, as Freeman makes clear, this happiness is only "*For the time being at least.*" The last paragraph of the story emphasizes how Diantha remains inherently attached to what her prism represents:

> Sometimes Diantha, looking from a western window, used to see the pond across the field, reflecting the light of the setting sun, and looking like an eye of revelation of the earth; and she would remember that key of a lost radiance and a lost belief of her own life, which was buried beside it. Then she would go happily and prepare her husband's supper. (65)

Like before, we find Diantha gazing from the window, this time caught in the light of the sunset rather than the moon. Although she is now—as Robert's wife—firmly tied to the domestic space, the tinge of regret she may feel at making such a personal sacrifice is made clear, as she reminisces over "that key of a lost radiance and a lost belief of her own life." Might the ambiguity of this perhaps not so "happily ever after" ending serve to give Freeman's readers a potential radiant glimmer of hope for an alternative queer narrative ending?[9]

Before her marriage, Diantha is indisputably queer. She does not belong to any categories that might identify her: neither girl nor woman, neither orphan nor daughter, neither masculine nor feminine, neither completely wild nor completely tame. She is, to quote Elizabeth Freeman, "out of time," whether for the supper bell or indeed any sort of expected heterosexual future, her delay in the face of marriage a queer disruption of chrononormative growth. It is not only her reluctance to grow into a heterosexual future of domesticity, marriage, and reproduction that "queers" her, it is also her "world-making" through the use of the prism, the creation of her sideways "land of never-never." Diantha's space of fairies forms a "nonsensical" resistance to "common" heterotemporal linearity and allows her to grow sideways, her imagined world resulting in a rejection from normative reality. When Robert appears, Diantha is reluctant to leave behind the queer potential of her prism and the inevitable burying of her nonnormative sexual desires. Yet, after her marriage, it seems that Diantha has chosen a "plain, common world" over her own "preposterous fancies" (65). However, the ambiguity of the ending allows the reader to conjecture that Freeman was perhaps nurturing for Diantha a hope for a queer futurity that can also be found in the writing of her contemporary, Sarah Orne Jewett, whose diary from 1867 shows that she wrote for an imaginary female reader "a hundred years from now," while Willa Cather called *The Country of Pointed Firs* "a message to the future" (qtd in Fetterley and Pryse 1).[10] This "message to the future" reflects the contemporary queer theory of José Esteban Muñoz, whose notion of "queer futurity" is a hopeful and enthusiastic future of liberation, "the warm illumination of a horizon imbued with potentiality" (1). Indeed, while Diantha's horizon of the setting sun implies a fading of color, one is also aware that the sun must rise again.

Understanding Freeman's fiction as a site of queer world-making and futurity enables contemporary readers to understand the subversive value of her work as an early example of historical queer potential. "The Prism" also allows one to note similar portrayals of narrative stalling in other short stories by Freeman (see "Arethusa" (1901) for example), as well as that found in the writing of her contemporaries. Kate and Helen in Jewett's *Deephaven* face a similar queer choice of whether or not to grow up, as does Sylvia in "A White Heron" (1886). Similarly, Sylvia's choice to stay in nature reflects that of Ellen in Alice Brown's "A Flower of April" (1900), who avoids her unwanted suitor by staying in the garden.

By leaving the ending of "The Prism" ambiguous, the reader remains unsure as to whether Diantha, a "divine flower," will grow *up* towards the "glaring light of . . . commonness" and eventually shrink and wither on the stem (much like Libby, who "was like a flower, which would blossom the same next year, and the next year after that, and the same until it died" 57–8), or whether she will one day again grow *sideways*, amongst the "broken lights across the fields," like the evergreen winding creepers of her hiding place in the undergrowth. Indeed, perhaps the burial of the prism was not a funeral but rather a planting, a quivering seed waiting in the darkness to grow and explode into a flower of all colors, a promise for the future, much like the biblical promise of hope through the symbol of the rainbow.

Works Cited

Agamben, Giorgio. *Infancy and History: The Destruction of Experience*. Translated by Liz Heron. Verso, 1993.
Ansley, Jennifer. "Geographies of Intimacy in Mary Wilkins Freeman's Short Fiction." *The New England Quarterly*, vol. 87, no. 3, 2014, pp. 434–63.
Bruhm, Steven, and Natasha Hurley. Introduction. *Curiouser: On the Queerness of Children*, edited by Steven Bruhm and Natasha Hurley, U of Minnesota P, 2004, pp. ix–xxxviii.
Cox, Palmer. *Queerie Queers with Hands Wings and Claws*. John D. Larkin, 1885.
—. *Queer People with Paws and Claws*. Hubbard Brothers, 1888.
Dyer, Richard. *The Culture of Queers*. Routledge, 2002.
Ensor, Sarah. "Spinster Ecology: Rachel Carson, Sarah Orne Jewett, and Nonreproductive Futurity." *American Literature*, vol. 84, no. 2, 2012, pp. 409–35.
Fetterley, Judith, and Marjorie Pryse. *Writing out of Place: Regionalism Women, and American Literary Culture*. U of Illinois P, 2003.
Freeman, Elizabeth. *Time Binds: Queer Temporalities, Queer Histories*. Duke UP, 2010.
Freeman, Mary Eleanor Wilkins. "The Prism." *The Uncollected Stories of Mary Wilkins Freeman*, edited by Mary R. Reichardt, UP of Mississippi, 1992, pp. 55–65.

"Gay." *Webster Dictionary*, 1913. <https://www.webster-dictionary.org/definition/gay> (last accessed 10 June 2022).

Halberstam, [Jack]. "Oh Bondage Up Yours! Female Masculinity and the Tomboy." *Curiouser: On the Queerness of Children*, edited by Steven Bruhm and Natasha Hurley, U of Minnesota P, 2004, pp. 191–214.

Halperin, David. *Saint Foucault: Towards a Gay Hagiography*. Oxford UP, 1995.

Hanson, Ellis. "Knowing Children: Desire and Interpretation in *The Exorcist*." *Curiouser: On the Queerness of Children*, edited by Steven Bruhm and Natasha Hurley, U of Minnesota P, 2004, pp. 107–36.

Jagose, Annamarie Rustom. *Queer Theory, An Introduction*. Melbourne UP, 1996.

Kendrick, Brent L., ed. *The Infant Sphinx: Collected Letters of Mary E. Wilkins Freeman*. Scarecrow Press, 1985.

Knatchbull-Hugessen, E. H. *Queer Folk: Seven Stories*. Macmillan and Co., 1874.

Muñoz, José Esteban. *Cruising Utopia: The Then and There of Queer Futurity*. New York UP, 2009.

Poochigian, Aaron. *Sappho, Stung with Love: Poems and Fragments*. Penguin, 2009.

Prins, Yopie. *Victorian Sappho*. Princeton UP, 1999.

"Queer." *Webster Dictionary*, 1913. <https://www.webster-dictionary.org/definition/Queer> (last accessed 10 June 2022).

Scahill, Andrew. *Malice in Wonderland: The Perverse Pleasure of the Revolting Child*. U of Texas, PhD dissertation, 2010.

Scott, Colin A. "Sex and Art." *The American Journal of Psychology*, vol. 7, no. 2, 1896, pp. 153–226.

Stockton, Kathryn Bond. "Growing Sideways, or Versions of the Queer Child: The Ghost, the Homosexual, the Freudian, the Innocent, and the Interval of Animal." *Curiouser: On the Queerness of Children*, edited by Steven Bruhm and Natasha Hurley, U of Minnesota P, 2004, pp. 277–315.

Warner, Michael. Introduction. *Fear of a Queer Planet: Queer Politics and Social Theory*, edited by Michael Warner, U of Minnesota P, 1993, pp. vii–xxxi.

Watts, Emily Stipes. *The Poetry of American Women from 1632 to 1945*. U of Texas P, 1977.

Notes

1. Freeman's early success was as a children's writer. She published the ballad "The Beggar King" in 1881 in juvenile periodical *Wide Awake*, followed by a proliferation of books and poems for young girls that established the author as a leading writer in the genre, a popularity that lasted decades (Kendrick 49).
2. While I have used the term "lesbian" in moments where I specifically reference lesbian literary criticism I will use the term "queer" for my own analysis, not just in an attempt to avoid the potential anachronistic or historically incorrect pitfalls provoked by the use of the term "lesbian" but also to open up the field beyond same-sex female desire and toward overlapping notions of complicated gender and autosexuality.
3. Stockton makes sure to underline that this is not an argument for the notion of arrested development, often used to discredit queer adulthood: "The grown homosexual has

often been metaphorically seen as a child. *Arrested development* is the official-sounding phrase that has often cropped up to describe the supposed sexual immaturity of homosexuals: their presumed status as dangerous children, who remain children in part by failing to have their own" (289). This interpretation is rooted in Freud and is evidently problematic, with Stockton citing its use by certain figures from the "American religious right" to uphold conservative values (289). This chapter does not aim to perpetuate the culture of comparing adult queerness to childish behavior, rather to propose that Freeman's spatial constructions of childish imagination can be understood as a way to achieve pleasurable "queer worlds."

4. The moon might also bring to mind queer-signifying Sappho, who used lunar imagery in many of her poems to describe feminine beauty (see "Off in Sardis" and "Star clusters near the fair moon dim," Poochigian 37, 79). Sappho, whose poems also bloom abundantly with flowers, was used by many female poets at the end of the nineteenth century to signify female autonomy and queer desire. See Prins and Watts for more on the Victorian re-appropriation of Sappho as a queer-signifying figure.
5. "La petite mort," from the French meaning "the little death," describes the death-like sensation felt post-orgasm.
6. Fetterley and Pryse use the example of the autoeroticism that can also be found in "A New England Nun." Their description of Louisa, who "desires to love herself" yet understands the "mismatch between her desire and her gender whose cultural script requires her to want marriage" might easily be applied to an older Diantha (317).
7. Intriguingly, the 1913 entry for "gay" in the Merriam-Webster dictionary defines the term as not just "Loose; dissipated; lewd" but also "an ornament" and "brilliant in colors."
8. By "witched" I mean to signify the ostracism of Diantha for her difference, her attachment to nature, and her non-normative threat. There are clear parallels between "witched" and "queered," both aligned with the notion of the other and positioned against or outside of society.
9. It is difficult to equate the character of a young Diantha who would ignore the bell, stand up to her stepmother, and take pleasure in her own difference, with the adult Diantha who passively accepts heternormativity and marriage to an unimaginative (and emotionally abusive) man. One might question why Freeman herself would want to adopt such a narrative outcome and indeed it is possible that such a heteronormative ending may not have been driven by Freeman's own desire to marry Diantha off suitably. Rather it may signify the market-driven conventions of nineteenth-century women's writing, as well as the expected magazine publication practices, which would never have allowed unpunished portrayals of female sexuality.
10. See also Sarah Ensor's "Spinster Ecology."

PART II

VIOLENT, CRIMINAL, AND INFANTICIDAL: FREEMAN'S ODD WOMEN

4

THE REIGN OF THE DOLLS: VIOLENCE AND THE NONHUMAN IN MARY E. WILKINS FREEMAN

DONNA M. CAMPBELL

When Edith Wharton wrote an introduction to *Ethan Frome* in 1922, eleven years after its original publication, she explained that she had written it because

> the New England of fiction bore little—except a vague botanical and dialectical—resemblance to the harsh and beautiful land as I had seen it. Even the abundant enumeration of sweet-fern, asters and mountain laurel, and the conscientious reproduction of the vernacular, left me with the feeling that the outcropping granite had in both cases been overlooked. (1)

In her autobiography, *A Backward Glance*, Wharton explained that *Ethan Frome* treated "life as it really was . . . utterly unlike that seen through the rose-coloured spectacles of my predecessors, Mary Wilkins and Sarah Orne Jewett" (293). Wharton's characterization of Freeman as drawing a world of "sweet-fern, asters and mountain laurel" through "rose-coloured spectacles," though typical of her time, gravely underestimates Freeman's portrayal of "granite outcroppings" by glossing over the underlying issues of poverty, isolation, and violence underlying much of Freeman's fiction.

Wharton's dismissive portrayal reflects some of the ways in which Freeman has been read by contemporaries and later critics. Praised by contemporaries such as W. D. Howells, but ignored in the era of modernism, Freeman's work underwent a revival in the 1970s and 1980s beginning with the Feminist Press edition of *The Revolt of Mother and Other Stories* (1974) and Marjorie Pryse's

Selected Stories of Mary Wilkins Freeman (1983), both of which focused on feminist themes of women's community and emphasized stories celebrating women's transgressions as resistance to a patriarchal social order. As Mary Reichardt observed in her review of Freeman criticism through 1987, however, this selective focus limited the range of contexts in which to read Freeman. Changes in feminism and a less idealized, more complex vision of women's relationships reveal a shift from "Freeman-the-feminist-communal activist" to "Freeman-the-Gothic-satirist." Stories such as "Luella Miller" in Alfred Bendixen's edition of *The Wind in the Rose-Bush and Other Stories of the Supernatural* (1986) and "Old Woman Magoun" in Reichardt's own *A Mary Wilkins Freeman Reader* (1997) challenged earlier feminist critics' views of the "positive, nurturing quality" in Freeman's work (Reichardt, "Mary Wilkins Freeman" 39). Sandra Zagarell likewise undercuts this 1970s and 1980s feminist vision by observing that *The Jamesons* is instead "a satire of the narrative of community" portrayed in Sarah Orne Jewett's *The Country of the Pointed Firs* (Introduction xxi).

Yet critics have often ignored Freeman's darker themes of theft, violence, and trauma, of acts that are not purely social resistance but actual crimes. The explicit crimes, particularly in her later work, range from kidnapping (*The Portion of Labor*) to neglect ("The Lost Ghost") and murder ("Old Woman Magoun," "The Long Arm," and *Madelon*). More unusual still is the fact that women are portrayed as aggressors and perpetrators in addition to victims. Mrs Magoun, Phoebe Dole, and Cynthia Lennox act deliberately and sometimes with deadly intent, often on initial impulses arising from quasi-incestuous desire, mistaken notions of innocence, or a wish both to dominate and to fuse with, by erasing the autonomy of, another human being. To emphasize this dehumanization, in many stories, Freeman employs a nonhuman surrogate, such as a doll or an animal, to encapsulate and signify the trauma or suffering in a way that renders it visible but still palatable to the nineteenth-century reader. A closer examination of Freeman's treatment of crime shows the ways in which strategies of power and dominance rely on nonhuman surrogates and their capacity to embody and sometimes to catalyze disruption and violence.

Nonhuman Surrogates: Dolls, Animals, and Ghosts

Freeman's many powerless surrogates include dolls, animals, and ghosts, all treated in ways that express the memory of trauma and abuse in her stories. As a means of mediating discussions of the unspeakable, these surrogates are never fully adult human beings but rather mimic their appearance or sentience with the exception of an absent key factor: nonhuman presences such as dolls and ghosts embody a physical resemblance without life, whereas plants and animals embody physical presence, sentience, and emotion without resemblance to human beings. In these ties of kinship with human hosts, Freeman's surrogates possess properties far beyond the touristic objects, souvenirs, or totemic emblems of empire that, as Richard Brodhead, Elizabeth Ammons, Sandra Zagarell, and many other critics have noted, are pervasive in New England regionalism. The material signifiers of poverty, violence, abuse, and trauma that these surrogates represent also align these stories with naturalism, as does the fetishistic use of objects, as Monika Elbert has argued. A further key to Freeman's surrogates is Bill Brown's observation that "in local-color fiction, the most recherché and retrospective of American genres, lies a prehistory of modernist materialism" (125). Freeman's prehistory of "modernist materialism" invests humble objects with freighted meanings that according to Perry Westbrook evoke the Puritan typological connection of human beings to plants and animals. Through the use of surrogates, Freeman emphasizes the dehumanizing patriarchal structures that pit women against each other, against themselves, and against children. Stories of violence show women and their surrogates as little more than the sum total of the aggressor's projected desires, unless the regarded-as-inanimate or powerless surrogate, or the woman she represents, strikes back.

First published in *Harper's Monthly* in 1904, "The Reign of the Doll" brings together two sisters, who had "quarrelled over the distribution of the property after their mother died" (286), through the medium of a misdelivered Christmas gift, the doll of the title. When Fidelia Nutting receives an unexpected package, her estranged sister Diantha, overcome with curiosity, hurries to her door from the house across the way, and the pair open the package to discover a doll, undressed except for an undergarment of "coarse muslin" (288). Drawn together by a shared impulse to dress the doll, they stay up all night making clothes for it and guiltily keep it for a time despite believing that it is meant for a nearby child. Fidelia tries to return it but learns that the child already has many dolls, so the sisters, "themselves . . . the children who loved the doll" (295), keep it and name it "Peace" (296), with the implicit blessing of the neighbors. The doll's squeaky utterances and its helpless state place it in the uncanny state of a nonhuman being that evokes human sympathy, in this case leading to a rapprochement between the sisters that the story suggests only an unbidden gift could accomplish.

"The Reign of the Doll" shows just how closely Freeman connects theft and the giving of gifts as a means of exchanging material goods. A common pattern in Freeman's early stories is that of a transgression such as theft, followed by remorse and reflection leading to moral growth, semi-public confession, and expiation, a classic Puritan cycle of redemption. The insertion of a gift into this process demonstrates how a crime may be expiated materially, through physical objects rather than words. The sisters technically steal the doll, in that they make little effort to find the actual recipient of the package, but their shared guilt draws them together over a small piece of stolen property that the community transforms into a gift. The gift of the doll balances and heals the cause of their estrangement, their inheritance of a larger piece of material wealth, their mother's property. Although not primarily a Christmas story, "The Reign of the Doll" fits Jana Tigchelaar's model of the gift as attending to "the needs of the community" (237) beyond the nuclear family, as it heals a rift between the sisters, whereas in later stories, Freeman follows the later nineteenth-century trend of "thinking about the gift . . . [as] a way of reflecting on capitalism, and vice versa" (3), as Hildegard Hoeller suggests. "The Reign of the Doll" includes both gift and theft: the doll, an unintended gift that is stolen by and then returned to the sisters as a gift, places them outside the market economy of property and inheritance that had initially separated them.

The doll in "The Love of Parson Lord" (1900) embodies Freeman's familiar theme of the inhumanity of doctrinaire Calvinism and the emotional abuse that religion requires in the name of godliness. Parson Lord's commitment to righteousness is expressed in his refusal to recognize his daughter Love's feelings or autonomy as a human being. Having dedicated Love to the service of God, Parson Lord allows her no freedom and no suitors since she is destined to do God's work. Epitomizing this enforced self-denial is Parson Lord's commitment to selling his fine apples to raise money for overseas church missions, without giving Love even a taste of them, a biblical symbol of the earthly pleasures and sexual awareness that he also wishes to deny her. Under his stern neglect and insistence on living life in the future rather than in the present, Love Lord "live[s] as under the self-regulating motive power of an automaton" (4), making her akin to the "homely, rustic" doll that she cherishes (7). When she finds her childhood doll, long hidden as a punishment, her father refuses to let her keep it. Starved of love, Love looks on the Squire's wife, the motherly Madam Diantha, "as if the lady were the Blessed Mary, and she a little papist" (14), a double defection from her father's affection and his religion.

When Love finds a beautiful doll in the attic, she assumes that Madam Diantha has given it to her and, like the sisters in "The Reign of the Doll," feels as though she is stealing it. Like Lily's doll in "Old Woman Magoun," it is a double for her: she carries it with its "pink face looking over her shoulder" (30), and it sends "her heart into blossom" (31).[1] In psychological terms, since her growth has been stunted by an absence of visible parental love, Love behaves much like an infant that conceives people as existing in absolutes: her sense of absolute love toward Madam Diantha matches her sense of absolute duty toward her father, and she cannot imagine him as the giver of the doll and other gifts she receives. Only by reading his diary after his death does Love realize that, although he had kept his vow not to permit her marriage to Madam Diantha's grandson, Richard Pierce, her father had arranged it and that he loved her after all. The story's first two dolls—the first one a gift from a motherly poor woman, which was then confiscated; the second seemingly a gift from a motherly rich woman but actually given by Parson Lord—teach Love how to love and keep her from becoming the third doll, the "automaton" and abstract emblem of her father's service to the Lord that he had trained her to be.

In *Understudies*, trees, plants, flowers, and animals are the surrogates for the inexpressible passions of humanity that rigid social norms do not permit human beings to express. As Susan Griffin has argued, the animal stories in *Understudies* are "fundamentally concerned with language" with "changing scenes in which the roles of human and animal are scripted, improvised, and rescripted . . . highlighting the semiotics of species" (512), practices that blur the boundaries of language and expression between human and nonhuman. In "The Parrot," from *Understudies*, these boundaries are blurred by a parrot that expresses the inner feelings of his owner, Martha, through mimicry of speech and actions. Martha is a New England woman, and he is a tropical bird, but the bright red of his plumage echoes the "compressed line of red" (195) of her lips and confirms his connection as the creature that speaks for her. Because of that connection the words that she cannot utter emerge from his beak: profanities, expressions of pleasure that the handsome minister is visiting—"He's come, Martha, damned if he ain't" (197)—and, more simply, extended repetitions of her name in a town that barely speaks it. Intuiting her pain, the parrot says, "poor Martha, why, poor Martha" as she sobs (200), and her ability to confide in him is like "a healing lotion on a burn" (201). When Martha falls in love with the town's young minister, who courts her for a year, she believes she is about to be married. However, the minister marries another, and when he and his bride come to call on Martha, the parrot destroys the minister's bride's bonnet by "plucking furiously at [its] roses and plumes" (201), the symbolically stolen plumage of both the parrot (feathers) and Martha (the roses of her cheeks when the minister calls). The parrot's revenge, or the meting out of emotional justice, makes Martha determine once and for all the question that has preoccupied her Puritan mind throughout the story: like Félicité with her parrot in Flaubert's "Un Coeur simple" (1877) his action makes her decide that he indeed has a soul.

The parrot's functioning as an emotional surrogate for Martha recalls other animals in Freeman's stories, and, like them, it has sentience and emotion without resemblance to the human form. Unlike the caged, unnamed canary in "A New England Nun," which represents Louisa Ellis's emotional agitation through movement but cannot speak or break free from its cage, the parrot flies free and has the power of speech. With its red plumage signifying passionate rage, power of flight, and profane language, it breaks the norms of the culture, even for birds, and gives vent to forms of expression that seem perverse. Like Aunt March's saucy parrot in *Little Women*, which nips at the dog and irritates Amy, the parrot is the unruly representative of a well-bred woman, whose class and gender should make her the ultimate in decorum but whose emotions erupt through the parrot in words that disrupt the social order. Furthermore, as a tropical bird, the parrot is flamboyantly an outsider in the town, a representative of the colonial trade and imperial power that constituted the economic power base, including the slave trade, that caused New England's rise to power in the seventeenth and eighteenth centuries and its acknowledged cultural dominance in the nineteenth. The parrot has power because it signifies colonial power: it is masculine, a redcoat, and an agent of its own will, choosing of its own volition to express Martha's anguish. As a nonhuman yet not a thing, it has movement and speech yet not the ability to observe decorum, and the uncanny nature of its seemingly random but pertinent utterances cuts through the polite fictions that Martha has been forced to endure in her silent courtship.

Children, Violence, and Trauma

The crimes and use of surrogates in the stories thus far are minor: the theft of dolls and the destruction of a bonnet scarcely rise to the level of a crime, yet they establish Freeman's pattern of using material objects to contain or to signify the otherwise irresolvable conflict at the heart of the text. In other stories, however, the logical consequence of confusing objects as human beings, or of allowing human beings to express their emotions solely through objects, is that the human being begins to behave in violent ways toward the objects of her affection, identification, and rage. As discussed earlier, previous surrogates were nonhuman, possessing physical resemblance without life (dolls) or a physical presence, sentience, and emotion without resemblance (plants and animals). In selected stories, however, Freeman challenges the limits of the surrogate by making it a child or a child ghost. The child has humanity, sentience, and emotion but lacks the agency of adult characters or, in the case of the child ghost, even the physical body of an adult human being, thus rendering it incapable of self-defense in a violent or traumatic situation. The child ghost combines the supernatural implications of never quite being able to attain the future (children) or to leave the past behind (ghosts). Their nonhuman, or non-adult human, presence in material space yet suspended time aligns them with the structures of regionalism's deep time.[2] The question of surrogates and their use and abuse, and of fetishizing a human creature, thus becomes far more serious and violent in *The Portion of Labor*, "The Lost Ghost, "The Long Arm," and *Madelon*.

Although its plot of striking workers has understandably received the bulk of critical attention, *The Portion of Labor* (1901) also tells an underlying story of trauma and abuse through the lonely childhood of one child (Robert Lloyd), the abduction of another (Ellen Brewster), and the attempted murder of a third (Amabel Tenny), often through the agency of a shared doll. When wealthy Cynthia Lennox sees eight-year-old Ellen Brewster and impulsively spirits her away to her own house, she sees the action as a rescue of sorts, a wish-fulfillment fantasy of the fairy godmother whose wealth elevates the child of poverty beyond the means of her parents. But Cynthia's decision to give Ellen a home ignores the fact that she already has one. Freeman critiques the conventional fantasy of the wealthy that lifting individuals out of wage slavery will engender gratitude and that such individual solutions, based in charity, a desire for possessorship, and a rich woman's whims, can effect systemic change. As a child and again as an adult, Ellen soundly trounces the idea that class mobility depends on nurture and the separation of children from their working-class roots. She succeeds despite rejecting Cynthia's offers twice, first as a child by escaping from Cynthia's kidnapping and then as an adult by refusing Cynthia's offer to send her to Vassar.

Freeman signals that Cynthia's treatment of Ellen is abusive in multiple ways. As in "The Love of Parson Lord," the love of a child for an aristocratic woman who showers her with gifts is based on a false perception: that the child's yearnings toward her captor/savior express a natural aristocracy that belies her working-class roots. The damage that Love Lord's father inflicts by too little attention to his daughter is less severe than that which Cynthia inflicts by focusing too much; but the helpless laughter, tender kisses, and other attentions that Cynthia lavishes on Ellen come perilously close to physical violation, especially since Ellen is being held against her will. In discussing *The Portion of Labor*, Leah Blatt Glasser rightly notes Ellen Brewster's later intense passion for her wealthy benefactress Cynthia, but their relationship began when Cynthia abducts Ellen as a child, transforming her into an object, a physical fetish. Never letting Ellen act for herself, Cynthia "washe[s] her and dresse[s] her, and curled her hair" (43) before subjecting her to the "tenderest violence" (43) of affection. Like the child in "The Lost Ghost," Ellen has one repeated question for Cynthia—"Where is my mother?"—and when Cynthia gives her a doll, a "ravishing creature in a French gown," Ellen can only ask, "Where is her mother?" (46). The material goods and extravagant kisses cannot substitute for the presence of Ellen's mother, any more than Cynthia's objectified vision of Ellen can substitute for the genuine love of Ellen's mother, Fanny Loud.

The doll is the medium through which Cynthia attempts to expiate her crimes against Ellen as a child, much as the offer of a Vassar education is the medium when Ellen is an adult. Cynthia treats Ellen as a doll, an inanimate object for her pleasure and entertainment, and as if in recognition, Ellen modifies the doll's clothes to more closely resemble her own. Nor is Ellen's captivity the only time that the doll has been used to pacify a captive child. When Robert sees the doll in the Brewsters' parlor, he identifies it as "my old doll" and laughingly accuses Ellen of being a "child kidnapper," showing that he intuits both Cynthia's crime and Ellen's silence (216). During his reign of owning the doll, however, he had "burned her head with the red-hot end of the poker to see if she would wake up" (216). As befits the masculinity and capitalism that he represents, Robert acts with detached violence against a helpless object that differs from himself, whereas Ellen exerts compassion toward it. Both act according to the impulses of their gender and class. That Robert could torture the doll foreshadows his later instrumental view of the workers at Lloyd's as objects, whereas Ellen's nurturing actions toward the helpless thing prefigure her solidarity with the workers.

The end result of treating human beings as surrogates for emotions occurs in the final plot of the threatened child: Ellen's Aunt Eva's attempted murder of her daughter, Amabel. Loss of work at Robert's factory leads Eva's husband Jim Tenny to abandon the family and take up with another woman, whereupon Eva, driven insane with jealousy and grief, tries to stab Amabel. Stripped of her clothing, the terrified child is "brown despite her blonde hair" (314), marking her as ethnically and racially Other like the immigrant workers whom Ellen addresses in her valedictory speech. Amabel is the body of the victimized working class, marked by skin tone as well as by her defenseless youth, and the chain of assaults that gradually intensify until they reach her signifies the multiplying effects of the abuses of capitalism. As Eva explains, Jim "was just taken up and put down by them over him as if he was a piece on a checker-board" (283), a naturalistic image of causality and power that encapsulates the power relations between owner and worker in an industrial system. And Amabel is the end of the line of causality: like the workers, she is the last in a chain of abusive circumstances and is expected to absorb the blows of those above her.

"The Lost Ghost" deploys the ghost of a child as the surrogate embodying trauma; like dolls, ghosts function as nonhuman presences embodying a physical resemblance without life. As Mrs Rhoda Meserve, formerly Miss Arms, recounts the story, she began to see the child ghost of the title during her days as a schoolteacher when boarding at the house of Mrs Dennison and her sister, Mrs Bird. Miss Arms, who has lost her own home and family, initially believes her to be a five-year-old child of the house. But when the little ghost brings Miss Arms's coat upstairs and says, in what will become her repeated refrain, reminiscent of Ellen's in *The Portion of Labor*, "I can't find my mother," Miss Arms recognizes that she is a spirit, grows faint, and wants to see "somebody or something like other folks on the face of the earth" (216). Only the material world, in the form of the smell of biscuits, brings Miss Arms back to reality. Yet for all of her otherworldly attributes, "the child," as she is called in the story, is astonishingly corporeal. In addition to fetching Miss Arms's coat, she gathers twigs for firewood, dries the dishes, and pulls the cat's tail before Mrs Bird admonishes her and she begins petting the cat instead. The cat "never seemed a mite afraid" (224) despite its being an animal typically "dreadfully afraid of ghosts" (224), another indication of the ghost's position between corporeal and spiritual worlds.

The playfully domestic details of the child ghost who wants her mother soon yield to a darker reality: while the child's father was away on a business trip, her selfish and promiscuous mother locked the child in an unheated room with no food and left the village, and the child starved to death after a week. Miss Arms sees the lost ghost as "a little white face with eyes so scared and wishful that they seemed as if they might eat a hole in anybody's heart" (214), a description that oscillates between embodiment and disembodiment, sympathy and fear: pity for the child's fear, wistfulness, and pale face; and hints of terror in the hunger that might "eat a hole in anybody's heart," not only a longing for her mother but a foreshadowing of the death by starvation at the heart of the ghost's narrative. The premeditated cruelty of leaving her child to starve makes the mother the inverse counterpart of Mrs Magoun, a "murderous mother," in Linda Grasso's term, who feeds her granddaughter to death (Grasso 18).

Throughout regionalist ghost stories like "The Lost Ghost," the quiet surface emphasis on regional community norms and the hidden terror beneath confirms the binary tensions on which the ghost story rests: between spirit and material worlds; the comforting pleasures of the hearth and the uncanny terrors of death and the world beyond; the New England impulse to remain reticent about the supernatural and the urge to unburden oneself to a sympathetic listener; and the community's vision of itself and the absence of true connection for those who are outcast or vulnerable. As in Sarah Orne Jewett's "The Foreigner," in "The Lost Ghost" the terror arises less from the appearance of the ghost than from recognition of one's failure to extend sufficient care, material or otherwise, to help another human being. In "The Foreigner," Mrs Captain Tolland sees the ghost of her mother and is comforted in her transition into death, but Mrs Todd, who witnesses the deathbed visitation, berates herself for the community's failure to extend true compassion to a stranger in Dunnet Landing. The child ghost has no such comfort during her own process of dying. She cries out for a mother who had abandoned her, but a neighborhood woman who "had waked up three nights running, thinking she heard a child crying somewhere" (231) fails to check on the child until it is too late, suggesting, as in "The Foreigner," the failure even of women's community to substitute for the maternal bond.

In theorizing the broader implications of child ghosts in nineteenth-century women's writing, Roxane Harde has argued that "the child ghost [is] a historical and politicized entity" that acts as "the basis of a principled rejection of injustice caused by capitalism" (Harde 190). Although capitalism is the indirect cause of the child's death because her father, a drummer (traveling salesman), must be absent from the family to earn a living, the mother's rejection of her child, first by making her a household servant and then by abandoning her, arises instead from a profound failure of parental love. After the child's death, the father returns and kills his errant wife and himself, but that form of rough justice cannot make reparation for the failure of all the adults in the story to save the child. Even the conclusion, in which the ghost leads Mrs Bird into death, "nestling close to her as if she had found her own mother" (327), seems but a bittersweet consolation for a failure of parental love that, as the story shows, transcends the grave, a sense of loss that lingers even after the body has departed. The child ghost is a surrogate for the terrifying abyss of the absolute failure of family and community that, wrapped in regionalism's snug layers of frame stories and distanced from the present, forms both a cautionary tale for Mrs Meserve and Mrs Dennison and a means of their forming a tighter bond of friendship.

"The Long Arm," which Freeman co-wrote with Joseph Edgar Chamberlin, and which won a $2,000 prize in the 1895 Bacheller Short Story Syndicate Short Story contest, draws on the Lizzie Borden murder case and the lesser-known, but sensational, murder trial of Alice Mitchell for killing her lesbian lover, according to Laura L. Behling. As its first-person narrator, Sarah Fairbanks, "a country school teacher, twenty-nine years of age" (2) reflects on the recent murder of her father, Martin. She is unsure whether she herself has murdered him and states that she will lay out the case but does not know if she is "for or against myself" (1). Based heavily on the Lizzie Borden case, the first half unfolds the murder three times over: first in the recollections of Sarah of that night and a straightforward narration of events that seems at first to point to multiple suspects; second, in the seemingly irrelevant detail of Sarah's engagement to Henry Ellis, forbidden by her father, which provides both herself and Henry with a motive for murder; and finally in her father's heated fight with Rufus Bennett, during which she saves his life by holding Rufus off with her father's pistol. Also borrowed from the Borden case are the inexplicable events that happen to and around Sarah: the always-bolted door should but does not keep out the murderer; her green silk dress sports bloodstains from a source that she does not remember; and she herself reports that, after her father's ultimatum that she never speak to Ellis again, she gives him such a look that "Father turned pale and shrank back, and put his hand to his throat [with 'purple finger-marks'], where Rufus had clutched him" (7). Time extends and becomes indeterminate: after the fight, she sits "until I could see by the shadows that the full moon had risen" (8), and "crie[s] herself to sleep" (9). The elision of time markers and Sarah's heightened perceptions provide further evidence of the uncanny nature of objects that seem to have agency or manifest physical phenomena.

The second half of the story, and the key to the crime, is not Sarah's story but the love triangle between her father, Martin Fairbanks; his next-door neighbor, the "sweet, weakly, dependent" Maria Woods, who weeps at his death; and her masculine-seeming "tall ... very pale and thin" companion Phoebe Dole ("Long Arm" 23, 22). Separated forty years before, Martin and Maria renew their engagement with a ring that Maria keeps hidden from the domineering Phoebe. When Phoebe learns of Maria's engagement to Martin, she steals the ring and uses a "cutting instrument" (15) to stab him and keep Maria for herself. As Behling, Reichardt, and other critics have pointed out, the coded lesbian relationship between the two provides a motive for murder:

jealousy and hatred of a rival, as in the Alice Mitchell case. The locked-room mystery of Phoebe's gaining access to the house is solved when Francis Dix, a detective sent by Sarah's fiancé Henry Ellis, discerns that a person with an extra-long arm could reach through the cat door and unlatch it. After Sarah notices at a church meeting that "Phoebe Dole's arm is fully seven inches longer than mine"—an additional gesture toward her greater-than-average height and other masculine physical traits—and reports this to Dix, Phoebe confesses. Not a child but "childlike," Maria is completely under the sway of the other's "stronger nature" and is treated as an object or fetish rather than as a human being by Phoebe, who with the logic of a domestic abuser decides to possess her totally by killing Martin.

Nobody's Totem: *Madelon*, Race, and the Revolt of the Woman as Doll

Madelon (1896) combines the crime story format of "The Long Arm" with the unflinching and perverse New England will of Freeman's best-known early fiction. Verging on the Gothic with its deployment of violence and characters who cling to their ideas of honor with an absolute intensity, *Madelon* addresses several of Freeman's preoccupations during this period of her career: a nuanced sense of race; unrequited love; the body, sexuality, and desire, including incestuous desire; and a rigid moral absolutism challenged by the dictates of human feeling. Like "The Long Arm," *Madelon* begins with a crime: Madelon Hautville, who is in love with Burr Gordon but believes he has trifled with her affections, stabs a man who grabs her and tries to kiss her as she walks home from a dance one dark night, believing he is Burr; he is instead Burr's cousin Lot Gordon, who survives the attack. The remainder of the novel is a crime story in reverse, for although everyone denies that Madelon attacked Lot, she nevertheless frantically confesses to everyone involved, to no avail. The mystery then becomes how she will prove her guilt rather than her innocence. As Burr, who disputed with Lot over inherited property and would gain by his death, sits stoically in jail for the attack, Madelon agrees to marry Lot if Lot will confess to a suicide attempt in order to free Burr. As the townspeople grow suspicious of Burr and Madelon, despite complicated plot developments that have cleared them both, Lot, wracked with consumption and sequelae from his wound, writes a suicide note exonerating them both and then kills himself, freeing Madelon and Burr to marry. Yet the message of the novel remains: a woman's expiation is not enough, nor is the truth, unless it suits the patriarchy to confirm it. In a patriarchal culture that casts women as innocents, she does not have the freedom to be a criminal and must convince the town of her guilt.

One of Freeman's few mixed-race heroines, Madelon Hautville is of Iroquois and French descent, a heritage that Freeman expresses in largely stereotypical ways: she has dark hair and eyes, a sexually evocative figure, and an initial lack of control over her own emotions. When she stabs Lot, "the mixed blood of two races, in which action is quick to follow impulse" causes her to cry out "kiss me again, Burr Gordon, if you dare" as she stabs him (38). Freeman emphasizes the classic dichotomy of the dark passionate woman and the fair sheltered one, with Madelon as a "red rose" in contrast to Dorothy Fair, Burr's fiancée, who is a "sweet-scented flower like a pink or a rose" (9). Furthermore, Dorothy's purity and fairness are literally hidden behind her father's housekeeper, a Black woman, reputedly a princess in Africa, who mutters in an indistinguishable thick tongue and who stands as a bulwark to protect Dorothy's whiteness. A representation of Dorothy's sexuality displaced onto a threatening Blackness, the never-named African housekeeper mediates between Dorothy and the world beyond, the Africanist presence that, as Toni Morrison has suggested, permits a fantasy of pure whiteness to exist. For example, after Madelon virtually kidnaps Dorothy and takes her on a mad sleigh ride to the jail to get Burr to tell the truth, Dorothy, who "shook like a white flower," is lifted from the sleigh by "the grimly faithful servant-woman" and carried to her bed (114). Absent a mother or other such surrogate to mediate between herself and her passions or the outside world, for Madelon "there was no rest and no sleep" (114) during her frantic rides across the countryside to save Burr.

A further key to Freeman's treatment of race and history is the villagers' response to Lot's stabbing. They stand ready to hang Madelon and Burr once Lot dies because they won't "have a man murdered to death in our midst by no French and Injuns nowadays" (359). By this point, Madelon has been exonerated, yet the racist mutterings of the white villagers would convict her regardless of her innocence. Too, the phrasing evokes the French and Indian War, the colonial past, and the violent appropriation of lands from the original inhabitants. *Madelon*'s setting of a Vermont village is across Lake Champlain from the tribal lands of the Iroquois (Haudenosaunee) confederacy of Oneida, Onondaga, Seneca, Cayuga, and Mohawks, lands that were colonized under English rule into New York and Vermont, respectively. The Hautville family structure alludes to matriarchal and matrilineal Haudenosaunee customs as well, for although her father and brothers remonstrate with Madelon, she exerts her freedom of action and conscience in a manner impossible in the patriarchal culture that surrounds Dorothy Fair, who exists as a surrogate for whiteness and must therefore be literally confined and guarded. Samaine Lockwood has argued that the work of Freeman and others showed "unmarried women as negotiating in the present an intimate relationship to colonial New England history . . . [with] the past as occurring across and thus shaping the late nineteenth-century present" (59). Madelon Hautville negotiates this intimate relationship with colonial history in a heterosexual context, without forming the "new and puzzling intimacies and erotic forms" (59) of same-sex partnerships that Lockwood sees as central to this endeavor. Her racial difference from the colonist-descended villagers empowers her to conceive of a new form of resistance to patriarchy that relies purely on her own strength as a nonwhite woman.

The fusion of past and present that Madelon embodies through the intersection of race and gender difference is confirmed through other allusions as well as an allegorical component in the tale of her struggle. Also racially marked, Madelon's tormenter, Lot, is seen as a "white fox" (18) by the villagers, although perhaps in keeping with the late nineteenth-century worship of the white colonial past, the nineteenth-century critic Horace Scudder refers to "Lot Gordon, the hero."[3] Lot fetishizes Madelon because she eludes him and he can possess her only through trickery and coercion, like the Iroquois lands that she represents. His attempts to force her into marriage and submission, to turn her into a surrogate of his domination with no will of her own, like Dorothy Fair, would require the helplessness of whiteness that Dorothy represents and that Madelon rejects. Freeman signals Lot's alignment with colonialism through his use of a quill pen, a curious Revolutionary-era remnant that suggests his links to the past; he tempts Madelon with fine imported silks and curios, recalling the import duties levied by Parliament in the 1760s that led to colonial resistance, including the Boston Tea Party, before the Revolution. As she does with all material goods that come with an ideology of submission attached, Madelon proudly resists him and spurns his luxury goods. After Lot frees her from their marriage contract, he tells her, in a speech that echoes Revolutionary rhetoric, "Treasure of house and land and fine apparel and furnishings may be a goodly inheritance, but our heirs would thank us more for power to draw the breath of life freely" (277) than to be beholden to a desiccated and sickly master who is "half a dead man" (277)—like George III.

Further setting the stage for the theme of colonialism and land appropriation, the relationship between the cousins Lot and Burr Gordon is established by the story of a will. Sons of a common grandfather, Lot's father "kept his property intact, never wasting, but adding from others' waste" while Burr's father "plunged into speculation . . . and when his father died had anticipated the larger portion of his birthright" (19). The key word "birthright," which Freeman also uses at the end of "A New England Nun" to evoke the story of Jacob and Esau, here fulfills the same function: the Gordon cousins' grandfather, an Abraham figure, provides an inheritance that Burr's improvident father, like Esau, squanders for a figurative mess of pottage, while Lot's father profits from the improvidence of his brother. Often interpreted as a parable of "civilized" self-control in the present to provide for future generations (Jacob) over the "primitive" satisfaction of immediate appetites (Esau), the story as Freeman reverses it in "A New England Nun" becomes one of seizing satisfaction in the present rather than prizing the acquisition of the world's gifts in the future, as signified for Louisa by Joe Dagget and matrimony. A further understanding if not endorsement of Esau's choice is W. E. B. Du Bois's framing of the parable as the triumph of colonialism over "the great majority of mankind, the peoples who lived in Asia, Africa and America and the islands of the sea, [who] became subordinate tools for the profit-making of the crafty planners of great things" (Du Bois 4). Seen in this context, Madelon's choice of Burr over Lot, of Esau over Jacob, confirms her choice of freedom, anti-colonial sentiment, and solidarity with the French and indigenous part of her heritage. It also demonstrates that the novel's defining action—her stabbing of Lot Gordon—is actually a vigorous blow toward bodily autonomy for Madelon and the new nation that she represents. The pitch of the novel is high, as Scudder suggests in his review, but so are the stakes for the new nation.

Conclusion

Freeman's use of surrogates to signify strong emotions and violence within her stories and novels serves several purposes. On the surface, it enables her to encode levels of violence, neglect, trauma, and abuse that would otherwise be out of keeping in the literary milieu and for the audiences for which she wrote. More significantly, however, the use of dolls, ghosts, animals, and other nonhuman representatives allows her to work within conventional traditions of Puritan typology and symbolism while providing a deeply unsettling look at the usual conventions. Casting the theft of a doll, or any theft, for that matter, as in "The Reign of the Doll," as a positive good is a transgressive act, much as Martha's parrot speaking for her is, but these are relatively light-hearted examples of Freeman's use of surrogates. More disturbing are the stories of how surrogates paper over neglect, as in "The Love of Parson Lord," or come to embody threatened (*The Portion of Labor*) or actual abuse ("The Lost Ghost"). Equally sinister are the attempts to treat adult women as objects of power and conquest, as in "The Long Arm" and *Madelon*. Sarah does not stab her father but believes that she might have done; and Madelon responds to an attempted sexual assault not unlike that of Tess's in Thomas Hardy's *Tess of the D'Urbervilles* by stabbing her assailant. Finally, Freeman's surrogates add an additional dimension of the uncanny to the stories in which they appear, raising as they do questions about power, agency, and emotional violence as well as the truly disturbing issue of the ill-defined borderline between the human and the nonhuman.

Works Cited

Ammons, Elizabeth. "Material Culture, Empire, and Jewett's *Country of the Pointed Firs*." *New Essays on* The Country of the Pointed Firs, edited by June Howard, Cambridge UP, 1994, pp. 81–100.

Behling, Laura L. "Detecting Deviation in Mary E. Wilkins Freeman's 'The Long Arm.'" *American Literary Realism, 1870–1910*, vol. 31, no. 1, 1998, pp. 75–91.

Bendixen, Alfred. Afterword. *The Wind in the Rosebush and Other Stories of the Supernatural by Mary Wilkins Freeman*. Academy Chicago Publishers, 1986, pp. 239–58.

Brodhead, Richard. *Cultures of Letters: Scenes of Reading and Writing in Nineteenth-Century America*. U of Chicago P, 1993.

Brown, Bill. *A Sense of Things: The Object Matter of American Literature*. U of Chicago P, 2003.

Campbell, Donna M. *Bitter Tastes: Literary Naturalism and Early Cinema in American Women's Writing*. U of Georgia P, 2016.

—. "Summers in Arcady: The Deep Time of Evolutionary Romance in James Lane Allen, Hamlin Garland, and Edith Wharton." *American Literary Realism*, vol. 52, no. 2, 2020, pp. 95–113.

Du Bois, W. E. B. "Jacob and Esau." Commencement Address at Talledega College, *The Talladegan*, vol. 62, no. 1, November 1944, pp. 1–6. <http://www.webdubois.org/dbJacobEsau.html> (last accessed 17 June 2022).

Elbert, Monika M. "The Displacement of Desire: Consumerism and Fetishism in Mary Wilkins Freeman's Fiction." *Legacy: A Journal of American Women Writers*, vol. 19, no. 2, 2002, pp. 192–215.

Glasser, Leah Blatt. *In a Closet Hidden: The Life and Work of Mary E. Wilkins Freeman*. U of Massachusetts P, 1996.

Grasso, Linda M. "Inventive Desperation: Anger, Violence, and Belonging in Mary Wilkins Freeman's and Sui Sin Far's Murderous Mother Stories." *American Literary Realism*, vol. 38, no.1, 2005, pp. 18–31.

Griffin, Susan M. "'Understudies': Miming the Human." *PMLA: Publications of the Modern Language Association of America*, vol. 124, no. 2, 2009, pp. 511–19.

Harde, Roxanne. "'At Rest Now': Child Ghosts and Social Justice in Nineteenth-Century Women's Writing." *Transnational Gothic: Literary and Social Exchanges in the Long Nineteenth Century*, edited by Monika Elbert and Bridget M. Marshall, Ashgate, 2013, pp. 189–200.

Hoeller, Hildegard. *From Gift to Commodity: Capitalism and Sacrifice in Nineteenth-Century American Fiction*. U of New Hampshire P, 2012.

Jewett, Sarah Orne. "The Foreigner." *Sarah Orne Jewett: Novels and Stories: College Edition*, edited by Michael Davitt Bell, Literary Classics of the United States, 1996, pp. 530–55.

Lockwood, Samaine. *Archives of Desire: The Queer Historical Work of New England Regionalism*. U of North Carolina P, 2015.

Morrison, Toni. *Playing in the Dark: Whiteness and the American Literary Imagination*. Harvard UP, 1992.

Pryse, Marjorie. Introduction. *Selected Stories of Mary E. Wilkins Freeman*. W. W. Norton, 1983, pp. ii–xiii.

Reichardt, Mary R. "Mary Wilkins Freeman: One Hundred Years of Criticism." *Legacy*, vol. 4, no. 2, 1987, pp. 31–44.

—. ed. *A Mary Wilkins Freeman Reader*. U of Nebraska P, 1997.

Scudder, Horace. Review of *Madelon*. *Atlantic Monthly*, vol. 78, August 1896, pp. 269–70.

Tigchelaar, Jana. "The Neighborly Christmas: Gifts, Community, and Regionalism in the Christmas Stories of Sarah Orne Jewett and Mary Wilkins Freeman." *Legacy: A Journal of American Women Writers*, vol. 31, no. 2, 2014, pp. 236–57.

Wharton, Edith. *A Backward Glance*. Appleton-Century, 1934.
—. Preface. *Ethan Frome*, Scribner's, 1922, pp. 1–5.
Westbrook, Perry D. *Mary Wilkins Freeman*. Revised edition. Twayne Publishers, 1988.
Wilkins [Freeman], Mary E. "The Long Arm." *The Long Arm and Other Detective Stories by George Ira Brett, Professor Brander Matthews, and Roy Tellet*. Chapman and Hall, 1895, pp. 2–66.
—. "The Lost Ghost." *The Wind in the Rose-bush and Other Stories of the Supernatural*. Doubleday, Page & Company, 1903, pp. 199–237.
—. "The Love of Parson Lord." *The Love of Parson Lord and Other Stories*. Harper & Brothers Publishers, 1901, pp. 3–81.
—. *Madelon: A Novel*. Harper & Brothers Publishers, 1896.
—. "The Parrot." *A New England Nun and Other Stories*, edited by Sandra A. Zagarell, Penguin, 2000, pp. 194–201.
—. *The Portion of Labor*. Harper & Brothers, 1901.
—. "The Reign of the Doll." *Harper's Monthly*, vol. 108, January 1904, pp. 285–96.
—. *The Uncollected Stories of Mary Wilkins Freeman*, edited by Mary Reichardt, UP of Mississippi, 1992.
Zagarell, Sandra A. "Crosscurrents: Registers of Nordicism, Community, and Culture in Jewett's Country of the Pointed Firs." *The Yale Journal of Criticism: Interpretation in the Humanities*, vol. 10, no. 2, 1997, pp. 355–70.
—. Introduction to Mary E. Wilkins Freeman, *A New England Nun and Other Stories*. Penguin, 2000, pp. ix–xxiv.

Notes

1. Emotional violence in *The Portion of Labor* is discussed in Chapter 5, "Where Are My Children? Race, Citizenship, and the Stolen Child," of Campbell, *Bitter Tastes: Literary Naturalism and Early Cinema in American Women's Writing*, pp. 218–22.
2. See Campbell, "Summers in Arcady."
3. See Scudder. Glasser notes that Scudder's review was one of the few positive reviews of the novel.

5

TRANSATLANTIC LLORONAS: INFANTICIDE AND GENDER IN MARY E. WILKINS FREEMAN AND ALEXANDROS PAPADIAMANTIS

MYRTO DRIZOU

In "A Poetess" (1890), one of Mary E. Wilkins Freeman's best-known stories, Betsey Dole, the protagonist, is a frail, childish-looking old maid who revels in the affective power of poetry. When her sentimental style becomes the target of the local minister's critique, Betsey loses her confidence and eventually her life, consumed by emotional and physical affliction. The story makes a strong point about changing literary mores, since the minister champions the modern style of urban magazines, which heralds the death of Betsey's poetry (and life). This experience of loss, however, is refracted by a deeper source of grief, the pain that results from losing a child. Betsey is called to write a poem that commemorates Mrs Caxton's son, Willie, whose death haunts the bereaved mother and triggers the poetess's sympathies. The childless Betsey admits to the difficulty of identifying with a mother's grief but uses poetry as a vehicle to visualize the "faces of children that had never been" (39) and to birth her own offspring, namely, her art. When she is crushed by the minister's critique, Betsey burns the offspring of her mind, committing a symbolic act of infanticide that precipitates her own demise. This poignant act, indicative of the vexed relationship between authorship and motherhood, becomes a dominant motif that takes different forms throughout Freeman's canon.

Later stories, such as "The Little Maid at the Door" (1892), "The Lost Ghost" (1903), and "The Wind in the Rose-Bush" (1903), make repeated references to infanticide as a gesture of communal or individual negligence.[1] These stories rely heavily on the Gothic to represent the pathos of lonely dead girls who come back to haunt childless, caring women.² As Beth Wynne Fisken points out, Freeman "return[s] again and again to the plight of an orphaned and neglected child, badly in need of safe harbor and a surrogate parent" (43). The spectrality of these children suggests Freeman's attempt to exorcise her own ghosts, especially the ones that evoked "unresolved tension with her own mother from her formative years" (Reichardt 111). Rooted as it might be in the relation to her mother, Freeman's representation of motherhood carries broader cultural and political stakes. As Donna M. Campbell argues in her contribution to this volume, Freeman uses nonhuman surrogates, such as dolls or animals, to show the complexities of violence and desire within a nexus of "dehumanizing patriarchal structures that pit women against each other, against themselves, and against children" ("Reign" 81). In her analysis of commodity fetishism in Freeman's fiction, Monika Elbert further contends that sentimental stories, such as the above-mentioned "A Poetess" and "The Reign of the Doll" (1904), displace maternal urges onto fetishized objects of desire, which thwarts a fulfilling experience of motherhood ("Fetishism" 196–7). It is Freeman's "otherworldly" Gothic stories, Elbert notes, that paradoxically resolve the "good vs. bad" mother dichotomy; in "The Lost Ghost" and "The Wind in the Rose-Bush" positive female characters take up neglected dead children whose ghosts become "fetishized versions[s] of the child they never had" ("Fetishism" 211). For Roxanne Harde, Freeman's child ghosts express her call for social reform, which Harde places in the context of a transatlantic conversation between British and American female writers, including Elizabeth Gaskell, Charlotte Riddell, Elizabeth Stuart Phelps, and Ellen Glasgow. While the focus on Gothic has allowed critics to convey the complexity of Freeman's representation of motherhood, it has limited the scope of analysis to mostly Anglo-American cultural contexts and literary genealogies.

Freeman's radical representation of motherhood, however, extends to a transatlantic mythic discourse that reaches beyond oft-cited Anglo-American contexts. Her recourse to the trope of infanticide, I argue, invokes a long lineage of deviant maternal figures epitomized by La Llorona, the Wailing or Weeping Woman that forms an integral part of Central and South American mythology. Just like ancient demonic figures who commit violence against children (such as the Jewish Lilith and the Greek Lamia and Medea), La Llorona is constructed as a witchlike character who drowns her children to take revenge on her husband's infidelity or neglect. Bemoaning the loss of her children, she wanders the earth wailing in remorse. In popular imagination, La Llorona is used as a threat to discipline unruly children while her punishment—she cannot enter Heaven without her children—is a cautionary tale for women who stray from conventional expectations about motherhood.

Recent scholars have emphasized the critical import of the story of La Llorona as an enduring parable of transgression, monstrosity, and loss, signifying infanticide as an act of resistance against oppressive patriarchal structures. Rooted in Central American mythology and influenced by European folklore—La Llorona's infanticide and punishment evoke the German legend of the Lady in White (*Die Weisse Frau*)—the story is a powerful example of cultural hybridity and a dynamic vehicle of social critique. La Llorona is often compared to the formidable Snake Woman of Central American lore. According to Aztec mythology, a few years prior to the Spanish conquest, a woman was seen circling around the walls of Tenochtitlán; she was wailing for her children and entreating them to leave in view of the impending annihilation of indigenous civilizations (León 6–7). Aztec representations of the Snake Woman show her face painted half-red and half-black, while later incarnations of La Llorona incorporate the treacherous identity of La Malinche, a mythical Mexican figure who allegedly betrayed her people to Hernán Cortés. José E. Limón eloquently reclaims La Llorona as a third female figure that goes beyond the polarity "madonna/whore" (embodied in the contrast between the Virgin of Guadalupe and La Malinche). As such, La Llorona is a positive female figure whose endless wandering becomes an expression of utopian longing for the Greater Mexican folk masses (413).[3] Domino Renee Perez has further stressed La Llorona's significance for "intercultural dialogue," since "she does not recognize any border, and similar figures appear across cultures" (9).[4] Such figures can be found not only in folk tales and mythic narratives but also in literary texts that deploy infanticide as the means of social, political, and economic critique.

Taking La Llorona as an intertext that evokes a complex problematic of motherhood—one that transcends space, time, and genre, and finds expression in various cultures—allows the transition from a merely comparative to a "relational ontology," to use Walter D. Mignolo's term (112). In Mignolo's view, this transition entails an active questioning of the structures of power in which every comparative reading is embedded (117). And to do so, scholars must turn to larger networks of relation, which, as Shu-mei Shih suggests, operate on a global scale and "manifest themselves on formal, generic, and other levels" (84); for Shih, this mode of "relational comparison" requires "close reading of the texts" as well as "sensitivity to world history, scaling both the textual and the global without losing sight of either of the scales" (84).

As a case in point, I turn to a close reading of "Old Woman Magoun" in the context of a wider, global network of Llorona figures that extends beyond (and thus decentralizes) Anglo-American literary and cultural genealogies.

"Old Woman Magoun" is one of Freeman's darkest short stories, originally published in *Harper's Monthly* in October 1905. The protagonist, Old Woman Magoun, acts as a surrogate mother to her teenage granddaughter, Lily, whom she has tried to shelter at all costs. When Lily's father, Nelson Barry, claims her as barter for his gambling debts, Old Woman Magoun facilitates her granddaughter's death to save her from men's evil grip. The plot culminates the treatment of infanticide in Freeman's earlier fiction, which represented the motives and consequences of infanticide rather than the *act* itself. Further, while "Old Woman Magoun" makes use of major Gothic tropes—such as the devious villain in the character of Nelson Barry—it is more realistic in mode and more sober in tenor than Freeman's earlier infanticide stories. As Campbell has suggested, the story "operates on three levels of discourse: a biblical level of the struggle between good and evil that parallels the white slave narrative, a fairy-tale level that relies on repetition and ritualized language for its effect, and a naturalistic and evolutionary level, using animal imagery and Darwinian themes" (*Bitter Tastes* 87). I here wish to add one more level, a mythic tradition of transgressive maternal figures (such as La Llorona), who kill as they love and protect as they murder. Reading Old Woman Magoun as a Llorona figure opens up the scope of the story to an alternative genealogy of motherhood, one that shifts the focus of gender discourse from women's "natural" vocation as vehicles of biological reproduction to their redemptive mission as formidable agents of justice who avenge female oppression. As Limón argues with regard to Mexican articulations of the Llorona myth, infanticide is not a "repressed resentment against child caring" but rather the extreme, albeit "humanly understandable," response to systemic "sexual and familial betrayal" (416). In this sense, infanticide is not an act of individual transgression based on malicious plotting or impulsive revenge but a collective—albeit problematic—verdict of socially mandated retribution for a wider community of women.

This female community is also matriarchal in its foundation. The presence of a strong matriarchal network existing outside patriarchy is central to New England literature, as critics such as Josephine Donovan have shown. Freeman often challenges this view, blurring the lines between men's and women's worlds in both social and economic terms. In her reading of "Old Woman Magoun," Elbert sees matriarchy as a relic which eventually surrenders to a male economy of capitalism. To safeguard her matriarchal family's integrity, Old Woman Magoun must sacrifice her granddaughter (and her sanity) by adopting the male virtue of economic self-reliance. For Elbert, the story's ending delivers a terrifying message insofar as it shows that women "must choose separatism and literally sever the bridge between the sexes" to maintain their own economy. As such, "Old Woman Magoun" is "Freeman's most pessimistic story" ("Devious Women" 267). The pessimism of the grim conclusion is hard to counter if one reads the story solely within its contemporary socio-economic context, namely, turn-of-the-century consumer capitalism. The story's mythic undertext, however, offers a more expansive view of Freeman's matriarchal discourse, placing Old Woman Magoun in a matrilineal genealogy of Llorona characters who seek social and economic emancipation in their respective cultures. This cross-cultural genealogy redefines Freeman's work not only as New England or US literature but also as *world* literature—a global intertext that goes beyond the Anglo-American canon and generates new critical contexts for Freeman's themes, plots, and characters.

In this vein, I develop the connections between Old Woman Magoun and Old Hadoula, the main character in Alexandros Papadiamantis's *The Murderess*, a novella that was originally serialized from January to June 1903 in *Panathinaia* magazine in Greece. While *The Murderess* appeared two years before "Old Woman Magoun," it would not have reached a US audience prior to Freeman's death in 1930; its first translation into English did not take place until 1977, partly due to the difficulty of rendering Papadiamantis's highly idiomatic regional dialect into English and partly due to the challenge of conveying the complexity of modern Greek society and literature to a geographically remote and culturally distant audience.[5] Even as Papadiamantis was fairly familiar with certain American authors, such as Mark Twain and Bret Harte (whom he had translated into Greek), he would not have come across Freeman's work, as scholars only know of Freeman's reception in Western Europe.[6] Hence, neither Freeman nor Papadiamantis are likely to have known each other's texts.

The goal of this essay, though, is not to linger on the limits of reception of each author's work; neither is it to make hypotheses on the authors' knowledge of the Llorona mythology. Rather, it is to show how elements of myth become useful hermeneutic tools that probe cross-cultural connections of social and literary discourses, as seen in thematically comparable texts. Both "Old Woman Magoun" and *The Murderess* pivot around similar plots: their Llorona-like protagonists are fierce grandmothers who murder their granddaughters—and other female children in *The Murderess*—to save them from a patriarchal system that commodifies women on the marriage market. The explicit focus on female offspring intensifies the depiction of infanticide as retribution for women's suffering. The texts' retributive discourse is refracted by a range of motifs that convey women's restorative power: their female protagonists display farming and building skills, enterprising resources, and healing properties that cure not only physical ailments but also social ills. In what follows, I show how this restorative vision works on a metanarrative level as well; it becomes the foundation for a comparative reading practice that recuperates the critical import of transgressive myth as a bridge between—and across—different cultures.

While the stories' cultural contexts differ, their settings are similar. Both "Old Woman Magoun" and *The Murderess* take place in small rural communities; the former in the remote hamlet of Barry's Ford in New England and the latter on the Aegean island of Skiathos in Greece. Both settings are described as rugged landscapes that resemble fortresses in sequestered lands. Perched in a mountain valley between earth and sky, Barry's Ford seems arrested in movement: "[b]elow it the hills lie in moveless curves like a petrified ocean; above it they rise in green-cresting waves which never break" ("Old Woman Magoun" 218). Freeman's diction— "moveless" curves, "petrified" ocean, and waves "which never break"—suggests a frustrated potential for change and creates an aura of nearly violent sterility: the "green-cresting" waves implode but never break, while the ocean-like hills are framed in a barren ("petrified") landscape. The metaphor of the petrified ocean water has biblical echoes: it evokes Lot's wife, who became petrified as a pillar of salt when she defied God's order not to look back upon fleeing the destruction of Sodom. Similarly unruly, Old Woman Magoun refuses to obey but her own authority, which helps her look forward rather than backward. Her "instrumental" effort to have a bridge built contributes to economic and social progress, since it aims at connecting the hamlet with the bigger, neighboring town of Greenham.

To achieve the construction of the bridge, Old Woman Magoun had "haunted the miserable little grocery, wherein whiskey and hands of tobacco were the most salient features of the stock in trade" and would repeatedly admonish the idle men who cowered before her words (218). The assertiveness of her manner is supported by her physical strength and self-reliance, which Freeman describes in clearly gendered terms: Old Woman Magoun's "strenuous feminine assertion" is contrasted to the "weakness of the [hamlet's] masculine element" (218). The strength of feminine assertion is a major motif of New England fiction, as seen in some of Freeman's widely anthologized stories, including "The Revolt of 'Mother'" (1890). As opposed to Sarah Penn's quiet demeanor and introvert authority, Old Woman Magoun's presence carries the explosive threat of thundering force. In a seemingly protective fashion, she "spread[s] her strong arms like wings"—not to gather her children but to send irresponsible, childish men to work (218). Her threatening character is reminiscent of La Llorona's popular aura as a haunting figure of discipline. According to an account of the story in Santa Fe, New Mexico, La Llorona appeared to an ill-tempered, drunkard father, who never attended church and set a bad example for his children. To remedy the situation, La Llorona would tie the father to the church door to lecture him until she managed to work a miracle by urging the entire community to behave responsibly as well (Kraul and Beatty 1 qtd in León 8). Just like Old Woman Magoun's, La Llorona's authority is constructed as a centripetal force that gathers the community around her command to further individual and social change.

Old Hadoula in *The Murderess* also configures herself as an instigator of change for her family's future and, as the story progresses, for the wider social body. Hailing from the craggy, northern part of Skiathos island, full of "untrodden spots, caves, and rocks" (83), Hadoula was born in the old settlement of the Castle, a secluded, uninhabitable village that was deserted after most people moved to the new town—reluctantly (and lamentably) at first but more decidedly later.[7] The deserted, infertile landscape parlays directly into Hadoula's fate. Her marriage dowry, a long-standing custom of Greek society, included a downtrodden house in the Castle and a wild, barren field in the north of the island, both of which Hadoula regarded as sterile foundation for her life. Along with the deserted property, her dowry contract itemized the household wares her husband would receive along with the bride. On the day of signing the contract, Hadoula stood among the blankets, covers, cushions, and sheets, as "motionless and grandiose as the pile of linen" (10). Her petrified mien, however, would turn out to be merely superficial. After she married, Hadoula took her fate into her own hands, building her own house with her hard work, intelligence, and thrift. As a healer of various ailments, Hadoula would diligently gather herbs that she exchanged to make profit and build what she would modestly call "'her little corner'" (19). Like Old Woman Magoun, Hadoula is proud and self-reliant. She lacks, though, the unalloyed "goodness" of soul that Freeman identifies in her protagonist ("Old Woman Magoun" 219). Hadoula's intelligence of mind, facility with words, and diplomacy in manner turn her into a morally ambiguous character who does not hesitate to steal from her father's nest egg to start her own. She considers her stealing justified as revenge for her scant dowry and the meagre future it would entail.

As Hadoula tries to make her slim dowry bear fruit, she blends the language of economic productivity with the discourse of women's biological fertility. As she reflects, "[t]he more the family increased, the more the bitter pills multiplied," leading to more financial burdens and economic difficulties. These reflections take place upon her granddaughter's birth, a sickly infant to whom Hadoula has been tending for two weeks. In contrast to the profitable accretion of economic capital, this infant is just another girl that has come to add unwanted trouble to the world. The infant's gender is inextricably linked to the economic discourse of capital, as every young woman will need a dowry to get married. Just like Hadoula who was given to her husband as part of a contract of exchange, women acquired value only in relation to—and *as*—property that would be exchanged for marriage. The economic foundation of women's objectification was also ideologically sanctioned. Upon her granddaughter's birth, Hadoula ruminates that she had always led a life of servitude to others: she had originally served her parents as a little girl and had subsequently become a slave (and a nurse) to her husband. This fate came full circle when she became a mother: "she became a slave to her children, and when they had children of their own, she was slave to her grandchildren" (1–2). Using words such as "slave" and "nurse" interchangeably, Papadiamantis questions a romanticized view of women's "natural" vocation as selfless caretakers. Instead, he constructs a systemic social and economic genealogy of slavery that stretches across generations and allows for no escape.

The socio-economic determinism of women's servitude is also at the heart of Freeman's story, since Old Woman Magoun's granddaughter, Lily, is treated as an asset that can settle her father's gambling debts. Critics, such as Linda Grasso and Donna M. Campbell, have pointed out the similarities between

"Old Woman Magoun" and the early twentieth-century "white slave narrative," in which women's bodies become sexual objects for circulation. The economic and sexual commodification of women in Freeman's story follows a cross-generational trajectory along the lines of female servitude I have pointed out in The Murderess. Nelson Barry's wish to use Lily (his daughter) as sexual capital to offset his debt perpetuates the destructive authority he had had over Lily's mother; the latter died at sixteen after being seduced, impregnated, and deserted by Barry, a man whose family stock is emphatically described as "vitiated physically and morally" (230). The deterministic overtones of physical and moral degeneracy accentuate Lily's inability to escape her fate, which is compared to a ticking bomb: Barry's claim on his daughter is a terrible but "long expected blow" (224). The delivery of this blow is set in motion by Sally Jinks, a minor, fairly simplistic character, who urges Old Woman Magoun to send Lily to buy some salt at the grocery store.

The store, an iconic site of capitalist exchange, turns into a marriage market, where Lily's fate is bartered between her father and the man to whom he is indebted. To foreground Lily's entrapment in a deterministic gender discourse, Freeman draws on mythic tropes: crocheting white lace and "loosening some thread from her spool" (221), Sally conjures the Fates of Greek mythology. Personified as three old women—Clotho, Lachesis, and Atropos—the Fates would respectively spin, allot, and cut the thread of human lives.[8] Bestowers of life and arbiters of death, the three Fates were often depicted clad in white, just like in popular representations of La Llorona as a white-garbed female figure who wielded the double-edged power of life and death. Lily's search for salt—a life-giving staple of subsistence and preservation often extracted by enslaved people—becomes a spinning wheel that unwinds the series of encounters leading to her death; with a gesture that is evocative of Clotho, Sally unravels white lace thread from her spool as she introduces the idea of Lily's walk to the store, which unfolds the latter's fortune (and the plot). Instead of using a character to personify Lachesis, though, Freeman draws attention to the socio-economic gender discourse that determines the (mis)fortunes of young women such as Lily. In her effort to shelter her granddaughter by keeping her in a protracted state of innocence, Old Woman Magoun takes on the role of Atropos, the "unyielding" or "unchanging" Fate, who would decide how a human being was going to die. Making this decision for Lily, Old Woman Magoun offers her a way out of the "clutch of a tiger," as the grandmother describes Barry's hold over his daughter (224).

As the story progresses, the portentous grandmother becomes an archetypal figure who not only avenges her daughter's death but also turns against a broader system of patriarchal power. As is the case with Papadiamantis's Hadoula who smothers her sick granddaughter right after her reflections on women's servitude, Old Woman Magoun decides to let Lily eat from a deadly nightshade after Barry has laid claim on his daughter's future. In her attempt to envision—and provide for—a different future for Lily, Old Woman Magoun assumes the aura of a "prophetess" who defers to a divine form of justice; as she enigmatically tells Barry, "'[t]he Lord will take care of [Lily]'" (226). At the very moment of allowing Lily to eat the deadly berries, Old Woman Magoun looks up to the white, wing-shaped clouds. Symbols of freedom and protection, these ethereal wings embody the grandmother's desire to shelter Lily against Barry's transgression on the young girl's freedom. Her own wings—the strong arms that would spread disapprovingly to disperse men to work earlier in the story— are now turned inward to protect Lily.

The intensity of the grandmother's protective instinct is reflected in the tightness of her grip, which startles and hurts Lily. Yet Old Woman Magoun ominously admits that she would never hurt her granddaughter "'. . . except it was to save [the latter's] life. . .'" (229). The redemptive aspect of infanticide, a central motif in several renderings of La Llorona's story, turns the murderous mother into a hand of divine intervention, "a protector against social and political forces that would destroy her children" (Perez 46). Wearing a black gown, cape, and bonnet, the grandmother becomes an archetypal agent of death that Freeman describes as a stranger with a terrible, inscrutable look and a difficult yet necessary choice: to sacrifice Lily only to keep her free. Addressing Lily in a "grand" and "exalted" voice, Old Woman Magoun assumes the formidable aura of an Old Testament divine figure (229; 232). At the same time, she does not lose the "tenderest love and admiration" she has for Lily, offering a compassionate vision of heaven to relieve the girl's pain (228).

The precise cause of Lily's fatal distress, though, is kept slightly ambiguous. When Lily visits an eminent lawyer and his wife—whom Old Woman Magoun entreats to have Lily adopted and, hence, saved from Barry—she eats sour milk and apples, which could be liable for her consequently ailing stomach. This food combination, Barry reflects later in the story, would also hurt Lily's mother. Drawing a continued narrative of distress, Freeman emphasizes that women's sources of physical (and emotional) pain stem primarily from men's social and economic authority. Both Nelson Barry and the lawyer are patriarchal figures who arbitrate women's fates in an absolute or patronizing fashion: the former repeatedly tells Old Woman Magoun that he *wants* (and will have) Lily while the latter is patronizing toward his wife as he mercilessly refuses to adopt the girl. By sketching this web of patriarchal authority, Freeman subtly justifies her protagonist's choice to turn her protective wings into means for a destructive salvation through an otherwise monstrous act. What is more, Freeman reconfigures the source and definition of monstrosity by choosing to present infanticide not only as the product of but also as the reaction *against* patriarchy. Hence, she redefines monstrosity as a collective gesture of agency rather than an isolated instance of aberration.

The line between individual and systemic responsibility is blurrier in *The Murderess*, since Hadoula causes (or chooses not to obstruct) the death of several female children, including her infant granddaughter, three girls drowned in wells, and a baby girl. In an ironic twist of her name—"Hadoula" stems from "hádi" (or "chádi"), the Greek word for "caress"—she physically suppresses these girls' breath by smothering or having them drowned. In her view, she offers the girls a chance to breathe free: she spares them a future of servitude while relieving their families of the dowry these girls would need for marriage. To sanction her actions, Hadoula seeks divine counsel in the remote chapel of St John in Hiding, a refuge for all who flee secret burdens or sins. Praying for a sign, Hadoula misinterprets her later encounter with young girls as divine license to kill, framing infanticide as a merciful deed that is already "decided" and left for her to execute (57). What Hadoula considers a divinely ordained mission is also a Malthusian gesture that facilitates death by disease to control the overpopulation of female children; in her mind, ". . . disaster is happiness and disease is health" if "grief is joy and death is life and resurrection" (36). Much as Hadoula's reflections ring with Christian echoes of salvation, they also point to a Darwinist rhetoric that champions natural selection and eliminates those who seem unable to survive. As critic Gina Politi has argued, Hadoula is the embodiment of a social Darwinist mentality that conflicts with human law and Christian morality (259). At the same time, Hadoula is an experienced healer who helps those she otherwise considers too weak to survive.

Early in the story, Papadiamantis notes that Hadoula provides cures for "the sick, for anaemic girls, for pregnant women and women after childbirth and for those with women's diseases" (18). After having two girls drowned, she tends to their sick mother and "experience[s] the rare and indescribable sensations of a murderess transformed suddenly into doctor to her own victims" (62). Hadoula's healing practice gives her a powerful, albeit fearful, witchlike aura that accords with La Llorona's construction as a *bruja* (witch) or the demonic qualities of sorcery associated with other murderous maternal figures, such as the Greek Medea. Hadoula's mother, in fact, would often be called a "witch" due to her cunning and knowledge of magic. Hadoula's cunning acquires particular significance in the context of her healing capacities: it allows her to manipulate her way out of blame (as in the drowning episode mentioned above) as well as to challenge the moral discourse by which blame is assigned. This becomes evident in Hadoula's encounter with Marousa, a woman she had helped with her herbs in the past.

Persecuted by the authorities, Hadoula finds refuge in Marousa's house. The two women's conversation reveals the shared knowledge of a past secret: Hadoula had helped Marousa abort an illegitimate pregnancy, relieving the latter of her "'troubles'" and "'tortures'" (80). Rather than criticize or mock Marousa—as other women did—Hadoula bravely administered potions, drugs, and massages to help a woman in need. What is more, this woman is "described" as a Jewess or, as rumor had it, Turkish, marking her as both racially and religiously deviant.[9] Marousa's vulnerability as an unmarried young woman moves Hadoula who decides to go against social and moral convention by helping her abort the baby. The controversial yet salutary outcome of Hadoula's help brings the two women closer, creating a strong feeling of mutual solidarity that hails from a shared experience of oppression: both women have faced the consequences of a patriarchal discourse that sanctions men's arbitrary power and irresponsible conduct. By killing the seed of this discourse, Hadoula helps birth a union that heals divisions of race, religion, and age, forging a bridge of solidarity among women.

The trope of the bridge is also central to the thematic and narrative structure of "Old Woman Magoun." As mentioned earlier, Old Woman Magoun was pivotal in the construction of a bridge that would remedy the isolation of Barry's Ford by connecting the hamlet to neighboring towns. The building process has the potential to restore unity within the hamlet as well, since it allows men and women to join their forces for a common purpose. This unity, though, is only temporary. It cannot overturn what is described as an irreversible gender difference: men have an incurable propensity to drink and a consequent lack of industry, responsibility, and entrepreneurship. When they see the slovenly constructed bridge, Old Woman Magoun and Lily concur that men are not "'very nice...'" (228). On one hand, the use of a generic adjective to describe male shortcomings is suggestive of Lily's childish disposition. On the other hand, it indicates the generalization of a gender difference— "'... take [men] all together,'" Old Woman Magoun says—that entrenches the gap between men and women. The use of negative structure in the sentence intensifies this gap while bringing the grandmother and the granddaughter closer: their bond is not only biological but also social, predicated upon a gender difference that solidifies the structure of women's authority.

Similarly, building tropes figure prominently in the gender discourse of *The Murderess*. Hadoula's husband is a boat-builder who is as irresponsible as the men that Old Woman Magoun summons to work: due to his tendency to drink, he can neither calculate his wages nor save money and make long-term investments. Taking on the role of manager and co-provider in their household (and thus reversing gender stereotypes), Hadoula has built a house through her cleverness, resourcefulness, and thrift. The incremental construction of the house reflects Hadoula's gradual accrual of profit and her growing power of authority: the first year she built four thin walls and a roof while the second year she floored three quarters of the house, enabling the family's move to what Hadoula would call her "'nest'" or "'refuge'" (12). As the product of Hadoula's thrift and enterprise, this nest has offered her more fulfillment than her biological offspring, especially the female ones, whose dowry should breed economic burdens on the household. In Hadoula's mind, the construction of the house had given her "the greatest joy of 'all her days'"; it allowed her to be productive in a way that defied women's exclusive role as vehicles for biological reproduction (12). Built on the craggy land of her dowry, this house—the fruit of Hadoula's own resources and labor—gave her the opportunity to take hold of her fate and heal the economic and emotional injury of her meager dowry.

Freeman emphasizes the healing properties of women's economic production at the end of her story as well. Old Woman Magoun is a farmer who, like Hadoula, values self-reliance: she uses her hands to grow the products that ground her self-subsistence. After Lily's funeral, Old Woman Magoun continues to trade the products of her labor yet not only for reasons of economic survival. Her regular trips over the bridge rehearse the memory of her trip with Lily whom Old Woman Magoun tries to rejoin as another wandering Llorona seeking her children: holding Lily's rag doll as one would carry an infant, Old Woman Magoun reproduces the image of Lily who would tend to her doll like a baby. Turning into her granddaughter's very image, Old Woman Magoun tries to recover the innocence and goodness she had tried to instill in Lily's soul: to raise the latter, Old Woman Magoun had "poured the goodness of her own soul into this little receptive vase [Lily] of another" (219). By the end of the story, the vases are turned: Lily's memory is poured into the grandmother in a reflexive gesture that creates the foundation for a new form of union, one that nurses the memory of loss into an ongoing journey of emotional recovery—and redemption.

In *The Murderess*, this journey is refracted through the polyvalence of water imagery. A symbol of fertility, sustenance, and rebirth, water becomes an instrument of death and a space of loss, as Hadoula facilitates the death of young girls in wells. In "Old Woman Magoun," Lily is also asking for water after having eaten the deadly berries and feeling "dreadful dry" (231). In the Llorona myth, water signifies not only the agony of loss but also the hope for rebirth: after drowning her offspring, La Llorona is tormented by remorse and wanders around bodies of water longing for her dead children. Unlike La Llorona, though, Hadoula wanders to flee—rather than recover—the specters of the children she has killed. Hunted by the authorities and haunted by her guilt, Hadoula seeks refuge in a Dostoyevskian underworld: she descends to the "Bad Valley" and hides in the "Black Cave," where the bubbly, brackish "Deadwater" besieges the exit in a violent caress that resembles her own lethal strokes (117). With "long growls of madness ... and sometimes a groan of pain and longing," the swelling tidal waves articulate the children's sobs that Hadoula has unwillingly internalized; the "dead chorus of little girls" increasingly envelops her breast and demands Hadoula's maternal affection (118, 120). To emphasize the inescapability of guilt, Papadiamantis points out that Hadoula imagines the dead girls' faces as rings in a tight necklace that hangs around her neck. Seeking escape (and redemption), she heads to the old hermitage of Ayi Sostis—the "Savior Saint"—to confess her sins. Right before Hadoula reaches the hermitage, however, she is drowned by the swelling tide. The final scene depicts Hadoula's struggle to survive in detail that evokes her previous acts of infanticide: water slowly covers her ears and nostrils just as she had quietly covered the mouth of two girls, her sick granddaughter early in the story and the shepherd's baby at the end. The plot comes full circle as Hadoula's own mouth fills with water, symbolically claimed by the girls who had drowned in wells.

At this climactic moment, Papadiamantis takes one step further than Freeman by identifying Hadoula not only with the girls' own image but also with their suffering bodies, united as they all are in the effort to take a last breath. At first glance, this union is framed as punishment, since Hadoula is trapped between the rising tide and the persecuting authorities, "midway between divine and human justice" (127). Upon closer reflection, however, Hadoula's death can also be interpreted as a moment of healing informed by the restorative power of memory. Turning toward the deserted shore, Papadiamantis's protagonist sees the barren field she had been given as dowry; the wistful tone of her final remark— "'[o]h, there's my dowry'"—is a bitter memory of the patriarchal discourse that has defined her life and driven her actions (127). This defining memory is also sealing the bond between Hadoula and other women, including the female children she has killed. As she joins these children (and drowns), Hadoula articulates the tenacity of this bond in an acknowledgement that bridges her experience with that of other women and girls.[10]

As I have shown, this experience extends beyond the fictional world or the cultural context of *The Murderess*. Placing Hadoula's and Old Woman Magoun's experience within the transgressive Llorona mythology has forged a discursive bridge of connection among female characters who would otherwise be treated as isolated cases of aberrant motherhood. Although Freeman and Papadiamantis conclude their stories differently—Old Woman Magoun wanders as another Llorona seeking her (grand)child while Hadoula dies with "[s]alt and bitter water fill[ing] her mouth" (126)—they both structure their plots around the identification between old women and female children. Thus, both authors chart a cross-generational pattern of female oppression, which can only be broken through the violence of death. Rather than a sterile ending, though, death triggers the restorative power of memory as a mode of recovering what is physically and emotionally lost.

If poetry helps Betsey Dole visualize the "faces of children that had never been" and imagine a room full of cherubic figures "with white wings" as she tries to revive the memory of a dead child ("A Poetess" 39), myth enables us to recover (and remember) the transgressive resonance of an alternative genealogy of motherhood. This genealogy—matrilineal in its foundation and matriarchal in its scope—situates Freeman's fiction within a wider nexus of literary and mythic texts, which retell old myths in new contexts of global historical relevance. Such contexts, including a nascent awareness across the Atlantic of the politics of gender, point to a diffuse and expansive network of global relations that call for new paradigms of comparison. In Shih's view, "relational comparison" excavates and activates "the historically specific set of relationalities across time and space," which can be "as much about form as content" (79–80). This comparative model sees literature as "participating in a network of power-inflected relations" that operate on multiple levels and require conceptual agility between the micro-scale of the textual—as in close reading—and the macro-scale of the global—in terms of social, cultural, and economic interconnections (Shih 84). Consequently, the fields of comparative and world literature become increasingly interconnected, mutually reflexive, and endlessly generative; in Freeman's case, reading her work *as* world literature generates new, comparative readings of widely discussed and broadly anthologized stories, including "Old Woman Magoun." Such readings can reach across culture and genre, as seen with La Llorona and *The Murderess*, a Central and South American myth and a modern Greek novella, respectively. We need to forge more of these bridges, as we create new spaces of exchange within (and beyond) Freeman studies.

Works Cited

Barakat, Robert A. "Aztec Motifs in 'La Llorona.'" *Southern Folklore Quarterly*, vol. 29, no. 4, 1965, pp. 288–96.

Campbell, Donna M. *Bitter Tastes: Literary Naturalism and Early Cinema in American Women's Writing*. U of Georgia P, 2016.

—. 'The Reign of the Dolls: Violence and the Nonhuman in Mary E. Wilkins Freeman." *New Perspectives on Mary E. Wilkins Freeman*, edited by Stephanie Palmer, Myrto Drizou, and Cécile Roudeau, Edinburgh UP, 2023, pp. 79–94.

Coutelle, Louis, Theofanis G. Stavrou, and David R. Weinberg. *A Greek Diptych: Dionysios Solomos and Alexandros Papadiamantis*. Nostos, 1986.

Donovan, Josephine. *New England Local Color Literature: A Women's Tradition*. Frederick Ungar Publishing, 1983.

Elbert, Monika M. "The Displacement of Desire: Consumerism and Fetishism in Mary Wilkins Freeman's Fiction." *Legacy: A Journal of American Women Writers*, vol. 19, no. 2, 2002, pp. 192–215.

—. "Mary Wilkins Freeman's Devious Women, *Harper's Bazar*, and the Rhetoric of Advertising." *Essays in Literature*, vol. 20, no. 2, 1993, pp. 251–72.

Fisken, Beth Wynne. "The 'Faces of Children That Had Never Been': Ghost Stories by Mary Wilkins Freeman." *Haunting the House of Fiction: Feminist Perspectives on Ghost Stories by American Women*, edited by Lynette Carpenter and Wendy K. Kolmar, U of Tennessee P, 1991, pp. 41–63.

Freeman, Mary E. Wilkins. "The Little Maid at the Door." *Harper's New Monthly Magazine*, February 1892, pp. 349–59.

—. "The Lost Ghost." 1903. *The Wind in the Rose-Bush and Other Stories of the Supernatural*, edited by Myrto Drizou, Hastings College Press, 2015, pp. 145–72.
—. "Old Woman Magoun." 1905. *A New England Nun and Other Stories*, edited by Sandra Zagarell, Penguin, 2000, pp. 218–34.
—. "A Poetess." 1890. *A New England Nun and Other Stories*, edited by Sandra Zagarell, Penguin, 2000, pp. 34–47.
—. "The Reign of the Doll." *Harper's New Monthly Magazine*, January 1904. pp. 285–96.
—. "The Revolt of 'Mother'." 1890. *A New England Nun and Other Stories*, edited by Sandra Zagarell, Penguin, 2000, pp. 64–78.
—. "The Wind in the Rose-Bush." 1903. *The Wind in the Rose-Bush and Other Stories of the Supernatural*, edited by Myrto Drizou, Hastings College Press, 2015, pp. 1–28.
Grasso, Linda. "Inventive Desperation: Anger, Violence, and Belonging in Mary Wilkins Freeman's and Sui Sin Far's Murderous Mother Stories." *American Literary Realism*, vol. 38, no. 1, 2005, pp. 18–31.
Harde, Roxanne. "'At Rest Now': Child Ghosts and Social Justice in 19th-Century Women's Writing." *Transnational Gothic: Literary and Social Exchanges in the Long Nineteenth Century*, edited by Monika Elbert and Bridget M. Marshall, Ashgate, 2013, pp. 189–200.
Kirtley, Bacil F. "'La Llorona' and Related Themes." *Western Folklore*, vol. 19, no. 3, 1960, pp. 155–68.
Kitsi-Mitakou, Katerina. "Aquatic Spaces and Women's Places: A Comparative Reading of George Eliot's *The Mill on the Floss* and Alexandros Papadiamantis's *H φόνισσα*." *Byzantine and Modern Greek Studies*, vol. 29, no. 2, 2005, pp. 187–202.
Kraul, Edward Garcia, and Judith Beatty, eds. *The Weeping Woman: Encounters with La Llorona*. Word Process, 1988.
León, Luis D. *La Llorona's Children: Religion, Life, and Death in the US-Mexican Borderlands*. U of California P, 2004.
Limón, José E. "La Llorona, The Third Legend of Greater Mexico: Cultural Symbols, Women, and the Political Unconscious." *Between Borders: Essays on Mexicana/Chicana History*, edited by Adelaida R. Del Castillo, Floricanto P, 1990, pp. 399–432.
Mignolo, Walter D. "On Comparison: Who Is Comparing What and Why?" *Comparison: Theories, Approaches, Uses*, edited by Rita Felski and Susan Stanford Friedman, Johns Hopkins UP, 2013, pp. 99–119.
Palmer, Stephanie. *Transatlantic Footholds: Turn-of-the-Century American Women Writers and British Reviewers*. Routledge, 2020.
Papadiamantis, Alexandros. *The Murderess*. 1903. Translated by Peter Levi. New York Review of Books, 1983.
Perez, Domino Renee. *There Was a Woman: La Llorona from Folklore to Popular Culture*. U of Texas P, 2008.
Politi, Gina. "Darwinist Text and Papadiamantis's *The Murderess*: A Suggested Reading." *Proceedings from the First International Conference of Comparative Literature: Connections between Greek and other Foreign Literatures*, edited by the Greek Association of General and Comparative Literature, Domos Publications, pp. 253–69.
[Πολίτη, Τζίνα. "Δαρβινικό Κείμενο και 'Η Φόνισσα' του Παπαδιαμάντη: Πρόταση Ανάγνωσης." *Πρακτικά Α΄ Διεθνούς Συνεδρίου Συγκριτικής Γραμματολογίας: Σχέσεις*

της *Ελληνικής με τις Ξένες Λογοτεχνίες*, Ελληνική Εταιρεία Γενικής και Συγκριτικής Γραμματολογίας, Εκδόσεις Δόμος, σελ. 253–69.]

Reichardt, Mary R. "'The Web of Self-Strangulation': Mothers, Daughters, and the Question of Marriage in the Short Stories of Mary Wilkins Freeman." *Joinings and Disjoinings: The Significance of Marital Status in Literature*, edited by JoAnna Stephens Mink and Janet Doubler Ward, Bowling Green State U Popular P, 1991, pp. 109–19.

Shih, Shu-mei. "Comparison as Relation." *Comparison: Theories, Approaches, Uses*, edited by Rita Felski and Susan Stanford Friedman, Johns Hopkins UP, 2013, pp. 79–98.

Notes

1. I am using the term "infanticide" in a broader sense to define the act of killing female, infantilized children. As I show in what follows, female children are sheltered or objectified in ways that keep them in a state of protracted childhood and prevent them from growing into mature women.
2. In "The Little Maid at the Door," Ann Bayley compensates for her daughter's loss by comforting the lonely "little maid" whose parents have been taken away. In "The Lost Ghost," the childless Mrs Bird is gradually consumed by her love for a ghostly girl who is seeking her mother. In "The Wind in the Rose-Bush," Rebecca Flint has no children or husband of her own, as she had to provide for her ailing mother; when her mother dies, Rebecca shifts her caring attention to her niece only to find out the latter has died because of her stepmother's neglect.
3. The term "Greater Mexico" signifies people of Mexican descent on both sides of the US-Mexico border. The term emphasizes connectedness—rather than division—across boundaries.
4. Some scholars, such as Bacil F. Kirtley and Robert A. Bakarat, have argued for La Llorona's European origins, noting thematic and narrative similarities to the "White Lady" (*Die Weisse Frau*) of German folklore and classical female figures (such as Euripides' *Medea*). The origins of the Llorona myth are beyond the scope of this essay, which develops the cross-cultural resonance and political import of such myths for early twentieth-century literary texts.
5. Alexandros Papadiamantis (1851–1911) holds a prominent position in the modern Greek literary canon, as he recorded the conflict between modernity and tradition in turn-of-the-century Greek society (and particularly his native island of Skiathos). His style is idiosyncratic; his language is an archaizing or "purist" (*katharévousa*) form of Greek with a lot of regional dialect, and his tenor is realist with many naturalist elements. Papadiamantis's work was mostly serialized in Greek newspapers and periodicals and was not collected in volumes until after his death. The first foreign translation of *The Murderess* was attempted by Octave Merlier and appeared in 1934 in French. For a succinct account of Papadiamantis's reception and oeuvre, see Coutelle et al.
6. For more on Freeman's reception in the British literary market, see Palmer.
7. Papadiamantis refers to his protagonist as "Old Hadoula" at the very beginning of the story. He later calls her simply "Hadoula," which is the name I use

throughout the essay. I retain this spelling for reasons of consistency, although the name can also be transcribed as "Khadoula." Other names by which Hadoula is called are "Jannis Frankissa" or "Frankojannou" to emphasize the relation to her husband, Jannis Frankos, which is one of possessorship according to Greek gender conventions.
8. The Greek Fates survived in Roman mythology as the "Parcae" (Nona, Decuma, and Morta) who determined human destiny in a similar way to their Greek counterparts.
9. After nearly four centuries of Ottoman rule, the designation "Turkish" carried mostly negative connotations for Greek people. Hence, to label someone "Turkish" would be to assign a deviant and allegedly barbaric identity to them. By Papadiamantis's time, the modern Greek state was still quite new, struggling to recuperate its territorial and cultural integrity.
10. Hadoula's death by water has often been interpreted as a return to the womb or a cathartic moment of expiation. For an interesting comparison of Hadoula's and Maggie Tulliver's death by drowning (in *The Murderess* and George Eliot's *The Mill on the Floss,* respectively), see Kitsi-Mitakou.

6

REDEFINING THE NEW ENGLAND NUN: A REVISIONIST READING IN THE CONTEXT OF *PEMBROKE* AND IRISH AMERICAN FICTION

AUŠRA PAULAUSKIENĖ

The title story of Mary E. Wilkins Freeman's collection *A New England Nun* (1891) has generated a vigorous debate. The scholars argue whether Louisa Ellis's refusal to marry signifies a preference for autonomy or a gesture of passivity driven by fear of sexuality and change. For many critics, the religious term *nun* is a metaphor for avoiding matrimony. Claiming that there are "two New England nuns" in Freeman's early short fiction—Louisa Ellis from "A New England Nun" and Louisa Britton from "Louisa"—Martha J. Cutter defines the nun as a woman "who decide[s] not to marry" (213). Janice Daniel, too, pairs the two Louisas as unconventional young women who choose singleness over the traditional "place" of marriage (70). When critics attempt to de-stigmatize spinsterhood, they use the term "nun" positively, associating it with women's autonomy. On the other hand, the term is used negatively when Louisa Ellis' self-isolation and sterility are condemned. In either case, the "nun" is equated with an unmarried woman while the meaning and connotations of the term—other than sexual abstinence—are either disregarded or used loosely.

As an example, Ben Couch acknowledges that Louisa "gives up society in order to serve her own higher purpose, her autonomy" similarly to a nun who "gives up sexuality and society" to serve God (188). Despite this awareness, though, Couch concludes that Louisa does not give up her sexuality; on the contrary, sexual pleasure "without the help of a man" is her higher purpose (197). The nun's vocation to serve God is replaced by her alleged pursuit of autoerotic desires. A similar mismatch between the definition and its application occurs in Susan K. Harris's analysis. Drawing on William Wordsworth's sonnet "Nuns fret not at their convent's narrow room" (1807), Harris defines nuns as eager seekers of "voluntary imprisonment," a site for production of "spiritual enlightenment" ("Mary E. Wilkins Freeman" 32). Yet her characterization of Louisa as a nun who "forsakes the world for a narrow existence" of cleaning, polishing, and sewing equates a nun's narrow cell with Louisa's narrow existence (36). Real nuns, however, practice ascetic living to achieve the transcendence Wordsworth is talking about.

The dominance of the feminist approach in Freeman's scholarship since the 1970s is partially responsible for such a loose interpretation of the Roman Catholic term "nun." True, nuns are not exclusive to Catholicism. However, the reference to a rosary at the end of the story seals Louisa's comparison to a *Catholic* nun, which offers a new perspective to consider Catholicism, a foreign element in Freeman's New England. Without claiming Freeman's special interest in Catholicism, I suggest that her definition of the term *nun* might be closer to its specifically Catholic definition than the definition offered by Freeman feminist critics who draw an equation between a nun and an unmarried woman. If Freeman does use the term metaphorically, the figurative meaning of the term encompasses her critique of the remnants of Calvinism, not only as a mode of gender oppression but also as a state of paralysis that parallels a Catholic nun's supposedly repetitive and stagnant routine.

Reading the story alongside other Catholic literary traditions, such as Irish American fiction, allows to examine the image of the nun as the Other in New England's Protestant culture at the turn of the twentieth century in the context of the idealized picture of this ecclesiastical figure drawn by religious insiders, in this case, Irish Catholics. Partially autobiographical texts by Kate Chopin, Kate McPhelim Cleary, James T. Farrell and Eugene O'Neill, written between the 1890s and the 1940s, feature Louisa Ellis's Irish female contemporaries yearning for a convent. Such Irish American texts challenge Freeman's image of the nun as a woman stuck in repetitive and sterile routines, but also echo her positive rendering of serenity and purity in Louisa's ritualized lifestyle. Freeman's wry admiration for the nun's life, I argue, echoes a similar portrayal of cloistered nuns in Chopin's "Lilacs" (1894). Freeman's contemporary with Irish roots, Kate O'Flaherty Chopin, was acquainted with Catholicism, as she was raised and educated in St Louis Sacred Heart convent from the age of six.

In my suggested reading, "A New England Nun" builds the foundation for Louisa's final naming as a nun; in fact, I argue that Louisa has converted into a nun *before* the story opens, and the intrigue is about whether Louisa will keep her nun's identity. Reading "A New England Nun" in the context of Irish American literature suggests that becoming a nun is a favorable solution in

Louisa's geographical and social environment. In this respect, Freeman's story *echoes* with select Chopin, Farrell, and O'Neill texts by representing a nun as freer and happier than a married woman.

On the other hand, the term is also endowed with a contrasting meaning of entrapment in the region's Puritan past. Read in the light of the novel *Pembroke* (1894), Louisa emerges as a *New England* nun. A comparison of Louisa Ellis to Barnabas Thayer on the one hand and Sylvia Crane on the other—both are characters of the novel *Pembroke*—uncovers distressing aspects of the term "nun" in Freeman's use of it, most importantly, an emotional paralysis caused by unbending habits. The metaphors of the tracks and the hunched back, that stand for the relics of the stiff Puritan will in the novel, can also be found, albeit in a more implied form, in "A New England Nun." Since the novel was published only three years later than the story, the latter could serve as a sketch for the extended study of New England character in *Pembroke*. Furthermore, the author's Introductory Sketch included in the 1899 edition of the novel explains Freeman's tone and attitude to her characters, alluding, I argue, to her earlier creation, Louisa Ellis.

In the Introductory Sketch to *Pembroke*, Freeman revealed her intention to write a study of abnormalities in the human will (iii). Historicist critics have noted a consistent development of this idea in her writing. Perry D. Westbrook praises Freeman as a "supreme" analyst of the vestiges of Puritan will in New England character (62). Donald R. Anderson, more recently, observes the influence of Puritan past on the "inaction" of the present (113). Susan Allen Toth sums up Freeman's favorite themes as "the gradual petrification of Puritan beliefs and the paralysis of Puritan will and vigor" (566). The paralysis of the will to act and live a full life, Toth claims, is symptomatic of the "spiritual decline" in nineteenth-century New England (567). In the Introductory Sketch Freeman not only diagnoses but also shows a way to heal the disease with compassion and care for others. When put in the context of *Pembroke*, Louisa Ellis emerges as a patient who does not overcome her spiritual disfigurement and remains a nun in her unredeemed state.

Puritan and Catholic Legacies in Freeman's New England

Stephanie Palmer reminds us that in nineteenth-century British reviews, the alleged Englishness of Freeman's characters "obscured the real Irish and French Canadians who inhabited the real New England" (76). The literary historian Ron Ebest points out that the United States provided a favorable environment for the Catholic devout (140). He draws on the historian John Cogley to suggest that nowhere else in the world "were so many Catholic children drilled as thoroughly" as in America's parochial schools (Ebest 140). During the second half of the nineteenth century, the number of all-girl private schools staffed by religious orders, such as the Sisters of the Sacred Heart, burgeoned from around fifty to over 700 (144). A staggering number of 88,773 nuns lived in the United States by 1920 (144).

Indeed, New Englanders coexisted with Irish immigrants since the middle of the nineteenth century. Edward Foster dates the arrival of the Irish in Randolph as the late 1840s, a few years before Mary E. Wilkins Freeman was born (4). By the 1880s the Irish had not only built houses on the land of former estates but owned Randolph's shoe factories (110). Therefore, Freeman encountered their presence from an early age and throughout her intermittent residence in the town to the extent that she could not have missed her community's attitude toward them. Foster states that "the Irish were hated, for they were Catholics and competitors for jobs" (4).

The divisions between Protestants and Catholics, as well as Anglo-Saxon and Irish stocks, were sharp due to the unapologetic ideology of nativism in the turn-of-the-century US. As a writer of Anglo-Saxon heritage and Calvinist descent, Freeman was revered by Anglo-British reviewers of her early fiction to which both "A New England Nun" and the novel *Pembroke* belong (Palmer 74). However, in her racial views Freeman remains as enigmatic as in her literary themes. Not accidentally, she appealed to Irish nationalist critics no less than she appealed to Anglo-Saxonist ones (Palmer 73). Besides, even independently of Freeman's views, Puritan and Catholic systems of beliefs as well as their cultural effects on Americans have had more commonalities than it may seem.

Both were restrictive, especially in matters of sexuality. According to Palmer, "Puritan" in the United States meant "old-fashioned and sexually repressed" (81). To draw an analogy, Charles Fanning points out a "deep puritanical streak" in the Irish culture, especially regarding matters of sex (32). Both Puritanism and Catholicism were patriarchal, but paradoxically, by making sexuality shameful, both diminished the status of men in the family. While both religious communities elevated mothers as guardians of morality in family and society, they trapped not only their daughters but also their husbands and sons in an outdated system of beliefs that had become part of a group's cultural identity. The mother who sacrifices her children to her faith is an archetype in Irish American literature and can be compared to Deborah Thayer of *Pembroke*. Deborah's character evokes associations with Julia Devlin in Elizabeth Cullinan's *House of Gold* (1970), a much later novel than Freeman's, with a similar theme of the cultural impact of religion that is generationally transmitted and sustained by the mother figure.

Brought into existence by historical circumstances, both sets of beliefs were exported to America and safeguarded through transmission across generations. As the early colonists leaned on Puritan values, such as will and tenacity, Irish immigrants to the US saw Catholicism as integral to their identity. As noted by Ebest, the Church for Irish Americans was a "source of solidarity, pride, and comfort" in the face of nativist prejudice (36). Both religions morphed to adjust to modern societies, but as Irish American literature captures the hold Catholicism still had on Irish Americans at the beginning of the twentieth century, Freeman records a similar process of difficult emancipation from certain legacies of Puritanism in nineteenth-century New England.

Catholic Allusions, "A New England Nun," and Irish American Fiction

"A New England Nun" is framed by Catholic images, such as a "nun" in the title, a rosary, and a repeated reference to a nun at the end. Yet less obvious allusions to Catholicism can be read in between these frames. One of the most cited details in the story is the protagonist's aprons. Daniel, for example, refers to Louisa's "precise and methodical" behavior, such as apron "removal and replacement," as "rituals" (71). She states that these rituals "help validate Louisa's identity" as a solitary but fulfilled creator of her own "place" (71). Extending this point, I argue that Louisa's domestic rituals evoke associations with religious rituals of the Catholic Church.

When going to the garden, the protagonist "tie[s] a green apron round her waist" to protect her dress against soiling (1). The green color as well as the "gingham" material are practical for gardening purposes; underneath she wears a shorter one of "calico" fabric, convenient for her sewing (3). The sewing apron serves to protect, but also hide, "still another," white "company apron" of "fine material" with "a little cambric edging on the bottom" that will enter into rotation when she has a guest (3). The rotation of the aprons can be interpreted as a religious act, allusive to Catholicism and pre-Reformation Christianity with their highly regulated order of wearing liturgical vestments and non-liturgical religious garments. More specifically and more related to Freeman's choice of the Catholic term "nun," the protagonist's apron may allude to the scapular, originally an item of clothing that was (and still is) part of the habit of monks and nuns. A scapular for those in the monastic life is a marker equivalent to the stole for a priest. Scapulars have differed in length; they were mostly at knee-length (although could be either longer or shorter) but were invariably designed as outer garments, open on the sides and originally joined by straps at the waist. In fact, monastic scapulars originated as aprons worn by medieval monks.

Ritual-like apron tying, untying, and rotation are very much in character with Louisa's ritualized lifestyle on the whole. "Slow and still in her movements," she takes "a long time to prepare her tea" before she "set[s] it forth" on the "little square table" that stands "exactly in the center of the kitchen" (2). The order, regularity, and repetition suggest a religious ritual. The luxury of the dishes, a "cut-glass tumbler," a "silver cream-pitcher," a china "sugar-bowl," and a "china cup and saucer," as well as the table linen, a "starched linen cloth," and a "damask napkin" remind us of the exclusive, designated items used by a Catholic priest holding a Mass (2).

In addition to these covert Catholic allusions, Louisa possesses nun-like character qualities. Freeman characterizes her protagonist as possessing "sweet serenity which never failed her," "acquiescing with" and accepting "with docility" her mother's counsel and her society's views on marriage as a woman's natural path, similarly to how a nun would humbly accept the regulations of the church (7). Although fourteen years have passed, Louisa "had changed but little" (8). To Joe Daggett's gaze, she is "every whit as attractive as ever," since she "still kept her pretty manner and soft grace" (8). Daggett registers her unchanged youthful looks and grace, the qualities that can be found behind convent walls in Chopin's "Lilacs."

Chopin emphasizes Sister Agathe's youthful innocence, although she is in her forties: "[h]er fair blonde face flushed and paled with every passing emotion that visited her soul" (539). The story was written soon after Chopin visited a friend, who, unlike her, had taken vows in the convent of their youth. The nun looked young and innocent, and in possession of beauty that would not diminish with age (Ebest 148). Such a portrait of a youthful nun as well as a secular woman's admiration for her made way into the story. Sister Agathe, according to Ebest, is "hopelessly naïve" about her worldly friend's lovers and suitors (153). Agathe's "unworldliness," I suggest, is her main appeal to Adrienne. The nuns' purity, like their youth, is preserved in the isolation from the corrupting influences of the outside world. That is why, driven by lilac smell-induced nostalgia, Adrienne takes an annual vacation to a convent.

In Freeman's story, equally innocent Louisa misses the signs of her fiancé's infatuation with Lily Dyer. Joe Dagget "colors" upon Louisa's mentioning of Lily's name and talks about the latter with a "sort of embarrassed warmth"; these clues, though, are lost on the girlishly naïve New England nun (4). Like Chopin's Adrienne, Louisa feels nostalgia for the life she will lose. Marjorie Pryse has pointed out "a tangible feeling of personal loss" in Louisa as she is "anticipating her marriage" (294). She gleans the sense of loss in the protagonist's mood right before her discovery that her fiancé is enamored with another woman.

During her evening walk, Louisa witnesses the fertility of "harvest-fields" on both sides of the road, as she walks, and the entanglement of shrubs and vines on either side of the wall, when she sits down (Freeman 12). She is immersed in the "mysterious[ly] sweet" air of a summer night (13) but at the same time "shut in" by these images of nature's reproductive vigor (12). Instead of anticipating to become part of this cycle of life, Louisa "look[s] about her with mildly sorrowful reflectiveness" (12). In a similar vein to the sense of loss that Pryse points out, Louisa's mood underscores her longing for the cloistered life she is about to give up.

Farrell describes a similar escapist fantasy from sexuality in his short story "Mary O'Reilley" (1928). An elderly unmarried protagonist, living a comfortable although unfulfilled life supported by her brother, rethinks her life's choices.

Having rejected one marriage proposal and having been too passive to pursue the man she was interested in, sensing life "shrinking and shrivelling inside of her," she recalls contemplating a convent at the age of thirty (53). To Mary, the convent represents not a religious calling but an escape from "the youth, love, laughter and babies of other people, and her restless thoughts" (53). Similarly, Louisa, fenced in by the lush nature, longs for an escape from heteronormative sexuality and the bustle of life that await her after the wedding.

In another reverie, Louisa misses her nun's life by juxtaposing it with the duties of married life she is about to enter. "Going about among her neat maidenly possessions," she feels as "one looking her last upon the faces of dear friends" (8). She frets over "features of her happy solitary life" and "graceful but half-needless" tasks she will be "obliged to relinquish" and simple pleasures of essence distilling and leisurely sewing she will have to "la[y] away" for "sterner tasks" her husband and mother-in-law will "devolve upon her" (9). Her present life of a nun seems freer and happier to her than the imagined married life. In this sense, a woman yearning for a nun's life echoes a similar, recurrent theme in Irish American fiction.

American writers with Irish roots link the idealized image of the nun among Irish American women with the scarcity of other options for women at the close of the nineteenth century. Freeman herself could not have read this literature—the texts I cite were published later than the collection *A New England Nun*. The examples I offer reveal the archetypal relation of Irish American women of Freeman's time with the real option of becoming nuns. That choice is seen as preferable to marriage, while the reasons for such preference emerge from the historical and social conditions in which these women lived.

At the end of the nineteenth century, the options for Irish American women were as limited as those of Freeman's New England women. They could be covered by marriage, or uncovered, but with one important distinction: an additional choice of becoming a Catholic nun. This alternative is imagined as a happier one than marriage in nineteenth-century women's texts, such as Chopin's "Lilacs," or Cleary's "The Stepmother" (1901). The allure of the convent continues to resurface well into the twentieth century, and in the fiction of canonical male writers, the already mentioned Farrell and O'Neill. Their highly autobiographical texts offer "literary inventions" that embody the "collective experience" of Irish American womanhood (Ebest 10). The fact that the writers used mothers and aunts as their prototypes makes that experience even more credible, especially when the portraits of convent-nostalgic women appear in the texts of multiple authors.

An Irish American woman's convent fantasy was most widely circulated by O'Neill in his world classic *Long Day's Journey into Night*. Although written in 1941, the play is set in 1912 and explores the psyche of an Irish American woman preoccupied with her girlhood past in nineteenth-century America.

Mary Tyrone's character is based on the writer's mother, Ella Quinlan O'Neill. She gave birth to her son Eugene in 1888 and got addicted to morphine. Mary Tyrone remembers herself as a "very pious girl" who "dreamed of becoming a nun" (104). These memories temporarily transform her from a bitter and tortured wife and mother to an "innocent" convent girl, who smiles "shyly" (107). That girl fell in love with James Tyrone and "all [she] wanted was to be his wife" (108). Mary regrets her choice, "You were much happier before you knew he existed, in the convent when you used to pray to the Blessed Virgin" (109). She longingly continues, "If I could only find the faith I lost, so I could pray again" (109). Looking at her wedding dress, Mary wonders what she had wanted it for. In a drug-induced trip to her youth, she longs for a purity of body and soul that would connect her to the Virgin Mary. "I'm going to be a nun—that is, if I could only find ... What is it I am looking for?" she asks (175). "I know it's something I lost," she says, "Something I miss terribly" (176).

O'Neill's mother's story is similar to Cleary's: they both developed a morphine addiction as a result of medical treatment for childbirth complications and both were demonized for it by the men in the family. Cleary bore six children on the Nebraskan frontier, despite her fear of childbirth, which she called the "black shadow," and endured the death of two of them, in addition to the battle with her eight-year-long morphine addiction and her husband's attempts to have her committed as insane. In the writer's partially autobiographical story "The Stepmother," a woman gives up her independent single life for the romantic notion of being a wife, a stepmother, and a mother. From then on, her life is determined by her husband's choices and failures.

Farrell's short story "Jim O'Neill" (1932), too, features a literary prototype of the author's mother, Mary Daly Farrell. Instead of being a homemaker, Liz O'Neill is a sloppy housewife and spends more time at the church than at the house. In her husband's words, she is "such a goddamn fool, praying all day in the church, until the janitors ha[ve] to ask her to leave" (60). But then he remembers his baby boy dying at his mother's breast and his own pain helps him to understand why she is in the church praying instead of "making things at home pretty and orderly," as an Irishwoman should (60). Although Liz O'Neill does not have a convent fantasy in this story, written from her husband Jim's perspective, the walls of the church appear more comforting to her than family life. Despite the solace Liz finds in a local church, it was the Catholic Church that "caught" her in the endless cycle of physical pain, grief of child loss, and grueling domestic work, and did so by forbidding any way of avoiding pregnancy, including divorce (Ebest 37). Not surprisingly, being a nun seemed a coveted route for escape. Nuns were free from subordination to husbands and their kin, pain and dangers of childbirth, and domestic duties (149). On the other hand, they did not escape "grueling" work in the convent (Ebest 149). Their days were "regulated around a strict schedule of duties," while their behavior was governed by many rules and closely monitored (150).

Nevertheless, the convent offered nineteenth-century women significant occupations that secular women, married or single, did not have. One of the Protestant suffragist speakers in Catharine Beecher's collected public addresses *Woman Suffrage and Woman's Profession* (1871), "praise[d] the Catholic hierarchy for creating convents" (Harris "Introduction" 16). In the words of the speaker, nuns as single women could exercise "higher ministry" than marriage; there they found "comfortable positions and honorable distinctions" (Catharine Beecher qtd in Harris 16). Many nuns were capable administrators, scholars, and teachers. Ebest points out that teaching nuns had a big advantage over secular teachers in the Boston area where Randolph is situated, since Boston public school district "refused to hire married women" (149). Freeman included this historical detail in the story "Louisa," where the protagonist loses her teaching position to Ida Mosley, but once Jonathan Nye starts courting her, Ida's family, sure of the impending marriage, "have Ida give the school up" (*A New England Nun* 405).

Despite their tenured jobs as teachers, as noted by Ebest, Massachusetts teaching nuns earned "less than one third" of the Boston elementary school teacher's salary (150). The pay should not have mattered, since the nuns were not allowed individual possessions. It may be surmised that the restrictions in nuns' lives balanced, if not outweighed, the freedoms. Yet a legitimate question may arise, that is, which feature of a nun's life might have become the bottom line for Freeman when defining Louisa as a nun.

Ebest observes that people may be tempted to assume that "their imaginations evacuated by the purgatives of dogma," the nuns were "rendered serene, obedient, and safely dull" (150). He uses the examples of Chopin and another distinguished woman of Irish American letters, Mary McCarthy, both schooled by the Sisters of the Sacred Heart, to suggest that those assumptions were false (150). Chopin and McCarthy revolted against the Catholic dogma but their disapprobation of the church was tempered by the positive memories about the nuns who had taught them (Ebest 176). Poignantly, in "Lilacs," Chopin idealizes Sister Agathe's innocence and kindness as well as the simplicity, modesty, and spirituality of nun's lives.

One passage in particular in Chopin's "Lilacs" echoes the conclusion of Freeman's story. In her lifestyle, Chopin's protagonist Adrienne, with her multiple suitors, an exciting acting career, and a luxurious house, is very unlike Freeman's ascetic and seemingly asexual Louisa. However, at the first smell of lilacs, Adrienne rushes to the convent where she stays in the company of another nun in a "spotless" bed placed on the "bare floors" of an "immaculately white" room; in fact, she does it "with subtle and naïve pleasure" (542). The order, neatness, simplicity, and peacefulness that lure the worldly Adrienne to a convent are also the ingredients cherished by Freeman's reclusive Louisa.

These texts published only three years apart, one by a writer with Irish Catholic roots and the other by a writer with Anglo-Saxon Puritan roots, present strikingly similar images of a nun's life. "The days of the fortnight which followed were in character much like the first peaceful, uneventful day of her arrival," as Chopin's narrator describes Adrienne's experiences at the convent (542). The conclusion of Freeman's story echoes in the image of a repetitive and peaceful existence of a nun: "She gazed ahead through a long reach of future days strung together like pearls in a rosary, every one like the others, and all smooth and flawless and innocent" (*A New England Nun* 17). Like Chopin's sentence that idealizes the simplicity and peace of a convent, Freeman's statement carries a similar tone of admiration. However, the positive connotations of "smooth," "flawless," and "innocent" future days "strung together like pearls in a rosary" contrast with the judgment implied by their "placid narrowness" and a suggestion that Louisa had "sold her birthright" of the "busy harvest of men and birds and bees" for the "pottage" of uneventful, isolated and loveless existence (17).

A Nun as the Metaphor for Stunted Life

It is precisely in the story's conclusion that the meaning of the term "nun" acquires the ambivalence built into the narrator's balancing between approval and judgment. The last sentence of the story leaves Louisa "prayerfully numbering" those flawless and innocent days, "like an uncloistered nun" (17). Pryse, who has analyzed the meaning of "uncloistered nun" defines it as free from prescribed heterosexual normativity. In Pryse's words, Louisa's choice of solitude "leaves her ironically 'uncloistered'" and "imaginatively freer, in her society, than she would otherwise have been" (295). A Catholic reader may understand the term to mean a nun who lives outside a cloister, or convent, or a woman who lives like a nun without taking a nun's vows. Even in this literal meaning, "uncloistered" promises a life that is freer than one regulated by patriarchal or religious rules.

Freeman may have been familiar with the Catholic definition when she named Louisa an *uncloistered* nun. However, the possible positive connotations of the term are complicated by the other religious reference in the story's ending, the comparison of Louisa to biblical Esau: "If Louisa Ellis had sold her birthright she did not know it, the taste of the pottage was so delicious" (17). According to Michael Tritt, who analyzed this allusion to Genesis, the Bible commentators "typically chastise" Esau, who is entitled to honor and spiritual blessings, but relinquishes his birthright "indifferently' for a bowl of pottage (37). Tritt's interpretation suggests that Freeman, too, chastises Louisa. In fact, the writer's attitude to her character has been a debatable subject in the criticism of "A New England Nun."

Jennifer Ansley points out that Freeman tends to sympathize with her characters' isolation in economically depressed New England towns (439). Ansley states that "the out-migration of labor," among other factors, isolated the women in rural spaces, and that Freeman "well understood" this (447). Considering that Louisa is one of the women isolated by her wage-earning fiancé's departure, Freeman's compassion could be expected. According to Ansley, however, Miss Ellis's character is exceptional. Louisa welcomes the solitude that her geographic and economic isolation creates and enjoys the fruit of her "ritualistic" homemaking labor as a guest to herself (448). Therefore, in Ansley's opinion, she does not need sympathy.

In my view, Ansley's argument about the impact of economic changes on relationships in the regions is fresh and compelling. Men's migration to cities freed them from the constraints of the family (Ansley 445). Women left behind in small towns had to find ways to queer their emotional attachments without physically leaving their restrictive geographical spaces (446). Building on Ansley's insight, I find Louisa's character exceptional but in a way that does garner sympathy from the author. In contrast to other female characters in Freeman's fiction, who forge relationships among themselves, Louisa's only human relationship is with her own self. For this reason, to apply Freeman's perspective on the residents of Pembroke to Louisa Ellis, she "is not to be pitied" for her "unhappiness," since she is happy with her limited life (Introductory Sketch vii). What is to be "reasonably lamented" is her "restricted view of life" that prevents a comprehension of her wasted life (vii).

It is possible to read "A New England Nun" as regret for unfulfillment, like "The Three Old Sisters and the Old Beau" (1896), analyzed as a parable of a wasted life by Toth. The "folly of unfulfillment" manifests in the characters "becom[ing] caught by habit" (566). As pointed out by Toth, Freeman herself used the expression "fixed in tracks" (566). Unable to "lift their feet and set them in another path," Toth explains, they "reject the passions of life without even knowing that they have made a choice" (566). Like the characters of *Pembroke*, I argue, Louisa is stuck in the tracks of repetitive habits. Unlike some redeemed characters of the novel, she does not get off her narrow track: "Placid narrowness had become to her as the birthright itself" ("A New England Nun" 17). This statement in the conclusion confirms Louisa's identity as a nun that marriage would have overturned.

In fact, Louisa's transformation into a nun happens earlier, during the fourteen years of Joe's absence. "Much had happened," says the narrator, "but the greatest happening of all—a subtle happening" was the change in Louisa that her mother and brother were "too simple to understand" (7). Unnoticed by them, "Louisa's feet had turned into a path" (7). The use of the phrase "the greatest of all" in relation to a mysterious happening allude to a spiritual change, such as taking a nun's vow in Catholicism. Besides its being autonomous and individualized, this path has other positive elements: it is "smooth maybe under a calm, serene sky" (7). But these positive features are outweighed by clear negatives: this path is "straight" and "unswerving," and "so narrow that there [is] no room for any one at her side" (7). Even three adjectives, *straight, unswerving*, and *narrow* evoke Freeman's metaphor of being "fixed in tracks," mentioned by Toth, while absence of "room for any one at her side" clearly alludes to the state of loveless-ness that Barnabas and Richard overcome in *Pembroke*, but Louisa fails to do in "A New England Nun."

According to Westbrook, conversion in Puritan descendants occurred as an "overwhelming emotionally charged surge of conviction of the reality of Christ and a consuming love for him" (57). In *Pembroke*, a deeply felt compassion for another catapults Barnabas Thayer and Richard Alger from reclusiveness to active love. Barnabas, the protagonist of *Pembroke*, is the main device for the author's extended metaphor of a spine that breaks under the burden of the ossified Calvinist legacy and only gets straightened out when Barnabas's love for Charlotte overcomes his rigid will. It is precisely such a conversion that is missing in the conclusion of "A New England Nun."

The track Louisa stepped into keeps her stuck in her decorous but seemingly useless habits. Her domestic work is self-serving, since she does not share the fruit of her labor with either the family or community. Her love is spent on objects. In Harris's apt phrasing, Louisa "sanctifies" house objects by her "loving care" and "lavishes all her love" on domestic routines ("Mary E. Wilkins Freeman" 37). Had the turn of the plot been different, marriage might have caused suffering, but would have also caused change, growth, and emotional communion. Feminist critics, who celebrate Louisa's selfishness as a rebellion against one of the main precepts of true womanhood, do not consider Freeman's views on individualism that she explained in the Introductory Sketch to *Pembroke*.

When presenting *Pembroke* to her readers as "a study of the human will . . . in different phases of disease," Freeman prescribed the remedy that in my reading links with a conversion: "the capacity of the individual for a love which could rise above all considerations of self" (Introductory Sketch iii). Barnabas Thayer is "the most pronounced exemplification of this theory" (iii). Barney's ailment and cure are portrayed allegorically as the straightening of a bent spine. He "was to [Freeman] as much the victim of disease as the man with curvature of the spine" (iii). The metaphor of crookedness marks the disease, while straightness signifies those who healed from the deformations of the will. He "was incapable of straightening himself . . . until he had laid hands upon a . . . purely unselfish love" (iii). Since Barney's emotional conversion has been discussed before, including by Freeman herself in the Introductory Sketch, I will track the story line of Sylvia Crane, the other character in the novel, besides Barney, who plays a role in the allegory of the curved spine. In her healed status, she can serve as a contrast to unredeemed Louisa.

The Metaphor of Deformity in *Pembroke*

In her intergenerational position in the Crane women dynasty, Sylvia is also instrumental in portraying the difficult generational disentanglement from tradition. Before leaving home, Sylvia rolls the same stone before the front door of the same house that two generations of Crane women have rolled before her (22). The eighteen-year-old courtship of Richard Alger has become a religion of her life, an "altar of love" on which she "laid her offerings" (26). Despite her lover's inaction, "love alone made the past years stand out for her" (25). If Sylvia suffers from a disease, it is schizophrenia of frustrated desire. Had Richard attempted to join her on the sofa, Sylvia would have arisen in feigned indignation, "propelled by stiff springs of modest virtue," perhaps rusty but still functional in Freeman's rural New England (27). She "had been trained" that love should be "concealed, with shamefaced air, even from herself" (27), and her redeeming act in the novel is a victory over puritanical secrecy and shame in matters of love.

The insurmountable obstacle of a stone at her door pushes her suitor back into his track "so hard he can't go out again if he wants to" (36). While after Richard's aborted courtship Sylvia worries on account of Richard missing hot meals and darned stockings, soon she starts to feel—and express—resentment at being jilted by a stubborn man. Her voice acquires a "curious impatient ring," her face a frown (37), and her movements "nervous jerks" (38). Not only her family but also Sylvia herself are shocked by a "certain vicious and waspish element which nobody had suspected her to possess" as if "some primal and evil instinct had taken possession of her" (38). From a meek "lamb" (40) Sylvia turns into a "crazy creature" (42).

Unknowingly using Barnabas as a stand-in for Richard, she breaks out of her restraining jacket of proper maidenly behavior. Sylvia looks "straight into his face" with a "strange boldness, her body inclined towards him," "pull[s] him down" to the sofa next to her, "[shrinks] close to him," "[lays] her head on his shoulder," and asks him to put his arm around her (170). When she realizes her error of mistaken identity, she turns on Barney "with sudden fierceness" (173). She accuses him of hurting her niece, Charlotte, and by implication blames Richard for hurting her, "all due to [their] awful will that won't let [them] give in to anybody" (174).

Sylvia's "impulse of rebellion," albeit "mild," indicates "perhaps some strain from far-off, untempered ancestors which had survived New England generations" (263). Freeman makes her a liminal character who is torn between the generationally instilled tradition and "strange" stirrings of pre-Puritan past. The metaphor of deformity that is fully developed through Barney's character is first applied to Sylvia. Her nature "had been warped to one side by one concentrated and unsatisfied desire" but as a woman who fought for and gained her love, she

Figure 6.1 "Sylvia never turned her head." *Pembroke*, 1894. Image courtesy of Thompson Library Charvat American Fiction Stacks, Thompson Library Special Collections, The Ohio State University Libraries.

has "regained her equilibrium" and "a certain quiet decision and dignity which bewildered everybody" (289). She used to be what may be called a crooked *nun*, "queer" and "slanted" in her sisters' eyes, but straightened out (289).

In "A New England Nun," the metaphor of crookedness may be implied by juxtaposing Louisa, who is sitting inside bent over her needlework, and Lily Dyer, who passes by outside "tall and erect and blooming" (16). While contrasted with Lily, Louisa can be paired with the willful Deborah Thayer from *Pembroke*. Freeman describes Louisa's path and Deborah's parenting in almost analogous language. Miss Ellis's path is "so straight and unswerving that it could only meet a check at her grave, and so narrow that there was no room for any one at her side" ("A New England Nun" 7). The path in which the sickly Ephraim "was forced to tread" was "so strait and narrow" that "it seemed as if his very soul could do no more than shuffle along where his mother pointed" (*Pembroke* 216).

Inferior to men in the public sphere, Puritan women were given authority at home. Since they were responsible for their children's righteousness and salvation, they gained a voice in matters of religion and morality. Similarly, Irish mothers were supposed to "provide moral and religious education" (Fanning 32). During the post-famine devotional revolution, the Irish hierarchy "consign[ed]" the family's "moral edification" to women (Ebest 108). "Endorsed and fortified by the Church," mothers became "the culture's moral magistrates," representing the church and Ireland (108). Matriarchal types that rule by manipulation or "by sheer force of will" (Fanning 31), present in Irish American texts, are recognizable in Freeman's fiction. Although her son looks more sick than usual, Deborah "steel[s] herself against that" driven by "high purpose" (239) due to her "position as the vicar of God upon earth for her child" (240).

If pride and stubbornness are symptomatic of the free will disorder, it is legitimate to wonder if the docile Louisa Ellis is afflicted by the same spiritual disease as Deborah Thayer, or Barnabas Thayer. I argue that in both the novel and the story, the ills of the will separate these characters from the spirit (or energy) that the author associates with love for a person, or, more broadly, one's neighbor. Should such a person be defined as a nun, Barnabas, before he is healed, could pose as one of Freeman's representative "nuns." Before his fateful visit to Charlotte's, Barney kisses a partition wall of his new house, overcome by "the joy to come to him within these walls" (7). After deserting Charlotte, he sits alone at his table "around which there would never be any faces but those of his dead dreams" (116). He lives like a "hermit," taking "solitary meals" in his unfinished house (167). As Sylvia had regained her equilibrium and true self by winning her love, Barney in the end "regains his old self" and "noble bearing" by putting compassion for Charlotte above his pride (329). On his way to Charlotte's to regain his love, he walks into a scene full of "life" and "resurrection" of spring nature (329), similar to the one Louisa Ellis calmly lets pass her by behind the window.

I would suggest, however, that neither Louisa's chastity nor her unconventional rejection of marriage earn Freeman's disapproval. Even her Catholic-like rituals receive the narrator's tolerant, meager admiration. If anything, the author's critique targets Louisa's inflexibility and withdrawal from human connection, as even her animals are separated from her love by cage bars and leashes. While becoming a nun and connecting to humanity through prayer and good works was an option for Freeman's Catholic contemporaries, her *New England* nun remains hostage to an inflexible, Puritan past. When placed in the context of the culturally ailing characters of *Pembroke*, Louisa Ellis's character emerges as a crooked nun—crookedness standing as a metaphor for the crippling effect of Calvinist doctrine of free will on nineteenth-century rural New Englanders, their narrowness and contentment with it serving as indicators of their spiritual malaise.

Louisa is not straightened out by a sudden surge of empathy that connects the reclusive characters of *Pembroke* to humanity. Therefore, the story leaves her in the unredeemed status of a nun. The term, as it is used in the conclusion of the story, stands for a no longer usable rigid will that blocks love for fellow humans. Having in mind the attitude of Puritans to Catholicism, it seems logical to associate loveless Louisa with the religion that Puritans sought to reform. On the other hand, the disorder of the will that earns the protagonist a Catholic appellation in the story is paradoxically a post-Puritan feature. As such, Freeman critiques not so much the Puritan beliefs or Puritan society of the past but the inability of her contemporary New England communities to develop, their inherited rigid wills resisting change and standing in the path of love, life, and pleasure. The indefinite article ("A") in the title is appropriate, since Louisa Ellis is one of many New England nuns.

Works Cited

Anderson, Donald R. "*Giles Corey* and the Pressing Past." *The American Transcendental Quarterly*, vol. 14, no. 2, 2000, pp. 113–26.

Ansley, Jennifer. "Geographies of Intimacy in Mary Wilkins Freeman's Short Fiction." *The New England Quarterly*, vol. 87, no. 3, 2014, pp. 434–63.

Chopin, Kate. "Lilacs." *The Heath Anthology of American Literature*, edited by Paul Lauter, 3rd ed., vol. 2, Houghton Mifflin, 1998, pp. 538–46.

Cleary, Kate McPhellim. "The Stepmother." *The Exiles of Erin: Nineteenth-century Irish-American Fiction*, edited by Charles Fanning, Notre Dame UP, 1987, pp. 236–44.

Couch, Ben. "The No-Man's-Land of 'A New England Nun.'" *Studies in Short Fiction*, vol. 35, no. 2, 1998, pp. 187–98.

Cullinan, Elizabeth. *House of Gold*. Houghton Mifflin, 1969.

Cutter, Martha J. "Mary E. Wilkins Freeman's Two New England Nuns." *Colby Quarterly*, vol. 26, no. 4, 1990, pp. 213–25.

Daniel, Janice. "Redefining Place: *Femes Covert* in the Stories of Mary Wilkins Freeman." *Studies in Short Fiction*, vol. 33, no. 1, 1996, pp. 69–76.

Ebest, Ron. *Private Histories: The Writing of Irish Americans, 1900–1935*. Notre Dame UP, 2005.
Fanning, Charles. "Elizabeth Cullinan's House of Gold: Culmination of an Irish American Dream." *MELUS*, vol. 7, no. 4, 1980, pp. 31–48.
Farrell, James T. *Chicago Stories*, edited by Charles Fanning, Illinois UP, 1998.
Foster, Edward. *Mary E. Wilkins Freeman*. Hendricks House, 1956.
Freeman, Mary E. Wilkins. *A New England Nun and Other Stories*. Harper & Brothers, 1891.
—. *Pembroke*. Scholar's edition, Harper & Brothers, 1894.
Harris, Susan K. "Mary E. Wilkins Freeman's 'A New England Nun' and the Dilemma of the Woman Artist." *Studies in American Humor*, vol. 3, no. 9, 2002, pp. 27–38.
—. "Introduction." *Nineteenth-Century American Women's Novels: Interpretative Strategies*. Cambridge UP, 1990, pp. 1–35.
O'Neill, Eugene. *Long Day's Journey into Night*. Yale UP, 1989.
Palmer, Stephanie. *Transatlantic Footholds: Turn-of-the-Century American Women Writers and British Reviewers*. Routledge, 2019.
Pryse, Marjorie. "An Uncloistered 'New England Nun.'" *Studies in Short Fiction*, vol. 20, no. 4, 1983, pp. 289–95.
Toth, Susan Allen. "Mary Wilkins Freeman's Parable of Wasted Life." *American Literature*, vol. 42, no. 4, 1971, pp. 564–7.
Tritt, Michael. "Selling a Birthright for Pottage: Mary Freeman's Allusion to Genesis in 'A New England Nun.'" *ANG: A Quarterly Journal of Short Articles, Notes and Reviews*, vol. 19, no. 4, 2006, pp. 34–41.
Westbrook, Perry D. *Mary Wilkins Freeman*. Revised edition, Twayne Publishers, 1988.

PART III

WOMEN'S WORK: CAPITAL, BUSINESS, LABOR

7

HUNGER STRIKES: QUEER NATURALISM AND THE GENDERING OF SOLIDARITY IN MARY E. WILKINS FREEMAN'S *THE PORTION OF LABOR*

JUSTIN ROGERS-COOPER

In Mary E. Wilkins Freeman's novel, *The Portion of Labor* (1901), set in the fictional New England factory town of Rowe, the wife of one of the town's three shoe factory owners, Mrs Norman Lloyd, is out on a sleigh ride during an economic depression. She happens to see the young Ellen Brewster out riding with her unemployed father Andrew, a former worker in Mr Lloyd's factory. Mr Lloyd frowns on the ride as wasteful; it indicates their lower-class status. By contrast, Mrs Lloyd comments on how "desperate" Ellen's family must feel to be spending down their savings, reasoning "they might as well get a little good time out of it to remember by-and-by when there ain't enough bread and butter" (120). Despite her feeling of sympathy for Ellen's family, Mrs Lloyd nonetheless reflects that "the world couldn't be regulated by women's hearts, pleasant as it would be for the world and the women, since the final outcome would doubtless be destruction" (121).

The gravity of Mrs Lloyd's pessimism is ironic on multiple levels. For one, the threat and reality of economic "destruction" in Rowe's working-class community occurs throughout the novel, causing panic, unemployment, and hunger; it was a "city of strikes" (120). The question of "women's hearts" also speaks to one of the novel's central questions: what is the relation between gender and solidarity in the novel, and how do women in particular feel and articulate solidarity within and beyond the working class, within and beyond the constraints of their sex? In a world before New Deal welfare capitalism, such questions were urgent in part because survival could be at stake. In this chapter, I will build on literary scholarship by Mary V. Marchand, Donna M. Campbell, and J. Samaine Lockwood to elaborate on the gendering of solidarity in *The Portion of Labor*. I will address how solidarity extends from women's queer or romantic relationships, and how those relations, together with the novel's heterodox generic style, advance received innovative interpretations of literary naturalism. In addition to pushing arguments about Freeman's work into wider discussions within the fields of American studies and labor history, I hope this chapter also provokes insights into Freeman's continuing relevance for conversations about the intersectionality of gender, race, and class identity, as well as issues of overwork, worker's rights, and regulation in an era of gig economies and platform capitalism. By providing a counterpoint to still dominant histories of striking male workers in the Long Gilded Age, this chapter speaks to what *The Portion of Labor*'s naturalist and sentimental modes teach us about the labors, performances, and emotions of historized forms of solidarity.

In particular, I elaborate on how Freeman characterizes the emergence of solidarity from the "queer women" characters in the text, or perhaps what Lockwood terms "romantic friendship" (Lockwood 9, 123). I imagine solidarity here as embodied states of intensified, shared sensation that arise from the performative, unwaged "work" that produces events of class conflict; that is, I understand class conflict through events produced and sustained by collective labors and performances, such as strikes, riots, protests, boycotts, and, ultimately, revolutions. Here, gendered forms of solidarity are intensified and shared sensations led, performed, and sustained by women—though not necessarily through an essentialized identification; in fact, Ellen's power as a voice of labor inspires both men and women in the text. In the novel, creating solidarities through non-normative gender expression or gender identity open possibilities for what Elizabeth Freeman calls "queer temporalities," or moments when characters, such as the protagonist Ellen Brewster, can create, suspend, interrupt, or redirect the normative times of New England factory life (E. Freeman xxii). I will attend to the moments in the text when such temporalities become visible, or when the "temporal order gets interrupted and new encounters subsequently take place." During these moments, the "empty homogeneous time" of personal maturation and capitalist command are interrupted by times that "propose other possibilities for living" (E. Freeman xxii). For example, I attend to how Ellen's performative labor as a strike leader emerges from the queer intimacy and desires formed by her homosocial and queer relations with other women, and how their shared feelings help to create, circulate, and reproduce the emotional and affective labor necessary for working-class forms of resistance, particularly the strike and how they end it. Through Ellen, Freeman narrates how women at the center of such relationships might create radical potential for solidarity by combining their intellectual and emotional labors to singularly activate resistance in a wider working class.

In this respect, *The Portion of Labor* has news to share with scholars and students beyond literary studies.

The Portion of Labor also is notable because it appears during an era when working-class narratives mostly focus on male waged labor. With this in mind, I contend that the novel's heterodox generic form reflects Ellen's queer exceptionalism in conversation with questions of genre. Freeman's innovations matter partly because of the novel's naturalist fidelities to traditions of labor fiction that envelop questions of class. Thus the novel is not unrelated to the work of Frank Norris or Theodore Dreiser despite its significant strains of sentimental-realism (after all, naturalism is a composite genre that includes traditions of sentimentalism and realism). Mary V. Marchand suggests we also emphasize *The Portion of Labor*'s relation to "reform novels" by Rebecca Harding Davis, Margaret Deland, and Elizabeth Stuart Phelps (Marchand 66–78, 65).[1] Marchand rightly argues *The Portion of Labor* contains an "intrinsically feminist perspective," and contends it "is distinguished by its radical analysis of American women's power and influence outside the home" (70). Indeed, in few other narratives of the period do we find women leading men in situations of class conflict and class violence. But Ellen is not *only* a naturalist character struggling for agency. We might see, then, *The Portion of Labor* as a naturalist reform novel about class conflict, and one whose generic imbrications help us locate Ellen as a figure of queer labor. By finding gendered forms of solidarity in and through the novel's queer temporalities and queer female relationships, Freeman works to queer naturalism through her figuration of Ellen as a New Woman.

As worker, intellectual, and striker, Ellen both embodies certain stereotypes of middle-class domesticity—she's beautiful, poised, and nurturing—and those of a working-class hero. Rendered as both intellectually charismatic and romantically desirable, she makes for a strange labor organizer (she promotes strikes, but not unions). She also couples nicely with Robert Lloyd, the son of the factory owner, and the manager responsible for the very wage cuts that spark the strike. Ellen thus contains contradictions. Yet these apparent contradictions help to define and figure queer naturalism in the novel; even as the town's capitalist economy constrains her potential, the spur for Ellen's labors of solidarity comes from within her and her relationships, rendered through queer desire and the singularity of her personality and performance of resistance.

Perhaps, then, we might define the novel's queer naturalism via Sandra A. Zagarell's arguments about Sarah Orne Jewett's *Country of the Pointed Firs*, and imagine the "textual discontinuities" in such "multivocal texts" as *The Portion of Labor* through an "identification of registers—distinct discourses with extra-textual coordinates" (355). In this sense, Freeman's representation of Ellen as exceptionally beautiful, intelligent, and charismatic, while also ableist, racialized, and innocent, exemplifies Ellen's embodiment of what Zagarell might call Freeman's, and the era's, ideological "cross-currents" (356). Ultimately, it is

Ellen's capacity to love other women that stimulates Ellen's choice to strike—or not strike. This cross-current in the text, I argue, has implications for genre: the novel offers the possibility of queer naturalism.

Feminizing Class Struggle

The Portion of Labor speaks to practices of class struggle by waged and unwaged women workers in the nineteenth century, and therefore addresses the conflict between capital and labor from a unique vantage. By presenting Ellen as a significant character within what Robert Ovetz calls the "uncivil war" during the Long Gilded Age, Freeman challenges standard representations of women in Victorian-era fiction (Ovetz 1). The shoe-workers in Rowe react and organize during an economic crisis that echoes the nineteenth-century long depression (1873–96), but in many respects the novel reimagines a neglected history of women's labor activism during the Long Gilded Age, such as the Lynn strike of 1860, when mechanization in shoe factories put the "family wage economy . . . in jeopardy," and the "active support of women" in the strikes helped project them "as a defense of traditional values" (Blewett 116, 120). In the Lynn strike as in the novel, women extolled the "duties of manhood" in striking; as we will see, similar rhetoric erupts at crucial times (Blewett 120). Yet when female characters like Ellen led the strike, their identities as shoe-workers were not necessarily "secondary to their role as female family members" (Blewett 121). Ellen also bears resemblance to the many women who participated in the 1877 general strike, and anticipates the Bread and Roses strike of 1912, when "female strikers challenged the economic order as well as the sexual labeling on which it was based" (Cameron 174). The women in *The Portion of Labor* belong within the cultural history of working-class women's labor struggles—although we should remember that in 1900, 50 percent of working women were "foreign-born," and many immigrant women's lives, and Black women's lives, "were consumed by the struggle to survive and assimilate" (Clinton 113, 119). If Ellen Brewster had been an immigrant or Black, the story probably would have been different.

Freeman focalizes the novel's politics through questions of gender and class, which we largely discover through Ellen, the working-class heroine. The novel's rearrangement of women's class relations through gendered forms of solidarity begins early in the text and prior to any factory troubles, after Ellen runs away from home. Freeman brings Ellen into contact with an upper-middle-class woman, Cynthia Lennox, who finds her downtown staring at a store window alone. In what will become a "romantic friendship," Freeman stages a collision through a girl and a woman from different classes whose relations stand in for larger relations of sympathy, if not yet solidarity—the moment is an antecedent to the encounter between Mrs Lloyd and Ellen that opens this chapter. Cynthia expresses concern for the young child standing alone, and she takes Ellen to her richly furnished home for care and nourishment. Later, Cynthia anonymously sends Ellen home on the counsel of her friend and eventual suitor, Lyman Risley. For Campbell, the relationship between Cynthia and Ellen presents a "complicated, class-infected relationship between women's bodies" (Campbell 222). Their relation offers a potential solution for subsequent conflict, like when Cynthia reveals her new interest in Ellen's mother, Fanny, when offering to send Ellen to Vassar. Cynthia and Ellen's meeting introduces how problems of class inequality might be repaired through sympathy or solidarity between women. Their introduction in front of a grocery window, too, signals how women across social classes might resolve together the problem of hunger and scarcity among the poor, rather than through unionized violence by working-class men. This question of hungry women will return at the novel's conclusion.

Queer Naturalism

Freeman elaborates on the novel's gendered class tensions through recognizable scripts of naturalist discourse with Ellen, Maria Atkins, and other characters. There are several meaningful exogenous and endogenous naturalist determinants in the plot: the capitalist economy, a sort of transcendental spiritual realm, and interiorized material forces of racialization and gender somewhat idiosyncratic to Freeman.[2] When Ellen first passes the Rowe factories, for example, she imagines

> vague terrors of what beside herself might be near unrevealed beneath the mighty brooding of the night . . . She was, as it were, in the mid-current of the conditions of her own life and times, and the material force of it swept away all the symbolisms and unstable drift. (14)

In language evoking Frank Norris or Upton Sinclair, here Freeman aligns the material force of capitalism as an influence on Ellen's personhood. Likewise, when Ellen is working "at her machine, her very individuality seemed lost; she became an integral part of a system" (398). At one point, Lyman tells Robert that Ellen had to work at the factory "because she was forced into it by circumstances . . . That mortgage had to be raised, and the girl had to go to work; there was no other way out of it" (371).[3] Passages like these firmly position Freeman's novel with naturalist thematic concerns. More importantly, such passages emphasize factory capitalism as an endogenous force delimiting the choices of Ellen and other working-class characters, but also as a force working *through* their bodies.

The force of factory capitalism comes into direct conflict with other forces acting on, within, and through characters like Ellen. Freeman renders gender as one such material force. Pointedly, she narrates it through a kind of interiorized unfolding from within Ellen's body. Yet the unfolding of Ellen's gendered interiority doesn't necessarily conform to the needs of capitalist class relations, much less to the expectations of traditional family relations. In ways that disrupt what Elizabeth Freeman calls "chromonormativity, or the use of time to organize individual human bodies toward maximum productivity," something inside Ellen grows excessive of her surroundings; she matures in ways that resist the social categories Victorians believed "natural" (3). Ellen's particular expression of feminine personality becomes activated: she emerges as a social force that takes unexpected directions, coming into conflict with capitalist economy and by extension the town's class structures. The force of such interiorized femininity at times even acts autonomously as it becomes visible; nor is it confined to women's bodies. For example, Freeman relates that Nahum Beals, one of the workers most sensitive to the town's inequality and who later assassinates Mr Lloyd the factory owner, "had a delicate, nervous face, like a woman's" (100). It is notable that one of Ellen's love interests in the first half of the novel, the kind and humble Granville Joy, also "had a face as gentle as a girl's, and really beautiful" (178).[4] For Freeman's characters, physical expressions of interiorized gender are not neatly naturalized in male and female bodies. When discussing Ellen, Robert's mentor Lyman reveals he dislikes such "strength in so young a girl," but promises Robert she "will make a more harmonious woman than girl, for she has not yet grown up to her own character" (372). Here, Lyman poses Ellen's gender identity through a framework of maturation that actually "naturalizes" periods of love and desire for women. It is a queer proposition not irrelevant to the lesbian continuum conceptualized by Adrienne Rich. Something natural inside Ellen is also queer.

The queer naturalism of gender expression in the novel, however, complicates how class conflict emerges and how gendered forms of solidarity circulate and emerge. For Freeman, solidarity is situationally dependent; it may be a reaction to conditions of scarcity from low wages or unemployment, but it is also relational and gendered, and inseparable from bodies, affects, and desires. Queer desires are particularly meaningful to the subsequent formation of solidarities between women who strike, but also because they attract women from different classes, such as Ellen and Cynthia. With implications for the development of feminine solidarity later, Freeman refers to Ellen's youthful contemplation of the "feminine element" around her in ways that queer her desires (140). Further, Ellen's queer desires partially extend from suggestions of gender performativity for Ellen and others, beginning with Ellen's observation, early in school, that she "did not think the boys, in their coarse clothes, with their cropped heads, half as pretty as the girls" (140). Her desire intensifies into a "fondest new love" for her teacher, Miss Mitchell. Her bodily desire for Miss Mitchell becomes part of how she learns, and part of why she longs to be a good student (150). Similarly, during a moment alone with Cynthia, Freeman explains that Ellen's feelings

> leaped towards her with an impulse of affection . . . A great love and admiration which had gotten its full growth in a second under the magic

of a look and a tone shook her from head to foot. She went close to Cynthia, and leaned over, putting her round, young face down to the elder woman's. "Oh, I love you, I love you," whispered Ellen, with a fervor which was strange to her. But Cynthia only kissed her lightly on the cheek, and pushed her away softly. (252)

Here, Ellen's desire for Cynthia is part of her personal maturation. The "impulse of affection" that shakes her suggests the ways that, later, such instincts of desire might inspire the bonds of solidarity. What is natural might be queer, and what is queer can gender solidarity.

The most pronounced illustration of the novel's elaboration of queer desire that ripens into solidarity occurs with Ellen's friendship with Maria Atkins's sister Abby; all three will later strike together. During their school days, Abby once asks Ellen if she is mad after talking. Ellen "pressed her round young arm tenderly against the other," and says, "I think more of you than any man I know" (229). Freeman elaborates:

The two girls walked on with locked arms, and each was possessed with that wholly artless and ignorant passion often seen between two young girls. Abby felt Ellen's warm round arm against hers with a throbbing of rapture, and glanced at her fair face with adoration. She held her in a sort of worship, she loved her so that she was fairly afraid of her. As for Ellen, Abby's little, leather-stained, leather-scented figure, strung with passion like a bundle of electric wire, pressing against her, seemed to inform her farthest thoughts. "If I live longer than my father and mother, we'll live together Abby," said she. (230)

This scene repeats later with variation: when discussing whether Ellen should attend Vassar, they do so in bed: "Abby was learning over her, caressing her, whispering fond things to her like a lover" (308). At a minimum, the scene echoes June Howard's contention that for Freeman "life and work affirm that sustaining relationships come in many forms," and that Freeman was a critic of the "hypervaluation of heterosexuality at the expense of other relations" (175).

Ellen's feelings for Abby are complicated, however, by their class position. On the one hand, after their rapturous encounter Ellen "quite ignored all about the sordid ways and means of existence, about toil and privation and children born to it," and realizes love "was the chief end and purpose of life" (231). On the other hand, her love for Abby affirms her desire to remain in toil and privation: when discussing her relationship with Robert, Abby tells Ellen, "There's a power over us which is too strong for girls," to which Ellen replies, "I will never be lifted out of the grind as long as those I love are in it" (305). In naturalist fashion, Ellen here tries to choose beyond the "power" delimiting her choices.

Freeman also locates feminine forms of solidarity among working-class women through deeply embodied relations of love. Freeman's innovation on naturalist fiction, and her comment on factory capitalism, occurs as a collision *between* forces that are exterior and interior to women's bodies. Within the context of queer naturalism, love is characterized as an interiorized force of attraction, and another material determinant expressed, but not overdetermined, by gender and sexuality. The modern femininity in *The Portion of Labor*, then, is inseparable from questions of gendering class consciousness and class conflict. We might thus revise Stuart Hall's famous remark on race and class—"race is the modality in which class is lived"—for how gender is an equally important "lived" embodiment of class in the novel (386). Freeman's attention to the contingent politics of intersectionality speak to why Freeman should be read today, again and anew.

Further, Ellen's regionally conceived racial identity isn't incidental to the narrative's queering of class relations. While the novel employs discourses of race and gender that echo strategies of other nineteenth-century authors, such as the "blackening of the working class," Freeman utilizes an idiosyncratic strategy of racialization threaded through a discourse of "wild blood" and "New England blood" (Lang 7; Freeman 72, 252). Freeman writes, for example, that Ellen had a "violent and intense temperament which she had inherited from two sides of her family" (190). She later describes Ellen as "in the full current of her own emotions, which, added to a goodly flood inherited from the repressed passion of New England ancestors, had a strong pull upon her feet," and that there was a "survival of the old Greek spirit" in her (261, 447). By contrast, fellow worker Sadie Peel's father is described as having a "Slavonic cast, although he was New England born and bred" (458). Her eventual suitor Robert even describes factory workers as a "different race" (499). Lockwood provides context for such passages by citing William Dean Howell's observations about "intimate racialized belonging" in Freeman's fiction, and further notes "the cultural context in which . . . racially charged delineations of sectionalized literary modes . . . were understood" (Lockwood 18). Campbell links the "treatment of race" in the novel to its "unruly naturalism" (200). While Freeman's characterizations of race in *The Portion of Labor* exist in tension with straightforward dimensions of white supremacy, such as perfectibility, normativity, and superiority, Ellen has inherited a range of traits from her "ancestors," with a diversity of positive and negative qualities. Ellen's racialization likely secures her sense of belonging and citizenship, and perhaps an exceptionalist New England whiteness; yet Ellen's interiorized racial character unfolds similarly to her gender expression, suggesting a linkage. In this sense, her racialization is inseparable from the interior forces shaping her queer desires. By locating Ellen's queerness in a racialized body, Freeman de-naturalizes normative assumptions about the sexuality of whiteness. In doing so, Freeman also complicates assumptions about the social construction of gender and race. Such complications are key for ongoing conversations about the relation of intersectional identities with class consciousness.

Performance and Solidarity

Ellen's relations of love and desire evolve within the Rowe's class conflicts, especially as she rises to become Rowe's leading intellectual and creative force. Her ascent begins early: her aunt Eva praises her reading and math ability in middle school. For a working-class girl, this is special. When Eva and Fanny defend their own lack of education to a neighbor, Eva admits, "We had to quit school. Folks can live with empty heads, but they can't with empty stomachs" (86). Ellen's intellectual development deepens as workers visit her home to discuss class conflict with her father; as she falls asleep, she listens to characters like Nahum Beals and Joe Atkins intently rue the town's inequality and injuries from the factory. Overhearing them, Ellen comes to feel a "conviction of the great wrongs of the poor of this earth and the awful tyranny of the rich" (123). Thus, Ellen's educational success fuses to her internalization of the moral economy of labor. This fusion propels the perception she is "smarter than all them boys and girls" in her class (183). Ellen practices the skills that will help her shape working-class futures at school.

Ellen's dual education at home and at school allows her to hone skills and develop knowledge that she will later use to perform the work of solidarity. The many forms of labor that solidarity requires—intellectual, social, and emotional—become increasingly intertwined in her maturation. Her development as a "remarkable scholar" continually intersects the problem of wage work, so that by high school, when her aging father is fired "on account of dullness in trade," Ellen's intellectual abilities become co-expressive with her social and emotional intelligence (154, 155). As economic recession appears and "the discontented ranks of impotent labor" fill the streets, Ellen's sensitivity to the "material force" of factory capitalism becomes a "blot upon the face of her happy consciousness of life" (152, 14, 152). She refuses to remain passive as the economy affects her family.

Further, her queer powers give her unique capacities to perform the arguments and arouse the emotions necessary for making solidarity for working-class actions. Her power of performance first erupts in her high school valedictory speech on "Equality," a "most revolutionary valedictory . . . written with a sort of poetic fire" (192). She describes the injustice done to labor in the "grand system of things," and Mr Lloyd complains to Lyman as Ellen's "clearly delivered sentiments grew more and more defined—almost anarchistic" (193). The audience of factory "employés and their families," many of them "of foreign blood," give a "storm of applause," and many women in particular "hallooed in a frenzy of applause" and even "stood up in their seats"

(193).[5] Through a vision of character and social life peculiar to the novel, in this scene Freeman presents Ellen as a singular figure of the working class, and as one uniquely able to perform the "almost anarchistic" forms of cultural articulation that generate both gendered and class solidarities. Ellen's performance opens a queer moment for the town: in particular, the solidarities she creates disrupt normative orders of class and gender. This moment foreshadows how she will later queer the time of capital with a time of striking.

Ellen's singular capacities inform her major relationships and the decisions that drive the novel's plot. Unflinchingly, she keeps to her convictions during her slow courtship with Robert; during a walk, she tells him people "can't think until they are fed," and as they pass the "great factories," she comments she doesn't "believe there has been another building in the whole city which has held so many heart-aches, and I always wondered if they didn't make ghosts instead of dead people" (276, 277). After graduation, she contemplates schoolteaching, working at the shoe factory, or attending Vassar (at Cynthia's expense). When she learns her unemployed father has been concealing the family's destitution and his stock speculation, she defers Vassar for factory work. While in the factory, she discovers "once and forever the dignity of labor," and "this army of the sons and daughters of toil" who "made possible the advance of civilization itself," even as a "girl of the people, with a brain which enabled her to overlook the heads of the rank and file of which she herself formed a part" (350). The novel doesn't treat her labor, nor that of other women workers, through the prism of middle-class domestic culture, nor through a lens of passive abjection. Rather, Ellen notices Abby "stitching vamps by the piece, and earning a considerable amount ... Abby was paying off a mortgage" (351). Abby might be subject to capitalism, but her wages also allow her to make choices. Factory labor isn't only a site of exploitation. It is also a site where women attempt to remake their lives.

Somewhat understandably, the genre conventions of the novel's conclusion belie some of the radical possibilities of the novel's political horizons—but not all. The queer desires Ellen experiences in girlhood partially recede as she becomes a "harmonious woman," as Lyman predicted to Robert (372). Class conflict and new romance, however, become entangled with Ellen's strength as the town's moral arbiter. After Robert assumes responsibility for the factory following his uncle's assassination, he "succeeded to all his [uncle's] unpopularity" after he discharges union leaders and replaces them with "non-union men from another town in their places" (444). When "a period of extreme business depression" soon recurs, he runs the factory at reduced "scale" in order to "meet expenses" and avoid layoffs, yet communicates none of his reasoning to the workers (444, 445). When Ellen sees the reduced wage list, she imagines he "was going to abuse his power of capital, his power to take bread out of their mouths entirely" (452). During this crisis, Maria Atkins becomes sick and yet still compels herself to work because of her and Abby's sick father. In a crucial question that goes unresolved, Abby asks, "I'd like to know what good it is going to do to work and earn and pay up money if everybody is going to be killed by it?" (449–50). In an age of globalized supply chains, ecological destruction, and climate change, Abby's question remains powerful well beyond the novel.

The contradiction behind Abby's question also defines the coming strike. The novel's presentation of the strike as a collective act led by women begins to reveal the text's queering of solidarity through gendered forms of class consciousness. It also stresses the singular, unwaged emotional labor that goes into the performances that create and sustain solidarity, especially passionate debate and emotional argumentation. Interestingly, the moral and emotional sentiments expressed by women, not union organizing, create the conditions of solidarity necessary for the strike. When Ellen and other women factory workers debate the strategy of striking, they cite winning support for sick families (notably, the same reason Ellen ends the strike). When some male union workers try to appropriate the debate, Ellen rebuffs the assumption that only the "union men would have something to say about it" (464). When asked what "poor men can do against capital unless they are backed up by some labor organization," Ellen replies by posing a power beyond organized labor: "When right is on your side, you have all the odds . . . I wouldn't submit" (465). Ellen claims that she would "do anything, at whatever cost to myself, to defeat injustice," and her mother Fanny expresses similar sentiments (474). Ellen eventually tells them, "If you men will do nothing, and say nothing, it is time for a girl to say and act" (477). Ellen continues, "If I were a man . . . I would go out in the street and dig—I would beg, I would steal—before I would yield—I, a free man in a free country—to tyranny like this!" (478). Here the *men* applaud and the sentiment to strike solidifies. Notably, Ellen wins the strike question through a language of masculinity. While she genders the strike as masculine duty and honor, she queers the relations of class conflict: she leads the strike as a woman, but does so in part by uniting men with women through a gendered discourse of manhood. In queering class consciousness this way, she creates forms of solidarity that spur revolt and find resonance beyond women in the factory. The queer time of the strike gestures to what Kathi Weeks imagines as worker projects of "self-valorization," and how they "multiply and increase their requirements, passions, and abilities in ways that cannot be satisfied within the limits of capitalist production" (149). Led by Ellen and other women's passions, the "self-valorization" of workers in this moment opens not just toward anti-capitalism, but also toward a form of gendered socialism.

Their debate before the strike nonetheless reveals the novel's radical horizon. In portentous naturalist terms, Freeman soon warns that Ellen was "bumping her head against the floor in her vain struggles for mastery over the mighty conditions of her life" (492). The strike's resolution begins when Ellen and Robert converse about the wage cuts. Robert says, "I could not prevent it," and goes on to say that the factory only met expenses and couldn't simply lose money (493). Then after a hard winter, Ellen's doubts grow during a confrontation with Abby. Tellingly, it is Abby who persuades Ellen to think differently, not Robert. During the earlier debate to strike, Abby had initially cautioned against it. Embodying one of the novel's primary cross-currents, she was compromising and fatalistic: "Bread without butter is better than none at all, and life at any cost is better than death for them you love" (473–4). This sentiment reappears when, thinking of families starving without wages, Abby tells Ellen, "I believe in bravery, but nothing except fools and swine jump over precipices" (514). She explains, "we haven't got a thing to eat in the house except potatoes and a little flour," adding, "[t]hose little Blake children next door are fairly starving" (514, 515). Moved by Abby's words, Ellen realizes "the cost is part of the principle in this world, and it has to be counted in with it" (516). She breaks the picket line, saying, "Strike if you want to . . . If you want to kill a girl for going back to work to save herself and her friends from starvation, do it" (527). Dramatically, an angry group led by the worker Amos Lee tries to shoot Ellen, but Risley intercedes (and survives his injuries). In quick succession, the strike breaks, wages are raised, and Ellen gets married.

Hunger Strikes

Such a conclusion is not without its problems, to be sure. Mary V. Marchand's assessment perhaps over-emphasizes the politics of the resolution: she writes that "Freeman's radicalism is ultimately circumscribed by prevailing definitions of femininity and women's proper place . . . [and Freeman's] representations of women are finally constrained by idealizing clichés that underwrote women's oppression" (70).[6] In conjunction with my arguments about gendered forms of solidarity in the novel, however, I would argue that Freeman's innovations within the naturalist tradition are significant for several reasons that go beyond the conclusion. Echoing Donna M. Campbell's sense that the "consolatory ending strikes a false note that calls attention to its own artifice," I read the resolution through Amy Kaplan's gloss on the "'unrealistic' endings of realist novels," which for Kaplan "embody the desire to posit an alternative reality which cannot be fully contained in the novels' construction of the real," and which "challenge our notion that the real is that which cannot be changed" (160). Indeed, such endings might be the "unruly naturalism" that for Campbell "transgresses the rules by its unevenness or excess" (4).

We should equally emphasize the politics of "excess" in the rising tension of the narrative as in its denouement. In the climax, for example, women rise to power through a masculine discourse of republican freedom. Furthermore, it is Ellen who ends the strike to protect women and children through the reasoning of Abby, who once whispered "fond things to her like a lover." Even in the absence of discourse about women's rights, suffrage politics, or union victory, the novel stresses the critical importance of the wage for women's survival in industrial capitalism, and the importance of women's powers to sustaining that survival. Crucially, Freeman reveals class tensions in part through the problem of hunger. It is noteworthy that when the strike's material effects on working families intensifies, and mimic the disabling effects of capitalist scarcity, Ellen then concludes the strike. Ellen's motivations to begin and end the strike center on her desire to improve the lives of working-class families. In that sense, a different form of gendered solidarity comes to matter more to Rowe's working-class community: the one felt for sick and starving families. Ironically, it's a solidarity that compels Ellen to end the strike.

Furthermore, the failure of the strike reveals the limits of not just striking to accomplish its objectives, but the power of capitalist economic cycles to overdetermine the lives and deaths of the working class. *The Portion of Labor* defies trite beliefs about the relation between hard work and success, not to mention the deserving and undeserving poor. Freeman's adaptation of the nineteenth-century reform novel into naturalist fiction staged a set of themes and problems that reflected the material conditions of wage labor in the industrialized, pre-welfare era. Perhaps none was more urgent and harrowing than the problem of subsistence wages and unemployment. Many families struggled to survive the laissez-faire capitalism of the nineteenth century and Long Gilded Age. The inability of capitalist markets to supply food to the working-classes—particularly during periods of unemployment, but also due to low wages—proved to be one of capitalism's most trenchant inefficiencies. With memories of the French Revolution and Irish famine still fresh at mid-century, the problem of hungry masses was also capitalism's major political liability. During the 1877 general strike in the United States, one of the slogans was "bread or blood," a phrase shouted by food rioters in England and Ireland since the beginning of the century. In turn, variegated cultures of reform, socialism, and labor unions emphasized hunger as one of the primary costs of laissez-faire immorality; during the collapse of Reconstruction, even Frederick Douglass argued the "master class" retained its power "of life and death" over Black Americans from the "power to starve them to death," a point later echoed by the twentieth-century Black socialist Hubert Harrison (81). So even if we accept the regression of the conclusion in terms of radical *feminism* and women's "power and influence," Ellen's choice to end the strike appears more complex if we remember she retreats to save lives (Marchand 70).

Ellen's choices bring us back to naturalism. Echoing June Howard, Jennifer Fleissner writes that Freeman's characters generally express an "emergent modern femininity," and address the paramount and political "question of women's relation to their own futures" (223).[7] As an example of what Howard and Kathy

Peiss call a "working-class version of the New Woman," however, Ellen manages to make her future in ways that are class specific, but which also transcend wage labor (Howard 159; Peiss 164). For Peiss, the working-class New Woman fashions herself through "activity in the public arena," and through her challenge to the "boundaries of domesticity and female self-sacrifice" seen in the embrace of "mixed-sex fun" in leisure activities and spaces (185, 6). By contrast, Ellen is an important working-class fictional innovation upon bourgeois figurations of the New Woman: she commands traditionally male public and private spaces, she leverages queer relations with other women to make choices, and she creates solidarity among working-class people to resist capitalist power. By creating a working-class New Woman character within a naturalist novel, Freeman effectively resets how naturalism works in the text. We should reflect further on how this kind of New Woman—one who cared for the survival of other "new women" in the working class—interrupts the naturalist logic that something inside or outside Ellen over-determined her fate. The tension between naturalist and sentimental discourse becomes a proxy for contemplating queer naturalism: in Ellen there's an excess that other forces cannot rule. To this end, I follow Campbell and Fleissner's interpretation of Freeman's naturalism; they write "sentimentalism is not antithetical but integral to naturalism" (6). Indeed, the cross-currents of sentimentalism and naturalism in *The Portion of Labor* represent continuing conflicts for working-class politics in the century or so after its publication. Freeman reveals an assumption that *working* women, waged and unwaged, are intimately positioned to articulate the moral economy of labor through relations of affection and solidarity. More importantly, they are crucial agents of modernity, with the power to make choices within lives of crisis.

So while the novel's conclusion might be interpreted as a reflex of melodramatic romance, its horizon of possibilities nonetheless opens toward feminist critiques of modern capitalism. Ultimately, Freeman suggests that class conflict requires women's voices and actions, but more crucially, she implies that such conflicts might be resolved through relationships between women, and by women leading men. This remains true whatever the conclusion, and still matters in places today where men, and governments of men, try to resolve crises of inequality and democracy without women's voices and passions. Freeman privileges gender relations as the moral center of impulses to reform and resist capitalism, and, memorably, she presents working-class women's survival through queer relations of sacrifice, love, and pleasure.

Works Cited

Blewett, Mary H. *Men, Women, and Work: Class, Gender, and Protest in the New England Shoe Industry, 1780–1910*. U of Illinois P, 1990.

Budd, Louis J. "The American Background." *The Cambridge Companion to American Realism and Naturalism: Howells to London*, edited by Donald Pizer, Cambridge UP, 1995, pp. 21–46.

Cameron, Ardis. *Radicals of the Worst Sort: Laboring Women in Lawrence, Massachusetts 1860–1912*. U of Illinois P, 1993.
Campbell, Donna. *Bitter Tastes: Literary Naturalism and Early Cinema in American Women's Writing*. U of Georgia P, 2016.
Clinton, Catherine. *The Other Civil War: American Women in the Nineteenth Century*. Hill and Wang, 1984.
Davis, Rebecca Harding. *Life in the Iron Mills and Other Stories*. 1861. The Feminist P, 1985.
Douglass, Frederick. *Selections from the Writings of Frederick Douglass*, edited by Phillip S. Foner, International Publishers, 1968.
Fleissner, Jennifer. *Women, Compulsion, Modernity: The Moment of American Naturalism*. U of Chicago P, 2004.
Freeman, Elizabeth. *Time Binds: Queer Temporalities, Queer Histories*. Duke UP, 2010.
Freeman, Mary E. Wilkins, *The Portion of Labor*. Harper & Brothers Publishers, 1901.
Glasser, Leah Blatt. *In a Closet Hidden: The Life and Work of Mary E. Wilkins Freeman*. U of Massachusetts P, 1996.
Hall, Stuart et al. *Policing the Crisis: Mugging, The State and Law and Order*. Red Globe P, 2013.
Harrison, Hubert. *The Negro and the Nation*. Cosmo-Advocate Publishing Co., 1917.
Howard, June. *Publishing the Family*. Duke UP, 2001.
Lang, Amy Schrager. *The Syntax of Class: Writing Inequality in Nineteenth-Century America*. Princeton UP, 2003.
Lockwood, J. Samaine. *Archives of Desire: The Queer Historical Work of New England Regionalism*. U of North Carolina P, 2015.
Marchand, Mary V. "Death to Lady Bountiful: Women and Reform in Edith Wharton's *The Fruit of the Tree*." *Legacy*, vol. 18, no. 1, 2001, pp. 66–78.
Ovetz, Robert. *When Workers Shot Back: Class Conflict from 1877 to 1921*. Brill, 2018.
Peiss, Kathy. *Cheap Amusements*. Temple UP, 2011.
Phelps, Elizabeth Stuart. *The Silent Partner: A Novel and 'The Tenth of January.'* 1871. The Feminist P, 1983.
Rich, Adrienne. "Compulsory Heterosexuality and Lesbian Existence." *Signs*, vol. 5, no. 4, 1980, pp. 631–60.
Weeks, Kathi. *Constituting Feminist Subjects*. Cornell UP, 1998.
Zagarell, Sandra A. "Crosscurrents: Registers of Nordicism, Community, and Culture in Jewett's *Country of the Pointed Firs*." *The Yale Journal of Criticism*, vol. 10, no. 2, 1997, pp. 355–70.

Notes

1. In terms of male narratives of the working class, I'm thinking of John Hay's *The Breadwinners* (1883), William Dean Howells's *Hazard of New Fortunes* (1889), Upton Sinclair's *The Jungle* (1905), and John Steinbeck's *In Dubious Battle* (1936).
2. In the beginning of Chapter 2, Freeman writes the "greatest complexity in the world attends the motive-power of any action" (12). She notes that Ellen couldn't explain why she ran away from home because "the answer was beyond her own power" (12).
3. Risley later adds, "that girl never went to work of her own free choice" (372).

4. During a mutual separation later, Granville "felt his throat fill with sobs, and swallowed compulsively. Along with this womanly compassion came a compassion for himself" (267).
5. When Ellen fends off debt collectors coming for her father, Freeman writes she had a "voice of pure command, and of command which carried with it the power to enforce" (326). Ellen's power of command is likely related to her "beauty which overawed" (190).
6. Marchand echoes what Leah Blatt Glasser calls the "regressive thoughts" of Freeman's character Lily in *The Whole Family* (91); Howard says Freeman's chapter in the collectively authored text "must be read selectively to make Lily a feminist heroine" (169).
7. I follow Fleissner and others in revising the long-held critical alignment of naturalism and masculinity. It is worth noting Louis J. Budd grouped Freeman with Crane and Dreiser as "realist/naturalists" who spoke to "the anxieties permeating the millions rather than from sequenced discourse with intellectuals" (Budd 24).

8

"IT WON'T BE LONG BEFORE THE GRIND-MILL GETS HOLD OF HIM": CHILD LABOR IN MARY E. WILKINS FREEMAN'S *THE PORTION OF LABOR*

LAURA DAWKINS

Mary E. Wilkins Freeman has been justly praised for her complex and sensitive portrayals of aging and impoverished women. As Mary R. Reichardt notes, Freeman's reviewers during her early career "marveled that one so young could write so compellingly about the plight of the destitute and the elderly" (viii). Yet in one of her most powerful novels, *The Portion of Labor* (1901), Freeman turns her attention away from the hardships of old age to anatomize the plight of the youngest members of society who are similarly imperiled by financial destitution. *The Portion of Labor* holds an important place in American literature as one of the few works of fiction that focuses on the controversial issue of child labor in the late nineteenth and early twentieth centuries.[1] As one who cherished fond memories of her own childhood,[2] Freeman deplored the theft of education, vitality, and individuality from generations of children who began to work for wages at an early age.

A long and ambitious novel, *The Portion of Labor* resists easy categorization, as several Freeman scholars have attested. Dorothy Berkson, for example, argues that Ellen Brewster, the novel's working-class protagonist, "resembles the pure, noble young heroines of Stowe and Dickens, young women whose spirituality is tested and developed through their exposure to the suffering of others" (150), yet Berkson notes that Ellen, "unlike her fictional predecessors . . . is more than just a spiritual influence, for she works and acts in the public political sphere" (165). Initially balanced "uneasily" between cultural paradigms of the "true woman" and the "new woman," Freeman's heroine, in Berkson's view, ultimately emerges as "essentially the same kind of 'angel in the house'" (165) familiar to readers of nineteenth-century sentimental novels. While acknowledging the "sentimental" aspects of *The Portion of Labor*, Mary V. Marchand places the work within a subgenre of women's industrial reform novels published during the late nineteenth and early twentieth centuries. Marchand contends that novelists such as Rebecca Harding Davis, Elizabeth Stuart Phelps, and Margaret Deland, as well as Freeman, "relied on the trope of industry as enlarged home, activist as public mother, reform as municipal housekeeping" (66). Although Marchand points out that these writers' heroines, unlike their "angel in the house" precursors, "lead, break, and settle strikes, form cooperatives, and pursue reforms," she finally concedes, with Berkson, that the novelists' representations of these spirited female protagonists remain "constrained by the idealizing clichés that underwrote women's oppression, . . . Freeman can finally only imagine women influencing reform through subordinate alliances with men" (70).

In contrast to Berkson and Marchand, Donna M. Campbell places *The Portion of Labor* in the tradition of American literary naturalism, specifically what she calls the "unruly naturalism" of women writers such as Edith Wharton, Kate Chopin, Willa Cather, and Ellen Glasgow, as well as Freeman. Campbell notes that these authors write classic naturalism "with themes of determinism, Darwinism, and death," but they transgress its boundaries with "unruly" features "such as sentimentalism, disability, and overt concern with social justice" (5). As Campbell argues, a novel such as *The Portion of Labor*, constituting a scathing indictment of oppressive factory conditions in industrial America, reflects what Donald Pizer has described as "naturalism's radical past . . . boldly and vividly depict[ing] the inadequacies of the industrial system which was the foundation of [the established order]" (7). According to Campbell, Freeman adheres to the "rules" of literary naturalism in depicting industrial workers as "cogs in the machine," but her tone of moral outrage throughout *The Portion of Labor* aligns her novel with the tradition of social protest rather than with the "clinical objectivity" of classic naturalism.

In attempting to classify *The Portion of Labor*, Freeman scholars have overlooked one popular subgenre of the late nineteenth and early twentieth centuries: what Robert Dowling has described as "moral realism, a fusion of the romantic and the pragmatic practiced by such reform writers as Charles Loring Brace, Helen Campbell, and Jacob Riis" (25). Reflecting the "transition from sentimentalism to realism, from a preoccupation with plot-driven pathos to social concerns," practitioners of moral realism, according to Dowling, combined elements of sentimentalism and realism with the overarching aim of reforming social ills. The best-known and most influential of these works of moral realism—Jacob Riis's nonfictional *How the Other Half Lives* (1890)—claims a place, as Hasia R. Diner attests, on "a selective list of American books that, on hindsight, unmistakably changed public opinion, began the process of altering public policy, and left an indelible mark on history" (vii). Riis's stirring portrait of exploited factory laborers and impoverished working-class families anticipates Freeman's similar concerns in *The Portion of Labor* a decade later. Given the public acclaim accorded *How the Other Half Lives* when it appeared in 1890, it seems likely that Freeman was familiar with the work when she began her own reformist portrayal of working-class poverty and oppression in industrial America.

However, Freeman's novel marks a significant departure from Riis's mode of "moral realism," specifically in her treatment of the serious social issue of child labor. Although both Riis and Freeman deplore the widespread employment of children in American industry, Riis, unlike Freeman, frequently locates the child laborer's parents or guardians as the source of the problem: "At the outset the boy stands condemned by his own to low and ill-paid drudgery, held down by the hand that of all should labor to raise him" (103). By contrast, Freeman places the blame for child exploitation unequivocally on the shoulders of factory owners and manufacturers. Throughout *The Portion of Labor*, she painstakingly demonstrates how working-class parents become trapped within a family wage economy in which older workers are discharged so that their preadolescent children, a cheaper source of labor, can fill the places they have vacated. Targeting the parents for "using" their children, as Freeman shows, deflects attention from an economic system in need of radical reform.

Indeed, Freeman arguably constructs a deliberate defense of the working-class family against the moral judgment of reformers such as Riis. As Diner has maintained, Riis's dissection of impoverished families often neglected "the dense networks of social life that gave meaning to the poor and that provided them with much of what Riis assumed they lacked: family life, neighborliness, morality, bonds of support, and even the ability to assert control over their daily lives" (xiv). These bulwarks—"family life, neighborliness, morality, and bonds of support"—are precisely the features of working-class life that Freeman focuses on in *The Portion of Labor*. While the author idealizes her heroine Ellen Brewster, her depictions of the working-class families surrounding Ellen are starkly realistic yet deeply sympathetic, underscoring parents' losing battles to improve their children's future and keep them out of the factories. Charging the captains of industry, not "greedy" parents, with the despoiling of childhood in "Gilded Age" America, Freeman implicitly rejects Riis's call for social intervention in working-class family life.

The Theft of Childhood

Freeman frames *The Portion of Labor* around an actual episode of child abduction that dramatically mirrors the theft of childhood within the working-class community she portrays. The novel's lengthy opening incident (spanning eight chapters) initially appears to function primarily as a plot device that enables the author to introduce her working-class protagonist to a member of the wealthy family into which she will eventually marry. Cynthia Lennox, meeting eight-year-old Ellen Brewster in the shopping district of the fictional New England town of Rowe after Ellen has fled from a family quarrel at home, exerts a subtly coercive force over the child as she urges Ellen to come home with her, "seem[ing] to have gotten her [Ellen] on some invisible leash" (20). The frightened child, who "stood sobbing, with a painful restraint, and pulling futilely from the lady's persuasive hand" (21), ultimately gains a "conviction of [Cynthia's] power, and she yielded to her unquestioningly" (24). Having gained "mastery of the child" (24), Cynthia keeps her in her home as a cherished doll—"wash[ing] her," "dress[ing] her," and "curl[ing] her hair" (43)—despite Ellen's frantic cries for her mother. When Ellen overhears that a massive search has been launched for her, she manages to escape the luxurious home in which she has been sequestered for one day and two nights, and returns to her own mother, who has grown increasingly terrified and distraught during her absence.

Freeman defuses the sinister implications of this incident by portraying Cynthia as a lonely woman whose abduction of Ellen emerges as a momentary act of derangement prompted by her recent loss of guardianship of a beloved young nephew. However, the author invites her reader to link the kidnapping of Ellen by a member of the upper class with the factory owners' ongoing appropriation of the young offspring of working-class parents, turning vibrant, strong-willed children into acquiescent, robotic laborers, bound by the same "invisible leash" that tied Ellen to the imperious Cynthia. Donna M. Campbell convincingly argues that the kidnapping incident in *The Portion of Labor* constitutes "an economic parable in which a child representing the strength, future, and capital of the working class is stolen to satisfy the needs, in this case the perverse maternal instincts, of a preternaturally youthful upper class whose vitality is sustained by the body and labor of others" (219). Tellingly, Ellen's aunt Eva, searching for her vanished niece, stops at the shoe factory where Eva has toiled since the age of fourteen, and "stares up at the windows, as if she meditated a wild search in the factory for the lost child" (51). Cynthia's commodification of the child Ellen as a rare "pearl" (20), a treasure she unlawfully secretes, parallels her factory-owning family's transformation of young workers into "piece[s] on a checker-board," "taken up" or "put down" at their masters' will (285). Watching the "boyish antics" of one of Ellen's playmates, Ellen's father Andrew remarks grimly, "Let him enjoy himself while he can, it won't be long before the grind-mill in there [the factory] will get hold of him, and then he'll be sober enough to suit anybody" (131). Resembling Ellen's thralldom to Cynthia, Rowe's working-class children fall helplessly into the devouring maw of the same factory that has depleted the youth and vigor of their parents.

Freeman also deploys the character of Cynthia—as well as that of Mrs Lloyd, the wife of the factory owner Norman Lloyd—to highlight the shortsightedness of reformers such as Riis who, she suggests, sought band-aid solutions to systemic social problems. Exhibiting what Joseph Entin, in another context, has called the "authoritarian benevolence of the progressive reformer," Cynthia asks the lost Ellen, with "a tone of indignation," "Tell me dear, where is your mother? She did not send you on an errand, such a little girl as you are, so late on such a cold night, with no more on than this?" (21). Freeman underscores the ironic implications of the factory-owning family's concerns about the treatment of working-class children in the following passage:

> [Mrs Lloyd]: 'Do you suppose that dear little thing was barefooted when she ran away?'
>
> [Lyman] Risley answered as if he had been addressed. 'I can vouch for the fact that she was not, Mrs Lloyd,' he said. 'They would sooner have walked on red-hot ploughshares themselves than let her.'
>
> 'Her father is getting quite an old man,' Norman Lloyd said, with no apparent relevancy, as if he were talking to himself. (166–7)

Although the significance of this dialogue is not immediately evident, Freeman soon reveals the "relevancy" of Mr Lloyd's observation when Ellen's father is subsequently fired from Lloyd's because he is "too old," and Norman Lloyd—apparently reminded by the conversation of the next generation waiting in the wings—employs Ellen, who is compelled to give up her college plans when her father is dismissed from his job. Mrs Lloyd's and Cynthia's misguided maternal solicitude about Ellen's home life—further indicated by Cynthia's angry inquiry, "Were they [Ellen's parents] harsh and cruel to her?" and Risley's prompt response, "You don't seem to consider that they love the child, possibly better than you can" (79)—expose their prejudicial views about working-class domestic environments as well as their blindness to their own family's complicity in robbing children of their education in order to increase personal profit. Freeman makes clear that the "web of surveillance through which the poor and disenfranchised were analyzed, regulated, and policed" (Entin 510) by some reformers neglected the most obvious culprit in stealing children's lives: unregulated (or poorly regulated) child labor in industrial America.

Freeman counters these reformers' stereotypes about working-class homes by demonstrating that Rowe's child laborers are endangered not by a dysfunctional domestic environment but by unstable employment and arduous working conditions. While Riis maintains, "The children of the poor grow up in joyless homes . . . Home to them is an empty name," Freeman's protagonist Ellen Brewster, like most of the workers in *The Portion of Labor*, "knew what it was to come home for rest and shelter after a day of toil, and she seemed to sense the full meaning of home as a refuge for weary labor" (363). As Diner has attested, Riis viewed the reform of the working-class family as the key to social progress, and "had no place in his vision . . . for the class-based actions of the urban masses to change their work lives through collective action, such as labor organizing" (xiv). In her portrayal of working-class families motivated almost entirely by the goal of creating better lives for their loved ones, Freeman shows that the damage child laborers incur takes place in the workplace rather than in the home and can be rectified only through the agency of workers' unions and political activism. Her tragic and memorable portraits of Ellen's fellow laborers illuminate their circumscribed destinies: the frail and consumptive Maria Atkins, who "felt vaguely as if she were in the grip of some mighty machine worked by a mighty operator" (309); the once-defiant Abby Atkins, "leather-stained and leather-scented" (230) from her tireless making of shoes; and Granville Joy, Ellen's first suitor, who becomes "one of the herd," pervaded by "the smell of leather that steamed up in his face from his raiment and his body" (237). Freeman's persistent references to the smell of leather that saturates the laborers demonstrates their dehumanization—the extent to which they have become identified with the commodities they produce.

A Family Wage Economy

As Katrina Irving has documented, many conservative social reformers sought to "impart those practices and skills" to the working-class woman "that would enable [her] to carry out her sentimental maternal role" (493). Yet policing the impoverished mother with the aim of persuading her to conform to middle-class ideals of domesticity, as Irving shows, "was more than a little ironic because such a position was not an option" for most laboring-class women, who "moved outside of the intensely privatized world of the home to which the True Mother was confined and upon which depended her claim to normative citizenship" (492). In *The Portion of Labor*, Freeman demonstrates that most members of working-class families, including children, were compelled through financial necessity to work for wages, making any culturally approved distinctions between "men's work" and "women's work" impossible to maintain. Far from being protected from the harsh realities of the working world, Ellen, in response to her wealthy suitor's inquiry as to whether the workers "have such a hard time," retorts bitterly, "I know they do. I think I ate the knowledge along with my very first daily bread" (277). Sacrificing schooling as well as the nurturing domestic space celebrated within middle-class American society, workers in Rowe experience "home life" for a few brief hours each day.

Indeed, Freeman reveals that factory workers in this New England shoe-manufacturing town can survive only by means of a family wage economy. The factory owners' desire for maximum profit prompts them to set up a system whereby older workers are continually demoted and replaced by younger ones—often young sons or daughters displacing parents. Ellen's friends Abby and Maria Atkins leave school and go to work at age fourteen when their ailing mother and father, broken down by years of toil, can no longer support the family; similarly, Ellen's mother Fanny and her Aunt Eva "had both stopped going to school at a very early age" (85) so that they could contribute to the meager family income. Eva tells her niece, "We had to quit school. Folks can live with empty heads, but they can't with empty stomachs. It had to be one or the other" (86). Ellen's father Andrew, determined that his bright, ambitious daughter will never give up her education for factory work, recognizes that he has no control over his own diminishing status as a worker at Lloyd's factory: "Though he was far from old, his hair was gray, his back bent. He moved with a weary shuffle. The men in the shop began to eye him furtively. 'Andrew Brewster will get fired next,' they said. 'The boss ain't no use for men with the first snap gone'" (155). Ultimately fired from Lloyd's, Andrew finds a lower-paying job at a rival establishment, only to lose that position to a child, as he laments to Fanny: "They've got a boy who can move faster in my place—a boy for less pay, who can move faster" (332). Compelled to give up her plans for college and take a factory job to help keep her family afloat, Ellen remains haunted by the image of her humiliated and despairing father, "exiled in his prime from his place in the working world by this system of arbitrary employment" (479).

Freeman's portrayal of the Atkins and Brewster families captures the oppressiveness of a system that traps the next generation in stasis, unable to rise through education because of the necessity for children to assume their displaced parents' working roles. In *Child Labor in America*, John A. Fliter has documented, "During the Gilded Age from 1870 to 1900, many business owners and stockholders favored the use of child workers in the name of greater profits. Children were paid less than women, who were paid less than men" (23). As Fliter points out, conditions like those that Freeman describes were typical in New England manufacturing towns in the late nineteenth century:

> It was a vicious cycle. Child labor depressed adult wages, but the income from working children was crucial to make ends meet. The social costs were steep, however. Early factory reports noted that a type of role reversal often existed: children and wives were employed while the father, unable to find work, remained idle, performed household chores, or took jobs with less pay. Children were being worked to death at an early age while adults, at the peak of their earning potential, could not find employment. (26)

Andrew's fervent hope that Ellen will escape factory life echoes the sentiments of many working-class families of the period, as Alan Dawley has attested: "Another measure of the [factory worker's] alienation was his wish that his children not follow him in the trade. But the family needed income, so what else was there to do? Since he had job contacts [there], his children became factory workers like himself because 'necessity compels it'" (130). In her portraits of the impoverished but proud Brewsters and other working-class families in *The Portion of Labor*, Freeman fiercely disputes middle-class charges of "parental greed" as the underlying motive for children's and women's labor in the factories.[3]

Lost Children

Freeman makes a strategic appeal not only to cultural ideologies of gendered "separate spheres" but also to nineteenth-century conceptions of childhood as a sacred, inviolate stage of human development. In *A Century of Childhood*, Mary Lynn Stevens Heininger has described the "cult of childhood" that emerged in Europe and was quickly embraced within Victorian and American societies, observing that Jean-Jacques Rousseau "had laid the foundation, asserting that, far from being corrupt, children were personifications of human morality in its most primitive and unspoiled state" (10). Reflecting what R. Macieski has called "the mythologies of childhood purity, innocence, and joy that were dominant in the culture of the era," Freeman portrays the child Ellen as a "little tender blossom" (58) and a "silver-stemmed flower" (13), whose face radiates "the absolute purity of curve and color of a pearl" (20), and whose "pretty baby mouth was curved like an inverted bow of love" (19). In keeping with Romantic notions that young children were endowed with a fineness of perception that inevitably dulled over the years, the narrator celebrates Ellen's innocent wonderment as she gazes into a shop window: "It takes a child or an artist to see a picture without the intrusion of its second dimension of sordid use and the gross reflection of humanity" (18). Although most of the novel focuses on Ellen as a young woman, Freeman begins *The Portion of Labor* with an extended depiction of Ellen's childhood so that readers can trace her sobering but necessary growth in awareness of social injustice and inhumanity in the "real" world.

Yet Freeman lingers over Ellen's childhood not only to chart her protagonist's development of social awareness but also to dramatize the mental and physical deterioration of Ellen's close friends and classmates as they leave school at a young age to become factory workers at Lloyd's. Freeman indicates that nineteenth-century sentimental views of childhood seem not to extend to the victims of child labor, setting descriptions of Cynthia's pampered nephew Robert, the "dear little boy" (45) who will become the owner of Lloyd's, against disturbing depictions of malnourished and sickly child workers at the profitable factory that supports Robert's life of luxury. As Karen Sanchez-Eppler has contended, the nineteenth-century working child's "need to labor [stood] in potent opposition to the burgeoning idealization of childhood as a life-stage appointed for play" (152). Freeman creates powerful portraits of young workers whose childhoods are abruptly truncated through economic necessity, with each portrayal illustrating a different loss: education (Abby Atkins), physical health (Maria Atkins), and individuality (Granville Joy). In combination, these portraits support Sanchez-Eppler's argument that the ways in which "childhood is imagined and inhabited provide one of the most potent mechanisms of class formation . . . [I]n nineteenth-century America childhood itself is increasingly recognized as a sign of class status" (151).

In her characterization of the Atkins family, Freeman illustrates how working-class parents' hopes for their children's future are repeatedly frustrated by their dependence on a family wage economy. As a schoolgirl, Ellen's closest friend Abby "was really brilliant in a defiant, reluctant fashion," and "when called out to recitation made the best one in her class" (143). In pondering the "world-wide question as to the why of inequality," the fiercely democratic Abby resists being "slighted in the distribution of things," and "her very soul rose in futile rebellion" (144). Yet this iconoclastic and keenly intelligent young girl, compelled to abandon her education and begin factory work after her elementary school years, undergoes a troubling metamorphosis. Her former awareness of injustice gives way to a self-protective acceptance of her "place" in life, and—most disturbingly—she begins to internalize the larger society's assertion of "natural" class distinctions. After Cynthia decides to financially support a college education for Ellen, Abby's sister Maria remarks, "I suppose we shan't see so much of you," to which Abby responds, "Of course we shan't . . . and it won't be fitting we should. It won't be best for Ellen to associate with shop-girls when she's going to Vassar College" (247). Distanced from the friend who continued her education and became valedictorian of her class, Abby "held [Ellen] in a sort of worship . . . she was fairly afraid of her" (230), subduing her own "fierceness of nature," and promising Ellen, "I'll work for you" (230). Unable to break the family cycle of underemployment by staying in school and fulfilling her own "brilliant" potential, Abby resigns herself to becoming "one of the herd" (237).

Freeman's depiction of Abby's sacrifice of her education for desperately needed family income reflected a harsh reality for many children of laborers in nineteenth-century New England. Macieski has noted that despite Massachusetts's "strong [legal] protections for children," the state nevertheless "had high levels of child labor" (49). Thomas Dublin has attested that, in the late nineteenth century, "children in Lynn [Massachusetts] shoeworker families contributed more than 41 percent of family earnings" (133). As Fliter confirms, most child laborers during the "Gilded Age" worked "seventy-two to seventy-eight hours per week," with the alarming result that

> reports from factory inspectors revealed a level of ignorance among child laborers that was almost inconceivable . . . Most of the children were between twelve and fifteen years old, and the average age at which

they started work was nine years. What little they had learned in school before going to work was long forgotten. Thousands could not write anything other than their name, and most could not read. (24)

William Moran has reported that middle-class businessmen and even some educators defended child labor, agreeing with one factory owner that "there is such a thing as too much education for working people sometimes" (132). In her portrayal of the Atkins family's struggle for survival, Freeman suggests that employing children as factory workers not only provided the factory's owners with a cheap source of labor but also ensured a stable work force, since children who left school to work could not expect better prospects in the future. By cutting Mr Atkins's work hours while he is still in his prime, Mr Lloyd can depend upon the daughters Abby and Maria to fill the gap. As Freeman makes clear, Abby's lost schooling and delimited future represent not simply collateral damage of the system but the outcome of a strategic plan on the part of the rapacious factory owner Norman Lloyd.

If the character of Abby embodies the factory's power to annihilate the intellectual potential of the next generation, Abby's sister Maria represents its ability to destroy that generation's physical vitality. As a schoolchild, Maria (in Ellen's estimation) is a "beautiful" girl with "an honest light in her eyes" (139). Yet her health begins to deteriorate as soon as she leaves school to begin factory work, and Ellen's subsequent recollections are of the young girl "coughing violently" (448), "coughing her life away" (479), unable to "speak aloud" (473). When Abby and Ellen urge her to stay home from work during a snowstorm, she "burst[s] out with a pitiful emphasis. 'I've got to go,' she said. 'Father had a bad spell last night; he can't get out. He'll lose his place this time, we are afraid . . . I've got to go to work; we've got to have the money'" (448). As Maria's health declines, she loses the will to survive: "Of late years all the fire of resistance had seemed to die out in the girl. She was unfailingly sweet, but nerveless . . . Maria was half fed in every sense; she had not enough nourishing food for her body nor love for her heart, nor exercise for her brain" (309). She recognizes that she is destined to work at Lloyd's, "as if [she] were driven by some more subtle machine than any in the factory" (309), for as long as she can maintain her precarious employment and her tenuous hold on life.

Freeman clearly draws her portrait of Maria from her own knowledge of persistent health problems among young industrial workers of the era. As Fliter reports, "Many dangers in the mines, factories, and mills degraded a child's health and sometimes resulted in loss of limb and life . . . Children who began work at an early age and labored more than ten hours a day, often at repetitive tasks for years, were commonly described as 'undersized,' 'delicate,' 'worn,' and 'puny'" (27–8). Although Freeman focuses on a shoemaking factory in *The Portion of Labor*—perhaps because, growing up in the shoe-manufacturing town of Randolph, Massachusetts, she was familiar with this industry—Maria's ailments, as Freeman describes them, more closely resemble those suffered by New England textile workers, who, as William Moran has pointed out, "were among the first Americans to be diagnosed with 'brown lung' or byssinosis... Eventually, 70 percent of the early mill workers died of respiratory diseases; the comparable figure for Massachusetts farmers at the time was 4 percent" (23). Moran notes that Margaret Sanger assessed the physical condition of 150 child workers from Lawrence, Massachusetts, ultimately testifying before Congress that the children "were very much emaciated; every child showed signs of malnutrition" and most of them "had swollen adenoids and enlarged tonsils" (209). Freeman's depiction of Maria's slow but steady decline in physical strength and vitality captures the "waste of child life" (162) tragically evident in New England factories at the turn of the century.

Freeman suggests that even those child workers who remained healthy often struggled with feelings of hopelessness and apathy. Granville Joy, Ellen's first suitor, displays the most dramatic psychological transformation among the young workers in *The Portion of Labor*. As a schoolchild, he is a "whirlwind" (131), a lively and irrepressible boy noted for his "youthful exuberance" and his "black eyes [that gazed] with a bold and cheerful outlook on the unknown" (129). When Ellen's father sadly acknowledges that "he'll be sober enough to suit anybody" when "the grind-mill gets hold of him" (131), his words are prescient. Granville is "a good scholar," of whom "many said it was a pity that he had to leave school and go to work," (265), but he loses his independent nature when he begins his job at the factory, and quickly (if reluctantly) accommodates himself to becoming "a cog in the machine." Accidentally meeting Ellen with Robert, the formerly self-confident Granville "saw himself [as] hopelessly common, clad in awkward clothes," and pervaded by the "smell of leather" (237). He considers himself interchangeable with other workers, telling Robert in "a sullen, bitter tone" that his employer's failure to recognize him is unsurprising, since "there are so many of us" (238). Granville's smoldering resentment emerges only in the "indescribably bitter emphasis" with which he repeats "so many of us" to Robert: "Suddenly his gentleness seemed changed to gall. It was the terrible protest of one of the herd who goes along with the rest, yet realizes it, and looks ever out from his common mass with fierce eyes of individual dissent at the immutable condition of things" (237). Granville, another "bee in the hive" (349), remains voiceless despite his internal rebellion.

The dehumanizing and mind-numbing effects of repetitive labor took an enormous toll on child workers of the era. In Lewis W. Hines's famous photographs of child laborers in the early twentieth century, the factory, as Richard S. Lowry observes, "appears as a demonic maternal machine, devouring childhood to produce a lifeless offspring that resembles nothing so much as zombies" (202). Alan Dawley has described the workers at shoemaking factories in Lynn in the late nineteenth century as "a silent congregation surrounded by the cacophony of moving machinery. Unlike the close conviviality of the [preindustrial shoemaker workshops], the factory workrooms heard little conversation and saw little human movement" (132). As Dawley elaborates:

> The [factory worker] worked steadily at a pace set by the external forces of the production line and enforced by the line foreman. If he slackened his pace, he threatened his own standard of living, either by risking firing or by cutting down his piece-wage for the day. Since he had no other source of livelihood, it is no wonder that a visitor to one of the factories noticed "the men and boys are working as if for life and scarcely stop to bestow a look on the visiting party." Such were the requirements of "system" in the factories. (95–6)

In *The Portion of Labor*, Ellen similarly notes the silent resignation among workers at Lloyd's, recognizing that each laborer "had no time for rebellion" if "he had to get his part of a shoe finished . . . so as not to clog and balk the whole system" (453). As Lowry reiterates, children introduced into this system at an early age came to resemble (as reflected in Hines's photographs) "not humanity, but the walking dead in children's bodies" (202).

Like Hines's photographs, Freeman's powerful prose portraits of young workers in *The Portion of Labor* dramatize their plight far more effectively than statistical reports by factory investigators. Lowry has contended, "Hines's photographs document the betrayal of New England values that placed a premium on education, telling a story of harsh industrial conditions and conveying the price of economic development and, perhaps, the callousness of a society that allowed its young to labor so early in life" (10). Similarly, Freeman's nuanced characterizations of Abby, Maria, and Granville capture the tragic exclusion of working-class children from idealized and sentimental nineteenth-century notions of childhood's innocence and joy. As Sanchez-Eppler has shown, "Throughout the nineteenth-century, while sentimental images of childhood as a time of delight, imagination, and love quickly proliferated, the role of children's labor in the household economy diminished far more slowly" (xx). Portraying the loss of education, health, and individuality among children who, prior to their labor in the factory, exhibited youthful vigor and intellectual promise, Freeman attempts to awaken the social conscience of the nation.

A Closed System

Although Freeman's outrage over the oppression of the working class in industrial New England registers clearly in *The Portion of Labor*, the novel's conclusion offers hope and reconciliation, seeming to temper and defuse the power of her protest. Examining Freeman's portraits of unconventional women, Leah Blatt

Figure 8.1 Child labor, making garters for Liberty Garters works. Mrs Finkelstein with Bessie, age 13, and Sophie, age 7. 127 Monroe Street, New York. Photograph by Lewis W. Hine, January 1908. Shutterstock.

Glasser has astutely observed that the author's tendency to pull back from controversial social messages reflected, in combination, her own ambivalence, her desire to reach a larger audience, and her reluctant compromises with nervous publishers. Yet the ending of *The Portion of Labor* appears so transparently insincere and so much at odds with what has come before it that the reader is tempted to credit only the latter two rationales, concluding that the novel's finale was either a tacked-on concession to a squeamish publisher or else the author's attempt to appease more traditional readers. The events contributing to the "happily ever after" ending of the novel are all lucky accidents, mirroring no fundamental change in the status quo: Ellen's parents receive unexpected dividends from her father's long-ago purchase of stock in a mining company; Ellen becomes engaged to Robert Lloyd, the factory owner who succeeds his uncle Norman; Abby plans to marry Willy Jones, a fellow worker; and Maria begins a courtship with another factory worker, John Sargent. The fact that Freeman shows that the conditions in the factory remain the same—wages are still low; children are still leaving school to go to work; Robert Lloyd still refuses to hire anyone connected with the union—suggests that she expects a careful reader to dismiss this tidied-up conclusion as a sop for her publisher or perhaps even a parodic facsimile of similar endings of nineteenth-century popular novels. What shines throughout the novel despite its conclusion is the author's moral indignation over the plight of "overworked and under-fed" factory laborers (267)—especially children.

The most dramatic indication that Freeman gives of the doom of working-class interests in Rowe is the failure of the strike that Ellen and other workers organize in response to a cut in wages. Ellen recognizes that her suitor Robert Lloyd "was going to abuse his power of capital, his power to take the bread out of their mouths entirely, by taking it out in part . . . he was deliberately going to cause privation, and even suffering where there were large families" (452). During the six weeks of the strike, as "times grew harder and harder" (511), Abby tells Ellen that many children in her neighborhood "are fairly starving. They are going around to the neighbors' swill-buckets . . . just like little hungry dogs, and it's precious little they find in them" (515). Even children too young for school, including Ellen's cousin Amabel, are enlisted in sewing at home on piecework that the family sells for a pittance: "That evening little Amabel . . . having divined the altered state of the family finances, was pulling out basting-threads, with a puckered little face bent over her work" (511). Acknowledging, "There are children starving and people dying," Ellen urges her fellow strikers to "accept Mr Lloyd's terms and go back to work" (516). With the strike settled "on the boss's [terms]" (522), the necessity for a family wage economy persists, and the cycle of underemployment for successive generations continues.

Although Robert, after business improves, ultimately rescinds the reduction in wages to regain Ellen's affection, the destinies of those workers who have grown up in the factory—Abby, Maria, and Granville—remain fixed. Abby remonstrates with Ellen, telling her she should never marry "just an ordinary man who works in the shop, and will never do anything but work in the shop . . . and have a lot of children to work in shops" (229), but in becoming engaged to another young laborer who has worked beside her for years, Abby accepts that fate for herself and her prospective family. Maria, whose health has continued to decline, becomes "worse again" (514) when financial hardship means no heat during the winter, yet she returns to work after the strike and, like Abby, becomes attached to a fellow worker at the end of the novel. Finally, Granville Joy, zealous in his defense of workers' rights during the strike, also resignedly returns to the factory, "very thin and pale" (542). The novel's "happy" ending for the Brewsters (questionable in Ellen's case, since Robert is hardly Prince Charming) does not extend to Ellen's fellow laborers, who will inevitably tread the track laid out for their parents, and almost certainly be faced with the need to send their own children to work. In demonstrating that nothing in Rowe truly has changed, Freeman undercuts the superficially positive outcomes in the novel's last chapter, leaving the reader with an image of defeated families trapped within a closed system.

Freeman published *The Portion of Labor* at a time when child labor had become a serious issue of concern among social reformers in New England. As Macieski has noted in describing the impact of Hines's photographs of child workers, "New England prided itself on its traditions of reform, so it came as a shock to some when Hines's photographs provided evidence that child labor was very much present in the region" (72). Freeman's novel surely provoked a similar reaction, since her portrait of ruthless factory owners and weary child workers dismantled familiar images of community-minded and progressive New England towns. Hugh D. Hindman has linked Massachusetts's failure to protect working children in the early twentieth century to the state government's reluctance to endanger the profits of factory owners (59). As Fliter points out, "The United States lagged behind England in the industrialization of the economy and was thus slow to learn the lessons about child labor exploitation from the British experience. . . . Whether out of greed, ignorance, or indifference, the United States repeated many of the same mistakes faced under British industrialization" (16). True reform did not happen until almost twenty years after *The Portion of Labor* was published.[4] The generation of children succeeding Abby, Maria, and Granville would not have escaped the "grind-mill."

As a popular writer capable of reaching large audiences, Freeman's literary voice emerges as one that, we may safely venture to guess, was instrumental in awakening the public consciousness to New England factory owners' exploitation of working-class children. At the turn of the century, when the nation, as Sanchez-Eppler has documented, "began passing child-labor laws and to view children working not as normative but as abusive" (xvii), *The Portion of Labor* stands out as a rare fictional treatment of an important social problem. Yet unlike reformers such as Jacob Riis, who relied upon social welfare programs and philanthropy to address the issue of urban poverty, Freeman suggests that the solutions to working-class hardship are much more complex. Implicitly indicting reformist campaigns that targeted the domestic life of laborers instead of focusing on systemic problems in industrial America, Freeman makes the human costs of the family wage economy starkly apparent in her intricate characterizations of workers whose youthful promise is stifled by their early induction into the robotic routine of factory labor. Her haunting portraits of child laborers, like her more familiar depictions of aging, impoverished women, expose the ills of industrial society and assert the nation's obligation to protect its most vulnerable citizens. Within a twenty-first-century America in which women and children make up the largest segment of the population living in poverty, Freeman's portrayal of the youngest victims of working-class oppression in the late nineteenth century remains sadly relevant today.

Works Cited

Berkson, Dorothy. "'A Goddess Behind a Sordid Veil': The Domestic Heroine Meets the Labor Novel in Mary E. Wilkins Freeman's *The Portion of Labor*." *Redefining the Political Novel: American Women Writers, 1797–1901*, edited by Sharon M. Harris, U of Tennessee P, 1995, pp. 149–68.

Campbell, Donna M. *Bitter Tastes: Literary Naturalism and Early Cinema in American Women's Writing*. U of Georgia P, 2016.

Dawley, Alan. *Class and Community: The Industrial Revolution in Lynn*. Harvard UP, 1976.

Diner, Hasier R. Introduction. *How the Other Half Lives*, by Jacob Riis. 1890. Norton, 2010, pp. vii–xv.

Dowling, Robert M. *Slumming in New York: From the Waterfront to Mythic Harlem*. U of Illinois P, 2007.

Dublin, Thomas. *Transforming Women's Work: New England Lives in the Industrial Revolution*. Cornell UP, 1995.

Entin, Joseph. "'Unhuman Humanity': Bodies of the Urban Poor and the Collapse of Realist Legibility." *Novel: A Forum on Fiction*, vol. 34, no. 3, 2001, pp. 313–37.

Fliter, John A. *Child Labor in America: The Epic Legal Struggle to Protect Children*. UP of Kansas, 2018.

Freeman, Mary E. Wilkins. *The Portion of Labor*. 1901. Gregg Press, 1967.

Glasser, Leah Blatt. *In a Closet Hidden: The Life and Work of Mary E. Wilkins Freeman*. U of Massachusetts P, 1996.

Heininger, Mary Lynn Stevens. *A Century of Childhood, 1820–1920*. Strong Museum, 1984.

Hindman, Hugh D. *The World of Child Labor: An Historical and Regional Survey*. Routledge, 2014.

Irving, Katrina. *Immigrant Mothers: Narratives of Race and Maternity, 1890–1925*. U of Illinois P, 2000.

Lowry, Richard S. "Lewis Hines's Family Romance." *The American Child: A Cultural Studies Reader*, edited by Caroline F. Levander and Carol J. Singley, Rutgers UP, 2003, pp. 184–207.

Macieski, Robert. *Picturing Class: Lewis W. Hine Photographs Child Labor in New England*. U of Massachusetts P, 2015.
Marchand, Mary E. "Death to Lady Bountiful: Women and Reform in Edith Wharton's *The Fruit of the Tree*." *Legacy*, vol. 18, no. 1, 2001, pp. 65–78.
Moran, William. *The Belles of New England: The Women of the Textile Mills and the Families Whose Wealth They Wove*. Thomas Dunne, 2007.
Pizer, Donald. "Late Nineteenth-Century American Literary Naturalism: A Re-Introduction." *American Literary Realism*, vol. 38, no. 3, 2006, pp. 189–202.
Ranta, Judith A. *Women and Children of the Mills: An Annotated Guide to Nineteenth-Century Textile Factory Literature*. Greenwood Press, 1999.
Reichart, Mary R. Introduction. *A Mary Wilkins Freeman Reader*, edited by Mary R. Reichart, U of Nebraska P, 1997, pp. vii–xxi.
Riis, Jacob. *How the Other Half Lives*. 1890. Edited by Hasia R. Diner, Norton, 2010.
Sanchez-Eppler, Karen. *Dependent States: The Child's Part in Nineteenth-Century Culture*. U of Chicago P, 2005.

Notes

1. William Blake and Charles Dickens, the most well-known British writers to expose the horrors of child labor in England, have few American counterparts. Although naturalist writers such as Stephen Crane, Upton Sinclair, and Jack London touched on the subject in their fiction, no important American novel besides *The Portion of Labor* treats the problem extensively. For a reference guide to American works of fiction about women and child laborers in textile mills, see Judith A. Ranta, *Women and Children of the Mills: An Annotated Guide to Nineteenth-Century American Textile Factory Literature*, Greenwood Press, 1999.
2. Although Leah Blatt Glasser suggests that Freeman may have chafed at the constrictions of being "pampered and protected by her mother," she acknowledges that Freeman shared an unusually close and nurturing relationship with her mother and resisted "parting with childhood" (11).
3. Richard S. Lowry cites a poster circulated by the National Child Labor Committee that proclaimed, "[Child labor] allows unsupervised, greedy manufacturers and parents to make a mockery of childhood." As Lowry counters, "The poster's connection between 'greedy manufacturers and parents' aptly captures the familial politics of child labor by suggesting how out of touch the movement was with the conditions that shaped much working-class family life" (196).
4. Hugh D. Hindman notes that child labor in the United States "peaked in 1890 and 1900 at 21.38 and 21.66 percent, respectively. By 1930, the labor force participation of ten- to fourteen-year-olds had fallen to 5.56 percent . . . Similarly, labor force activity rates of fourteen- and fifteen-year-olds peaked to 30.9 percent in 1900 and, by 1940, had declined to 5.2 percent. After 1967, the Department of Labor changed the definition of the US labor force, restricting it to those aged sixteen or older, and we stopped counting fourteen-and fifteen-year-olds" (295).

9

LITERARY BUSINESSWOMAN EXTRAORDINAIRE

BRENT L. KENDRICK

The distinguished accolades enjoyed by Mary E. Wilkins Freeman are numerous and well known. At the start of the twentieth century—when her career was at its height—she and Mark Twain were considered America's most beloved writers. She was the first recipient of the William Dean Howells Gold Medal for Distinguished Work in Fiction (1925). She was among the first women elected to membership in the National Institute of Arts and Letters (1926). And the bronze doors at the American Academy of Arts and Letters in New York (installed at its West 155 Street Administration Building in 1938) bear the inscription, "Dedicated to the Memory of Mary E. Wilkins Freeman and the Women Writers of America."

What is not well known, however, is the magnitude of Freeman's phenomenal financial success as a nineteenth-century literary businesswoman extraordinaire.[1] Freeman started her long career in the early 1880s and in 1883 received an inheritance from her father of $962.90 in cash and one-half interest in his Brattleboro, Vermont, business property valued at $5,000 (Marlboro District Probate Court). Yet after her death in 1930, the value of her estate at the height of the Great Depression—even after her personal property had been auctioned off at embarrassingly low prices—came to a grand and spectacular finale of $117,285.41 (Brown). Adjusted for current inflation and putting aside for the moment all the particulars, that would be equivalent to starting out with $24,214.38 in 1883 and ending up with $1,779,365.41 in 1930 when the stock market was at its worst.

By any standard, that's quite a financial success story. It's extraordinary, in fact, considering that during Freeman's early adolescent years in Brattleboro, Vermont, her family were "reduced to proud and shabby gentility," as biographer Edward Foster notes, especially when the purse became so lean that they moved into the home of Reverend Thomas Pickman Tyler and his wife, and kept house (37, 42). Freeman's father slipped more and more into the background and "the neighbors thought of him as a 'putterer' and as one who was always doing little services for others, partly perhaps to maintain his own dignity" (37). Yet those same economic and social frustrations instilled in her a "driving, compulsive demand for prestige and financial security" (132).

Freeman's is perhaps an even greater financial success story, considering that at the start of her career, she maintained, "I know so little about business and business customs" (Freeman, Letter 8). While her modesty may have been becoming, making such a claim was nothing more than a big fib, not too unlike the one she told when she moved Sarah Penn into the barn in her "The Revolt of Mother." Late in life, she declared that there never was in New England a woman like mother and that she had sacrificed truth when she wrote that story ("An Autobiography" 75). She did the same thing when she claimed that she knew little about business and business customs. Or was it simply that she was not *consciously* aware of all that she knew about business—of all that she had learned about business from her father, through his successes as well as through his failures?

Admittedly, publishing-house business customs may have seemed remote at the start of her career, but Freeman was no stranger to general business. After all, her father, Warren E. Wilkins—by trade an architect and builder of some note, having been trained in the tradition of Samuel McIntire of Salem (one of America's most celebrated craftsmen-architects)—ventured into the business world in 1867 when he moved his family from Randolph, Massachusetts, to Brattleboro, Vermont. On 1 January of the previous year, he entered into a co-partnership with Orin Slate of Brattleboro, to run a dry goods business under the name of Slate and Wilkins. Their joint business continued until 1868, when, by mutual consent, it was dissolved. On 1 January 1869, Wilkins entered into a new co-partnership with Willis Tuxbury, and the two of them continued the dry goods business and invited "all Slate and Wilkins' old customers, and all others" to do business with them ("Copartnership," *Vermont Phoenix*, 5 January 1866; and "Copartnership," *Vermont Record and Farmer*, 29 January 1869). Their partnership did not last long. On 11 March 1870, a large advertisement appeared in the *Vermont Phoenix* captioned "Hard Times." No doubt it was a declaration not only of Warren Wilkins's own challenging financial times but also of Brattleboro's challenging financial times. The advertisement announced a "ten percent off sale for thirty days on Black Silks, Black Alpacas and Other Dress Goods." What's more significant is the name that appears at the end in a large font: "W. E. Wilkins" (3). From that point forward, "W. E. Wilkins" was sole proprietor of the dry goods store. By June—and continuing regularly thereafter—large advertisements appeared in the *Vermont Phoenix*: "Save Your Money / by / Purchasing Your Dress Goods / of / W. E. Wilkins, / at the / New-York Store" (4). The upscale marketing strategy would have made his own household as well as Brattleboro's citizenry take notice.

By late 1871, Wilkins decided to leave his business. On 8 September, his "Closing Out Sale" advertisement appeared in the *Vermont Phoenix*: "Contemplating a change in my business and in order to reduce my stock as much as possible by the first of May, I shall close out all my stock of dress goods at greatly reduced prices" (4). The final closing-out sale announcement appeared in the *Vermont Phoenix* on 15 March 1872, with some additional language: "This is a BONA FIDE sale, and means Business. This sale will continue until all is sold" ("Great Closing Out Sale of Dry Goods").

Warren Wilkins left his dry goods business, but he did not leave his business ventures. The details are somewhat sketchy, but it is known that he kept ownership of his property—the Steen & Wilkins Block—apparently renting the downstairs of what had been his dry goods store to Newton and Rose—proprietors of a new drug store ("Local Intelligence," 17 October 1873). He rented the upstairs space at various times to Mrs S. E. Baldwin (a "hair worker") and to Mrs E. A. Weatherhead (a "dress maker") ("Brattleboro Business Directory"). His rental scheme was so successful that by 1876 he was "finishing off some very pleasant and desirable tenements in the second and third stories" ("Our Own Vicinity," 17 March 1876).

Additionally, his ongoing business endeavors found him looping back to his original architectural and building trade. He "enlarged the capacity" of the Steen & Wilkins Block, "greatly improving its appearance" ("Our Own Vicinity," 12 November 1875). It appears that he secured the contract for building an additional exit for the Brattleboro Town Hall ("Local Intelligence," 8 March 1873). He built a house on Mechanic Square for George E. Crowell and two more for Crowell on Forest Square ("Local Intelligence," 3 October 1879; and "Local Intelligence," 18 June 1880). And he built for himself a double-tenement house on Grove Street, heralded by *The Vermont Phoenix, and Record and Farmer* as "a model for its class and an ornament to the street" ("Local Intelligence," 29 October 1880). Two years later—in the fall of 1882—Wilkins left to work on a construction job in Gainesville, Florida. He died there on 10 April 1883 ("Local Intelligence," 20 April 1883).

During this period—from 1866 when Freeman was about fourteen until 1882 when she was thirty—business matters (e.g. buying trips to New York, the law of supply and demand, the rise and fall of prices, the best means of advertising, the disadvantages of charge sales)—would have entered into the Wilkins family household conversation just as surely and just as readily as fam-

Figure 9.1 Steen-Wilkins Block, Brattleboro, Vermont. Stereocard from the 1870s or 1880s. Collection of Brent L. Kendrick.

ily news or the weather or town gossip. Even if her father did not ultimately enjoy the full success that he had hoped for when he moved the family to Brattleboro, it seems likely that Mary Wilkins would have learned *something* about business from her father's many years of business successes and failures.

This much is factual. When her father died, she received $962.00 in cash and one half-interest in his Brattleboro business property, valued at $5,000. What she did with the cash is unknown. However, she kept the property, just as her father had kept it after he closed his dry goods store. Further, she rented it out—just as her father had rented it out—and she used the investment dividends to support herself and those who depended on her.

Managing the property for her was Charles F. Thompson, a notary public and treasurer of the Brattleboro Gas Light Company. His letter of 24 January 1895 is typical:

> Dear Friend,
>   I enclose usual Statement & ck. for $115.40. Mrs. Russell who lives in the No. Tenement up Stairs is behind 1 mo. She is having a hard time this winter but she will pay. She is a good tenant. I hope you are very well. Were you here on this crisp, pleasant morning, with our now fine sleighing, I should delight to take a fine pair and whisk you along over some of our fine roads and give you a regular Vt. airing.
>   Sincerely Yrs
>   C. F. Thompson

Thompson's "usual statement" itemized rents received from seven tenants as well as expenses for insurance, water rents, moving snow, and painting floors. The check for $115.40 represented earnings for one quarter. Adjusted for inflation that would be about $3,050.30 today. Clearly, from the time she came into her inheritance, she realized the importance of investments, especially if carefully managed (Thompson).

Another document from this period is important to highlight as well. It's a page from an undated will, seemingly written around 1895, since it mentions her story *The Long Arm*. It is noteworthy for several reasons. First it discloses that even then Freeman owned stock in the Boston and Albany Railroad and in the New York, New Haven and Hartford Railroad. Second, it shows clearly that she wanted her family to benefit from her Brattleboro property. Rather than leave it to them outright, however, she left her uncle and her cousin only the income from the property:

> G. E. Wilkins. One half income from my real estate in Brattleboro Vermont. Same to revert to Hattie P. Lothrop, upon his death. Hattie P. Lothrop, one half income from real estate in Brattleboro Vermont but upon condition that said property is . . .

Unfortunately, that unfinished sentence concludes the only surviving page of the will. The verso, however, shows several calculations, the largest of which is $17,260, presumably the minimum value of Freeman's 1895 estate (Freeman, Undated Will). Adjusted for inflation, that would be equivalent to about $507,647.06 today.

Freeman's response a few years later to the question, "What would you do if you had a million dollars?" rings true:

> I should portion out to various people sums varying from two hundred to five hundred dollars a year, after the fashion of annuities. I might go beyond five hundred in some cases, but I think not. . . . To such, of frugal habits, a very little a year would mean independence . . . I doubt in any case I should give any considerable sum outright. I think it is safe to assume in the case of any older person or persons who are in financial straits that they are either lacking in ability to manage money if they have it, or are victims of that persistent misfortune which seems to follow some people, and it would not be wise to intrust them personally with the principal. It would be advisable to have it safely invested for them. ("If They Had a Million Dollars")

Clearly, Freeman knew how to manage money. Clearly, too, she knew how to invest it.

While Freeman's business ability seems to have come from her father, he was not the only businessman in her life. In fact, she seems to have surrounded herself with businessmen, and, as Charles Johanningsmeier observed in his "Sarah Orne Jewett and Mary E. Wilkins (Freeman): Two Shrewd Businesswomen in Search of New Markets," neither writer was "so naïve as not to realize that men controlled much of the monetary capital in the late nineteenth century, not only in the publishing industry but also the world at large" (81–2).

Four other men who played roles in Freeman's life were businessmen: Ellis Hollingsworth, Isaac Tolman, Nathan Tolman, and Charles Manning Freeman. This is not to suggest that any of these men—other than Charles Manning Freeman—would have had any direct influence on her business dealings. However, it does seem to suggest that she felt comfortable and at home in a world where men controlled much of the money.

Until now, Hollingsworth has remained a rather elusive mystery, although Freeman discusses him in her 28 April 1886 letter to Mary Louise Booth, editor of *Harper's Bazar*:

> No: Mr Ellis Hollingsworth wont do as an incentive to the novel, for I am all over being in love with him by this time. I have not seen him since, and of course could not stay in love with him, unless I did. Then he is the

sort of man, one could be very fond of but not be in love with anyway. However, he would be very nice to write about, if he were not a little too elegant for my kind of story. (Freeman, Letter 13)

The details about *when* or *how* or even *if* Freeman might have been in love with Hollingsworth are unclear. This much is known. Hollingsworth was born in 1860, in South Braintree, less than four miles from Randolph where she was born in 1852 and lived until 1867 and once again from 1883 until 1902 when she married. He became a prominent paper manufacturer, having entered the business under his father—founder of Hollingsworth & Whitney Company. When he died in 1917, he had amassed $2,000,000, largely in real estate. Clearly, he was a business success ("Autumn Weddings: Littlefield-Hollingsworth"; "Died: Hollingsworth"; "Hollingsworth Estate").

The second man was Isaac S. Tolman. In 1893, the Randolph gossip making the rounds went like this: "Was Dolly Wilkins setting her cap for Isaac even while everyone knew he was virtually engaged to that nice Mabel Leach?" (Foster 121) The point here is not the possible romantic connection. Rather, it is the fact that Isaac Tolman was a highly successful Boston broker and partner in the banking firm of Rogers and Tolman. Recalling Freeman's will fragment from around 1895, it would not be unreasonable to speculate that Tolman might very well have served as a financial advisor of sorts, especially since the will shows that Freeman had begun developing an investment portfolio early in her career (Freeman, Undated Will).

After Isaac married, Randolph residents felt certain that Freeman would turn to his cousin, Nathan Irving Tolman, a buyer for Boston Dry Goods (successors to Jordan, Marsh, and Company) and, subsequently, treasurer of the Randolph Savings Bank. If a romance existed—and it might have: Tolman, after all, was in the dry goods business, just like Freeman's father—it did not go far, because he married Edith Porter in 1901, and no recollections of a romance with Freeman linger in Tolman family lore. However, they remained in contact until his death in 1925 (Kendrick, "General Introduction" 17). And at no time would that contact have been more important—from a business perspective—than in 1916.

On 25 February of that year, Mary Elizabeth Wales—Freeman's childhood friend and constant companion from 1884 until Freeman's marriage in 1902—gave Freeman a promissory note for $5,000. It was not the first time that she had financially supported Mary Wales and the Wales family. In fact, she started providing much-needed financial assistance as early as 1884 when she moved back to Randolph and rented the whole north side of the Wales house. Later she loaned all of the royalties from one of her early novels to Mary Wales (Foster 59–60, 141). Apparently, more money was needed, especially after family patriarch John Wales died in 1897. The next year, before publication of Freeman's *The People of Our Neighborhood*, she wrote to Edward Bok of Curtis Publishing on 15 April:

> Will you please have the agreement for the book publication of Neighborhood Types, and Village Amusements made out in the name of my friend here—Miss Mary Elizabeth Wales—and have the royalties thereon sent to her? I want to make her a little present, and think perhaps my interest in a little book will answer as well as anything.

Further, even after Freeman's marriage, she was "helping" Mary Wales as late as 1909 (Foster 181).

The promissory note of 25 February 1916, ended up in litigation. A few months later—on 8 June—Wales drew up her last will and testament. In it, she remembered her "dear and devoted friend Mary E. Wilkins Freeman of Metuchen, New Jersey," and left her "as a keepsake one article of furniture or jewelry which she may select, within a reasonable time after the probate of this will." In a codicil, she remembered her "dear friend Charles M. Freeman of Metuchen, New Jersey," and left him "all my Books and Manuscripts" (Last Will and Testament). But the will made no allowance for the $5,000 owed her friend, no doubt because she expected to repay it in a timely way as she had repaid other promissory notes and because, when she wrote her will, she had no idea that she would die just a few months afterwards, on 4 August 1916.

The fate of the books and manuscripts left to Dr Freeman is unknown, as is the keepsake that Mary Freeman selected. But this much is known. Freeman wanted what was rightfully hers. As one who knew how to manage money, she entered into a court battle, even though it implicated two friends—Mary Elizabeth Wales and N. Irving Tolman. On 16 October 1919, in the Commonwealth of Massachusetts, County of Norfolk, she filed a "Notice of Suit":

> An action at law this day has been brought against N. Irving Tolman, executor of the will of the above-named deceased [Mary Elizabeth Wales] in favor of Mary Wilkins Freeman, of Metuchen, in the State of New Jersey, being an action of contract, the writ dated today, and returnable to the Superior Court for out County of Norfolk the first Monday in January 1920, ad damnum, seventy-five hundred (7500) dollars, based upon a promissory note given by the deceased to the plaintiff, dated February 25, 1916, for five thousand (5000) dollars. ("Mrs. Freeman, Author, Sues on $5000 Note")

The battle was ongoing, continuing as late as 1928. On 23 January, Freeman congratulated Harper & Brothers on winning a law suit to "prevent the illegal use of authors' material by the surreptitious printing of it for readings and recitations." She was among the pirated authors, and she received a check for $45.00. But the revealing point in the letter is the following comment: "I realize the cost of the legal proceeding. I have had a note non-collected for more than eleven years, and must finally if I receive anything waive interest and a fifth of the face" (Freeman, Letter 492). She is referring, of course, to Mary Wales's promissory note. Grasping? No. Practical? Yes. Or, as she herself put it some years later, "It requires a large sum of money conservatively invested to produce a sufficient income, and there is not a living person to stand back of me. The bulk of my husband's estate I gave to his family" (Freeman, Letter 495).

The fourth businessman in her life was Charles Manning Freeman, whom she married on New Year's Day, 1902. Dr Freeman graduated in 1884 from Columbia College of Physicians and Surgeons, afterwards serving as a Medical Examiner at the Bureau of Pensions in Washington DC. He abandoned his medical profession in 1889, returned to Metuchen, New Jersey, and began working at his father's coal and lumber business. At Dr Freeman's own request, his name was added to the business letterhead—Manning Freeman and Son Coal and Lumber Company—but for the next ten years, he was paid a weekly salary. However, when his father died on 6 October 1899, Dr Freeman became sole owner. After Dr Freeman and Mary E. Wilkins married, he continued to run the business, and during the years that followed, Dr Freeman—with the help of the company's manager and assistant manager—built up the business more than his father might have imagined.

If Dr Freeman was a dollar and cents sort of man—and he was—he had married a dollar and cents sort of woman—and she was. At an early point in their marriage the relationship between the New England spinster and her businessman husband was particularly strained: "they were about to part, because of a difference of $12.50, which both being too tight about money to concede—they postponed the parting until they could agree upon said sum" (Silzer).

Much further on in their marriage, the coal and lumber business faced some seemingly serious economic challenges because Metuchenites had run up an unpaid $67,653.38 coal bill. On 13 January 1916, Dr Freeman (who purportedly did not believe in advertising) ran a front-page advertisement in the hometown *Metuchen Recorder*, appealing to all those who had run up debt to pay their bills. In the middle of the page, in 24-point type, appeared the figures "67,653.38". Above and below was an open letter to the public, bewailing the fact that he had been generous in extending credit, and now he wished to collect the large amount owed him. Dr Freeman commented: "The results have been very satisfactory. You see, the people of Metuchen were aghast, when they realized how much was owing our firm and they have promised to make every possible effort to pay up" ("Advertises His Bad Bills").

Mrs Freeman had this to say: "Charlie is not much on literary style, but his letter has produced pleasing results. If the 500-word letter brings in the

$67,653 it will be more than anything that length I ever wrote brought me" ("Mrs. Freeman Lauds Her Husband"). While many people in Metuchen noted that the style of the "Pay Up" letter did not resemble Mrs Freeman's style in the least, *The Boston Globe* commented: "This way of collecting is original enough to have been an idea of Mary E. Wilkins' own" ("Editorial Points"). It may well have been, especially considering what would have been, no doubt, Mrs Freeman's keen recollection of the ongoing dry goods store advertisements that her father published in newspapers during her Brattleboro years. As intriguing as it might be to speculate about the mastermind behind Dr Freeman's appeal to his Metuchen debtors, what's more intriguing requires no speculation. When he died in 1923, the final accounting of his estate totaled $213,435.39 (Middlesex County Surrogate's Office, New Brunswick, NJ).

Aside from the businessmen in Freeman's life, consider this. Her father's business slogan was "Quick Sales and Small Profits," a strategy used to guarantee cash flow. To link that slogan to Freeman's own genre preference may bring outcries of heresy. But the suggestion, nonetheless, warrants consideration, especially in any reappraisal aimed at discovering different modes of viewing her work. Freeman started with poems, religious ones. She moved on to children's verses. Next, she wrote verses and stories for *Wide Awake*. Then she wrote her prize tale, "A Shadow Family." And, finally, came "Two Old Lovers," her first story for adults, published in *Harper's Bazar*. It brought $25.00, her first check that can be identified as the progenitor of countless others to follow, at higher and higher and higher amounts. Early on, Freeman had established her best pace and her best métier, both artistically and financially.

Years later, Fred Lewis Pattee expressed his admiration for Freeman's *vers de société* lyrics, for her 1890 lyric "Now Is the Cherry in Blossom," and for her children's verses. "The lyric gods," he concluded, "certainly were good to you, and I hope you have not disappointed them" (Pattee, Letter to Freeman).

Freeman responded: "I wrote no more *vers de societe*. No more Cherries in Blossom. My dear Sir, do you remember I wrote you that I had to earn my living? I did not write this, but I also had an Aunt to support. How could I have accomplished these absolutely necessary feats on poetry" (Freeman, Letter 442).

Perhaps she couldn't accomplish those "necessary feats" on poetry alone, but she could by working multiple genres. Poetry. Short Stories. Dramas. Novels, published first serially in the magazines, and afterwards as books (sometimes simultaneously in Britain and the United States), and after that dramatizations and motion pictures. She wrote prose as well. Freeman's literary canon includes three plays, fourteen novels, three volumes of poetry, twenty-two volumes of short stories, and fifty uncollected short stories and prose essays, and one motion picture play. Working together, her pursuits of those various genres brought in a steady cash flow, approximating the spirit of her father's "Quick Sales and Small Profits."

Further, throughout her prolific career, Freeman had the good business sense to ally herself almost exclusively with one publisher, Harper & Brothers. She remained loyal by sending the firm her best adult fiction. Aside from the obvious advertising benefits offered by such a leading publishing house, its various magazines—*Harper's Bazar*, *Harper's Monthly*, and *Harper's Weekly*—provided an immediate outlet for the initial publication of her short stories and the serial publication of her novels. After appearing in the magazines, both the short stories and the novels could be issued by Harper & Brother as books. Freeman enjoyed double profits.

Freeman was also a candid and shrewd negotiator. Charles Johanningsmeier's article "Sarah Orne Jewett and Mary E. Wilkins (Freeman): Two Shrewd Businesswomen in Search of New Markets" explores how both writers were "not shy about forwarding their own interests in the world of print, and nowhere is their business acumen more apparent than in their relationships" with the Irving Bacheller and the S. S. McClure syndicates (58). Syndication helped them to gain a nationwide audience, often exceeding one million readers. In Freeman's case, it gave her money to help support herself after her father's death in 1883. She sold "The Emmets" (in 1884) and "A Wayfaring Couple" (in 1885) to McClure (64). Finally, it allowed them "to reach out to individuals who had never before enjoyed their work and who might now—they hoped—be sufficiently engaged to buy their books, thereby increasing their incomes" (70). Jewett and Freeman, in the hope of increasing their income and their readership, "were quite willing to enter this competitive male world of late-nineteenth century publishing" (81).

Within the world of publishing, Freeman's most common tactic was to pit one publisher against another. For example, she wrote *Wide Awake*, "I don't think I ought to write these stories under $30, $15 per thousand. I get $20 [per] thousand from 'The Youth's Companion,' for a similar length" (Freeman, Letter 85). She once told the *Woman's Home Companion*, "The Harpers (voluntarily) raised their price, and paid me four hundred for the last story. Do you feel like paying me as much? I know you said you would pay me as much as the Harpers but I mentioned a less price" (Freeman, Letter 379). As a final example, when Elizabeth Jordan asked Freeman to write a story for *Harper's Bazar* in 1910, Freeman replied, "I want to, but at the risk of appearing mercenary. Mr Duneka has agreed to meet my terms of $500 per story (I can obtain more elsewhere) and do you want to pay so much?" (Freeman, Letter 400).

Sometimes she was even more straightforward. When *Pembroke* was published in book form, she was quick to ask for 15 percent rather than 10 percent royalty on the first thousand copies (Freeman, Letter 131). When *Century* published her story "The Prism" and offered a payment equal to that given ten years earlier for "Emmy," she pointed out readily that other stocks had gone up and that her prices had risen as well (Freeman, Letter 308). In

1903 she quickly informed Elizabeth Jordan that she could write a $300 story just as easily as a $200 one (Freeman, Letter 337). At the end of her career when reprints brought $20, she distressingly made the case that they were worth twice that amount (Freeman, Letter 489).

Freeman also knew that business success was related to sales potential. She knew that she had to consider the public's reading tastes. She wrote to Fred Lewis Pattee on 5 September 1919: "Most of my own work is not really the kind I myself like. I want more symbolism, more mysticism. I left that out, because it struck me people did not want it, and I was forced to consider selling qualities" (Freeman, Letter 441). She realized that she had to be mindful of what was fashionable in literature and that she had to consider the needs of her editors and publishers.

This willingness to write toward market demands and market needs goes all the way back to the start of her career when she was beginning to make a name for herself. Frequently, editors sent her illustrations to use as springboards. On one occasion, she wrote a poem to accompany a masquerade. Initially it was "too worldly": the editor wanted something more religious. Freeman revised the poem but told a friend that she had been tempted to send with the second effort a note saying, "One question I would ask / Will this goody-goody poem / Sanctify a mask?" (Morse).

This same willingness to subject her creative impulse to editorial demands carried over to her longer fiction. Thus, it becomes clear why holiday stories figure so prominently in her canon and why her canon is so uneven. In a way, she approached writing as practically as her father approached his building trade or his dry goods profession: gauge the customer's needs and meet it, always with an eye toward pleasing the customer.

The final observation regarding Freeman's success as a businesswoman is this. She knew that if fiction is to sell, it must be promoted. Admittedly, promoting her works was largely her publishers' responsibility. But Freeman was more than willing to lend a helping hand or to offer unsolicited suggestions. For example, both Theodore Dwight and James Russell Lowell praised *A Humble Romance*. She wasted no time in asking permission to publish their letters, noting that sales "would be greatly increased" (Freeman, Letter 35). When *The Heart's Highway* was attacked by critics, she made arrangements for her friend Kate Upson Clark to write a favorable review (Freeman, Letter 320). And just before publication of *By the Light of the Soul*, she suggested that copies be sent "about with the hope that somebody may say a kindly word for it" (Freeman, Letter 378).

Further, she was not above prodding her publishers to bring out her books in time for holiday sales. She even refused to allow photographs of herself to be used in connection with her work because they did more harm than good. And, as late as 1927, when a friend told her that it was impossible to procure her *Best Stories*, she promptly chastised her publisher: "*Cant* you push it? This is not good business, if you will kindly excuse me for so stating, for *you* or for me." She wanted her fiction to sell, and she stood ready to promote it (Freeman, Letter 490).

Freeman's extraordinary business strategies all paid off remarkably well. As emphasized above, the value of Freeman's estate after her death was impressively high, even during the darker days of the Great Depression.

Of that amount, stocks and bonds made up the lion's share: $107,690.32 (adjusted for inflation, $1,633,795.97). The diversity of the securities (bonds and shares) is both staggering and fascinating: American Colortype Company; American Telephone and Telegraph; Atchison, Topeka and Santa Fe; B. F. Goodrich; Canadian Pacific Railway Company; Endicott Johnson Corporation; Francisco Sugar Company; International Securities Corporation; Lincoln Mortgage and Guarantee Company; New England Power Association; Northern Pacific Company; Pennsylvania, Ohio & Edison; Pennsylvania Railroad Company; Sheffield Steel; State of New South Wales; Union Pacific Railway; United Cigar Store; William Feline & Sons. Two investments had no value: 600 shares in Bohemia Gold Mining and 2,334 shares in Crystal Consolidated Mining Company (Brown, "Inventory and Appraisement").

Her investments alone brought annual dividends of $5,340.68 (adjusted for inflation, $83,046.28). The per capita income for New Jersey at the same time was about $735 (adjusted for inflation, $11,429). Massachusetts fared just slightly better with an approximate per capita income of $761 (adjusted for inflation, $11,896) (United States Department of Commerce).

Again, not bad for a writer who maintained that she knew little about business and business customs, especially considering that as early in her career as 1895 (evidenced by her will fragment) she owned stock in the Boston and Albany Railroad and in the New York, New Haven and Hartford Railroad. The die for her keen business acumen had been struck at least by then.

One remaining fact establishes, without a doubt, that the die had been struck long before that. It is critical to keep in mind that when her father died she received $962.90 in cash and one half-interest in his Brattleboro business property, the Steen-Wilkins Block. She held on to that property and, through its rentals, enjoyed a lifelong source of income (just as her father had enjoyed rental income from the property in his final years). Whether that income was large or small is irrelevant. What is relevant is that *she held on* to the property and used it as an investment. That property was the last item in her estate to be settled. In July 1931, it was sold to the Brattleboro Home for the Aged and Disabled ("Home for Aged Buys Property").

Over the course of a career that spanned nearly fifty years and through nothing more than her astute business acumen—and, obviously, the power of her pen—Mary E. Wilkins Freeman wrote her own phenomenal story of fame and fortune, with few parallels among nineteenth-century American women writers.

TWO-DAY AUCTION SALE

Antiques, Rugs and Housefurnishings

at 159 Lake Ave. Metuchen, N. J.

Wednesday, May 21st, 1930
Thursday, May 22nd, 1930

All the Personal Property from the Estate of the late

Mary E. Wilkins Freeman

Starting each day at 10.30 a. m.—D.S.T.—RAIN or SHINE

Hundreds of Pieces must be sold at Some Price to settle the estate. Many Antiques and Wonderful Rugs are among the Furnishings. Goods consist in part of the following: Kitchen Utensils, Garden Tools, Odd Dishes and Glass, Beautiful Sets of Glassware and China, Rugs, Mahogany Lowboy, Dressing Tables, Bookcases, Chests, Screens, Fireplace Sets, Andirons, Stands, Beds, Chest of Drawers and Bureaus, Carved Post Bed, Couches, Settees, Lamps, 600 Books, Mirrors, Candlesticks, Blankets, Draperies, Prints and Oil Paintings, Desks, Chairs of All Kinds, Silverware, Bedding, Linens and Towels, Sewing Machine, Bric-a-Brac, Wicker Furniture, Growing Plants, Corner Cupboard, Dropleaf and Gateleg Tables, Franklin Fireplace, Windsor Chair, Piano and Music Rolls, Inlaid Card Table, Clocks, Teakwood Stand, Ornaments, Baskets, Heaters, Typewriter, Radio Set, Electric Fans, and many other articles too numerous to enumerate will be offered. This is an exceptionally fine lot of goods and one of the sales you can't afford to miss. All to be sold by order of the administrator.

P. S.—HOUSE OPEN FOR INSPECTION OF GOODS MORNING OF SALE AT 9:00 A. M.

Remember the date and don't miss this sale

THOMAS BROWN, Administrator
174 Smith Street   Perth Amboy, N. J.

TERMS OF SALE---CASH

Figure 9.2 Broadside auction for Mary E. Wilkins Freeman Estate. Collection of Brent L. Kendrick.

Works Cited

"Advertises His Bad Bills." *Brattleboro Daily Reformer*, 15 January 1916, p. 3.

"Autumn Weddings: Littlefield-Hollingsworth." *Boston Daily Advertiser*, 3 October 1895, p. 8.

"Brattleboro Business Directory." *Vermont Farmer and Record*, 29 March 1872, p. 4; and 2 May 1873, p. 4.

Brown, Thomas. "Inventory and Appraisement." 12 April 1930, Middlesex County Surrogate's Office, New Brunswick, NJ.

"Closing Out Sale." *Vermont Phoenix*, 8 September 1871, p. 4.

"Copartnership." *Vermont Phoenix*, 5 January 1866, p. 4.

"Copartnership." *Vermont Record and Farmer*, 29 January 1869, p. 4.

"Died: Hollingsworth." *Boston Herald*, 15 March 1917, p. 15.

"Editorial Points." *Boston Globe*, 15 January 1916, p. 10.

Foster, Edward. *Mary E. Wilkins Freeman*. Hendricks House, 1956.

Freeman, Mary E. Wilkins. "An Autobiography." "Who's Who—and Why. Serious and Frivolous Facts about the Great and the Near Great." *The Saturday Evening Post* 190 (8 December 1917), pp. 25+.

—. Letter 8 to Mary Louise Booth and Anna W. Wright, 17 March 1886. *The Infant Sphinx: Collected Letters of Mary E. Wilkins Freeman*, edited by Brent L. Kendrick, Scarecrow Press, 1985, pp. 63–4.

—. Letter 13 to Mary Louise Booth, 28 April 1886. *The Infant Sphinx: Collected Letters of Mary E. Wilkins Freeman*, edited by Brent L. Kendrick, Scarecrow Press, 1985, p. 69.

—. Letter 35 to Theodore Frelinghuysen Dwight, 9 November 1888. *The Infant Sphinx: Collected Letters of Mary E. Wilkins Freeman*, edited by Brent L. Kendrick, Scarecrow Press, 1985, p. 91.

—. Letter 85 to Elizabeth Anna Farman Pratt, 30 September 1891. *The Infant Sphinx: Collected Letters of Mary E. Wilkins Freeman*, edited by Brent L. Kendrick, Scarecrow Press, 1985, p. 132.

—. Letter 131 to Harper & Brothers, 9 June 1893. *The Infant Sphinx: Collected Letters of Mary E. Wilkins Freeman*, edited by Brent L. Kendrick, Scarecrow Press, 1985, p. 156.

—. Letter 308 to Robert Underwood Johnson, 16 April 1901. *The Infant Sphinx: Collected Letters of Mary E. Wilkins Freeman*, edited by Brent L. Kendrick, Scarecrow Press, 1985, p. 252.

—. Letter 320 to Kate Upson Clarke, 31 January 1902. *The Infant Sphinx: Collected Letters of Mary E. Wilkins Freeman*, edited by Brent L. Kendrick, Scarecrow Press, 1985, p. 285.

—. Letter 337 to Elizabeth Garver Jordan, 19 May 1903. *The Infant Sphinx: Collected Letters of Mary E. Wilkins Freeman*, edited by Brent L. Kendrick, Scarecrow Press, 1985, pp. 294–5.

—. Letter 378 to Frederick Atherton Duneka, 6 October 1906. *The Infant Sphinx: Collected Letters of Mary E. Wilkins Freeman*, edited by Brent L. Kendrick, Scarecrow Press, 1985, p. 320.

—. Letter 379 to Hayden Carruth, 9 November 1906. *The Infant Sphinx: Collected Letters of Mary E. Wilkins Freeman*, edited by Brent L. Kendrick, Scarecrow Press, 1985, p. 132.
—. Letter 400 to Elizabeth Garver Jordan, 28 February 1910. *The Infant Sphinx: Collected Letters of Mary E. Wilkins Freeman*, edited by Brent L. Kendrick, Scarecrow Press, 1985, p. 335.
—. Letter 441 to Fred Lewis Pattee, 5 September 1919. *The Infant Sphinx: Collected Letters of Mary E. Wilkins Freeman*, edited by Brent L. Kendrick, Scarecrow Press, 1985, p. 382.
—. Letter 442 to Fred Lewis Pattee, 25 September 1919. *The Infant Sphinx: Collected Letters of Mary E. Wilkins Freeman*, edited by Brent L. Kendrick, Scarecrow Press, 1985, p. 385.
—. Letter 489 to William Harlowe Briggs, 10 December 1927. *The Infant Sphinx: Collected Letters of Mary E. Wilkins Freeman*, edited by Brent L. Kendrick, Scarecrow Press, 1985, pp. 418–19.
—. Letter 490 to William Harlowe Briggs, 20 January 1928. *The Infant Sphinx: Collected Letters of Mary E. Wilkins Freeman*, edited by Brent L. Kendrick, Scarecrow Press, 1985, pp. 420–1.
—. Letter 492 to William Harlowe Briggs, 23 January 1928. *The Infant Sphinx: Collected Letters of Mary E. Wilkins Freeman*, edited by Brent L. Kendrick, Scarecrow Press, 1985, pp. 421–2.
—. Letter 495 to William Harlowe Briggs, 1 February 1928. *The Infant Sphinx: Collected Letters of Mary E. Wilkins Freeman*, edited by Brent L. Kendrick, Scarecrow Press, 1985, pp. 422–4.
—. "Undated Will, ca. 1895." Collection of Brent L. Kendrick.
—. Unpublished letter to Edward W. Bok, 15 April 1898. Collection of Brent L. Kendrick.
"Great Closing Out Sale." *Vermont Phoenix*, 15 March 1872, p. 4.
"Hard Times." *Vermont Phoenix*, 11 March 1870, p. 3.
"Hollingsworth Estate." *Quincy Patriot. Quincy Daily Ledger*, 14 April 1917, p. 3.
"Home for Aged Buys Property." *Brattleboro Daily Reformer*, 3 August 1931, p. 1.
"If They Had a Million Dollars." *Ladies Home Journal*, XX (September 1903), p. 10.
Johanningsmeier, Charles. "Sarah Orne Jewett and Mary E. Wilkins (Freeman): Two Shrewd Businesswomen in Search of New Markets." *The New England Quarterly*, vol. 70, no. 1, March 1997, pp. 57–82.
Kendrick, Brent L. General Introduction. *The Infant Sphinx: Collected Letters of Mary E. Wilkins Freeman*, Scarecrow Press, 1985, pp. 1–31.
"Local Intelligence." *Vermont Phoenix*, 8 March 1873, p. 2.
"Local Intelligence." *Vermont Phoenix*, 17 October 1873, p. 2.
"Local Intelligence." *Vermont Phoenix*, 3 October 1879, p. 2.
"Local Intelligence." *Vermont Phoenix*, 18 June 1880, p. 3.
"Local Intelligence." *Vermont Phoenix*, 29 October 1880, p. 2.
"Local Intelligence." *Vermont Phoenix*, 20 April 1883, p. 3.
Marlboro District Probate Court, Brattleboro, Vermont, 31 May 1884 (Volume 31, p. 287).
Middlesex County Surrogate's Office, New Brunswick, NJ.

Morse, Allie. Letter to Thomas Schuler Shaw, 20 February 1932. Shaw Scrapbook. The Library of Congress, Rare Book and Special Collections, Washington DC.
"Mrs. Freeman, Author, Sues on $5000 Note." *Boston Herald*, 13 January 1920, p. 3.
"Mrs. Freeman Lauds Her Husband; Metuchen Appeal." *Perth Amboy Evening News*, 15 January 1916, p. 1.
"Our Own Vicinity." *Vermont Record and Farmer*, 12 November 1875, p. 5.
"Our Own Vicinity." *Vermont Record and Farmer*, 17 March 1876, p. 5.
Pattee, Fred Lewis. Letter to Mary E. Wilkins Freeman, 13 September 1919. Pattee Library, Pennsylvania State University.
"Save Your Money." *Vermont Phoenix*, 10 June 1970, p. 4.
Silzer, Henrietta W. Letter to Thomas Schuler Shaw, 20 February 1932. Shaw Scrapbook. The Library of Congress, Rare Book and Special Collections, Washington DC.
Thompson, Charles F. Letter to Mary E. Wilkins, 24 January 1895. Collection of Brent L. Kendrick.
United States Department of Commerce, State Personal Income: 1929–1982. U.S. Government Printing Office, 1984, p. 8.
Wales, Mary Elizabeth. "Last Will and Testament." Probate Court, County of Suffolk, State of Massachusetts.

Note

1. Unless documented otherwise, this chapter is based on my *The Infant Sphinx: Collected Letters of Mary E. Wilkins Freeman* (Scarecrow, 1985), the most comprehensive account of Freeman's life and letters to date. The volume includes 517 letters housed in more than fifty library and personal collections, located through: *American Literary Manuscripts: A Checklist of Holdings in Academic, Historical, and Public Libraries and Museums, and Authors' Homes in the United States* (1961 and 1977); the *National Union Catalog of Manuscript Collections* (1959–62 to present); an independent survey of 361 libraries that I conducted in 1974; dealers in autograph letters and manuscripts; and individual collectors of Freeman memorabilia. A comprehensive listing of these collections can be found in "Calendar of Letters," *The Infant Sphinx* (533–40).

   The edition expanded Freeman's biography extensively by exploring the five major periods of her literary life as reflected in her letters: "Raising Wonders in a New Literary Field" (September 1875–March 1891); "Deviations from My Usual Line of Work" (April 1895–August 1897); "A Hopeless Sort of Chase of Myself" (September 1897–December 1901); "Tiptoeing along the Summit" (January 1902–November 1918); and "Obstacles in the Path of Pleasure and Duty" (April 1919–February 1930).

   Since the publication of *The Infant Sphinx*, many libraries in the United States and in Europe have made comprehensive inventories of their manuscript collections available online. As a result, I have found new Freeman letters that were not known to exist when *The Infant Sphinx* was published, and I continue my efforts to locate still more.

   At this point in my research, the new letters are numerous enough—especially when combined with extensive new biographical information gleaned from an in-depth review of newspapers in the United States and in Europe, many of which are available today online—to warrant a more comprehensive publication that updates Freeman's life and letters. Toward that end, I am working on a two-volume work tentatively titled *Dolly: Life and Letters of Mary E. Wilkins Freeman*. Volume I: *The New England Years (1852–1901)* and Volume II: *The New Jersey Years (1902–1930)*.

Aside from my ongoing work on *Dolly: Life and Letters of Mary E. Wilkins Freeman*, much scholarship remains to be done, especially in the areas of establishing complete and reliable bibliographies along with publishing authoritative texts of Freeman's works. Charles Johanningsmeier provides a thorough discussion of these scholarly opportunities in his "The Current State of Freeman Bibliographical and Textual Studies" (*The American Transcendental Quarterly*, vol. 13, no. 3, September 1999, pp. 173–96).

10

DECONSTRUCTING UPPER-MIDDLE-CLASS RITES AND RITUALS: READING MARY E. WILKINS FREEMAN'S STORIES ALONGSIDE MARY LOUISE BOOTH'S *HARPER'S BAZAR*

AUDREY FOGELS

Launched in 1867, *Harper's Bazar: A Repository of Fashion, Pleasure and Instruction*, was marketed as a high-end fashion magazine aimed at an upper-middle-class audience of (white) women. Fashion, together with articles about manners, diet, health, furniture, and household management were naturally important subjects for the magazine; so were serialized novels, short stories, and poems—sometimes written by prominent authors. Delivering a discourse on upper-middle-class domesticity, the *Bazar*'s didactic columns taught women how to dress, what to buy and how to behave; in fact, it could be said that the magazine literally *fashioned* the identity of its readership into a socially acceptable one, where commodities played a key role. This conflation of gender with consumption, which promoted and reinforced the idea that to be a woman was to be a consumer, was a trademark feature of *The Bazar*,[1] and would define the idea of American womanhood for a long time.

And yet, focusing on the outstanding personality of its first editor, Mary Louise Booth,[2] Paula Bennett has shown that *The Bazar* had also a covert but clear feminist agenda. If Mary Louise Booth was at the head of a genteel fashion publication whose aim was to sell clothes and fashion women's identity, Bennett explains, "[her] commitment to the women's rights movement was steadfast throughout her adulthood" (226). Indeed, using her editorial privilege to "seed *The Bazar* with articles, poems, illustrations, and fiction critiquing traditional gender and class values and advocating a women's right to substantive education, meaningful work and a decent wage" (Bennett 228), Booth sought to raise upper-middle-class women's awareness of the world in which they lived. She gave them tools they could use to turn their social advantage to contribute to society, something which was made possible since "the audience of *Harper's Bazar* consisted primarily of women who, because of their class privilege, *were best positioned to take full advantage of such reforms as the magazine favored*" (Bennett 228, my emphasis).

It is in the context of this covert but well-identified feminist perspective that I propose to read some of the stories Mary E. Wilkins Freeman published in *The Bazar* and to examine the role they played in the indirect but persistent feminist discourse of Booth's editorial line. Indeed, through a spatial and temporal distancing provided by archaic regional settings, quaint and lower-middle-class characters, and New England provincial surroundings, Freeman's stories work as mirrors to the world of *Harper's Bazar*, pointing to the ways affiliations of gender and class function as prerequisites to social acceptance. Interestingly, such distancing makes visible, and I will argue ultimately questionable, the privileges of upper-middle-class membership. Providing *Harper's Bazar*'s readers with means of self-reflection and self-revelation, my contention is that Freeman's tales do not so much "def[y] *Harper's* concept of women" (Glasser 39) or undermine the objectives of the magazine (Elbert, "Devious Women" 253)[3] as work hand in hand with the magazine's subtle material, contributing in various ways to bringing its feminist agenda to the foreground.

Focusing on tales that explore the strict gender expectations, the destructive financial strains and the unhealthy competitive relationships that characterize women's lives in the post-bellum consumer culture, I will concentrate on the ways Freeman's stories contribute to enriching Booth's covertly reform-minded magazine. Indeed, shedding light on the detrimental role consumer culture plays in the lives of nineteenth-century women, as it develops rigid gender constraints, financial hardships, and exclusionary practices, Freeman's stories underwrite *Harper's Bazar*'s feminist stance, providing their own perspective on the issues tackled by the magazine. I argue that, if *Harper's Bazar* "provide[d] the wherewithal on how to achieve the golden looks and the model home" (Elbert, "Devious Women" 259), the narratives, illustrations, and other material Booth chose to publish in its columns had another story to tell, one in which Freeman's narratives had a say. Freeman's most critical stories shed light on one of Booth's more subtle agendas, underscoring the feminist stance present in the magazine's many anonymous editorials or poems. From their own fictional vantage point, these texts often deepen, sometimes modulate, but always enrich *The Bazar*'s covert engagement with feminist issues. Read in this way, one can see how Freeman's stories and Booth's magazine are not so much dissonant or juxtaposed (Elbert, "Devious Women" 258) as complementary, working together but through different means (anonymous editor's column and fictional tales) to give their readers the tools to question their own lives. In the end, while the publication might have made some women feel "incomplete, unsatisfied and even neurotic" (Elbert, "Devious Women" 259), it also undeniably provided them with the means to put their own choices and assumptions in perspective.

Despite their persistent feminist agenda, neither Booth's position nor Freeman's work can be read as univocally feminist. Whether it was because her economic situation constrained her to write stories the public wanted—because she herself was ambivalent about rebellion or simply because she needed to be accepted—many of Freeman's stories were indeed simply sentimental "without the suggestion of subversion" (Glasser 41).[4] Similarly, critics have underlined the extent to which *Harper's Bazar* was filled with countless conventional domestic texts; they have also underlined how Booth was a "bundle of contradictions" (Elbert, "Devious Women" 257) interested in frivolous commodities and fashion. Still, replacing Freeman's stories in their editorial context as well as reading *Harper's Bazar* in light of the texts Booth chose to publish in the magazine, emphasizes the heterogeneity of their respective works, even as it underscores their underlying coherent commitment to feminist concerns.

Of Bonnets and Caps: Questions of Gender and Fashion

Published in the 26 May 1883 edition of the *Bazar*, "A Mistaken Charity"[5] is the story of deaf Harriet and blind Charlotte, two old and physically deformed women who live happily in their leaky house out in the country. Their self-reliance and quaint happiness is threatened by the arrival of the charitable Mrs Simonds and her desire to make things right. Against the will of the two old women and that of her own husband, who cannot see the use of dislodging the old women from the life they have chosen for themselves, she sends Harriet and Charlotte to a Home where they are forced to dress and behave properly. Soon, however, the two sisters, who were clever enough to keep the key to their house, find a way to escape back to their own home where the blind Charlotte finally sees "chinks," openings in her future. All's well that ends well and the two sisters' sojourn in the poorhouse comes across as a disagreeable but short-lived experience.

As many critics have underlined, the story celebrates American self-reliance and the creation of an alternative, critical space; the story is also a critique of middle-class benevolence and its implicit gender constraints. In this story, the symbolic violence generated by Mrs Simonds's supposedly benevolent intervention[6] undeniably offers a clear critique of the rigid gender models upheld by genteel upper-middle-class women. Focusing at length on Mrs Simonds's desire to rectify the two sisters' physical appearance and crooked bodies, the story highlights the ferocity of Mrs Simonds's gender standards and the pain caused by implementing them. Forced into leaving their home for a more "proper" one, the sisters fall apart; they start to cry "pitifully" and "tremble all over"

(Freeman, "A Mistaken Charity" 320). Once they have arrived at the almshouse, they cannot get used to either their white lace caps or to the delicate neckerchiefs which they have to wear and which come across in this context more as a prisoner's uniform than as what they are meant to be, namely, dainty clothes. When the two sisters finally decide to escape, they "hung with 'grim humor . . . the new white lace caps with which [they] had been so pestered, one on each post, at the head of the bedstead so they would meet the eye of the first person who opened the door" (Freeman, "A Mistaken Charity" 321). Comically replaying a grim episode from American history, the white bonnets hung triumphantly on bed posts like scalps brandished by Indians in a sign of victory, Freeman hereby points to the "tender violence" that characterizes nineteenth-century genteel behavior, where the domestic space has also become the place of "intrusive intervention[s] of the empire."[7] The image of the caps impaled on their posts subtly evokes the symbolic violence at work in class relations, as would-be directors of decorum belonging to the upper-middle-class attempt to coerce lower-class citizens into so-called "proper" behavior, going so far as to occupy and colonize the intimacies of their very rooms.

This criticism of society takes on a gender twist when it is read alongside two items published in the same issue of the *Bazar* which mirror and reinforce one another: a set of engravings entitled *Ladies' Summer Bonnet* advertising fashionable new summer bonnets together with an unsigned article describing the upcoming new summer fashion. While these two different texts both contribute to showing how essential bonnets and fashionable accessories are to the season's new trends, in the light of Freeman's tale, they take on another meaning: bonnets and other such trendy accessories come across as arbitrary props operating as systems of control that manage and "fashion" bodies into a prescribed identity; they are the visual signs of one's consent to a set identity which Charlotte and Harriet refuse. Their rejection of any attempt to direct their behavior is also obvious in the sisters' choice not to subject their bodies to what can be seen as systems of control developed by the rising cosmetic and fashion industry. With their twisted and hairy bodies standing as testimonies to their refusal to bend to middle-class injunctions of gender propriety, Charlotte and Harriet have turned away from the lures of corsets, creams for a beautiful complexion, wigs, products for removing superfluous hair on lips, faces, arms, magical oriental creams to make one's skin fairer, and even a cure for deafness appearing in *Harper's Bazar*'s columns. Turning down the offer of bonnets Mrs Simonds had taken out for them (as well as the numerous kinds of props sold in the magazine's columns), Harriet and Charlotte refuse to fashion their bodies according to the norms imposed on them, calling attention, by this act, to the vacuity of such rites. To the end, deaf, blind, with hair on their chin and a limp in their gait, Charlotte and Harriet remain true to a "natural self," underlining the extent to which social identity is the result of social performance.

Figure 10.1 "Ladies' Summer Bonnets." *Harper's Bazar*, 26 May 1883, p. 12. Image courtesy of the Home Economics Archive: Research, Tradition, and History (HEARTH) Collection, Albert R. Mann Library, Cornell University.

Placed in a magazine whose overt vocation was to promote fashion and dress, Freeman's tale not only shed a critical light on the relation of upper-middle-class women to the fashion industry and its models, but perhaps also set her readers thinking about the kind of social role they wanted to play in the 1880s. Indeed, according to Bennett, under Mary Louise Booth's editorship, *Harper's Bazar* was characterized by "an anxiety" about what an upper-middle-class white woman would do with the new choices she had: would she exploit her social advantage in order to become the pleasure-seeking consumer she was expected to be or would she opt to make use of her social advantages by contributing to society, sensitive to the needs of those less privileged than herself? Read in the magazine's larger context of the question of women's mission in society, Freeman's tale contributes to the debate, as it stages a woman, Mrs Simonds, who has become a social actor but is nonetheless on the wrong track.

What's more, if Charlotte and Harriet end up happy, back in the house in which they have chosen to live, they nonetheless remain characters who are invisible to society, having refused to don the bonnets of a recognizable middle-class identity, and will live on unseen, on the margins of society. Their decision not to follow the prescriptions of fashion and to stay true to their selves shows how it is possible *a contrario* to rebel against fashion codes that produce subjects whose visibility in society rests largely, and ironically, on self erasure and the suppression of oneself. The way post-bellum prescriptive gender norms menace women's identity and integrity is explored at length in "A Modern-Day Dragon"[8] published in *Harper's Bazar* on 14 June 1884. In this tale, Mrs Ayre forbids her son David to court Almira King, the woman he loves, because she is overdressed while her mother, Mrs King, is, on the contrary, underdressed. "Peculiar," Mrs King has always been a manly woman who had taken charge of the family farm even when her husband was still alive: "she was an odd figure, short and stout, with a masculine width of shoulders. Her calico dress cleared her thick ankles, her black hair was cut short, and she wore a man's straw hat." As for her daughter Almira, she is introduced as somewhat too frivolous, too feminine, dressing up in an excessive manner from the start: "A girl was tripping up the aisle below, dressed in a pink silk gown, bewilderingly draped and pleated. She wore a little white crape bonnet with a knot of crushed roses." Either over frilly or not frilly enough, too feminine, or not feminine enough, the women of the King family, a name which already presages a form of gender trouble, do not correspond to what at their time is expected of their gender.

However, as the tale will show, fashion and culturally sanctioned gender imperatives are not easy to be simply put aside since clothes literally *fashion* a woman into a socially accepted being and determine her membership in a community. Realizing that her appearance is at the source of her daughter's sentimental sorrows, Mrs King decides to transform herself into a respectable woman, aligning her appearance with what is expected of her: "She had on a *decent long* black dress and a *neat* bonnet. Her short hair had given way to a *braided* knot. She sat in the pew and listened *solemnly* to the sermon, regardless of the attention she excited" (my emphasis). Like an actress dressing for a part—"Mrs. King *tied on* her new switch with *infinite* difficulty, *arrayed herself* in her long skirts, and walked a mile and a half to see David Ayre's mother" (my emphasis)—, her physical transformation heralds her consent to the performance of gender even as its ritualization underlines its artificiality. But Mrs King's adoption of the expected codes of femininity comes too late: she dies having tried to please a community that will not accept her in return. Despite the story's sentimental ending —the young couple Almira and David do end up together—, it cannot mask a central point: women who do not abide by socially sanctioned gender codes can be punished, and sometimes harshly so. While the rigidity of the mother-in-law and her strict belief in "proper" gender norms is stressed in a tale that compares her to a dragon, the cost for Mrs King, who has chosen to dress differently from the fashion of the time, and for her daughter, who is mocked and rejected by the community of women for being overdressed, is also made apparent. The gender defiance that paved the way to happiness for Charlotte and Harriet is not without its dangers. Better perhaps to look within the safe bonds of a socially sanctioned identity to find one's own rather than step out of the system altogether.

The tale's ambiguous message regarding women's relation to gender codes and fashion is taken up in an essay published a couple of pages after Freeman's story and entitled "Devotion to Clothes." Here, the anonymous author opposes two types of women; the first type is criticized for her obsession with clothes while the second is lauded for her interest in books and education. The essay then goes on to list to a series of morally elevated hobbies ("books, their crayons, their scales and exercises") that might seem more worthwhile for women to engage in. It ends on a mischievously playful note, concluding that a woman obsessed with clothes can find solace in the fact that "her mind is perpetually agitated, and she has no time for ennui, or to ask, with Mallock, if life is worth living." The writer clearly lampoons the fashionable woman for her frivolity and mindlessness, but the metaphor of fashion as a form of literature suggests a more ambiguous relation to fashion: "the dressmaker is her *encyclopedia*, and the sewing-machine her hobby; she walks abroad, not for exercise, but for *exhibition*, and a new suit or a *novel* fashion is as precious to her as a twelfth-century vase to a collector of *curios*" (my emphasis). While it can be frivolous, fashion is a real language whose grammar is complex, as shown in the following passage, published in the 14 July 1888 issue of the magazine, in its regular column dedicated to clothes, *New York Fashions*:

> RED, white, and blue, the national colors, prevail in seaside toilettes. They are used singly for the entire costume, or in combinations of any two of the colors, in stripes, and there are also white serges with plaids or merely crossbars of both red and blue together. The white serges of fine quality with stripes or bars of color are chosen for morning toilettes at the sea-shore, . . .

The assertive tone and prescriptive quality of the article conveyed by the present tense leaves no room for doubt: in fashion, every detail counts, an idea once again taken up and made clear in the very next pages of the *Bazar*, which features numerous engravings of diverse corsages, sundry styles of lace and assorted trimmings for various bonnets. If *Harper's Bazar* is undeniably a fashion magazine, whose aim is to sell its affluent and fashion-conscious readers the latest trends in clothing and consumer goods, it also juxtaposes different points of view on fashion. Taken individually, short stories, editorials, and engravings each say something different about fashion, some underscoring its centrality while others signal its futility. Read together, these textual and visual discourses offer readers what can be seen as complementary and diverse tools to think about fashion critically. In some ways, understanding the many shades and nuances of fashion's complex semantics is not only a means of survival in certain social circles; it is a sure way to remain critical of its ever-encroaching influence. In this context, Freeman's tale "A Modern Dragon" contributes in its own way to the debate as it points to the rigidity of fashion expectations all the while showing the cost of stepping outside of its expected codes.

OF MEN AND WOMEN; THINKING ABOUT ECONOMIC (IN)DEPENDENCE

Social visibility and acceptance are linked to well-recognized gender norms; they are also a function of one's financial situation and more specifically are related to the problem of women's economic dependence on men.[9] That such a theme should find a place in *Harper's Bazar* and in Freeman's stories is little wonder considering Louise Booth's and Freeman's own lives. Freeman's experience as an author who had to earn her own living and as the daughter of a woman forced to bear the consequences of her husband's economic failures help explain her lifelong concern with money. In 1876, her parents were forced to give up their little cottage and in 1877, the family moved into Reverend Tyler's house where Freeman's mother was hired to serve as housekeeper: "The monetary concern intensified when she realized she did not intend to marry and gain the economic stability that would come with such a step" (Glasser 43). As for Booth, her commitment to such topics can also be explained by her political beliefs and her personal life: "Single, without resources, and self-taught, Booth had supported herself during her apprentice years the ways so many working women did, by sewing, for two years toiling as a vest maker" (Bennet 230). Faced with the impact of financial issues on their own choices and lives, Mary Louise Booth's publication and Mary E. Wilkins Freeman's works register those concerns.

It is because they have lost their fortune owing to imprudent male relatives that the pensioners of "Sister Liddy" (2 March 1889) have become invisible to the outside world. Indeed, set in what could be read as a parody of Winthrop's "City Upon a Hill"—in an almshouse which stands on rising grounds but which no "eyes could see" because it stands for an inverted ideal—"Sister Liddy" reiterates the constraints brought about by lack of financial affluence and women's dependence on men. Destitute and invisible to the outside world, living in what looks like a closed-off community, the women of the almshouse spend their time harping back to their past glories, evoking the role of their relationships to men in their social downfall: "She was a single woman and had lost all her property through an *injudicious male relative*" (Freeman, "Sister Liddy" 329, my emphasis). As they recall their financial downfall, the women of this story implicitly raise the question of women's financial dependence on men, and corollary themes, such as marriage, divorce, and property laws. The episode at the end of the tale, when the sickly young woman is saved by her lover, who finally comes to rescue her from her lowly life in the almshouse, comes across as a relief and participates in the tale's sentimental and conventional "happy end." However, the tale's resolution also clearly suggests what little control women have over their financial situation and thus over their lives, illustrating how dependent on a man's life and fortune a lower- or middle-class woman was.

Similarly, in the story "A Modern Dragon," if Mrs King decides to dress like a man, it is not only because she is from the start a "stout hired girl" but also because her husband being "incapable himself of carrying on this little farm," she has had to earn a living on her own. Clearly, then, if Freeman's tales portray women whose lives were far removed from the lives of *Harper's Bazar*'s readers, they nonetheless reflected the financial changes of fortune that could in fact affect the lives of *all* women, no matter their wealth and status. In "Sister Liddy," the wealth of the now destitute women, underlined by the self-aggrandizing repetition of "I had," points to the social and financial height from which they have fallen. Ultimately, all women are in a fragile situation, something which was true of all American women who, in Bennett's eyes, were particularly at risk given the sentimental education given to them, making them unprepared to manage their estate or their finances in the event of the decease of their spouse (Bennett 236).

In suggesting how these women's fates are linked to their financial situations and the question of their dependence on men, Freeman offers her readers a means of thinking about a theme often present in *Harper's Bazar*, namely, the link between women's financial status and any possibility of self-development. Bennett has shown that if Booth did not write Gail Hamilton's four-part discussion of married women's property rights legislation or Higginson's column entitled "Women and Men," she was nonetheless responsible for their publication just as she was for the publication of Freeman's story about the dangers of women's financial dependence on men. The next article in the very same issue is one written by Elizabeth Champney that deals with Vassar College, extolling the college for having promoted women's education and providing them with the possibility of studying anything from chemistry to history, gymnastics to Romance languages, mathematics to physics. Concluding how "it has become *fashionable* to be erudite," the article suggests that women's education can provide a means of alleviating women's financial fragility.

Freeman's tale had given voice to the women who have lost everything because of an imprudent husband; *Harper's Bazar* provides its readers with what can be read as a set of thought-provoking solutions, namely, articles emphasizing the importance of economic independence and education in women's lives. Read together, Freeman's tales and the essays published by Booth establish a link between women's self-development and financial security, offering its readers the means to find solutions to those complex issues.

No More Jobs and the Reign of Commodities; How to Reconcile the Irreconcilable?

Financial insecurity not only leads to social downfall; it also triggers feelings of exclusion, breeding resentment and spite amongst women, feelings central in the tale "A Stolen Christmas,"[10] one ironically published in the 24 December 1887 issue. In this story Mrs Poole is introduced as envying her slightly richer neighbor, Mrs Ely, a feeling exacerbated by the approach of Christmas and by her desire to buy her orphaned grandchildren presents. While Mrs Poole is seen as a covetous, albeit poor, soul who envies Mrs Ely out of benevolent feelings arising from her desire to be generous with her grandchildren, Mrs Ely is portrayed as a hypocritical woman who revels in her many possessions, symbolized amongst other things by her lace curtains. Unable to scrape up enough money to buy her presents, Mrs Poole ends up by stealing toys for them at the local shop, so that they can have a proper Christmas.[11] While the act is to an extent morally condemned, because it robs her of some of her Christmas spirit—this is one way to read the title—, Mrs Poole is not otherwise punished by the plot. On the contrary, she is triply rewarded at the end since her son-in-law finally finds a job and sends her money; her rival's possessions perish in a fire, making Mrs Poole the richer of the two, and she herself finds out that the toys she had stolen had in fact been hers all along since the shopkeeper, recognizing in her a good soul, had set them out for her to have. The sentimental moral seems clear: being a good woman, Mrs Poole needn't have stolen, for however dire her situation, her true nature was recognized all along by Mr White— and arguably by the reader. In many ways such an ending can be said to contribute to the upper-middle-class reader's sense of entitlement and self-satisfaction, justifying the *Bazar*'s readers' inaction since Mrs Poole is rewarded by somebody *else*.

Still, more than a shoplifter, Mrs Poole comes across as the victim of a system that makes her an outsider. Indeed, the tale indicates how the consumer economy that is gaining momentum in the 1880s, and which is based on the continual acquisition for more and more goods, breeds exclusion and resentment. Unable to buy the numerous offerings of the Emporium, the local shop, Mrs Poole's experiences a "complete moral revulsion": her morals "gyrat(ed) into a wild somersault," making her become something she never would have otherwise been, an unlawful person, a shoplifter. However, as the victim of a system which encourages material possession at any cost, she is not so much to blame as the society from which she is excluded and the economy which makes it impossible for her to carry out her trade any longer: "Marg'ret was a tailoress, but she could *now get no employment at her trade*. The boys all wore 'store clothes' in these days" (my emphasis). Clearly, the new and booming consumer economy based on manufactured goods excludes some people from the job market, turning them into outsiders. Robbing honest folks of the chance to work and "of the chance to airn," even as it was producing more goods to buy, this new economy to which ironically a magazine like *Harper's Bazar* owed its existence, was casting aside those who could not afford to participate.

Harper's Bazar was based on the growing consumer economy of post-bellum America, but the printed material that appeared in it from the 1860s to the 1880s continued to concentrate on "lower middle class and working-class women—mill girls, shop girls, and, above all, women in the garment industry—and on families that had to make do on $500 a year ... or considerably less" (Bennett 240). In other words, in the midst of a new and changing economic system, the condition of women who like Mrs Poole were experiencing a transformation in their lives was a constant concern of the magazine. Illustrating the despair and feeling of exclusion experienced by those unfit to contribute to the new system, Freeman's tale focuses on Mrs Poole's distress, emphasizing the time spent worrying about what she is unable to afford: her sleepless nights spent thinking about the presents for her grandchildren, the time spent coming up with alternative solutions, her feeling of guilt produced by her envy of Mrs Ely's means, her social unease at the thought of not belonging:

> Finally those animals of sugar and wood, those pink-faced, straight-bodied dolls, those tin trumpets and express wagons, were to Marg'ret as the fair apples hanging over the garden wall were to Christiana's sons in the *Pilgrim's Progress*. She gazed and gazed, until at last the sight and the smell of them were too much for her.

Obsessed by her inability to consume and hypnotized by a profusion which is simply "too much for her," by becoming a shoplifter, Mrs Poole passes from being a citizen who is symbolically excluded to one who is actually so.

Freeman's "A Gala Dress"[12] published close to another symbolic moment of the year, on 14 July 1888, proposes a complementary perspective on the exclusion brought about by lack of financial resources as it stages the story of two sisters who have decided to exclude themselves from society because they do not have the financial means to buy a gala dress. Indeed, convinced that a proper middle-class woman can only participate in social gatherings if she wears the right dress, the sisters, who own only one silk dress between the two of them, believe they have no possibility of sharing in social events. Like in "A Stolen Christmas," much of the tale concentrates on the strategies these destitute women develop to find a solution to their predicament. In their cases, they spend their time customizing their one and only silk dress over and again, tearing off and sewing back on either a silk or a velvet trim, each time one of them wants to use their single dress for a different purpose. The Babcock sisters live in constant fear their financial status will be discovered; and while the people of the town attribute their secretive behavior to what they think is their odd and condescending personality, the tale clearly links their stand-offish attitude to their dire financial situation. The fact is, the moment they inherit money, they feel allowed to participate in the town's different social events and can once again act "normally," strolling along the streets of the town like any other inhabitant. Functioning like an inverted mirror of the *Bazar*'s upper-middle-class readership, the tale illustrates once again how financial affluence and means determine social acceptance and belonging.

The same issue of exclusion and money is taken up, albeit in a different tone, in a cartoon that is published at the end of the December 1887 issue of *Harper's Bazar*. The drawing represents an obviously lower-middle-class woman who is strolling in what must be a zoo and who "soliloquizes" as she looks at a caged-up seal: "Arrah. An' that oi moight be wan av thim crathers, an' wear a sale-skin sacque all the year roun'" (Annex 4). The woman's Scottish-sounding accent and dress, together with her preposterous desire to be a seal to enjoy the luxury of seal skin clearly distances her from the *Harper's Bazar*'s readers, just as Mrs Poole's financial distress clearly differentiates her from them too. Still, published just a few pages after Freeman's story, it reasserts the feeling of exclusion experienced by those who do not have the means to participate in the widespread consumer economy and gives them a voice, however comical it might be. Visual and textual messages evoke in their own way the high cost of a changing economy for some American women even as they serve to comfort others' sense of entitlement by mocking outsiders or preparing elite readers to become future consumers.

The final message is ambiguous indeed since the readers will be able to buy what Mrs Poole in the tale longs for but cannot afford. In fact, the objects she covets throughout the tale are actually the very same ones advertised at the end of the magazine (together with engravings and the names of shops where they can be bought) and hence made available as Christmas presents for the readers of the *Bazar*—"animals of sugar and wood, pink-faced and straight bodies dolls, tin trumpets, express wagons." Still, if such an ending serves to consolidate the empowerment of the upper-middle-class readers of *Harper's Bazar*, the feelings of disempowerment and the various social strategies Mrs Poole, the Babcock sisters, and the comic character each deploy cannot simply be brushed aside. Their narratives function as reminders of the kind of exclusion faced by women when the economic system changes and when they are unable to keep up with social demands.

What, to the American Woman, is Your Fourth of July?

Finally, Freeman's tales also explore the social consequences brought about by the growing importance of material possessions in women's lives, that is, the consequences for women's sense of themselves as a community.[13] "A Stolen Christmas," for example, does stress the resentment and envy that exists between Mrs Poole and Mrs Ely, a theme that Freeman also takes up at length in "A Gala Dress" (14 July 1887), where the Babcock sisters and their nosy neighbor, Matilda Jennings, are pitted against each other throughout the plot. Unlike the two sisters who, since they have nothing proper to wear, refuse to participate in the town's social events, Matilda Jennings prefers to wear her worn-out dress, however shabby it is. Although she can't figure out why the sisters never go out together (the fact they only have one silk dress to share with each other is a secret only the reader knows), she senses that they are hiding something and, throughout the story, tries to find out what it is.

One Fourth of July, when she is on a picnic with Emily, Matilda Jennings manages to avoid a nest of firecrackers but, purposefully, does not warn Emily to step aside. The latter's silk dress gets scorched as she unwittingly walks on the crackers. Emily is desperate because it means her secret will be discovered since the dress is burnt beyond repair. But when an old aunt of the sisters dies, she and her sister inherit two silk dresses, which finally makes it possible for them to participate in social events together. The final twist in the story comes when having inherited two new dresses, the two sisters want to give their old, scorched silk to Matilda who confesses that she had let Emily walk on the crackers so she would ruin her garment.

The story reveals a lot about small town gossiping and jealousy;[14] it also highlights the effects of social and economic competition on women's lives, suggesting how violent women's relationships can become.[15] Indeed, if nothing serious really happens to Emily in the tragicomic plot, the fact that Matilda Jennings does not warn her suggests the extent of her resentment and how far she is willing to go to punish her for her secrets and pride, with the tale calling attention to the way a system based on material acquisition produces disharmony amongst women, opening up rifts that could lead to more serious forms of violence.

That this act of violence against another woman should take place on a 4th of July, when the entire nation is out celebrating Independence Day, comes across as an ironic comment on the idea of women's independence, an issue that can be said to be at the heart of *The Bazar*'s feminist stance altogether. If the Babcock sisters and Mathilda celebrate Independence Day in their own way by having a picnic in the park, the tale underlines how they cannot free themselves from their envy and jealousy of one another and how tied they are to their lack of economic independence and autonomy.

Significantly, "Women's Share in the Fourth," published a few pages after the tale, provides a placating answer to the narrative of national/domestic disharmony explored by Freeman's tale. Indeed, in an attempt to show that all American women can share in the Independence Day celebrations, the essay, which is seemingly addressed to suffragist women, underlines how more traditional women did participate in Fourth of July celebrations: "We are sure it will be admitted by the most demanding suffragist that women, after all, have their full share in the celebration of Independence Day." The article goes on to explain that whether they are chosen because of their beauty and fair complexion to read the Declaration of Independence or whether they spend sleepless nights worrying about the possible injuries their sons might incur in what the article calls the "murderous revelry" of that celebration, these homebound women are as deserving of recognition as the more outspoken ones. Indeed, as they fret over the dangers of the fireworks and crackers, the mothers, sisters, and aunts that the essay describes—who are in fact no other than the readers of *Harper's Bazar* themselves—take part in the Fourth of July celebration in their own way, "do[ing] their share." Unlike Freeman's tale then which highlights disharmony, the essay reads as "a rite of assent"[16] erasing tensions and discord to emphasize how all women participate in the national celebration.

Hence, taken together, both article and short story tell a complex story of a community made up of diverse women who are at times at war with one another but who each, in her own right, is as deserving as the other to take part in celebrating American Independence. Shedding light on the feats of ordinary women, the story and the article valorize types of behavior most probably favored by *Harper's Bazar*'s readers, but in the end makes room for all of them as it puts side by side (and, hence, on the same level) suffragists and women whose concerns are primarily domestic. Still, while the column argues for the recognition of the place of *all* women in the celebration, providing a multifaceted portrait of American women, Freeman's tale also hints at the economic realities that still need to be overcome if any genuine independence and sense of community is to be reached. As it points to this unsettled issue, her narrative serves to fuel yet again the unresolved debate over women's actual independence and rights, and provides *Harper's Bazar*'s readers with the critical tools to question their own lives and choices.

Conclusion

The dialogue Freeman's stories establish within the fabric of *Harper's Bazar* in the years Mary Louise Booth was its editor often helps to underscore the magazine's covert feminist mission even as it contributes to placing Mary E. Wilkins Freeman's texts in a rich web of feminist issues and debates. Freeman's more critical texts, shedding light on the magazine which in turn provides themes and contexts for them, clearly participate in *Harper's Bazar*'s covertly feminist editorial line. Read in the thick cultural context of the high-end publication, which maneuvers between sometimes contradictory goals, Freeman's stories serve to illuminate the underlying assumptions of class, gender, and race that govern women's lives. If falling off the social ladder and financial fragility is a threat evoked in many of Freeman's texts, stable hierarchical racial categories appear like ultimate safeguards against complete loss of identity. When all else is lost, whiteness remains.[17] Still, if Freeman's narrative redoubles *Harper's Bazar*'s implicit racial agenda, something which was to become more intense after the Fifteenth Amendment was passed, the compulsive insistence on racial purity present in her stories can also be seen as a sign that race too might not be, after all, so unquestionable. Foregrounding the different ways in which one becomes a visible female citizen, Freeman narratives help reveal how *Harper's Bazar* not only instructed its readers in the art of becoming proper upper-middle-class women but *also* provided them with feminist tools, participating actively in what Paula Bennett has called *Harper's Bazar*'s art of "subtle subversion." ("Devious Women" 225). Making visible what the profusion of *Harper's Bazar*'s traditional content might render opaque, Freeman's polyphonic stories help bring to the fore and reinforce *Harper's Bazar*'s subtle feminist messages, namely, those linked to the impact of an increasingly rampant consumer culture on post-bellum American women's lives and self-development. Interestingly, the very multiplicity of Freeman's voices, at once sentimental and rebellious, enables her to fit in what is in fact a polyphonic publication, working to undermine *Harper's Bazar*'s very foundations even as it consents to them. Conversely, envisioning the magazine in the light of Freeman's tales underlines how heterogeneous the magazine really was, ceaselessly blurring as it did the frontier between subversion and conservatism, culture and commerce, public and private.

As a cultural site of contradictory voices and stances, *Harper's Bazar* comes across as a multilayered, syncretic, and heterogenous fashion publication, something which Freeman's multi-voiced narratives help underscore. In the end, what reading Freeman alongside *Harper's Bazar* demonstrates is the commitment of both Mary E. Wilkins Freeman and Mary Louise Booth to an often indirect, sometimes ambiguous, but always persistent feminist agenda, one enriched by the fertile friction produced by the dialogic encounters of Freeman's many stories and Mary Louise Booth's policy of publishing. That such a feminist agenda should find its way in the frivolous contents of a high-end fashion magazine should come as no surprise. Like Freeman herself who was a "fashionable feminist," trying to "establish standards of behavior for feminists and fashionable alike" (Glasser 240), *Harper's Bazar* was a culturally rich publication,[18] one which attempted to bridge the wide gap between frivolity and political engagement while being aware that its readers might be attracted to both.[19] Interestingly, far from offering a monolithic feminist agenda portraying one type of woman only—the white, upper-middle-class one—Booth's and Freeman's texts deal with questions of gender, class, and race that make room for other lives and experiences. Addressing notions like entitlement, white privilege, economic inequality, and social invisibility, their century-old texts make visible "invisible" systems of control and, as such, offer present-day readers invaluable critical and imaginative tools to map new worlds.

Works Cited

Abelson, Elaine. *When Ladies Go A-Thieving; Middle-Class Shoplifters in the Victorian Department Store*. Oxford UP, 1989.

Bennett, Paula B. "Subtle Subversion: Mary Louise Booth and Harper's Bazar (1867–1889)", *Blue Pencils and Hidden Hands, Women Editing Periodicals, 1830–1910*, edited by Sharon M. Harris, Northwestern UP, 2004, pp. 225–43.

Bercovitch, Sacvan. *The Rites of Assent: Transformations in the Symbolic Construction of America*. Routledge, 1993.
Elbert, Monika M. "Mary Wilkins Freeman's Devious Women, 'Harper's Bazar,' and the Rhetoric of Advertising." *Essays in Literature*, vol. 20, no. 2, 1993, pp. 251–72.
Endres, Kathleen L., and Therese L. Lueck, eds. *Women's Periodicals in the United States, Social and Political Issues*. Greenwood Press, 1996.
Fetterley, Judith, and Marjorie Pryse, eds. *American Women Regionalists: A Norton Anthology*. Norton, 1992.
Freeman, Mary E. Wilkins. "A Mistaken Charity." *American Women Regionalists: A Norton Anthology*, edited by Judith Fetterley and Marjorie Pryse, Norton, 1992, pp. 314–23.
—. "Sister Liddy." *American Women Regionalists: A Norton Anthology*, edited by Judith Fetterley and Marjorie Pryse, Norton, 1992, pp. 323–33.
Garvey, Ellen Gruber. *The Adman in the Parlor, Magazines and the Gendering of Consumer Culture, 1880s to 1910s*. Oxford UP, 1996.
Glasser, Leah Blatt. *In a Closet Hidden: The Life and Work of Mary E. Wilkins Freeman*. U of Massachusetts P, 1996.
Harper's Bazar, December 1887, Annex 4.
Hoganson, Kristin. *Consumers' Imperium, The Global production of American Domesticity, 1865–1920*. U of North Carolina P, 2007.
Rodier, Katherine. "Lucy Stone's and the *Woman's Journal*." *Blue Pencils and Hidden Hands, Women Editing Periodicals, 1830–1910*, edited by Sharon M. Harris, Northwestern UP, 2004, pp. 99–120.
Stoler, Ann, ed. *Haunted by Empire: Geographies of Intimacy in North American History*. Duke UP, 2006.
Wexler, Laura. "Tender Violence: Literary Eavesdropping, Domestic Fiction and Educational Reform." *The Culture of Sentiment: Race, Gender and Sentimentality in 19th Century America*, edited by Shirley Samuels, Oxford UP, 1992, pp. 9–38.

NOTES

1. While the link between consumption and the magazine industry had been a given of the magazine industry from the start, with advertisers financially supporting the publications that touted their commodities, the gendering of consumption became increasingly pronounced in the 1880s and 1890s: "As consumption was increasingly seen as gendered, components of consumption transactions were increasingly framed as gendered as well, playing out a scenario of man as the forceful seller and woman as the receptive buyer" (Garvey 174).
2. The Harper Brothers' new venture was quickly successful, something which was largely attributed to the astuteness and savvy of first editor Mary Louise Booth (1867–99). A historian and well-known translator of French and German literature whose intellectual interests and lower-middle-class origins were, at first glance, far removed from the upper-middle-class world of high fashion and consumption of her readers, Mary Louise Booth was recognized as a brilliant intellectual and a shrewd businesswoman. She perfected the journal's formula thanks to her keen taste for quality artwork and writing and by 1880, twelve years after its publication, the magazine increased its circulation to 80,000, which was an unprecedented success in publishing business (Endres).

3. According to Monika Elbert, Freeman's stories are at odds with *Harper's Bazar*'s editorial line. Indeed, she reads them as offering either contrapuntal commentaries on (or naïve reinforcement of) the magazine's supposedly mindless celebration of idle women engrossed in consumption and frivolity: "Certainly, the idleness is juxtaposed with the diligent nature and industrious ways of Freeman's positive characters, but certainly, too, the domestic prop or fashionable dress item becomes the icon for both the Freeman heroine and the *Harper's Bazar* peruser of ads" (Elbert, "Devious Women" 253). Later, Elbert adds: "Thus, models, female audience, fashion reporters, and Freeman's heroines all have this in common—the love affair with a commodity" ("Devious Women" 254). If, in the end, Freeman's characters "learn to find pleasure and solace in something beyond consumer culture," Elbert argues that "Freeman quite subversively undermines the objectives of *Harper's Bazar* and certainly of the ads which support it" ("Devious Women" 254). I argue that while Freeman does have an argument with consumerism, she carries it out in a magazine that shares many of its critical ideas.
4. In her essay entitled "The Girl Who Wants to Write," Freeman speaks of writing as something a girl may not want to do out of "some seething of the central fire of genius" but "for money with which to buy a French hat" (Glasser 41). While Leah Blatt Glasser is certainly right when she explains that beneath this futile-sounding comment which fits so perfectly gender expectations there is the idea that "the French hat itself reflects the very 'seething fire' that her own statement satirically rejects and has nothing to do with the woman's concern for style" (Glasser 41), the metaphor clearly shows that Freeman was attracted to both fashion and money. Still, as I argue in this essay, these facts are not antithetical to more feminist concerns.
5. Unless otherwise mentioned, all references to Mary E. Wilkins Freeman's stories will be taken from *American Women Regionalists: A Norton Anthology*, edited by Judith Fetterley and Marjorie Pryse.
6. As Laura Wexler suggests, "In this aspect sentimentalization was an externalized aggression that was sadistic, not masochistic, in flavor. The energies it developed were intended as a tool for the control of others, not merely as aid in the conquest of the self . . . it aimed at the subjection of different classes and even races who were compelled to play not the leading roles but the human scenery before which the melodrama of middle class redemption could be enacted" (15).
7. Ann Stoler argues that "[m]atters of the intimate are critical sites for the consolidation of colonial power . . . management of these domains provides a strong pulse on how relations of empire are exercised, and . . . affairs of the intimate are strategic for empire-driven states" (4).
8. References to this story come from the text available at the following site: <http://wilkinsfreeman.info/Short/ModernDragonHR.htm> (last accessed 22 July 2022).
9. For more on this subject of Freeman as a savvy businesswoman, see Brent Kendrick's chapter in this volume.
10. References to this story come from the text available at the following site: <https://digital.library.cornell.edu/catalog/hearth4732809_1454_048> (last accessed 22 July 2022).
11. For a study of this theme in the Victorian era, see Elaine Abelson.

12. References to this story come from the text available at the following site: <http://wilkinsfreeman.info/Short/GalaDress.htm> (last accessed 22 July 2022).
13. For a study of the tensions that existed within the American feminist movement especially as it expressed itself in American magazines, see Katherine Rodier.
14. For Monika Elbert, this story is another example of Freeman's exploration of tensions among women. For her, the supportive networking system between women in Victorian America is not viable in Freeman's world (Elbert, "Devious Women" 270). While this might be true, Elbert does not underline enough the cause of this tension, which is to be found in the rising consumer economy.
15. If Monika Elbert also shows the extent to which the economic realities of Freeman's time stymie her heroine's development and distort relationships among women, she locates the problem within women themselves more than in consumer culture itself. In her words, "All the repetitive and monotonous activities of Freeman's fetishistic women—the incessant sewing and cleaning, the frenzied shopping and collecting, and the obsessive baking and inordinate saving—can be seen as symptoms of their thwarted creativity" (Elbert, "Displacement" 210). For Elbert, if consumer culture creates false needs and desire, the problem comes from women's own "inchoate desires" and "inarticulate longings." As I read these stories, the heroine's activities are not the signs of neurosis but of their power to reclaim a space of their own; these attitudes are not the sign of an inner flaw (thwarted creativity) but rather the consequence of a destructive system.
16. See also Sacvan Bercovitch's seminal work.
17. In "Sister Liddy", the importance of whiteness in the construction of a visible self is underlined by the repetition of the adjective "white" used to qualify clothing and to signify a form of essence ("I was allers real white myself"). The reference to a dark complexion further underlines the centrality of whiteness: "I remember you had a real handsome blue bunnit once, but it warn't so becomin' as some you'd had, you was so *dark-complected*," remarked the pretty old woman, in a soft, spiteful voice. "I had a *white* one, drawn silk, an' *white* feathers on't, when I was married, and they all said it was real becomin'. I was allers *real white* myself. I had a *white* muslin dress with a flounce on it, once, too, an' a black silk spencer cape" (Freeman, "Sister Liddy" 329).
18. While Elbert notes that *Harper's Bazar* was a "journal of mixed messages," she does not recognize the critical quality of the magazine nor does she contemplate the idea that those messages could have any impact on the female readers: "Surely these words fell in the deaf ears of Harper's unheeding women" ("Devious Women" 258).
19. In her study on women, nineteenth-century domesticity, and the American home as a fertile "contact zone," Kristin Hoganson also underlines the agency of American middle-class women: "These women did more than dumbly respond to prescriptive literature and the market-place; they asserted agency through shopping, decorating, and dining preferences and their choice of leisure and reform activities" (8).

PART IV

PERIODIZATION RECONSIDERED

11

MOBILIZING THE GREAT WAR IN MARY E. WILKINS FREEMAN'S *EDGEWATER PEOPLE*

DANIEL MROZOWSKI

Mary E. Wilkins Freeman is not a writer that appears in discussions of the literature of the Great War, yet a slender selection of stories in her 1918 collection *Edgewater People*—"The Liar," "Both Cheeks," and "The Soldier Man"—engage with the war in prominent and surprising fashion. In her introduction, Freeman suggested that she wanted to represent how communities came to resemble individuals; her portrait of Edgewater in a time of international conflict registered the energies and identities of mobilization, and the rich passions of pacifism and militarism. With their depictions of the home front during the Great War, these stories remain under-covered additions to the canon of American war writing, challenging our understanding of the typical modes of representing war experience. They reveal some of the resilience and flexibility of Freeman's recognizable style, including her penchant for the mundane choices that make up everyday ethics, the small yet dramatic reversals of fate and fortune, and the powerful illusions people make and embrace.

Yet *Edgewater People* presents few of the ideological signs marked by historians of the Great War. Freeman's collection holds little to no interest in European or ethnic loyalties; it offers no clear or direct Progressive Era obsessions with reform; it refuses to parrot the enlightened assumptions of Wilsonian foreign policy. But these stories enter, often directly, into the maelstrom of conversation over one of the largest social experiments ever undertaken in America: the mobilization of millions of people towards an overt war effort in 1917–18. The precise numbers are staggering. The Great War institutionalized the modern mass American military by transforming it from a peacetime outfit of under 300,000 active troops and reservists into just under 4 million soldiers, three quarters of whom were conscripted. Mobilization on this scale involved an energetic propaganda that mixed volunteerism and coercion in order to convert American popular opinion away from Woodrow Wilson's famous palliatives—"impartial in thought as well as in action," his declaration of neutrality in August 1914, and "He has kept us out of the war," his 1916 reelection campaign slogan—towards a modern fight to make the world safe for democracy. Conscription broke with tradition, altering the meaning of US military service and citizenship in dramatic and swift fashion. In order to blunt the force of the draft, Jennifer D. Keene confirms that most popular representations depicted the Great War as a kind of moral crusade, "filled with broad ideological pronouncements by American civil and military leaders and a quest for adventure by citizen soldiers" (1). Yet Freeman's fiction suggests how deeply and ambivalently Americans argued during the war itself over the meaning of service, beyond broad ideological pronouncements and military fantasy. Her fiction can help open up a period of military and literary history mostly known through representations produced retrospectively, in the great flowering of war memoirs and novels a decade after combat that continues to define the war.

Still, I do not want to imply that there is an easy correspondence between the composition and publication of Freeman's war fiction and the challenges and propagandas of modern mobilization. Commentators like Lewis Mumford assert that the United States (like most pre-war nations) was gripped by a "collective psychosis" of imagined peace long before an official declaration of war, and American economic policies and goods as well as ideological sympathies and charities played powerful roles long before deployment (275). Any totalizing homology between her stories and mobilization risks a synchronicity and a political sympathy that poorly suits the actuality of America's evolving relationship to the conflict. And, as I hope to show here, Freeman's fiction fits uncomfortably along the complex gaps between the various versions of the war effort circulating in 1917–18. Steven Trout argues that modernist and patriotic visions of the war emerged at different points, and much of the contemporaneous fiction drew from cherished traditions of American soldiering, what he calls "affirmative interpretations of modern warfare and military service" (12). Though Freeman's work might draw from contextual headlines, and it might dramatize the private anxieties of broad political arguments, it was neither completely affirmative of nor deeply invested in the ideologies of mobilization. Out of this rich ambivalence, Freeman imagined an idiosyncratic and instructive home front electrified by and yet hesitant about the dramatic energies of a mobilizing society.

"Everything is Different Since the War"

Freeman's absence from the canons of Great War writing can be explained not only in terms of typical accounts of aesthetics and ideology, but also through the economics and expressions of gender. As mobilization, combat, and then return and re-habituation rewired gender norms, writers came to express atavistic dread about masculine vitality through the spatial geographies of home and front. American women actively participated in wartime relief, peace, and military preparedness organizations, including the Army Nurse Corps, the Red Cross, and welfare workers for the American Expeditionary Forces; they registered the war's traumas in some of the most eloquent works of the period, from Edith Wharton to Jessie Redmon Fauset. Yet the common cultural imperative still ruled: men trained and fought and died, and women gardened and knitted and mourned. Pearl James writes persuasively about the ways in which anxiety about masculinity, predating the war in the form of fears about degeneration and decadent torpor, emerged in the wartime misogynistic trope that "conflates femininity with the home front" (30). This bluntly ideological version of the home front was perhaps most legible in the constant circulation of visual iconography, from posters to films, hoping to harness traditional feminine virtues, like a nurturing domesticity, towards national service and sacrifice. Even generally acknowledged texts of a Great War canon like Willa Cather's *One of Ours* (1922) faced this gendered scrutiny; H. L. Mencken famously dismissed her novel because it lacked plausibility, fought out not in France, but in a "Hollywood movie-lot" (James 32). The gendered experiences and representations of the war as a space of strenuous masculinity and male sentimentality were seemingly closed to writers like Freeman.

But her age also seemed to invalidate her wartime writing. Freeman understood the War personally as a pivotal moment in her career, diminishing her audience and eroding her reputation. As she suggested stoically in a letter to an effusive fan in 1928, such "[praise] does not happen nowadays, I think the War stopped that too" ("To Edith O'Dell Black," 16 December 1928, *The Infant Sphinx* 428). When diplomatic relations faltered with Germany in early 1917, Freeman was in a period of personal disintegration that included Charles Freeman's business disasters, his long slide into addiction, and her own deteriorating health. As early as 1919, Freeman would write Fred Lewis Pattee with melancholia: "I do know, and have always known, my accomplished work is not the best work of which I am capable, but it is too late now" ("To Fred Lewis Pattee," 5 September 1919, *The Infant Sphinx* 382).

Literary history stops telling the stories of writers who seem to age out of and work well beyond their convenient historical sections of anthologies. This is particularly true in the later stages of a writer's career, when the problems of aging and dying are intertwined with the passing of once familiar circumstances and mastered fashions. By 1926 the Great War was a personal marker of sweeping changes in general literary taste. As Freeman wrote to Jean O'Brien in that year: "Everything is different since the War, and since even the pre-war days for I think the change antedated the War . . . As nearly as I can understand the situation, there is in arts and letters a sort of frantic impulse for something erratic, out of the common" ("To Jean O'Brien," 27 February 1926, *The Infant Sphinx* 401).

Her statement echoes more famous modernist invocations, like Ezra Pound's command to "make it new" or Virginia Woolf's famous 1924 declaration that "On or about December 1910 human nature changed" (320), but Freeman's war stories hold few of the tropes now considered typical of the period: they contain no Gothic battle pieces; no confrontation with death, stoic or otherwise; no traumatic silence. The very idea of Great War literature, perhaps unshakeable now and certainly influential enough to be default, is that the experience of modern war made the realistic mode perverse, even immoral. Its experiences required a rejection of the kind of traditional realism Freeman was associated with in favor of more modernist aesthetics of allusions and cryptology. But if we call modernity's dominant emotions sensation and outrage or its experiences displacement and exile, I'm not convinced we can't place Freeman within that rubric. Hostility, disenchantment, fragmentation, discontinuity, and transition are all touchstones for her wartime writing.

In turn, the mobilization fiction of *Edgewater People* offers us an opportunity to rethink the standard stories we tell about a generation of realist writers active and publishing well within the periodized confines of modernism. The war's immense gravity warped not only those lost writers coming of age in its wake, but it also altered the trajectories of those writers trained in the late nineteenth century and confronting the realities of the twentieth. Freeman's own sense of her career ending is undercut by the very vigor of her attempts to grapple with the meanings of the Great War. Though three stories out of a prolific fifty-year career make for a slim archive, they are potent reminders of the war's impact and Freeman's talent. As wartime narratives about mobilization by an older woman realist, these stories might be situated uncomfortably in literary and cultural history, yet they can help unsettle an entrenched system of periodization that so often fails to recognize the potencies of the war writing of women, let alone the possibilities within the long arc of an artist's life.

The Great War Comes Home to Edgewater

Of the three *Edgewater* stories, "The Soldier Man," first published in *Harper's Magazine* in September 1916, bears the most tangential relationship to the war itself. A hard luck gardener, Henry Ludd, is caught between duty to his mother and love for his fiancée in just the sort of tense family geometry typical of Freeman's best work. It includes Gothic flourishes that add a sinister subtext, as Ludd seems to be both symbolically and literally starved by his self-contained mother, a woman whose youthful countenance and implacable demeanor suggest wicked motives. The echoes of the Great War are metaphoric and elusive, but still compelling within "The Soldier Man," as Freeman leans on a linguistic index of martial imagery to invest the story of Henry Ludd with a kind of grandeur. His garden itself becomes a locus of meaning, gesturing towards economic sustenance, home-front rationing, and even the scene of battle, as it burns down in a dramatic climax that intimates arson on the part of his mother. Yet Freeman suggests that this soldier man thrives through duty and labor, finding himself, at the end of the tale, once again without his fiancée, under the watchful eye of his wicked mother, striving happily with military precision and effort.

Though one would be hard pressed to claim "The Soldier Man" as war literature, the context of the Great War helps explain its linguistic registers, its questions about private motives and public purposes, and its existential depiction of labor. Henry Ludd is just the sort of character Freeman explored her entire career: dignified yet struggling, seemingly content yet engaged in fretful ritual, intriguing but ultimately unknowable to his community. As the story sounds out themes of devotion and renunciation, loyalty and sacrifice, Ludd earns the epithet "Soldier Man" from the townsfolk:

> It may have been from his almost painful erectness of carriage, as if he would disavow all the burdens of his life and keep in step with the rank and file of the successful who had lived to see the fulfillment of their hopes of youth; it may have been from his speed of movement, which suggested attack upon labor itself with a stern purpose of conquest; it may have been for some subtler reason in the character of the man which people recognized but could not specify. It is certain that, laboring year in and out without the personal benefit which a man has a right to expect from his toil, he labored like one under marching orders, which were not for him to disregard or question, but to obey with his cheerful might. He charged the fertile ground with seeds. His flowers and vegetables, standing in brave order of life, might have been a host which he commanded, not for self, but for something beyond his humble outlook. (439–40)

Freeman constructs a narrative position that achieves a simultaneous intimacy and distance, recognition and estrangement. The reader is aligned with the townsfolk through this narrative voice, but we are never given assurance of that "something beyond" that might lend Ludd motive. This is as deft a description of a character as Freeman offers in her fiction, marshaling meaning most clearly through military metaphors as a way to explain the relentless toil of a fellow being, and yet the core of logic is almost vertiginously empty. Despite the descriptive insistence on conquest and command, Ludd's life, as seen from this narrative position, seems to be missing an authority that might direct his speed and effort away from raw, impoverishing masochism. All the resonance of military might—his "speed of movement" and "stern purpose of conquest" as he charges "the fertile ground with seeds"—is not only sterile but also ironic. This irony echoes in the mockery of the title's uncanny doubling of *soldier* and *man*, suggestive of both a defensive overcompensation and a playful children's toy, and underlines the odd and unproductive eroticism of Ludd's efforts. With his fiancée once again driven away by his returning mother in tale's end, the implacable and mechanical Ludd attacks his work "with his old magnificent energy," back to the struggle which is "after all, the love of his life" (472).

The question of motivation was no small problem for the mobilization of a mass public, especially given the relentless accounts of devastation from the deadlocked Western front, and Freeman would register it obliquely in "The Soldier Man." But "Both Cheeks," published first in *The Saturday Evening Post* in November 1917, bluntly considers the emotional energy of debts and retribution as fuel for war mobilization. A young man of enlistment age, James Lord, begs his old uncle Zenas to call in a demand note from another much wealthier uncle, the suggestively named Uncle Abel, so James can join the AEF without the weight of Zenas's financial dependence on his conscience. Zenas remains adamant as the last pacifist holdout of the entire town, refusing to indulge his nephew on the moral grounds of scriptural authority and, as the story suggests, the firmer foundation of personal stubbornness.

Zenas inhabits a depleted place, as everything from his rooms to the furniture to the man himself is directly referred to as "old." He pointedly refuses to modernize his house with the comfort of steam heat, and even the youthful James Lord works in an antique shop. Nothing seems vital or forceful about the physically shrunken and delicate Zenas except for his recalcitrance, as he is incapable of calling in a legitimate debt or rightfully asking a neighbor to house a troublesome dog that stalks his doorstep. Yet the story turns on a dramatic reversal, revealing a kind of inner strength in Zenas that belies his exterior—a slumbering volcanic power that can be converted to violence as easily as political conviction.

Disgusted and disturbed by his uncle's refusals, James leaves the house, replaced by a neighbor, Thomas Dodd, a frequent verbal combatant with Zenas who pantomimes the usual war-mongering stump speeches and mocks Zenas for wanting to send a peace delegation to the Germans. Freeman dramatizes their opposed values with a nearly allegorical precision, and their argument is staged with ironic symmetry: neither man is a particularly charismatic exemplar of their respective position, as the blustering Dodd reads as boorish, and the mild Zenas remains demure. Even when the vituperative Dodd calls him a traitor, Zenas resists with a whimpered dissent.

Their argument becomes pedantic as they quote and misquote scripture at each other, taking umbrage over the 'turn the other cheek' biblical doctrine espoused famously in Matthew 5. "Both Cheeks" begs a blithely easy reading: Freeman is merely giving the ideological presuppositions for and against mobilization through temperamentally matched mouthpieces. But she undercuts this discursive mythology in boisterous fashion. Enraged, Dodd claims that he will give the pacifist a chance to practice what he preaches; the cantankerous neighbor rises up and strikes Zenas, and when the old man literally turns the other cheek, Dodd strikes him again. The story swerves: instead of turning both cheeks, the slight, delicate Zenas brutalizes his rival, grappling the man to the floor, smashing his head repeatedly against the sofa. The fight is ridiculous and comic, yet furious and savage, with the warmonger on the defense and the peace advocate now "dangerous and terrible." The narrator assures us that Zenas always knew that "he could fight. He would not, perhaps, have been a pacifist if he had not known that" (407).

With the beating stopped by James and two younger neighbors (one of whom is a recent enlistee), Lord offers a surprising response when asked why he flew in the face of the Bible: "Scripture doesn't say what's to be done when the second cheek is hit" (411). Dodd does the rhetorical work of connecting this "second cheek" interpretation to the doctrine of American militarism, citing German sabotage of American factories and ships, as well as the infamous sinking of the *Lusitania*, as examples of the repeatedly struck second cheek. But it is Zenas, "shocked and exalted," who offers the more visceral and intimate reading of his own conversion: he now yearns for a "terrible victory" over Germany. Like Dodd, the Germans should be beaten "on the sofa, body and soul" (414). The telescoping and collapsing of frame here—from the international scene of conflict to the literal domestic space of the sofa—is freighted with sincerity and sentimentality in equal measure. "Both Cheeks" suggests just how riven with ironies and contradictions the efforts of mobilization were: the pacifist becomes the most capable fighter; the dealer in antiques hopes to fight in this most modern of wars; the personally repellent Dodd, without any of the gentlemanly graces of Zenas, serves as the mouthpiece for the entire town; and the real victory is with the beaten, as the bruised Dodd rises triumphant in their argument.

By tale's end, old Zenas is infused with enough war zeal to rise from his bed to emphatically declare that he *will* curb the rascal dog, he *will* call in that demand note, and he *will* support his nephew's enlistment. His transformation is not only forceful and moral, but also described as modernizing and timely: "He was now of his day, the dreadful Day for all the world" (419). The double signification of day / Day seems no minor point in this story, as it oscillates between pathos and poignancy, between ridiculousness and savagery, and between the modern present and mythic time. The once slumbering power of the demure old man now awakens to the present crisis; he rises as a fearsome, testamentary patriarch. When asked by James how he can thank him, old Zenas Lord replies in the final line of the tale: with "the head of Germania on a charger" (419). Antiquated and mythical, this concluding line is so overwrought, so overdetermined, that it threatens to undermine the seriousness of his transformation. Is the story mocking the conversion of the meek and mild into a bloodthirsty demander of heads on platters? Or reveling in the submerged strength of a generation of Americans who missed out on the glories of the Civil War and have now aged out of the Great one? Regardless, "Both Cheeks," indelibly marked by Freeman's own concerns and style, suggests not only how the Great War garnered the attentions of an older generation of realists, but also how professional, mature writers bent the Great War to their own styles and to their own investments.

If "The Soldier Man" exemplifies how the war might serve as a potent linguistic resource, and "Both Cheeks" dramatizes bluntly if ironically the arguments of mobilization, "The Liar" should be the most enduring of her war stories: it is troubling, rambling, and oddly powerful. As two older women sew and talk, Freeman weaves a scene torn directly from the omnipresent recruitment posters, built on the expectations of proud mothers reaffirming the masculine honor of their fighting sons. Mrs Dickerman's son Sammy is still in

Figure 11.1 "She told them it was Leon's, and that he had fought in it." Women at the washing line, doing the work of nationalist propaganda. *Harper's Monthly*, November 1917. Image courtesy of *Harper's Magazine*.

training but will soon graduate, and she is envious of Mrs Selma Woodsum, whose son, Leon, is already in the trenches of France. But Selma is the titular liar: she has allowed the villagers to believe, through acts of omission and deft imprecision, that her son is bravely in the vanguard of the US Army. Leon is *actually* a daredevil pilot for a traveling circus, a position his mother abhors because of its tawdry associations with purportedly "bad" people. With Leon on his way home after an extended illness, Selma steals the ink-stained uniform of Mrs Dickerman's Sammy, and hangs it on her own laundry line, the comedic ink stain now a badge of courage legible to all her neighbors.

Contemporary readers would call this act a bit of stolen valor. But the initial frame of the tale also deploys a rich set of linked images of peaceful domesticity and violent war: knitting and digging, ink stains and blood stains, circus stunts and weapons training. This semantic confusion lies at the center of the story. When the visibly ill Leon returns on the train, the townsfolk greet him as a wounded soldier, and his mother nurses him in home isolation. Neighbors swing by to pay a respectful visit to the returned hero, including a one-time paramour of Leon's, Aggy Nelson, who builds up a rich fantasy surrounding Leon. To each question—"is—he wounded?" "Blind, or—disfigured?" Selma responds with knowing silence, and Aggy fills in the gaps with ready-made romanticism (294). The story is filled with inadvertent liars.

"The Liar" suggests how easy it is to tell a false war story—about the things the villagers carry, rather than those of the soldiers. In light comedic touches, the townsfolk think Leon is blind, marveling at his ability to move around the familiar spaces of town. But the story is far less interested in Leon than in Selma, who is continually referred to as youngish-looking, childish and impulsive. As Selma tells the truth to her own older suitor, Luke Gleason, a postmaster in town, they try to parse out why she's built up this rich web of lies. The story turns on the suspense of revelation: when will the false war story collapse in on itself—and why does Selma lie in the first place? It is, after all, her own desires that drive her into the lies of omission. Better to be a fake soldier than an actual circus performer.

Luke steps in to solve all the narrative problems: he fixes it so Leon can join the Canadian air force as a pilot, and he will finally marry Selma so that she won't be alone. But the story never offers a satisfying reason for Selma's lies, and it cannot neatly tie off a major question: why go to war at all? For Freeman and most professional American writers, the War was "Over There," as the song went—France really, and not the Middle East or the Eastern Fronts—but still an ongoing event imagined as a place not like Metuchen or Brattleboro. Freeman was professionally involved in what John T. Matthews calls "institutions of representation"—outlets of print culture that made the war *over there* real to an American audience (217). For most of those outlets in 1917, Mr Wilson's War was what Robert H. Zieger describes as "a potent mixture of

Christian redemption, American exceptionalism, and determination to rescue European moral and cultural values from the folly of Europeans" (1). The war mobilization of American culture revolved around an ideology of popular reconciliation—a way to cleanse the body politic of labor unrest, racial strife, and masculine withering.

"The Liar" first appeared in the November 1917 issue of *Harper's Monthly*. The Selective Service Act of 1917, enacted on 18 May, authorizing the federal government to raise a national army through conscription, haunts the issue. Freeman's story appears early, tucked between conventional romantic poetry and reports of Amazonian adventures, but it is joined by a host of voices on the war. Edith O'Shaughnessy reports on diplomacy with Mexico now in the light of mobilization. A colonel of the US army describes the organization of the new forces. An editorial responds to concerns about the political collapse of Germany upon defeat. A series of drawings of Bethlehem Steel show off weapon production. Even William Dean Howells, from the august Easy Chair, reviews Sir Oliver Lodge's spiritualist memoir of his son, Second Lieutenant Raymond Lodge, killed in the Great War. Howells finds the medium scenes tedious and silly, but he speaks to a culture bracing itself for mourning when he asks why spiritualism is on the rise: "Is it because the dead are *superabounding* now beyond the ratio of all the past pestilences and a most powerful people is dedicating itself, body and soul, to the destruction of human life in the most murderous war that ever was?" (882).

An article by Ida M. Tarbell, the famous muckraking journalist, pairs most directly with "The Liar." In "Mobilizing the Women," Tarbell describes the debate raging in the Council of National Defense on how to use women in the work of the war effort. The Council hoped to forge a national organization of women towards two major objectives: food security, from garden productivity to home conservation, and reform propaganda, aimed at protecting the morals of children in the looser times of war. But Tarbell locates a more personal struggle for agency for women against the momentum of mobilization: "If these women had been called in times of peace, it is probable that they would have felt that they had a right to say no, if their judgment so dictated. But this was war, and it seems not to have occurred to any of them that it was a possible thing to say no, any more than it occurs to the honorable-minded boy who is drafted to rake up reasons why he shall not go into the Army" (106–7).

What is of interest to the November 1917 readers of *Harper's*? Issues of mourning, of food, of weapon production, of gender economy, of diplomacy, of the reconstruction of Europe. Essentially, the construction of an informed, engaged home front in support of a new mobilized national army. "The Liar" is embedded in this stream of issues, an important part of the articulation of "structures of feeling" about the war as a collective effort but also about the war as a deep complication of individual agency.

But this story doesn't embrace patriotic gore or the defense of civilization as a means towards war mobilization. Freeman actually wrote those kinds of pieces for other outlets—the pabulum of patriotic statements used in charity volumes hastily assembled and sold in support of various causes. Like many equally famous peers, Freeman contributed a short paragraph praising American mobilization in defense of an abused France in *For France*, edited by Charles H. Towne for Doubleday, Page, and Company in 1917. In *America in the War*, edited and illustrated by Louis Raemaekers for The Century Company in 1918, Freeman offered a poem, "Wake Up, America!", that declares America a Christ-called savior smiting the devilish Hun. "War is Over," she writes, once America wakes up to this righteous fight (34).

Her war fiction contains no such overt messaging. "The Liar" actually makes the case for a kind of conspiracy that lies at the heart of respectability—the very sort of respectability evinced in propaganda posters and charity volumes. Though far from pacifist, her tone in fiction is more complex than virulent patriotism, suggesting that a tissue of lies can support enlistment as easily as any hymn to the republic. The psychic structures of her wartime characters remain ambiguous; they are cantankerous, illiberal, guided less by communal ideology and more by their own private will.

"The Liar" ends as ambiguously as any of her great canonical stories. As Luke declares to Leon: "You are going to make the stories true, my son . . . There are more reasons than one for going to war." No specifics are offered; no summation is provided. And perhaps no single patriotic or personal reason would satisfy. The ink stain may very well become blood; the circus stunts may very well become evasive maneuvers; Selma's lies will, indeed, become a kind of truth. But Leon's fate is unresolved.

Freeman wrote a kind of war resolution by imagining a soldier's journey home in the slim story "The Return," published in the *Woman's Home Companion* in August of 1921. It contains many of the hallmarks of her earlier fiction: a long engagement complicated by a fresh courtship; promises and duty bristling against inclinations and desires; a kind of eccentricity magnified into a grand strangeness. The story is in the vein of stereotypical homecoming narratives. While recovering from a gruesome facial wound in France, Dick breaks off his engagement with Ellen Hale. Ellen, conflicted already by her courtship with a non-combatant, Lee Abbott, struggles with various moral questions about her duty: will Dick be horrifically scarred? Should she dutifully marry a man she doesn't love and who seems to have rejected her because of his traumas?

The story resolves these problems in a memorable, dreamlike conclusion in which the triumphantly returning soldier, face perfectly reconstructed, passes the waiting Ellen by, without even a glance, on a parade back to his mountain home. The narrator suggests that his experiences in service to his country have led him to an elevated love, his mind now a praise song of patriotism so potent

Wake Up, America!

This was done to Canadians by the Huns

AMERICA wakes! The White Christ has called her;
She has seen the devils abroad in His world;
Evil vaunting himself has appalled her;
To the War-wind of Heaven her flag is unfurled!

America wakes—with his murder and lust
Let the Hun take the path he has carved into hell.
No longer blaspheming the Cross with his trust.
America wakes, the sick world shall be well.

America wakes—God's last peace-lover,
God's fighter to death, when her peace is assailed.
Shout, sing, fling out the flags, War is over;
When America battles, right has prevailed!

MARY E. WILKINS FREEMAN.

Figure 11.2 "Wake Up, America!" *America in the War*. Image courtesy of Trinity College, Connecticut.

Figure 11.3 Image opposite "Wake Up, America!" in *America in the War*. Courtesy of Trinity College, Connecticut.

that no mortal woman could interrupt. But what is most interesting here in this late story is that this return cannot be described from an inside perspective—not Dick's or Ellen's or Lee's. The tale of Dick's maimed face, his recovery, and his triumphant processional are told and retold through letters, through gossip, through second- and even third-hand accounts. The wounded man's experiences and interior are unknowable, only accessible through an overblown, beatifying ideology that appears more grotesque than the wounds of the war. An ideology that feels implacable, even inhuman.

Freeman's Obscured Mobilization

Critics of Great War Literature, from Keith Gandel and Pearl James, have suggested that the United States' "experience of the war was deeper and more traumatic than has been acknowledged generally" (James 9). And yet writers of Freeman's generation are still largely absent from the scenes reincarnated by literary historians. Despite the vagaries of literary tastes, Freeman's war fiction, I believe, bears out the real strengths of her work—the sensitivity to the inner life and its oblique frustrations; the counterbalance between public reputations and private meaning; the almost complete lack of overt moralizing; the plots that undercut expectations; the endings that imply yet withhold wisdom. Though the stories are patriotic in spirit—boys go off "Over There" with the blessing of family and friends—the specific representation of that patriotism is shaded and warped under her vision in a way that is decidedly Freeman's own. The pacifist beats his lifelong friend; the son plays out his mother's lies; the wounded veteran returns as a monstrous paragon to patriotic stoicism. That is, her stories are on conventional subjects performed unconventionally. There is always something in her fiction that defies total comprehension—what Elizabeth Meese calls the "unreadable" images that resist determining textual meanings in Freeman's best writing.

Beyond the aesthetic pleasures of her later work, which are plentiful and surprising, and the research gratifications found in the entire scope of her career, which might help loosen or tighten the threads of literary periodization, the war fiction of Mary E. Wilkins Freeman is particularly relevant and even invaluable to us today. It is not unfair to call ourselves a mobilized society, whether we are actively enlisted or not. Americans live in a perpetual home front shaped by and shaping our own forever wars, fought by volunteers, by private armies, by drones, and by economic sanctions. A fiction that explores lies about enlistment and experience, that dramatizes lifelong pacifism giving way to righteous jingoism, that outlines the inexpressibility of homecoming, that registers the role of militarization as a framework for domestic meaning, might be worth considering at the close of twenty years of occupation of Afghanistan, at the center of a nexus of almost 800 military bases around the globe, in a culture with a nearly $800 billion dollar defense budget. Can we long afford to ignore our own cultural ambivalence towards a weapon like the GBU-43/B Massive Ordnance Air Blast, horrifically known as the "Mother of All Bombs," dropped in Afghanistan on 13 April 2017? Freeman's characters, confronted with the realities of modern war and having lived too long to enjoy peace but born too early to see combat, might have something to tell us about those contradictions. And in Freeman's resistance to butchery and her ambiguity towards pacifism, we might sketch out the beginning of a home front ethos that neither embraces slaughter nor condemns combat but somehow tolerates both.

I don't want to argue the merits of the entire collection—critics from Perry Westbrook to Leah Blatt Glasser have rightfully suggested that *Edgewater People* might be her weakest. I also don't want to offer a final verdict on her war fiction. My sense is that Freeman was still a vital if waning voice in American letters in 1917—that for her readers and her publishing partners, her voice on the Great War resonated in ways that might be difficult to recreate now. But there is truly an undeniable sense of an ending in her work of this era. As Selma says, early in "The Liar," "I'm too old to try to keep up with the styles" (284). Yet that only tells a slanted truth. Selma goes on to claim that when the new styles mean "going around without holding up your skirts, or letting them trail in the dust, I believe in following them no matter how old you are" (284). This point of adaptation and resilience, even if incomplete, resonates clearest as Freeman struggled to evolve her style to meet the pressures of the war. To find, in the face of personal and professional diminishment, something that would suffice.

Works Cited

Freeman, Mary E. Wilkins. *Edgewater People*. Harpers, 1918.

—. *The Infant Sphinx: Collected Letters of Mary E. Wilkins Freeman*, edited by Brent L. Kendrick, Scarecrow Press, 1985.

—. "The Liar." *Harper's Monthly*, November 1917, pp. 758–71.

—. "The Return." *Woman's Home Companion*, August 1921. <http://wilkinsfreeman.info/Short/Return.htm> (last accessed 22 July 2022).

—. "Wake Up, America!" *America in the War*, edited by Louis Raemaekers, Century Company, 1918.

—. "We Are With France." In *For France*, edited by Charles H. Towne, Doubleday, Page and Company, 1917.

Gandal, Keith. *The Gun and The Pen: Hemingway, Fitzgerald, Faulkner and the Fiction of Mobilization*. Oxford UP, 2008.

Glasser, Leah Blatt. *In a Closet Hidden: The Life and Work of Mary E. Wilkins Freeman*. U of Massachusetts P, 1996.

Howells, William Dean. "Editor's Easy Chair." *Harper's Monthly*, November 1917, pp. 882–5.

James, Pearl. *The New Death: American Modernism and World War I*. U of Virginia P, 2013.

Keene, Jennifer D. *Doughboys, The Great War, and the Remaking of America*. Johns Hopkins UP, 2001.

Matthews, John T. "American Writing of the Great War." *The Cambridge Companion to the Literature of the First World War*, edited by Vincent Sherry, Cambridge UP, 2005, pp. 217–42.

Meese, Elizabeth. "Signs of Undecidability: Reconstructing the Stories of Mary Wilkins Freeman." *Critical Essays on Mary Wilkins Freeman*, edited by Shirley Marchalonis, G. K. Hall, 1991, pp. 157–76.

Mumford, Lewis. *The Culture of Cities*. Harcourt Brace, 1938.

Pound, Ezra. *Make it New*: Essays. Faber & Faber, 1934.

Tarbell, Ida. "Mobilizing the Women." *Harper's Monthly*, November 1917, pp. 841–7.

Trout, Steven. *On the Battlefield of Memory: The First World War and American Remembrance, 1919–1941*. U of Alabama P, 2010.

Westbrook, Perry D. *Mary Wilkins Freeman*. Revised edition. Twayne Publishers, 1988.

Wilson Woodrow. "Address to Congress on War with Germany, April 2, 1917." *World War I and America*, edited by A. Scott Berg, The Library of America, 2017.

—. "Statement on Neutrality, August 18. 1914." *World War I and America*, edited by A. Scott Berg, The Library of America, 2017.

Woolf, Virginia. "Mr. Bennett and Mrs. Brown." 1924. *Collected Essays, I*. Hogarth Press, 1966.

Zieger, Robert H. *America's Great War: World War I and the American Experience*. Rowman & Littlefield, 2000.

12

A CACOPHONY OF VOICES: FREEMAN'S MODERNISM

MONIKA ELBERT

A striking painting entitled *The Factory Village* by J. Alden Weir that hangs in the Metropolitan Museum of Art in New York depicts a cultural moment that inspired many realist authors, even so-called local color writers—the incursion of industrial life into a bucolic rustic landscape. Weir, who had studied in late nineteenth-century France and had the utmost contempt for their Impressionistic painters, returned to America and, ironically, became one of the Impressionistic School of painters in New England. His painting does tend to whitewash the reality of this commercial intrusion, as the factory stands in harmony with the picturesque town and the lovely verdant foliage. The museum label is quite striking in pointing out how Weir "celebrates New England industry—symbols of progress in harmony with Nature." The description goes further: "A large tree spreads its protective canopy over two telegraphy poles, in the extreme foreground, as well as over the smokestack and spool shop (with tower) of the Willimantic Linen Company's Connecticut factory." And as a final note, to undermine the complacency and beauty of Weir's painting, the museum label concludes that in this "tranquil scene," there is "no sense or hint of the company's labor woes or financial problems."

Just so, in terms of literary criticism of Mary E. Wilkins Freeman, the assessment has been to make her work seem far more peaceful and bucolic than it is, but Freeman is very much aware of the incursion of the industrial into the rural. In the past, many critics, such as Josephine Donovan, have focused on two major turn-of-the-century New England women writers, Mary E. Wilkins

Figure 12.1 Julian Alden Weir, *The Factory Village*. Superstock.

Freeman (1852–1930) and Sarah Orne Jewett (1849–1909), as gentle local color writers who wrote nostalgically about rural New England landscapes and who were out of touch with the increasing commercialization of the late nineteenth-century United States. Even Edith Wharton looked down upon them as writing through "rose-colored spectacles."[1] I would like to share another view: both authors were extremely aware of the dangers that modern corporate culture, materialistic strivings, and economic monopolies posed to the individual wanting to live in harmony with nature and with their townspeople. They are as invested in a critique of capitalism as Charlotte Perkins Gilman demonstrated in her well-known treatise, *Women and Economics* (1898).

Though my focus here will be on Mary E. Wilkins Freeman and the dearth of critics who focus on her sense of capitalism and its attendant economic woes, it is telling that recent critics have recently paid more attention to Jewett's sense of undermining capitalistic economics in her works. In the case of Sarah Orne Jewett, one can find devastating landscapes beset by a modern sense of economic profit in several of her stories, most notably those stories connected with her Gothic writing, in which man-made products often seem demonic or possessed (see Elbert and Ryden). In many of her journal entries or in her correspondence with friends such as Annie Fields, Jewett bemoans the onslaught of an industrial America having no compunction about invading the New England landscapes and destroying trees and other vegetation as well as neighborly ties.

It is far from a complacent view of happy rural life. In addition, in such stories as Jewett's "The Failure of David Berry" (1891) and "A Businessman" (1885), there is a strong yearning for life as it used to be, an age of craftsmanship that reinforced the worker's connection to nature, and a nostalgia for a time in which "homespun" objects rather than manufactured goods rendered men and women part of a more wholesome natural landscape of producing and giving. Sarah Way Sherman has presented Jewett's lament about the incorporation of New England in "The Gray Mills of Farley" in neighboring New Hampshire. June Howard ("Unraveling Regions") and Sandra Zagarell show the intrusion of the capitalistic marketplace (and urban tourists) into the supposed provincial Jewett landscapes, whereas Mark Storey shows the idealization of Jewett's rural landscapes by urban tourists, and Kent C. Ryden (in *Sum of the Parts*) shows a darker, less than pristine view of Jewett's, Freeman's, and Wharton's rural landscapes. Although Howard in her recent book, *The Center of the World*, focuses on Jewett, in the few pages she looks at Freeman's work, specifically on *The Jamesons* (1899), she astutely comments on whether "local color is empathetic or touristic, an insider or an outsider narrative" (47).

My study goes one step further to problematize the manner in which the outsiders and insiders interact and are perceived. Although Kent Ryden looks at folkloric ways in defining the rural, he privileges the actual inhabitants—not the "surveyors and cartographers" who superimpose meaning on the rural landscape but those who actually inscribe meaning as a result of "the daily experience of inhabiting a locality," what he calls a "lived sense of place" (*Mapping the Invisible Landscape* 69). I also agree with Mark Storey, who suggests that "representations of rural life can provide a more geographically intricate understanding of nineteenth-century modernity" (19). Although Storey's focus is on urban modernity, he does concede that the countryside does express the same types of anxiety: "although the city feels and looks like the pre-eminent expression of modernity and the exemplary geo-social site for elucidating what modernity constitutes, the spaces that wear those changes less overtly are not only still relevant but might actually provide a distinct, de-centered perspective on the same conditions" (19). Storey does not consider Freeman in his study, but his vantage point aids in a consideration of Freeman's modernism.

Although Freeman has traditionally been seen as a regionalist writer (or early on in literary history, she was assigned the pejorative "local color" definition), that category of "regionalism" and her writing career span the periods of realism/naturalism through modernism. Freeman's stories, especially those I consider revolving around the encroaching industrial landscape, are marked by a type of nihilism and isolation that is reflective of both naturalist and modernist tendencies. The despair of the naturalist protagonist struggling with economic woes is similar to that of the modernist character, although the latter time period includes the possibility of total global destruction by an influenza epidemic and World War I (which Freeman also writes about in her *Edgewater People*, published in 1918). Today especially we can understand what it means to live in pandemic times, and the sense of isolation that is warranted. The solipsistic protagonists, who need to fend for themselves, on their own terms, are already apparent in Freeman's bucolic writings, but the feeling is accelerated in her more industrial, urban, and wartime settings. Regionalism and modernism are not incompatible or incongruous: recent critics have noted the arbitrary assignment of literary time periods and illustrate how modernism does not disqualify regionalism. Guy Reynolds reads larger national concerns in Willa Cather's *My Antonia* (1918), so that the regional perspective is moved to a modernist platform. Similarly, Dathalinn O'Dea locates the modernist malaise in the regionalist dynamics of *Dubliners* (1914). John N. Duvall rethinks literary modernism to include "all imaginative writing that responds to the intense forces of modernization that occur from the 1890s to the eve of World War II" and shows how writers "whose regionalism is associated with realism and naturalism . . . contribute to an understanding of modernism" (243). In arguing for Freeman as a modernist writer, I'd like to show the breadth of her writing, as she moves from simple pastoral landscapes to industrial wastelands to alienated wanderers.

Mary E. Wilkins Freeman is aware of the displacement of the individual and their family by capitalistic enterprises even early on in her writing career. In many of her late (unrecognized) stories, Mary E. Wilkins Freeman presents characters who take on the panic of other modernist protagonists and writers—namely a sense of confusion and displacement arising from too much commotion or too many interruptions associated with early twentieth-century living. These markers of civilization—the telephone, the train, the car, hotels, and department stores, and, finally, a World War—all intrude upon the protagonists' psyche to create a type of alienation that ultimately disrupts their lives or even destroys them. There is no solace in nature in these later Freeman stories. There are nuances of desperation, isolation, numbing silences, and suicidal tendencies in these works that are akin to those moments of despair and devastating indictments of the capitalist landscape in other (modernist) writings, such as Edith Wharton's *Ethan Frome* (1911), James Joyce's *Dubliners*, Sherwood Anderson's *Winesburg Ohio* (1919), and D. H. Lawrence's "A Rocking-Horse Winner" (1926). It is perhaps surprising to find the angst of industrialization in seemingly complacent "local color" authors like Freeman and Jewett. My analysis moves from Freeman's late nineteenth-century stories, which show an alarm about consumerism, commercialization, and the rise of factories, to the twentieth-century stories, veritable examples of Freeman's forays into modernism with its concomitant despair. Stories from both periods show the increasing disempowerment of the individual to create their own environment or to find meaning in an (imagined) erstwhile domestic haven or bucolic landscape.

The End of an Era, the Exodus from Nature

Impending doom wrought by factories and displacement from trains is already characteristic of Freeman's late-nineteenth-century stories. Thus, for example, in "A Wayfaring Couple" (1885), we hear about a rather dismal settlement: "These poor, little houses were all alike: they had been built expressly for the operatives in the Saunders cotton mill" (1). The only positive image among the "row of little cheap houses . . . on each side of the narrow, dusty street" is the house of David May: "There was not a tree in the whole length of [the street] except in front of David May's house. A slim, young maple, carefully boxed in around the trunk, stood close to his gate" (1). This small bit of life among the squalor of the industrial town sounds hopeful, until we hear that David May has been fired by the foreman, Lem Wheelock, who always had a "spite" against him (it is later revealed that he had been sweet on David's wife). Clearly the Saundersville factory is not unionized, as David laments his fate, in a local dialect: "The boss jist called me into his office, an told me they wouldn't need my services no more, an' paid me what was owin' me, an' that was just $10. I tried to talk, but he kep' on writin' in a book an' didn't seem to hear me . . ." (2). In her manner of protesting, David's wife, Minty, distressed that they must move, pulls the flowers out of her front-yard garden as her statement of ownership: "The new folks shan't have my flowers! They shan't" (3). They set off looking for a new job and a new home: she takes with her a basket of her flowers, some domestic knick-knacks, and family keepsakes, but regrets the fact that she can't remove the maple tree to replant at her new home. Although David advises her to take the train and meet him in White River, where he hopes to find a job, the wife won't hear of abandoning him. Finding no employment at White River, they move on to the next town, Waterbury, which also proves disappointing. Lamenting the fact that they have no family to fall back on (nostalgic for an earlier New England landscape), they find refuge in an abandoned farm. David goes off to a neighboring town, Bassets, in hopes of finding a job at a tub factory, but that journey fails, as well. They settle for a temporary abode in an abandoned farmhouse, which shows as much deterioration as the apple tree adjoining the kitchen door: "The tree had deteriorated like the house; some of the limbs were dead, and its apples were not the fair, large things that they had been. They were small and knotty" (5). The incursion of the industrial has damaged nature. Depressed and tried, David falls ill, and having no horse for an old rusty carriage they find in the dilapidated barn, his wife, after making him comfortable in the cart, maneuvers herself into the sulky and proceeds to drag him three miles into the town of Bassets, where she finds medical help and a kind neighborly woman, Mrs Marsh, takes them in during his convalescence. The foreman at the local tub factory promises him a job. The story ends with Minty singing, and a neighbor remarking on her pretty voice, which reminds her of "a bluebird singin', when he first comes back in the spring" (10). This story, like several other late-nineteenth-century stories by Freeman revolving around economic woes, ends on a happy note, with a return to nature or neighborly love. This would not be the case of Freeman's twentieth-century stories, which show grim prospects of economic solvency and communal love.

Before moving on to her most devastating pronouncements against twentieth-century civilization, I will point to a few other instances in her late-nineteenth-century stories that shed light on her increasing anxiety about a capitalistic society. "Two Old Lovers" (1883) includes David Emmons, a lethargic worker, a throwback to Irving's Rip Van Winkle, who is so somnambulistic as a result of the New England town, Leyden, turning more industrialized-weary, that he doesn't have the gumption to propose (until the final deathbed scene) to his girlfriend, Maria, who has cared for him and patiently waited for his proposal. Most importantly about this story, Freeman shows the development of the quintessential New England factory town in her description, and its subsequent decline. There is a type of uniformity about the village:

> Leyden was emphatically a village of cottages, and each of them built after one of two patterns: either the front door was on the right side, in the corner of a little piazza extending a third of the length of the house, with the main roof jutting over it, or the piazza stretched across the front, and the door was in the center." (n.p.)

Moreover, we hear about the history of the town, and its subsequent demise:

> when one Hiram Strong put up his three factories for the manufacture of the rough shoe which the workingman of America wears, he hardly thought he was also gaining for himself the honor of founding Leyden. He chose the site for his buildings mainly because they would be easily accessible to the railway which stretched to the city, sixty miles distant. (n.p.)

The evolution into a working town rather than a commuter town takes away the characters' individuality:

> At first the workmen came on the cars from the neighboring towns, but after a while they became tired of that, and one after another built for himself a cottage, and established his family and his household belongings near the scene of his daily labors. So gradually Leyden grew. A built his cottage like C, and B built his like D. They painted them white, and hung the green blinds, and laid out their flower beds in front and their vegetable beds at the back. (n.p.)

We then hear that Hiram Strong's heirs have died off, and it appears that business has slowed down a bit, to the point that the workers had "begun to drone a little like the factories. 'As slow as Leyden,' was the saying among the faster-growing towns adjoining theirs" (n.p.). The shoe factory workers seem content enough though their faces were "a little pale" because of their "indoor life." The factory buildings themselves are "great, ugly wooden buildings . . . Their outer walls were black and grimy, streaked and splashed and patched with red paint in every variety of shade, according as the original hue was tempered with smoke or the beatings of the storms of many years" (n.p.). David Emmons, although a slow suitor, has the distinction of being very individualistic as a gardener, a throwback to the quintessential pioneering man: "If David Emmons was slow, his vegetables were not. None of the gardens in Leyden surpassed his in luxuriant growth" (n.p.). Emmons is an interesting throwback to individualism gone awry in the industrial town. Moreover, his example shows that not just creative female protagonists in Freeman's oeuvre attend to their gardens.

In other Freeman stories of the late nineteenth or early twentieth century, economy is always a factor in the characters' development or demise. At times, consumerism gets out of hand and makes the females lose a sense of themselves, as in the shopping spree described in "One Good Time" (1897)[2] or causes maternal neglect in the too-materialistic woman ("The Lost Ghost," 1903). Or, women, dispossessed in a system that doesn't include protection for solitary or poor women, lose their lives or their progeny, as in "Sister Liddy" (1891) or "Old Woman Magoun" (1905). However, there are also stories that have women giving up any patrimonial privilege to an estate or land, as in "Evelina's Garden" (1896)—in which Evelina saves her sense of self and then wins the day and gets her beloved (and her father's estate), anyway—and women who silently but firmly go against their husband's will and resist a rampant materialism (embodied in barn-building) for the sake of the daughter's domestic security (embodied in a home) in "The Revolt of 'Mother'" (1890). There are those falsely accused of stealing and those desperate enough to steal, as in "Calla-Lilies and Hannah" (1887) and "A Stolen Christmas" (1887), and those who escape the poorhouse to go back to their small hovel of a real home ("A Mistaken Charity," 1883). And there is even a moment when a Christmas ghost in the shape of a hard-working girl knocks on the door, is invited in, and intercedes for the sake of a man who has welcomed her into his family but who has been accused of stealing after losing his promissory note ("The Twelfth Ghost," 1889).

Women who are stuck in factory life have a chance in some of Freeman's early-twentieth-century fiction. In "For the Love of One's Self" (1905), Amanda Dearborn silently suffers as a worker in a shoe factory, but the view of "a tall spruce-tree" outside the window keeps her going. At the start of the story, she bemoans her fate: "Nobody knew how the girl hated her work in the great factory, or how she hated life, yet endured it with a contemptuous grimness" (106). The best day for her is pay day: "she came the nearest to happiness when she went to the savings-bank to make a tiny deposit" (107). She resists participating in talk about strikes, "although her sympathies were entirely with the party who wished to strike" (107). Her financial security is just too important: she needs the pay check to cover her expenses at the boarding house where she lives and also to bestow Christmas presents on her cousins. One of the foremen at the shoe factory, Frank Ayres, becomes attracted to Amanda, even though his brother tells him, "She is the homeliest of the lot" (111). For Christmas, Frank sends her a box of candy, but she can't believe it was meant for her and sends it back. The ending of the story has him presenting her with candies one more time, walking her home to the boarding house, and having them commiserate about the recent deaths of their mothers: Frank tells her of his interest in purchasing her late mother's house which is on the market, and the suggestion is that there will be a "happily ever after." There is another such implausible happy ending in Freeman's novel, *The Portion of Labor* (1901), in which the strong female protagonist, Ellen, a worker in the shoe factory, leads a strike and is able to tame and domesticate the factory owner, Robert. As Leah Blatt Glasser points out, the transformation for both can only go so far: "Freeman tames Ellen in the conclusion, perhaps aiming to appeal to a wider audience of men and women" (189). But it is not a complete sell-out: "Although Robert's approach to the workers will change, Ellen will marry Robert and come around to share some of his perspective when she considers the hardships the strike has caused" (Glasser 189).

At times, there are happy endings for males who resist, at least temporarily, their pre-ordained roles as protectors and wage-owners. For example, in "The Balking of Christopher" (1912) the main character, Christopher, suffering what seems like a case of neurasthenia, laments to the local minister that he just can't go on working and basically goes on strike:

> "I ain't going to plow the south field. I ain't going to make a garden. I ain't going to try for hay in the ten-acre lot. I have stopped. I have worked for nothing except just enough to keep soul and body together. I have had bad luck. . . . I have never in my life had a chance at the spring or the summer. This year, I'm going to have the spring and summer . . ." (406)

He leaves his savings for his wife, and he goes off to spend a kind of transcendentalist life at his "shack" on Silver Mountain. Christopher embraces the sugar maples, and at the end of July, he returns earlier, announcing to his wife, "I am better than I ever was in my whole life, Myrtle, and I've got more courage to work now than I had when I was young. I had to get rested, but I've got rested for all my life" (413).[3]

A variation of "The Balking of Christopher," somewhat less happy, can be found in "the Elm-Tree" (1903), in which an independent man, David, who, though slightly crippled from a life of work, "was in spirit a revolutionist and anarchist," (8) falls on hard times when the new house he is building is reclaimed by the bank: "The bank in which his savings were stored had failed, and there was nothing to meet the payments for the stock. He sold the house and the field at a miserable sacrifice. . . ." (7). Shortly after the loss, he suffers another hardship—the death of his wife, and he becomes quite bitter. The new proprietor of the home, Thomas Savage, finds the new house burned down; David is blamed by many, but his good friend Abner Slocum believes that Savage's wife had been to blame, for she was always "dreadful careless about fire—used to carry live coals in a shovel all over the house" (18). His friend and daughter take David in, so that he is not forced to go to the poorhouse, but David is slightly addled. In the end, he takes pride in the oak that had stood on his property and announces that his real house is his beloved elm, which he had venerated throughout his life. The neighbors are somewhat stunned as he talks about his tree as his home: "It's the handsomest house in this town, and it's all mine. Nobody else had it painted green, and it's higher than the meetin'-house . . . Nobody is going to build cupolys nor bay-winders on that" (39). The neighborly consensus is that "He's out of his head" (40).

Modernist Isolation

In many of Freeman's darkest twentieth-century stories, those that verge on a modernist malaise of isolation, there are no easy endings or places of refuge (certainly not in nature). Men cannot resist their expectations as breadwinners and businessmen, and women are stuck in a sense of the past that precludes their coming to terms with their aging bodies and déclassé backgrounds. Social climbing seems for the twentieth-century protagonists of Freeman as irresistible as for women in Wharton's fiction, and World War I allows unmanned men to find their manhood. As I mention above, the markers of civilization—the telephone, the train, the car, hotels, and department stores—will all undo the protagonists' sense of security and purpose. To illustrate, I will examine four stories "Humble Pie" (1904), "A Guest in Sodom" (1912), "Sweet-Flowering Perennial" (1915), "The Cloak Also" (1917), and briefly two chapters of a compilation of stories, *Edgewater People* (1918; namely "The Liar" and "A Retreat to the Goal").

"Humble Pie" (1904), an early example of Freeman's forays into modernism, shows a woman, Maria Gorham, who wants to impress upon her neighbors her class status. She books a summer vacation in "a great mountain hotel," which turns out to be a disaster as those of a higher class will shun her and ridicule her outdated clothes (of which she had been so proud in her little village). As a schoolteacher, and an independent woman who inherited her mother's house five years prior, she is proud of her social position: "She was entirely fearless. So quietly poised was she in her own self esteem that it had never occurred to her that anybody could have any ill will, or even any uncomplimentary feeling, toward her" (82). She imagines herself "good-looking" and "industrious" as the townspeople have described her in such positive terms. She is embarrassed that her friend Emma uses the wrong words, and she resists the advances of Emma's brother Dexter Ray, who seems to her awkward and shy, has a decent job as a pharmacist, a position she finds boring: "he seemed to have no interest except in measuring out drugs and dispensing with soda water" (84). Her obsession, as she packs her suitcases, is with her many outfits (which will turn out to be dated). Her friend Emma, as her cheering squad, exclaims, "I guess there won't be many to that hotel where you are goin' that has any prettier things than you" (83). Maria tries to brush off the compliment, but she herself believes she will be the most dazzling woman at the resort. Although "secretly dazed at the wild extravagance into which she was about to launch . . . a spirit of defiance had suddenly seized her" (86). Bored, though, "with the very sight of all the old articles of furniture, which has heretofore been to her almost like members of the family" (86), she is committed to going. Moreover, she laments the fact that "fate had not provided her" with a more attractive suitor than Dexter. When her friend Emma advises her to simply go on a "fifteen-dollar excursion" to spare expenses, Maria gets more irate and declares that if she had to go "with a rabble," she would prefer staying "at home" (86). And Maria insists that she intends to "take the money out of the bank" (86) because she really needs a change and her nerves are hot. Dexter is willing to take her to the railroad station in his buggy, Maria's arrogance cannot abide that kind of transportation; she opts for a stage-coach, "a relic preserved with pride," which has her tripping and tearing "the hem of her gray mohair" (89). She realizes later that she was in a regular train compartment, but that the wealthy ladies had "all been on Pullman coaches. It had never occurred to Maria to take a Pullman coach" (89). In the mountain wagon to the resort, two young girls appear to be mocking her dress and their mother does not seem to even notice her. Her travel to the hotel, in a stagecoach, then a train, and finally a mountain wagon, already presages the feelings of alienation she will experience in hotel life.

This "mountain" retreat is not the type of natural setting the early Freeman had described in her homey rural stories of New England. This is more like a Wharton setting, where the characters are disrupted by their retreats into ostentatious vacation environments and false relationships. On the first evening at the resort, Freeman's protagonist Maria makes the mistake of wearing a sacque, while all the other ladies wore "low neck gowns" and looked "askance at her sacque" (90). The entire vacation goes from bad to worse, so that Maria learns the meaning of humiliation and humility: she keeps wearing the wrong fashion, the black flies bite her face, the hotel physician is called in to care for her swollen face, and only one woman speaks to her during her first two weeks at the hotel; during the last two weeks, no one speaks: "Maria was, on the whole, more lonely than she had ever been in her life, and she did more thinking" (93). In one of the few happy endings of her more modernist stories of alienation, the main character allows herself to accept her lowly self, as she writes Emma and Dexter in advance about her intention to invite them both over upon her return home. As Emma realizes, her friend has been "eatin' humble pie" (94), and she happily welcomes her home as her future sister-in-law.[4] In the remaining stories I analyze, there is no hint of comic relief.

In "A Guest in Sodom" (1912), Freeman again resorts to a modern pleasure that would give modern man a sense of achievement and pride: this time, not a trip to a resort, but ownership of an automobile. Benjamin Rice sells off much of his land to acquire a car, a mark of prestige. However, the automobile turns out to be a sad excuse of a car, and even though he returns it to a dealer to receive a new one, he is cheated as he discovers it's the same old faulty car. Benjamin subsequently has a stroke, and we hear the narrator/friend, at the very start of the story, saying, "His mind was run over and killed by the machine, if minds can be run over and killed" (148). The surviving family members agree that the purchase of the car was the beginning of the end for the father. His wife argues that it undermined Benjamin's trust in the world: "Findin' out wah an awful wicked place this world he was livin' in was, and what kind of folks there was in it, just broke his heart" (148). Moreover, it was a personal affront to the father's sense of saving: "Poor pa didn't make a god of his money, but he knew the worth of it, through he and his father before him workin' so hard to get a little laid by, and losin' so much was an awful shock to him" (148). The father would save, but in terms of his spoiling the daughter, he "didn't spare money where she was concerned" (148). She was able to attend "the Means Academy in Rockland, and then her father bought a type-writer for her, and she took lessons" (148). Like Narcissa in "One Good Time," he begins to splurge, but the consequences are more grave. He sells his "nine-acre lot" to purchase the car and afterwards even buys a fur coat for himself. His rationale is that he now "wants to have a little fun" before he gets too old, and he complains that he'd never had much except his "board and lodgin'" for all his hard work. The purchase proves to be catastrophic, as Benjamin, who is simple and knows nothing about money, gets taken in by the local swindler, Sammy, who is considered a genius by the townspeople for his clever ways of making money. Sammy, who is an agent for the Verity Automobile Advance Company of Landsville, Kentucky, talks Benjamin into purchasing from that company, even though it is far away and has the dubious distinction of being funded by "The Variable Tea-Kettle Corporation of Vermont." But the con man convinces him that "it's the best car on the market, and there's millions back of it" (151).

From the start, there are problems with the car: it is hard to crank, and Benjamin cannot learn the art of cranking. The car breaks down, and he and his family are stuck in a distant town; though his wife and daughter take the train home, he is forced to walk home to save money as the car purchase and upkeep was exorbitant. He laments to his friend that he has been duped, that he thought the car was made of better steel, and he has an epiphany: "I'm afraid I've thrown my money away, and, worse than that, I'm afraid there is more wickedness in the world than I've ever dreamed of" (153–4). The car is shipped back to Kentucky, with Benjamin footing the bill. A new car is shipped to him within six weeks, but it turns out that they just have sent him the same old car, painted anew. (Evidence was that his wife's lost gold breastpin reappeared mysteriously in the "new car.") Benjamin has a breakdown and what seems to be a stroke, and the doctor attributes his downfall to "progress": "that good, simple man has encountered the deadly juggernaut of progress of the times, and has gone down before it" (157). For the remainder of his life, Benjamin sits in the car every day, with his fur coat on, and with his "shakin' hand on the wheel" (157), as he periodically toots the horn: he believes "he's goin' forty miles an hour" (158). It is a grotesque and horrifying display of consumerism.

Similarly, in the story "The Cloak Also" (1917), a good-natured and kind but too trusting man, Joel Rice, is hoodwinked into being a much too generous merchant. The process is a bit reversed, as Rice doesn't spend money on himself, as in Benjamin's case, but saves for others. It was his childhood dream to own a dry goods store in town: "As a child he had played at keeping store, with a soup-box for a counter and pins for the currency of the realm" (248). But even as a child, his ventures as an entrepreneur prove unsuccessful:

> Even when he had disposed of countless stock of cups, of sweetened water, of bits of broken china gathered from back yards, of green apples and the cores thereof, and his customers had not only defrauded him of pins, but had mocked him . . . he remained sublime in his determination that when he was a man he would "keep store." (248)

The dream of his life was to own "a little retail dry-goods store in a country town" (248). His mother sends him to a nearby business school, and after graduation, he becomes a bookkeeper in a local factory. He marries a local woman, a music teacher, who "brought him enough money to pay off a mortgage on the house." They have a child, and his wife Susan inherits five thousand dollars from an aunt who has died out West. She opens an account in the town bank as she contemplates what to do with the money. Of course, Joel's childhood dreams are awakened, and he talks his wife into using the money to purchase a dry goods store in Racebridge, Maine. The more rational wife is suspicious about his business sense, but allows him his dream to own and run a store, and so they move. When they get to the town, she realizes that the store is seriously lacking: "not one-tenth of it but is out-of-date. It means buying new if there is to be any store. Poor Joel has been cheated, cheated!" (251). He makes a business trip to New York for the spring trade, and he is hoodwinked into buying all the wrong products from the wholesale retailers. More trouble starts when the good-natured Joel allows the local customers to buy on credit, and his life's dream catapults him into an anguished state of poverty. His wife does inherit more money from a distant cousin, which allows him to reinvest with new goods from New York, but he doesn't enforce the pay by cash rule, so he continues to lose money. His wife gives music lessons, and she takes in sewing; Joel turns peddler to make up for his failing business. World War I starts, but they have no time to think of anything besides their impending poverty. Joel does find some comfort in "attributing his failure to succeed, as a peddler of shop-worn and antiquated goods, to the war" (262). One day he invites the townspeople to his store to preach how unchristian they have been in not settling their accounts with him. With much bravado, he exclaims, "You have robbed me of my coat; I have given you my cloak also" (266). He ultimately commits suicide (throwing himself into the river), an act which guilts the town into paying their debts to the surviving widow and child.

In "Sweet-Flowering Perennial" (1915), Freeman presents Mrs Clara Woods, "a middle-aged woman, with nothing to distinguish her from a thousand other middle-aged women" (228). This sense of anonymity and insignificance is common to the later aging Freeman protagonists. We are introduced to Clara at the bank, cashing "one of her modest dividend checks." She is warned by a customer at the bank, a wealthy tenant of the boarding house where she lives, not to return home as several of the young tenants have scarlet fever. Woods considers staying at a hotel ("a quiet hotel for those of her ilk," 228) but chances upon a childhood friend in the bank, someone of a "higher class," who invites her to sojourn with her; Clara recalls that "Selma lived in the suburbs, in a very wealthy town" (231). The lure of staying with her friend in a gorgeous house is great, so she gladly accompanies her. At first, Clare seems thrilled and almost thankful that the scarlet fever made her find refuge there: her bedroom is huge and has a nice view, and she has a luxuriating bath in her own tub, an experience not easily afforded her in her boarding house: "Clara had, though she was commonplace, a love for the beautiful amenities of life, whose lack irritated her" (235). However, the time Clara spends there seems phantasmagoric—as telephone calls seem to interrupt the peace of the household, and Selma is frequently being called away by train to "attend business" in New York to meet with a lawyer; in the end, this type of modernist ghost story has Selma reliving her past love, and Clara trying to make sense of it. Selma apparently is able to seem perennially young in her garden of perennials, and from day to day, she appears to be alternately young and old. Clara tries to make sense of this and believes that Selma can magically transform into the beauty she was as a young woman, or that Selma's niece (Selma's lookalike) is staying with them in a room of her own for several days. Clara finally appears to witness a love scene between the young Southern lawyer, Mr Wheeler, and Selma, and the enamored Wheeler takes his leave when Selma announces that the niece he found so captivating has left. Instead, Wheeler exclaims that Selma must have resembled the niece a great deal in her youth, and there is a strange ghostly embrace between the two, making the reader not sure if this was real or a vision of lost youth: "Clara saw the two make what was apparently an involuntary movement, and Selma had kissed the young man, and he had held her for a second like a lover" (246). All of these modernist Freeman stories present an unfathomable or desperate kind of ending that makes the readers question their own sense of false priorities and pretensions or lament the passing of time.

The striking finality of some of Freeman's later stories in *Edgewater People* (1918) attest to her darkening vision for the fate of mankind, especially in the context of World War I, which brought a type of disillusionment that was adopted by modernist writers. "The Liar" shows a mother's lament that her son, Leon, has joined the popular Barnum and Bailey Circus, ironically labeled "The Greatest Show on Earth." She feels that if anyone knew the truth, it would bring shame to the family, so when her friends come to visit, she always tells them he is fighting in the trenches of France—in order to preserve the family reputation and safeguard his manhood. Leon also cannot abide the thought of remaining in New England, which explains his escape to the traveling circus:

> A little New England village with conservatism in its backbone was not for him. He was alien to it. He could not live in the narrow, monotonous environments and remain true to his instincts. No man who lives contrary to his instincts of life makes a success of living. Small wonder that the boy had fled when that little traveling show had struck its shabby tents in the vacant lot below the house three years ago. (181)

Sounding rather Heminwayesque, the boy decides to escape by finding adventure in war, and thereby also pleasing his mother. He realizes that she would not "make a fuss about my enlisting and going to fight in the trenches, and maybe never set eyes on me . . ." (177). His Uncle Luke advises Leon to enlist as a pilot, as he had done stunts in a plane in the circus. Leon advises his mother that he will make her proud by his enlistment: "your smart son flying an aeroplane, and covering himself with glory thick as eagle feathers, and you as proud as Punch, when he comes home with his coat so covered with badges of honor . . ." (179). The picture he evokes leaves out the real possibility that he might come home in a body bag, but his uncle advises him that going to war is the right thing to do, so as to make the stories that his mother, "the Liar" of the story, told about his bravery true.

The final story in the *Edgewater* collection, "A Retreat to the Goal," offers a strange account about another reconciliation between a mother and a son, although the ending is happier than in "The Liar." The prodigal son of this tale has led an erratic life out in the world, and finally has a hankering to go home. Sounding a lot like a lost Hemingway or Fitzgerald character, the main character John Dunn decides that he cannot live such a lost life with his business comrade any longer. He had been on the "verge of success," but he sees it as an "ill-wrought success" (285). We hear that at the "very threshold the man had turned himself about and beat the most ignominious and most glorious retreat of humanity, the retreat of the sinner from the strongholds and fleshpots of sin" (285). Although he was "hardly past middle-age," he looked old (286). Having no money, he sets off for the countryside, and chances upon his parents' homestead. They don't recognize him, but they take him in to do various chores, work the fields, and manage the father's store. He is deemed a hard worker, and they learn to trust him and make him almost part of the family. It turns out that the mother recognized him early on, but she has waited to tell the family because she wanted him to be worthy of being called son: "I wanted to make sure that my son had come back" (314), and after the revelation scene, he is granted his old bedroom. John takes refuge in his early home and takes on desultory work on a farm that is clearly not impoverished, but not the stuff of urban travelers' fantasies, and the mother's welcome home is a curious form of love and punishment. This is an interesting story with which to end the final Freeman short story collection: it is as if Freeman has some nostalgia for early New England life, even though the twelve stories included in the collection are dark and dismal and belie any such possibility of a homecoming. If Freeman's early stories gave us, now and then, a glimpse of peacefulness, a slight restoration in nature, or a momentary renewed sense of home, her last volume would plunge the returning war-weary hero or aimless traveler into a type of solitary confinement within his mind.

Works Cited

Donovan, Josephine. *New England Local Color Tradition*. New York: Ungar, 1983.

Duvall, John N. "Regionalism in American modernism," *The Cambridge Companion to American Modernism*, edited by Walter Kalaidjian, Cambridge UP, 2005, pp. 242–61.

Elbert, Monika. "The Displacement of Desire: Consumerism and Fetishism in Mary Wilkins Freeman's Fiction." *Legacy*, vol. 19, no. 2, 2002, pp. 192–215.

—. "Mary Wilkins Freeman's Devious Women, *Harper's Bazaar*, and the Rhetoric of Advertising." *Essays in Literature*, vol. 20, no. 2, 1993, pp. 251–72.

Elbert, Monika, and Wendy Ryden. "EcoGothic Disjunctions: Natural and Supernatural Liminality in Sarah Orne Jewett's Haunted Landscapes." *ISLE: Interdisciplinary Studies in Literature and Environment*, vol. 24, no. 3, Summer 2017, pp. 496–513.

Freeman, Mary Wilkins. "The Amethyst Comb." *A New England Nun and Other Stories*, edited by Sandra A. Zagarell, Penguin, 2000, pp. 286–99.

—. "The Balking of Christopher." 1912. *Mary Wilkins Freeman Reader*, edited by Mary R. Reichardt, U of Nebraska P, 1997, pp. 400–13.
—. "The Cloak Also," *Uncollected Stories*, pp. 248–67.
—. *Edgewater People*. Harper & Brothers, 1918.
—. "The Elm-Tree." *Six Trees*. Harper & Brothers, 1903, pp. 3–40.
—. "For the Love of One's Self," *Uncollected Stories*, pp. 106–24.
—. "A Guest in Sodom," *Uncollected Stories*, pp. 148–58.
—. "Humble Pie," *Uncollected Stories*, pp. 82–94.
—. *The Portion of Labor*. Harper & Brothers, 1901.
—. "The Slip of the Leash." *Uncollected Stories*, pp. 95–105.
—. "Sweet-Flowering Perennial." *Uncollected Stories*, pp. 228–47.
—. "Two Old Lovers," *Harper's Bazaar*, March 1883, <https://americanliterature.com/author/mary-e-wilkins-freeman/short-story/two-old-lovers> (last accessed 14 January 2022).
—. *The Uncollected Stories of Mary Wilkins Freeman*, edited by Mary R. Reichardt, UP of Mississippi, 1992.
—. "A Wayfaring Couple." *Utica Weekly Herald*, 26 May 1885, <http/wilkinsfreeman.info/Short, public.wsu.edu/~campbelld/amlit/freeman.htm> (last accessed 14 January 2022), pp. 1–10. Rpt. in *A New England Nun and Other Stories*. Harper & Brothers, 1891.
Glasser, Leah Blatt. *In a Closet Hidden: The Life and Works of Mary E. Wilkins Freeman*. U of Massachusetts P, 1996.
Howard, June. *The Center of the World: Regional Writing and the Puzzles of Place-Time*. Oxford UP, 2018.
—. "Unraveling Regions, Unsettling Periods: Sarah Orne Jewett and American Literary History." *American Literature*, vol. 68, no. 2, June 1996, pp. 365–84.
O'Dea, Dathalinn. "James Joyce the Regionalist: The *Irish Homestead, Dubliners*, and Modernism's Regional Affect." *Modern Fiction Studies*, vol. 63, no. 3, Fall 2017, pp. 475–501.
Reynolds, Guy. "Willa Cather's Case: Region and Reputation." *Regionalism and the Humanities*, edited by Wendy J. Katz and Timothy R. Mahoney, U of Nebraska P, 2008, pp. 79–94.
Ryden, Kent C. *Mapping the Invisible Landscape: Folklore, Writing, and the Sense of Place*. U of Iowa P, 1993.
—. *Sum of the Parts: the mathematics and politics of region, place, and writing*. U of Iowa P, 2011.
Sherman, Sarah Way. "Jewett and the Incorporation of New England: 'The Gray Mills of Farley'." vol. 34, no. 3, Spring, 2002, pp. 191–216.
Storey, Mark. *Rural Fictions, Urban Realities: A Geography of Gilded Age American Literature*. Oxford UP, 2013.
Weir, Julian Alden. *The Factory Village*. 1897. The Metropolitan Museum of Art. New York.
Wharton, Edith. *A Backward Glance*. Charles Scribner's Sons, 1934.
Zagarell, Sandra A. "Troubling Regionalism: Rural Life and the Cosmopolitan Eye in Jewett's *Deephaven*." *American Literary History*, vol. 10, no. 4, Winter, 1998, pp. 639–63.

Notes

1. Edith Wharton, *A Backward Glance*, Charles's Scribner's, 1934, p. 293. Wharton seems to want to make herself seem superior to Freeman and Jewett by focusing on "life as it really was in the derelict mountain villages of New England," as she portrays it in *Ethan Frome* (1911) and in *Summer* (1917). But she seems a little myopic in her assessment, as if she really hasn't read Freeman (or Jewett, for that matter) deeply enough to see the darkness of their country villages.
2. See my essays on rampant consumerism in Freeman's stories: "The Displacement of Desire: Consumerism and Fetishism in Mary Wilkins Freeman's Fiction" and "Mary Wilkins Freeman's Devious Women, *Harper's Bazaar*, and the Rhetoric of Advertising."
3. See also "The Slip of the Leash" (1904), in which Freeman presents a male character, Adam Anderson, who had "lived in one of the far Western States, on a fine farm which he himself had wrested from the wild" (95). He describes his children as being too civilized, as they play piano and play croquet, whereas when he was a boy, he had a more rugged life "playing with a shovel and a hoe in grim earnest for his bread and butter" (95). Craving the experience of being a wild man in nature again, he frees himself from the domestic bonds, at least momentarily.
4. See also Freeman's "The Amethyst Comb" (1914), which could be taken from the pages of Wharton's "Old New York." Miss Jane Crew periodically takes the train to New York to visit her childhood friend, Mrs Viola Longstreet, and to go shopping in the department stores. She is slightly envious of Viola for making a wealthy marriage (albeit to a much older man), and retaining her youthful beauty so that she can draw interesting young men into her circle after her husband's death. She is a kind of merry widow, who delights in overspending on clothes and jewelry and in surrounding herself by the likes of the young fop, Harold Lind, who enjoys the good life and knows something about jewelry. His modernist devil-may-take-it attitude is summed up by his appearance, which seemed to say, "Look at me—I am absurd and happy; look at yourself, also absurd and happy; look at everybody else likewise; look at life—a jest so delicious that it is quite worth one's while dying to be made acquainted with it" (291). He ends up stealing Jane's amethyst comb from her traveling jewelry box to present it as a gift to Viola. Jane is too polite and kind to bring up the theft to her friend, but she quickly leaves and has second thoughts about ever seeing her (and her bad company) again. But Viola eventually has to give up her beautiful domicile and way of life because she was hoodwinked out of her money by types like Harold. As if to return nostalgically to a better more rural homespun past, Freeman has Jane taking Viola in at her simple country home, with the "pine-tree" (ever the source of joy and hope for Freeman) growing outside Viola's room (298).

13

UNDERGROUND INFLUENCE: SYLVIA TOWNSEND WARNER'S PASTICHE OF MARY E. WILKINS FREEMAN

STEPHANIE PALMER

Of course a poet might be influenced by, or could himself or herself influence, a writer one has never heard of and who was not widely read (or read at all), but this would necessarily limit both the interest of the claim of influence and also the pleasure of detecting, or suspecting, echoes and allusions.

Marjorie Garber, "Over the Influence"

Influence thus provides a way of discussing the overtly singular within the plural or universal, and distinguishes instead of relativizes the orders of things.

Mary Orr, *Intertextuality: Debates and Contexts*

Freeman impressed, repelled, and motivated American women writers like Edith Wharton and Kate Chopin.[1] Freeman's influence makes her more important to twentieth-century literature than critics normally account for. These writers' interest in Freeman proves that her accomplishment went underground, but survived, during the period between her death in 1930 and her recovery in the 1970s. Freeman also influenced the British writer Sylvia Townsend Warner. Warner (1893–1978) was active from the 1920s until the 1970s. She is more popular with lesbian and communist enthusiasts than canonical critics of high modernism.

In 1966, Warner published an essay on Freeman, "Item, One Empty House," in *The New Yorker*, a magazine Warner referred to as her "gentleman friend, my regular," a joke that sexualized her economic arrangement with the magazine that benefitted her and her partner Valentine Ackland so decisively (Rattenbury 146). In the more than 150 fictional and nonfictional contributions that Warner made to *The New Yorker* between the 1930s and the 1970s, "Item, One Empty House" is the only piece that discusses an American writer. This singular piece reflects on where sexually nonconforming women writers fit in national literary histories. It offers a theory and model for transatlantic female influence. After using it to demonstrate that Freeman is an important precursor to Warner, I compare Warner's fiction of the 1960s to Freeman's most characteristic fiction of *A New England Nun and Other Stories* (1891), the Freeman volume Warner claims to have picked up by chance, and to Freeman's more sexually explicit story, "Evelina's Garden" (1896).

Working through the theories of influence proposed by Harold Bloom, Sandra Gilbert and Susan Gubar, Rita Bode, and others, I argue that transatlantic female-to-female influence during Warner's era arose out of a choice, rather than an obligation, and was motivated not only by anxiety (although anxiety surely plays a part) but by a wide array of emotions including triumph, nostalgia, rage, and contentment. When it comes to analyzing female-to-female influence, Bloom is partially useful and partially in need of the refinements proposed by feminist scholars. There is a rivalrous, negative element to Freeman's influence over Warner, in that Warner claimed Freeman to reject modernism, self-aware metropolitan culture, the cramped opportunities for single women in the nineteenth century, and Elizabeth Wade White, a romantic rival from Warner's past. Yet there is a reparative, positive element as well, in that Warner affiliated herself with Freeman to celebrate realism and stories of hunger and privation. The key difference between Bloomian influence and progressive female-to-female influence is that Warner rejects not the literary precursor herself but the social conditions under which the precursor had to live and write. In rejecting the precursor and forging her own path, Warner seeks originality for both artistic and social reasons; she works toward an acceptance of a wider variety of sexual and economic activity. The claim of influence grants both authors agency: Freeman because she is strong enough to invite response from later generations, and Warner because she is discerning enough to choose her own precursor. To say that Freeman influenced Warner bequeaths both writers a mantle of greatness, of "classic" status, that they deserve.

Theories of Women's Transatlantic Influence

Many of the critics who have theorized influence lately have mourned its unfashionable status. Andrew Elfenbein avers that "[b]usiness as usual is not advancing knowledge about influence in literary criticism" (506). Elfenbein finds that literary critics have been stuck in Harold Bloom's categories—the ephebe, the strong precursor, the swerve away from one's ancestors, and purgation—even when they do not cite him, and he complains that literary critical discussions of influence often "gesture toward psychological processes that are not made explicit" (482). Marjorie Garber wonders why Bloom closed down further work on influence. Vernon Shetley reminds readers that the negativity of Bloom's model sparked much of the initial reaction against him, including from feminist and African American critics, who posited anxiety-free models of influence for writers in their own traditions. Elfenbein proposes that scholars classify different types of influence according to heuristics empirically tested by psychologists to lead people to reject or accept arguments, including "creating reciprocity, striving for conformity, acceding to authority, [and] maintaining consistency" as well as "demonstrating reactance," the psychological motivation most close to Bloomian influence (495). In other words, influence need not arise out of a state of anxiety. Garber and David Greven separately argue that a theory of influence requires a concept of a unitary canon that literary studies and creative writers have lost. Despite the problems inherent in conducting an influence study in the twenty-first century, though, these critics compellingly argue why the study of influence needs to be kept rigorously in the critical vocabulary.

One of the ways this chapter seeks to keep influence in the critical vocabulary is to refine Gilbert and Gubar's concept of the "female affiliation complex," a concept which they develop in relation to modernist women writers of the same generation as Warner, although Warner is not one of Gilbert and Gubar's examples (165–224). In the "female affiliation complex," modern women writers enjoy a choice between matrilineage and patrilineage because of the newly legitimated literary contributions of their female predecessors. They feel burdened by their matrilineal predecessors even when they choose to self-consciously affiliate themselves with women to escape the binds of patriarchy. Warner demonstrates that she, too, shares a female affiliation complex when she chooses to write about Freeman—except that in Warner's case, there seems to be less of a "complex," of an anxious, warped relation to the predecessor, than Gilbert and Gubar imply.

In another examination of female modernist influence, Cyrena N. Pondrom studies the meaning of the rhetorical act of an overt claim of influence, when a writer *says* she is influenced by another writer. As Pondrom shows, Edith Sitwell wrote in a preface that one of her poems was influenced by Gertrude Stein. Pondrom argues that the singular overt claim is strategic, stemming from Sitwell's feminist determination to render Stein more canonical. Warner's essay is a rhetorical act similar to Sitwell's preface. Warner overtly announces her motivation for reading Freeman and implicitly acknowledges Freeman's influence upon her own work; even though Warner readers can spot other writers who influenced Warner, the overt claim stands. Mary Orr's statement in the epitaph defines influence study (in contradistinction to intertextuality study as performed by Myrto Drizou in this volume) as an analysis that winnows down literary history to a few key contributors. Such a move is assuredly unfashionable these days, and it is one that is often detrimental to writers like Freeman and Warner, who are passed over in favor of others who slot more easily into the canon.

In fact, both writers' reputations have suffered in similar ways. Freeman is assured a place in literary history as a regionalist, but this place is seen as less important than realism or naturalism. Even during her day, as Donna M. Campbell argues, Freeman could not be trusted to produce texts that fit easily into the generic categories that the powerful editor William Dean Howells wanted to cultivate because her work was too symbolic, melodramatic, sentimental, romantic, and at times even exotic; in Campbell's words, Howells considered Freeman an "untrustworthy realist" (115). Similarly, Elizabeth Powers argues that Sylvia Townsend Warner is not considered a classic writer, citing Warner's long career, her indifference to metropolitan self-aware literary culture, and the lack of anyone to carry on Warner's critical legacy through scholarly collections, which are just appearing in the twenty-first century.

The mixture of emotions that Warner felt for Freeman is closely related to the transatlantic crossing. The fact that Freeman is American and Warner is British makes Warner all the more detached from Freeman. Transatlanticism as a paradigm developed in response to earlier models of literary influence which treated US writing as inevitably dependent on its predecessors. In contrast, transatlanticists argue that oceanic crossings involve multi-way traffic, although as Meredith McGill has commented, the critical habit of using transatlanticism to trace the dissemination of British influence has not abated (161–5). Close readings of women's transatlanticisms have offered new models of influence. Scholars have argued that, rather than wrestling with strong precursors, women writers have thought laterally across the Atlantic (in Susan Manning's phrase) and allowed the other side to be different. For example, Rita Bode argues that the lines of influence between Harriet Beecher Stowe and George Eliot are blissful rather than rivalrous; Stowe and Eliot simply reach for similar ideas in their fictions. Stowe and Eliot's correspondence foregrounds their distinct national identities, but "instead of seeing in national separation a divisive barrier, they consistently transform it into a means of explanation and reconciliation for their differences and disagreements" (192). Bode's approach follows from other feminist criticism in positing women's literary relations as free from anxiety, as Shetley attests. To say that women's influence is *entirely* free from anxiety, however, overlooks the rivalry that arose early in the twentieth century when more and more women writers grew ambitious for literary careers (Stout 53). Such rivalries make some of the aggressivity of Bloom's theory of influence newly relevant to female-to-female influence. Rivalry is traceable in Warner's essay about Freeman, to which I will now turn.

"Item, One Empty House"

Warner's "Item, One Empty House," regarded as literary criticism by Freeman critic Shirley Marchalonis and as a story by Warner critic Michael Steinman, is an admiration of Freeman's craft and an imitation of Freeman's short story writing.[2] It demonstrates the breadth of Warner's interest in American literature. Warner submitted the hybrid essay/story to the *New Yorker* in May 1965 (Warner to Maxwell, 27 May 1965). Warner was 71 years old then, and her diary entries express contentment, although she worried about her partner Valentine's ill health, and she suffered occasional bouts of writer's block after the *New Yorker* rejected one of her stories.[3] This was a problem because most of the 1960s Warner-Ackland household income came from this periodical, and Warner's account with the *New Yorker* was overdrawn because she was immersed in writing a biography and unable to produce new fiction.[4] Although it may have been written or dusted off merely to pay the bills, "Item, One Empty House" rewards close scrutiny. It purposefully confuses times and places, as if to dramatize the socially constructed nature of literary critics' ideas about national literatures, literary periods, and literary greatness—questions that were also occupying the emergent feminist literary critics who would soon reissue some of Warner's novels with Virago.

The piece begins when Warner is an awkward and lonely English visitor to a bohemian house party in the farther reaches of Connecticut during Prohibition, where partygoers are purposely international, drinking bootlegged whiskey, and "talking about Joyce and Pound and melting pots" (120).[5] When she retires to her room and sees the moonlight, she writes, "I began to think about Mary Wilkins and to reflect that perhaps at the moment I was the only person in New England to be doing so" (119). The fact that she calls Freeman "Wilkins" might arise out of determination to privilege spinster lives. Indeed, Warner identifies Freeman as a "spinster" in the essay, and she—who in the 1920s was sexually active but unmarried—associates spinsterhood with quaintness and reclusiveness, perhaps timidity, in contradistinction to the decidedly more wicked Maupassant:

> The spinster and the bachelor . . . He would have thought her a quaint character and put her into one of his stories. She would have surmised him to be a bad character and kept him out of any story of hers. (120; ellipses in original)

The moonlit scene is reminiscent of Hawthorne's "The Custom House," and it links Freeman with the romantic literary tradition in New England while turning Freeman into a kind of mad woman in the attic. Warner explains that she had known Freeman for some time because "she was left to read on unassisted," true to Warner's reputation for being a maverick (119). She initially picked up *A New England Nun* on a shelf of miscellaneous books in a spare room in a country house in Cambridge. She noted the absence of a real nun or any "animated lives" but "found something nearer to the bone" (120). Although letters between Warner and her *New Yorker* editor, William Maxwell, make it clear that Warner only added the "E" to Freeman's name as a sop to dictionary rectitude—and hence did not seem to know or care what the "E" stands for—the "E" stands for Eleanor, which was the name of Warner's mother, who did not approve of Sylvia's unconventionally unfeminine childhood and adolescence (Warner to Maxwell, 26 November 1965; Harman 13, 37–8). In this sense, Freeman serves as a kind of non-biological mother for Warner.

In Connecticut, Warner recalled that it was Freeman's control of detail that gives

> these stay-at-home stories a riveting authenticity. The details have the flatness of items in an inventory. Item, one green-handled knife. Item, one strip of matting, worn. They don't express, or symbolize; they exist by being there; they have position, not magnitude. (120)

In this memorable passage, Warner evokes Freeman's realism, the capacity for the details in her stories to signify because they express a certain time and place. Warner singles out a story about "starving on a wintry mountainside" as illustrative of Freeman's "carnality" (121). The detail may refer to the story from the same collection, "A Wayfaring Couple" (1885), in which a laid-off cotton factory operative and his wife wander the countryside looking for work and squat in an abandoned home.

In the 1960s, Warner mourns that her younger self lacked the confidence in her own convictions. She muses that, "if I had had the courage of my convictions downstairs, when everyone was talking about Joyce and Pound and melting pots, I would have said, 'Why don't you think more of Mary Wilkins?'" (120). At the time she was insecure about her grasp of Freeman, afraid that she'd encounter a guest who would "cross-examine my admiration" (121). Under imagined cross-examination, but not necessarily from her own feelings, she finds Freeman an imperfect model:

> And then I should have been forced to admit that she couldn't get to grips with a man unless he was old, eccentric, a solitary, henpecked, psychologically aproned in some way or other; that she never hazarded herself; that she was a poor love hand; that lettuce juice too often flowed through the veins of her characters instead of blood. Though in one respect I would have fought hard for her carnality; she wrote admirably about food, about hunger, about privation, starvation even. (121)

Warner's praise for Freeman is double-sided: she drew sustenance from Freeman's belief in the dignity of the quiet life and her ability to render it large and meaningful through marketable literary fiction. True to Warner's own Communist sympathies, she lauds Freeman's focus on hunger and privation. At the same time, Warner contributes to a larger argument that Wilkins's stories are sexually repressed and therefore must be relegated to the nineteenth century.

With her humorous characterization of the cocktail conversation about "Joyce and Pound and melting pots," Warner distinguishes herself and Freeman from metropolitan modernism, which she sees as male, parrot-like, and oblivious to questions of social justice. The remark conveys an anxious literary rivalry in which a white woman writer expresses nervousness about multiculturalism. Here, Warner might be interpreted as saying that the Americans should focus on the problems suffered by their own people instead of accepting immigrants or worrying about James Joyce, both of which would be illiberal sentiments. I argue though that the essay as a whole, as well as Warner's life record, imply that it is fashions, not foreigners, which should be avoided, in favor of socially conscious realism, rather than whiteness per se.

Warner reports that she woke up in the morning after that horrible whiskey evening and took a walk. Somewhat implausibly, a short distance away from the fine home of her hosts is a singular house, "a frame house of two stories, lean and high-shouldered, standing a little back from the roadside. It had an air of obstinacy asserting its verticality against the indifferent, snow-covered horizontality all around" (122). It looked empty and forsaken, with grey paint scaling off it and streaks of damp. A week ago or more someone had left footprints in the snow that suggested an entry into the house and no exit. The detail suggests that the someone might still be in the house, and perhaps Warner should check to make sure the person is all right. Warner is just an observer, though, and she remains loitering unobtrusively outside. Warner's evocation of this house serves as a pastiche of a Freeman story of deprivation and loneliness. The essay concludes, "I had come on a story by Mary Wilkins—a story she did not finish" (122).

This pastiche of a Freeman story seems significant. Warner's essay mourns that Freeman's achievement has not been recognized. The essay suggests, rather like feminist literary critics would soon do, that the works of Freeman were unfinished, under-read, and overflowing with new ideas and voices. Whereas male literary historians had been busy relegating Freeman to the nineteenth century, a time of prudery and known, cramped achievements, Warner implies that Freeman's accomplishment was somehow unfinished. The comment opens Freeman's fiction to new analysis. It invites readers to read her oeuvre beyond the most anthologized stories, for example. The comment about a story Freeman did not finish calls to mind the tension between the middle of Freeman's stories and the endings. Although it would be wrong to overgeneralize, the middles of Freeman's stories touch on subversive possibilities, while the endings often tie together plot threads in marriage or other conventional methods of closure.

This strategy is common among nineteenth-century women writers, who hid the subversive nature of their fiction beneath conventional overplots (Harris 30–5).

When Warner backs away from the decrepit house, she concedes Freeman's fictional territory and returns to her own. This is a tactful and considerate expression of sisterhood. Present-day feminists often view expressions of sisterhood with caution, because they can overlook shades of difference between authors. Warner's epigrammatic essay seems, though, like a viable model for a rhetorical claim of transnational female affiliation. She does not erase the class difference between herself, the daughter of a schoolmaster at a prestigious private school, and Freeman, the daughter of a failed artisan. Nor does she attempt to override national and local peculiarities and claim more knowledge of New England than she actually has. She does not cross the boundary, but walks up to it, makes a thoughtful encounter with a like-minded author of her choosing, and returns to her own side.

Rejection

In "Item, One Empty House," Warner rejects many things: the fad for modernist abstraction, the old-fashioned definition of a spinster, and romantic betrayal. But she does not detract from Freeman's achievement. Marchand argues that Wharton's rewriting of Freeman does not reject Freeman per se but the women's culture which Freeman represented in Wharton's mind ("Cross Talk"). Something similar happens with Warner's rewriting of Freeman. Warner's rejection of various aspects of literary culture makes Bloom's theory of "purgation" relevant. In purgation, a writer purges outdated or difficult-to-achieve aspects of a precursor's work and hence truncates not only the precursor, but also the writer's self, and in the process, curtails himself as he slips near to solipsism (Bloom 115–38).[6] "Purgation" is an obscene term, and one unfortunate in the case of a writer like Freeman, who was purged from the canon during the Cold War era, like other female and sexually nonconforming writers. Suffice it to say that Warner sifts and separates the elements that intrigue her about Freeman and literary culture and rejects some of them.

By affiliating herself with Freeman instead of Joyce and Pound and melting pots, Warner affiliated herself with realism, not modernist abstraction, even though her own realism in *Lolly Willowes* (1926) and *Mr. Fortune's Maggot* (1927) is mixed with fantasy elements. While other celebrated British novelists of the 1920s were realists, like E. M. Forster and Mary Webb, modernism was clearly becoming more fashionable.[7]

It was as if Warner chose Freeman to let even her "gentleman friend" the *New Yorker* know that despite her multiple tangled financial connections to the United States, she would choose her artistic connections. A letter from Warner's *New Yorker* editor, William Maxwell, remarks that Freeman carried no positive cachet in the United States in the 1960s: "Sarah Orne Jewett is read, though not ravenously, but Mrs. Wilkins is, as you say, not" (Maxwell). In the essay, in order to highlight the affiliation between Freeman and herself, Warner exaggerates her own meekness and smallness. During her 1929 trip to the United States, Warner was 35 years old and had enjoyed an independent income for some time; first she scraped by as a co-editor of the ten-volume compilation *Tudor Church Music*, and next she earned money from publishing a volume of poetry and three novels. Much of this income came from American sources, since *Tudor Church Music* was funded by a grant from the Carnegie Foundation, and her novels earned her more royalties from American than British sales (Harman 85). The *Herald Tribune* invited Warner to New York as a guest critic, and the New York literati treated her as a celebrity (Harman 84). It was in New York that Warner first met an upper-middle-class American from Middlebury, Connecticut—Elizabeth Wade White.

Soon after this trip to New York, in October 1930, Warner became lovers with Valentine Ackland, in a supportive, passionate relationship that lasted until Valentine's death in 1969. Elizabeth Wade White came to visit Sylvia and Valentine in 1935, and Elizabeth became lovers with Valentine from 1938 to 1939 and again in the 1940s. Sylvia's "marriage" with Valentine was an open arrangement in which Valentine took other lovers, but Valentine's relationship with Elizabeth nearly tore Sylvia and Valentine apart. Sylvia deeply mourned the prospective loss of Valentine and grew furious at Elizabeth's constant pleading for Valentine to move to America.

Letters attest to the intimacy and trust Sylvia developed with Elizabeth: "I am leaving New York tonight and I feel that I am leaving, not a city, but, a friend," Sylvia wrote, in March 1929.[8] In the same letter, she expressed excitement about her eagerly anticipated trip to New England, where Elizabeth had her roots, of which she was deeply proud:

> I must just send for a line before I go to say that I have set foot in New England. Not very far in: only the wooded country round Westport. But that has been enough to show me how well-loved a countryside it must be. I saw it under snow: with the squirrels looping from bough to bough, dislodging a powder of tiny icicles.

Westport, Connecticut in the 1920s was already shifting from an agricultural and manufacturing economy to becoming a suburban destination for New York's artistic set. Despite this, the letter codes Westport as rural New England. The landscape matches the landscape under snow described in the 1966 essay. Other letters to Elizabeth Wade White in the Warner archives and in the collection, *The Akeing Heart*, edited by Peter Judd, attest to the passionate friendship between Sylvia and Elizabeth; Elizabeth was Sylvia's protégé; Sylvia worked hard to convince Elizabeth to trust her inner moral compass more than her conservative upper-middle-class parents and pursue her intellectual ambitions and sexual inclinations. Sylvia wrote to Elizabeth's mother that Elizabeth was rejecting her [Freemanesque] "Puritan conscience" (Warner to Mary White 164). Despite Sylvia's best efforts to respond to the love triangle with tolerance, however, she felt violated. New England once meant "Elizabeth Wade White" to Warner. Hence, the region held sharply negative associations. By rewriting New England as the home of Freeman, Warner reopens a scarred-over wound and heals it for good. Thus, there is anxiety behind Warner's rhetorical claim of being influenced by Freeman, but it is not the anxiety of Freeman's influence in the classic sense of that term. Warner claimed Freeman to reject White.

Affiliation

The Warner-Freeman connection contains many strands, which are not only reactive. There are artistic affinities between Freeman and Warner, and readers acquainted with both can read intertextually to see what Freeman might have become had she lived in a freer era. Both writers value the physical and material. Both mix the realist aesthetic with other techniques. Both are masters at the short story form, beginning and ending abruptly, *suggesting* rather than saying outright, and securing attention and illuminating character through physical detail. What Glen Cavaliero said of Warner is often equally true of Freeman: both writers have a "tart, unjudging awareness of the quirks and perversities of human nature" and "a feeling for the long littleness of life and a flair for making its dissection entertaining" (45). In their stories about humble, often humiliated people, there is both humor and pathos (Camfield).

In their novels and short stories, Freeman and Warner depict the fierce and only sometimes constructive energy behind the seemingly meek exteriors of humble male or female characters. Rather than idealize narrowness, both writers mourn the isolation or pettiness of small lives. Although both writers are limited in their representations of racial others, they largely detached themselves from nationalist master narratives of Americanism or Anglocentrism by parodying imperialist or patriarchal wills to power. Lolly of Warner's bestselling 1926 novel *Lolly Willowes*, who becomes a witch to escape meddling family members, resembles Freeman's spinster heroines. Although the novel received prominent attention in the United States, there is no evidence that Freeman read it, as to the best of our knowledge, she avoided new fiction in her final years. Because Warner's lesbian relationship with Ackland is well documented, Warner critics have speculated whether the witch in *Lolly Willowes* signifies lesbianism. Gay Wachman argues that the witch signifies differently, as "celibate contentment" (78). Celibate contentment with undercurrents of non-normative desire is certainly one of Freeman's key themes. The Reverend Timothy Fortune, the anti-hero of Warner's novel *Mr. Fortune's Maggot*, experiences a crisis of faith concerning the holiness of his life work similar to that undergone by Betsey Dole about her poetry in Freeman's "A Poetess" (1890); after becoming a missionary on a Polynesian island, Fortune discovers his only convert secretly worships pagan gods. Guy Stoat of Warner's "The View of Rome" (1962) recalls the sisters Charlotte and Harriet Shattuck of Freeman's "A Mistaken Charity" (1883) in that out of desperation to get home from the County Hospital, he concocts a story for the nosy nurses about a step-niece named Hattie who will spend the winter with him, when he actually longs to go home to a life of solitude with a cat named Hattie.

Warner's "A Love Match" (1964) echoes Freeman's short stories in its quiet, unsensationalist style and its exploration of closeted transgressive relationships experienced by secretly strong women. "A Love Match" is a droll story of brother-sister incest that goes undetected by the English villagers of Hallowby. The relationship between Celia and Justin Tizard begins when Justin is on leave from the Battle of the Somme, suffering from shell shock. Celia comforts him, they embrace, and make love. It is Celia, three years Justin's senior, who first identifies the relationship as "good": "'Now we've done it,' he said; and hearing the new note in his voice she replied, 'A good thing, don't you think?'" (105). Celia also takes the lead in deciding to return to England from France, choosing a home, and composing the couple's public face for their judgmental neighbors; she prevents the neighbors from thinking her a "dangerous woman" (110) by raising money for charity at their parties. Celia's leadership happens only behind closed doors, however; the neighbors consider Justin the head of the household. It is only in private that the couple, "safe within their brick wall, cast off their weeds of middle age, laughed, chattered and kissed with an intensified delight in their scandalous immunity from blame" (110). The quiet village unsuspecting of the perverse drama in their midst, respectable characters enjoying a quiet revolt, and the queer possibilities behind veneers of middle-aged village folk are reminiscent of Freeman's tales of defiance. Both Freeman and Warner can be said to be engaged in what Gay Wachman calls "crosswriting," when lesbian writers explore lesbian relationships in the guise of other transgressive relationships.

"A Love Match," like many of Warner's stories from the 1960s, touches on anxieties about aging, one of Freeman's major topics. Sexually active women were supposed to be young, according to the British as well as the North Americans. Celia's leadership role in the Tizard marriage ends when poison letters arrive claiming to know about the true nature of her relationship with Justin. The letters "taunt Celia with being ugly, ageing and sexually ridiculous" and they rip "through her self-control and made her cry with mortification" (116). Justin hypothesizes correctly that the letters are from the young neighbor Mary Semple, who has been propositioning a rather bewildered Justin behind Celia's back. The experience prompts the couple to change: "on that Sunday morning the balance between Justin and Celia had shifted, and never returned to its former adjustment" (120). Celia insists that Justin take the lead and make decisions, while she herself "became slightly frivolous, forgetful and timid" (120). She gains weight and begins to enjoy pick-me-up holidays. A neighbor notices and assumes that Celia is going through the Change and feels sorry, not for Celia, but for "poor Mr. Tizard" because "the Change wasn't a thing that a brother should be expected to deal with" (120). As the bombs of World War II begin to drop, the conventional villagers consider Celia a silly old woman while Justin is still a hot number. Warner's interest in aging women might have reignited her interest in Freeman.

Warner wrote that "lettuce juice too often flowed through the veins of [Freeman's] characters instead of blood" (121), and one can spot Warner's comparable willingness to consider the sexual dimension of her characters' quest for independence and fulfillment. Yet in her rejection of lettuce juice flowing through the veins of Freeman's characters, Warner overlooks moments in Freeman's fiction where desire, even sexual desire, is broached. Warner's reading of Freeman is incomplete, then. Even in networks of female, queer affiliation, writers misuse and misconstrue each other, and my reading of "Evelina's Garden" demonstrates how. This story, I argue, reveals sexual desire in an encoded, "cross-writing" way.

Like "A Love Match," "Evelina's Garden" features a garden wall—in this case, a "high arbor-vitae hedge" poorly tended by an irresponsible English gardener who lets it grow too high for the taste of the nosy neighbors (155). Behind this hedge, carrying out their passions in secret, live the aging Evelina Adams and her young first cousin once removed, Evelina Leonard. After a rejection by a suitor, Evelina Adams channels her life energy into tending her lovely garden and spending her winters distilling flower petals into perfumes. The image of the garden is a familiar image from Freeman's fiction of the culture that women were encouraged to cultivate, viewed ambivalently both as a prelapsarian feminine realm apart from patriarchal culture or New Womanhood, and a cramped realm of obsession and wasted energy: "The roses and pinks, the poppies and heart's ease, were to this maiden-woman, who had innocently and helplessly outgrown her maiden heart, in the place of all the loves of life which she had missed" (162).[9] When Evelina Adams dies, her will stipulates that the young Evelina must tend the garden faithfully and remain a spinster or be cut off from her inheritance. Evelina's suitor with an overweening Puritan conscience breaks off the engagement so that Evelina can continue to live in prosperity. Frustrated at his mistaken rectitude, Evelina sneaks out during a moonlit night to ruin the garden, in a fit that exemplifies the strength and resourcefulness hidden beneath her girlhood and meekness, as well as Freeman's droll manner of combining mimesis with hyperbole and tall tale:

> But at one o'clock in the morning young Evelina stole softly down the stairs with her lighted candle, and passed through into the kitchen; and

> a half-hour after she came forth into the garden, which lay in full moonlight, and she had in her hand a steaming kettle; and she passed around among the shrubs and watered them, and white cloud of steam rose around them . . . And then she set to work and tore up the roots with her little hands and trampled with her little feet all the beautiful tender flower-beds; all the time weeping, and moaning softly: "Poor Cousin Evelina!" (190–1)

The boiling water is salted and kills the shrubs decisively. The parataxis adds understatement and a casual tone to what is actually a violent destruction of the garden as a vehicle for the sublimation of sexuality. Now Evelina and Thomas Merriam are free to wed. In an odd plot development, a codicil in Evelina Adams's will ensures that Evelina Leonard will keep the house so long as she marries Thomas Merriam, so the story's moral quandary dematerializes: "Evelina's Garden" has one of Freeman's overly neat endings that defuses tumultuous energies. In addition to the beautiful garden and the overly neat ending, several elements in the story are familiar to readers of Freeman: there is a mother-daughter conflict as in "Louisa" (1890) or *Pembroke* (1894), and a series of misunderstandings between courting characters as in "Amanda and Love" (1890). What is striking about this story is that the violent ruination of the garden hints at the depth and seriousness of Evelina's desire to wed. Freeman treats this desire not as sexual desire per se but as desire for matrimony, which she links to women's generational, biological destiny: Evelina "looked up in his face with her blue eyes, through which the love of the whole race of loving women from which she had sprung, as well as her own, seemed to look" (191). Evelina is coded as white in this passage, a coding that might disqualify her from having sexual passion in the conventional thinking of Freeman's generation. But the passion involved in destroying the garden suggests a passion that is not merely obedient to the calls of past generations. Lettuce juice does not flow through Evelina Leonard's veins.

Against conventional notions of career-mindedness, Sylvia Townsend Warner affiliated herself with Freeman in 1966, just before feminist literary criticism became a keyword on university campuses, and decades before Warner's own work would receive the kind of scholarly attention granted to writers of critical acclaim. Given that Freeman was American and forgotten and Warner was British and still present, this decision was paradigmatically a choice rather than a family obligation, an affiliation, rather than an inheritance.[10] It was a choice that seems refreshingly free of anxiety, or of what Gilbert and Gubar call an affiliation "complex," in that Warner read whatever she wanted to and developed the courage of her own conviction to not only read in private but discuss in public her appreciation for Freeman's realism and writing about hunger, privation, and carnality. Freeman's influence over Warner is a case of influence that overturns

Bloom's and Gilbert and Gubar's focus on anxiety as the canonical psychological motivation. Warner rejected significant things when she mulled over her affiliation for Freeman: a romantic rival, unhelpful literary fashions, the *New Yorker*'s hold over her finances and sense of self as a writer, and the Victorian comparable silence around matters of sexuality. But she did not reject Freeman herself or Freeman's accomplishment. For Warner, Freeman maintains her reputation for being a spinster, but the word is associated with depth and breadth of experience. Warner's appreciation might be just one of the underground manifestations of Freeman during the early Cold War era which are worthy of further exploration. Like Warner, readers can affiliate themselves with Freeman today, for her short story prowess, her intriguing cross-writing, or her stubborn feminisms, recalling earlier readings, and devising new ones, without necessarily claiming a family resemblance to themselves or their nation.

Works Cited

Bingham, Frances. *Valentine Ackland: A Transgressive Life*. Handheld P, 2021.

Bloom, Harold. *The Anxiety of Influence: A Theory of Poetry*. Oxford UP, 1973.

Bode, Rita. "Belonging, Longing, and the Exile State in Harriet Beecher Stowe and George Eliot." *Transatlantic Women: Nineteenth-Century American Women Writers and Great Britain*, edited by Beth L. Lueck, Brigitte Bailey, and Lucinda L. Damon-Bach, U of New Hampshire P, 2012, pp. 188–208.

Camfield, Gregg. "'I Never Saw Anything at Once So Pathetic and Funny': Humor in the Stories of Mary Wilkins Freeman." *American Transcendental Quarterly*, vol. 13, no. 3, 1999, pp. 215–31.

Campbell, Donna M. "Howells' Untrustworthy Realist: Mary Wilkins Freeman." *American Literary Realism, 1870–1910*, vol. 38, no. 2, 2006, pp. 115–31.

Cavaliero, Glen. "The Short Stories." *PN Review*, vol. 8, no. 3, 1981, p. 45.

Donovan, Josephine. "Silence or Capitulation: Prepatriarchal 'Mothers' Gardens' in Jewett and Freeman." *Studies in Short Fiction*, vol. 23, no. 1, 1986, pp. 43–8.

Elbert, Monika M. "The Displacement of Desire: Consumerism and Fetishism in Mary Wilkins Freeman's Fiction." *Legacy*, vol. 19, no. 2, 2002, pp. 192–215.

Elfenbein, Andrew. "On the Discrimination of Influences." *Modern Language Quarterly*, vol. 69, no. 4, 2008, pp. 481–508.

Freeman, Mary E. Wilkins. "Amanda and Love." *A New England Nun and Other Stories*, Harper & Brothers, 1891, pp. 288–304.

—. "Evelina's Garden." *A Mary Wilkins Freeman Reader*, edited by Mary R. Reichardt, U of Nebraska P, 1997, pp. 155–93.

—. "Louisa." *A New England Nun and Other Stories*, edited by Sandra A. Zagarell, Penguin, 2000, pp. 48–63.

—. "A Mistaken Charity." *A New England Nun and Other Stories*, edited by Sandra A. Zagarell, Penguin, 2000, pp. 11–21.

—. *A New England Nun and Other Stories*. Harper & Brothers, 1891.

—. *Pembroke*. Northeastern UP, 2002.

—. "A Poetess." *A New England Nun and Other Stories*, edited by Sandra A. Zagarell, Penguin, 2000, pp. 34–47.

Garber, Marjorie. "Under the Influence." *Critical Inquiry*, vol. 42, no. 4, 2016, pp. 731–59.
Gilbert, Sandra M. and Susan Gubar. *No Man's Land: The Place of the Women Writer in the Twentieth Century, Volume I: The War of the Words*. Yale UP, 1988.
Greven, David. "Introduction: Hawthorne and Influence: Reframing Tradition." *Nathaniel Hawthorne Review*, vol. 42, no. 1, 2016, pp. 1–15.
Harman, Claire. *Sylvia Townsend Warner: A Biography*. Minerva P, 1991.
Harris, Susan K. *Nineteenth-Century American Women's Novels: Interpretative Strategies*. Cambridge UP, 1990.
Hogg, Emily J., and Clara Jones. Introduction. *Influence and Inheritance in Feminist English Studies*, edited by Hogg and Jones, Palgrave Macmillan, 2015, pp. 1–9.
James, David. "Realism, Late Modernist Abstraction, and Sylvia Townsend Warner's Fictions of Impersonality." *Modernism/Modernity*, vol. 12, no. 1, 2005, pp. 111–31.
Judd, Peter Haring. *The Akeing Heart: Passionate Attachments and Their Aftermath: Sylvia Townsend Warner, Valentine Ackland, and Elizabeth Wade White*. Peter Haring Judd, 2012.
McGill, Meredith. "Contribution to Roundtable on *Poetics of Character: Transatlantic Encounters 1700–1900* by Susan Manning." *Journal of American Studies*, vol. 49, no. 1, 2015, pp. 161–5.
Mann, Susan Garland. "Gardening as 'Women's Culture' in Mary E. Wilkins Freeman's Short Fiction." *New England Quarterly*, vol. 71, no. 1, 1998, pp. 33–53.
Manning, Susan. *Poetics of Character*. Cambridge UP, 2013.
Marchand, Mary V. "Cross Talk: Edith Wharton and the New England Women Regionalists." *Women's Studies: An Interdisciplinary Journal*, vol. 30, no. 3, 2001, pp. 369–95.
—. "Death to Lady Bountiful: Women and Reform in Edith Wharton's *The Fruit of the Tree*." *Legacy*, vol. 18, no. 1, 2001, pp. 65–78.
Maxwell, William. Letter to Sylvia Townsend Warner, 26 July 1965, transcription by Michael Warner, Sylvia Townsend Warner Archive, Dorset History Centre, STW.2012.125.0691. Quoted with the permission of the *New Yorker*.
Menke, Pamela Glenn. "The Catalyst of Color and Women's Regional Writing: *At Fault, Pembroke*, and *The Awakening*." *Southern Quarterly*, vol. 37, no. 3–4, 1999, pp. 9–20.
Orr, Mary. *Intertextuality: Debates and Contexts*. Polity, 2003.
Pondrom, Cyrena N. "Influence? or Intertextuality? The Complicated Connection of Edith Sitwell with Gertrude Stein." *Influence and Intertextuality in Literary History*, edited by Jay Clayton and Eric Rothstein, U of Wisconsin P, 1991, pp. 204–18.
Powers, Elizabeth. "On Situating Sylvia Townsend Warner: How (Not) to Become a 'Classic' Writer." *Yale Review*, vol. 104, no. 4, October 2016, pp. 88–100.
Rattenbury, Arnold. "Plain Heart, Light Tether." *PN Review*, vol. 8, no. 3, 1981, pp. 46–8.
Shetley, Vernon. "Negative Influence." *Genre*, vol. 45, no. 1, 2012, pp. 195–213.
Steinman, Michael. Afterword, *The Music at Long Verney: Twenty Stories*, by Sylvia Townsend Warner, Harvill P, 2001, pp. 189–93.
Stout, Janice. "Starting from Rome: Literary Rivalry, Dorothy Canfield, and Willa Cather's Death Comes for the Archbishop." *Studies in American Fiction*, vol. 43, no. 1, 2016, pp. 51–72.
Wachman, Gay. *Lesbian Empire: Radical Crosswriting in the Twenties*. Rutgers UP, 2001.
Waid, Candace. *Edith Wharton's Letters from the Underworld: Fictions of Women and Writing*. U of North Carolina P, 1991.

Warner, Sylvia Townsend. *The Diaries of Sylvia Townsend Warner*, edited by Claire Harman, Chatto and Windus, 1994.

—. "Item, One Empty House," *Critical Essays on Mary Wilkins Freeman*, edited by Shirley Marchalonis, G. K. Hall, 1991, pp. 118–122. Also rpt. in Warner, *The Music at Long Verney: Twenty Stories*, edited by Michael Steinman, Harvill P, 2001, pp. 149–56.

—. Letter to William Maxwell, 27 May 1965, transcription by Michael Warner, Sylvia Townsend Warner Archives, Dorset History Centre, STW.2012.125.0691.

—. Letter to William Maxwell, 26 November 1965, transcription by Michael Warner, Sylvia Townsend Warner Archives, Dorset History Centre, STW.2021.125.0691.

—. Letter to Elizabeth Wade White, 1 March 1929, Sylvia Townsend Warner Archives, Dorset History Centre, STW.2012.125.0082. Copyright Sylvia Townsend Warner Estate.

—. Letter to Mary White, 19 November 1938. *The Akeing Heart: Passionate Attachments and Their Aftermath: Sylvia Townsend Warner, Valentine Ackland, and Elizabeth Wade White*, pp. 163–4.

—. *Lolly Willowes*. Penguin, 2020.

—. "A Love Match." *A Stranger with a Bag and Other Stories*. Faber and Faber, 2011, pp. 94–122.

—. *Mr. Fortune's Maggot*. Virago, 1978.

—. "The View of Rome." *A Stranger with a Bag and Other Stories*. Faber and Faber, 2011, pp. 135–50.

Notes

1. Candace Waid, Pamela Glenn Menke, and Mary V. Marchand are only a few of the critics who have uncovered Freeman's influence on these writers. Waid's *Edith Wharton's Letters from the Underworld* (92–121) departs from Wharton's well-known comments about Freeman and Jewett being her "predecessors" by arguing that Freeman and Wharton engaged in sibling rivalry, in that both Freeman and Wharton were associated in their day with realistic, dark, and iconoclastic readings of New England. Memorably, Waid reads intertextual echoes between two texts from 1905 that feature women named Lily who are subjected to male sexual violence, Wharton's *The House of Mirth* and Freeman's "Old Woman Magoun." In "Cross Talk," Mary V. Marchand argues that Wharton was not ambivalent about Freeman but about the women's culture her work symbolizes. In "Death to Lady Bountiful," Marchand reads Wharton's *The Fruit of the Tree* (1907) as a reaction against a tradition of women's fiction that delineates middle-class women's roles in industrial reform. Although Marchand includes Freeman's *The Portion of Labor* (1901) in that tradition, Justin Rogers-Cooper and Laura Dawkins show in this volume how uneasy a fit this is. Menke argues that Chopin's development between her novels *At Fault* (1890) and *The Awakening* (1899) is linked to her admiration for Freeman's *Pembroke* (1894).
2. Marchalonis implicitly treats the piece as literary criticism by including it in an anthology of literary criticism. Steinman identifies the piece as a "story" (193).
3. Valentine Ackland's breast cancer was not diagnosed until 1968, but she suffered from various ailments earlier in the 1960s (Bingham 256–7).

4. Harman 265–73. Warner wrote wryly about aging at this time as well. In March 1961, she wrote in her diary, "how shabby and displumed I have let myself become, I have *consented* to becoming" (Warner, *Diaries* 272, her italics). In April 1964, she wrote, "It is not N.Y. who are the task masters: but age and failing powers, and rising expenses" (Warner, *Diaries* 291).
5. All page numbers to "Item, One Empty House" refer to the Marchalonis edition.
6. Although both precursor and ephebe are female in this essay, and their femininity is an important aspect of the argument, Bloom's theory is so masculine that I hesitate to change the gender pronoun of his schema.
7. David James argues that Warner's novels of the 1930s (written just after her trip to New England in 1929) participate in a larger return to realist aesthetics among British women writers intent on revivifying narrative mimesis to critique contemporary social oppression. His compelling argument suggests that Warner's ruminations about Freeman's realism in the moonlit room of 1929 was part of important new developments in British women's fiction.
8. This letter is quoted with permission, copyright The Sylvia Townsend Warner Estate.
9. On the garden as a feminine realm, see Donovan and Mann. On women's culture as a site of obsession and cramped lives, see Elbert.
10. Emily J. Hogg and Clara Jones have recently critiqued the notions of "inheritance" and mother-daughter generational relationships from a feminist perspective, arguing that the notions overinvest the past with too much unity, which makes it difficult to criticize the mother writer, and excludes some women from the canon.

14

UNTIMELY FREEMAN

CÉCILE ROUDEAU

> The contemporary is the untimely.
> Roland Barthes, *Lectures at the Collège de France 1979–80*,
> quoted in Agamben.

Dates matter. Born in 1852 in Randolph, Massachusetts, Mary E. Wilkins Freeman was a woman and a writer of her time and age. A housebuilder's daughter, she grew up in a divided country, lived and worked through Reconstruction America, and died a celebrated writer, while the United States and the world were confronted with the disastrous results of capitalism gone wild. As this collection of essays has shown, Freeman also responded to the spirit of her time; her stories and novels register the social upheavals brought about by rapid industrialization, the changes in women's lives and gender relations, the rise of xenophobia in a new imperialist age, the trauma of war, again, in the early twentieth century, and the philosophical questioning of the stability of the self under the assault of modernism. Freeman, that is, needs to be read "in time."[1]

But Freeman's texts are also responding to the pressures of our present. Uncannily so. What would it mean, this chapter asks, to read Freeman out of time? To free her, and us, from the bonds of nineteenth-century epistemologies, and let her texts "speak back" to us and resonate with our own concerns, however anachronistically? Jennifer Fleissner, in her essay "Historicism Blues," has pointed to the failings of one version of "historicism" that affirms above all "the *pastness* of the past—its inability to speak back to the present-day position that organizes it" (702). Such a card has been played again and again;

from Fred Lewis Pattee to Perry D. Westbrook, early critics have largely contributed to attaching Freeman to a place, New England, itself the epitome of a past that was no more. On the other hand, a forced contemporaneousness has also taken its toll on nineteenth-century literature. Presentism, as Fleissner and others have observed, has its own pitfalls, one of them being to turn the past into a mere foil to our enlightened present, as if the past existed only "in order to irradiate the virtues of the present" (Fleissner 702). This version of teleological thinking is "a methodologically untenable presumption" (Coviello 13) that would exhaust what happens in Freeman's texts—diegetically, poetically, philosophically—in the discourses that are ours today. This is *not* what "Untimely Freeman" proposes.

By focusing on the untimeliness of Freeman, this chapter stakes out a third position: somewhere between, on the one hand, the injunction to historicize, and *only* historicize, and, on the other, the lures of a colonizing presentism that appropriates a text for the benefits of our time only. Reading Freeman as untimely pressures the linearity of our modes of reading the nineteenth century. It entreats us to focus on the staggered and the inchoate; not so much on how the text might be a harbinger, a proto-text, of our present, as on the "unforeclosed possibilities" that would (or would not) come to be and may have disappeared from view.[2] Reading Freeman as untimely means reading her works from our present—what else can we do?—without ever taking our present as the only heuristic pivot. It invites us to meet her *as if* she were our contemporary, and by contemporariness we understand, with Agamben, "*that relationship with time that adheres to it through a disjunction and an anachronism*" (41). The key here lies in the "as if condition,"[3] the back-and-forth movement between, and within, our present and hers, which is also the condition of empathy. Reading Freeman as untimely, then, that is—reading her "now" as always out of joint—allows her present and ours to meet in an unsettled and unsettling contemporariness, a shared *productive* dischrony and a form of empathy *through time*.

Starting from this unstable juncture of temporalities, this chapter considers two of Freeman's late turn-of-the-century collections of animal and plant stories, *Understudies* (1901) and *Six Trees* (1903), and reads them neither as the end point of her critical regionalism, nor as precursors of what we—inhabitants of a post-Enlightenment natureculture—have learned, but rather as fictional forays into alternative "distribution(s) of the sensible" (Rancière) that have not yet come to pass. Both collections, I argue, unsettle the forceful historical continuity and epistemological arc that, we were taught, culminate in our binary ontologies (animals vs. humans). Instead, they propose to twenty-first-century readers uncanny continuities generative of vibrant demarcations and queer fictional oddkins that pressure our understanding of her—and our—heuristic tools and a prioris.

Uncanny Continuities

In 1901, Harper & Brothers published *Understudies*, a collection of stories that may be best introduced by looking at the cover of the first edition—adorned with six cameo portraits linked by garlands. In the center, a name stands in golden letters, Mary E. Wilkins. The profiles, however, are not those of angry spinsters, narrow-minded ministers, or miserly farmers that had been so common in her stories up to that time. Rather, readers are witness to a different set of protagonists—a horse, a dog, a parrot, a monkey, a squirrel, and a cat—understudies, all of them, if we believe the title chosen for this collection.[4] Mimicking "the arrangement of actors' head shots on a playbill," as noted by Susan Griffin in one of the few scholarly readings of this collection (511), the cover may have come as a surprise to the many fans of Wilkins's tales and romances.

True enough, *Understudies* does not quite fit into Freeman's oeuvre—at least, at first sight. Apart from a recent critical interest in this collection as her "first volume of ecofiction" (Dixon 166), it has remained, perhaps in accordance with its title, backstage. These studies are, however, only deceptively marginal, and not at all picturesquely outmoded. I read them instead as Freeman's testing ground for a radical shift from essentialization to performance, from the belief in a self-bounded identity to a "relational epistemology" in which knowledge of "self"and "others" starts with and as relation.[5] Not only do the stories partly strip humans of their hegemony as social—and narrative—agents; they also sidestep our ingrained anthropological dualisms, nature/culture, human/nonhuman, without necessarily eroding the boundaries between them. If they "speak back" to us, then they do so from a present that is not ours yet uncannily continuous with it; as such they open up our present to a new contemporaneousness that however precludes any coincidence—of ourselves with ourselves, of themselves with themselves. And they do so by hijacking us into the world of fiction. Thus begins "The Cat":

> The snow was falling, and the Cat's fur was stiffly pointed with it, but he was imperturbable . . . It was night—but that made no difference—all times were as one to the Cat when he was in wait for prey. Then, too, he was under no constraint of human will, for he was living alone that winter . . . He was quite free except for his own desires, which tyrannized over him when unsatisfied as now. ("The Cat" 3)

Entering the world of fiction, not unlike entering the world of the theater, implies that we willingly suspend our disbelief, in this case, that we divest ourselves of what French anthropologist Philippe Descola calls our "naturalism" and shift to "animism." In *Beyond Nature and Culture* (2005), Descola defines naturalism as the belief in a radical discontinuity of interiorities between the

Figure 14.1 Front cover of *Understudies*, 1901. Image courtesy of Thompson Library Charvat American Fiction Stacks, Thompson Library Special Collections, The Ohio State University Libraries.

human and the nonhuman, combined with an acknowledgment of a continuity between our physicalities. Conversely, animism is the belief in a continuity of interiorities (here the "desires" nagging the Cat, his sense of freedom) and a discontinuity of physicalities (here, the bristling "fur"). In order to develop an animal narrative, Freeman's *Understudies* tap into the possibilities of animism; she bets on the continuity of interiorities between animals and humans to accommodate the mental and experiential scheme of non-Western modes of identification that are not so much *past* ontologies as *alternative* ways of distributing the sensible in the present.

In Freeman's "The Cat," the Cat is the hunter, providing fresh food to the ailing stranger "with yellow hands like yellow claws" (10). Once the Cat has brought the prey to the old man, the narration creates a non-intuitive yet potent structure of feeling between them both:

> *both the man and the Cat* looked wolfish . . . When the rabbit was half cooked, *neither the man nor the Cat* could wait any longer. The man took it from the fire, divided it exactly in halves, gave the Cat one, and took the other himself. Then *they* ate. (11–12, my emphasis)

Freeman does not merely anthropomorphize the Cat. She only deceptively takes up the trappings of the old-time fables or Elizabethan allegories à la Ben Jonson. As readers, we do *not* encounter ourselves as specimens of the human condition in an animal guise; what we encounter is the possibility of an encounter with "others" that are fictionally revealed to live and think and feel in continuity with ourselves. The adverb "both," or, further down, the pair "neither . . . nor" put the man and the cat on the same footing; they are impatient together—"wolfish," adds the narration, as if mischievously pointing to a third term that is less a term than a blurry and blurring qualification. Turned into equals, "they" then eat—one subject, however plural.

The love story between the man and the Cat, which is played while the Master is away and the Cat serves as his understudy, does not turn the Cat into a human, though. Not quite. Freeman does not fall back on the autobiographical formula, that of Anna Sewell's *Black Beauty: The Autobiography of a Horse* (1877) and others. By assimilating animal psychology to that of humans, these animal autobiographies persisted in colonizing the other, making the other fit in the highly self-centered scheme of the autobiographical genre. The challenge of Freeman's *Understudies* is instead to find a form that allows for *another* story to be told *together with* the human plot. This other non (hetero-) normative story takes place outside the village and in the Master's absence, between the acts, as it were, before the curtain is raised again on the world as we know it.

Upon the return of the Master to his home and property, the plot is indeed resumed. The Master and the Cat must be reacquainted like an old couple who has seen better days, and it is pathetic; "[t]he Cat had his bird to himself, for his master had his own supper already cooking on the stove" (15). Queer suffixes have yielded to the law of separation—the raw and the cooked, the animal and the human, and the last sentence of the story tells as much: "he and the Cat looked at each other across that impassable barrier of silence which has been set between man and beast from the creation of the world" (16). This clausula sounds like a provocation. The sudden resurgence of the biblical injunction of absolute separation between the human and the nonhuman does not quite fit into the diegetic arc of a tale that has gone very far, maybe too far, in the reshuffling of categories. As often, in Freeman, the ending of the tale disappointingly caters to the expectations of the most conservative readers. "The Cat" is no exception. Yet, something is amiss:

> But the tobacco was gone; not a dust left . . . Suddenly many features struck [the Master] as being changed. Another stove lid was broken; an old piece of carpet was tacked up over a window to keep out the cold; his fire-wood was gone. He looked, and there was no oil left in his can. (15–16)

Between the acts, something has happened, the trace of which bears no easy explanation. What is missing is the trace of another story, another temporality, and another performance of the present—that of the Cat and his lover—which Freeman's understudies can accommodate, without entirely being able to integrate it in the weaving of the tale. Freeman's animism pluralizes the present. Ontologies with a deeper history continue to carry their own efficacy into the tale's unsettled "now"—Freeman's and ours.[6]

Another of Freeman's understudies, the sixth and last of her animal tales, also proposes a shift in ontological regimes, an unsettling of binary epistemologies—animal vs. human. In "The Doctor's Horse," the reader of regionalist sketches, from Sarah Orne Jewett to Elizabeth Stuart Phelps, will easily recognize the figure of the country doctor on his daily rounds. Freeman's story, however, would not be much of a story if one focused on the figure of the doctor only. The doctor's life—we learn it from the horse's mouth—is no storied life. Nor is the horse's for that matter:

> The horse seemed to live his life in a perfect monotony of identical chapters . . . The same stall, the same measure of oats, the same allotment of hay . . . All the variation which came to his experience was the uncertainty as to the night calls. ("The Horse" 88)

In order for a story to emerge that is *not* the insipid story of the doctor nor that of the domesticated animal, something must happen. What happens, in Freeman's tale, is a shift in ontological regimes, dramatized as the sudden capacity of the animal, first described as one who "had no disturbing memories, and no anticipations" (88), to know and remember who he is. Put differently, the horse evolves into an individualized consciousness aware of itself as continuous through time—into a historical self, that is.

To take neuroscientist and philosopher Antonio Damasio's terms, fiction, the possibility of fiction, is indexed on this transition from "core" to "extended consciousness"—i.e. from a consciousness that provides the organism with a sense of self here and now to a consciousness that encompasses "the organism's past and its anticipated future" (3). And not only is the story made possible *because* of this transition, fiction also *performs* this transition with its own tools.

One day, as the doctor's niece sits in the doctor's buggy, the horse, sensing a "current of terror behind him," suddenly feels as if an electric current were "firing his blood" (92). Granted, the narration's vocabulary is here reminiscent of evolutionary discourse—the horse reacts in accordance with his race and becomes what he should never have stopped being: a fiery undomesticated colt. Another lexicon, however, emerges—that of knowledge and consciousness: "At last he knew, by her terrified recognition of it, his own sovereignty of liberty ... He was again himself—what he had been when he first awoke to a consciousness of existence ... He was no longer the doctor's horse, but his own" (93–4). No longer an animal with neither memories nor anticipation, the horse acknowledges the continuity of his self and the consciousness of his existence as a historical being. Has the tale gone too far? It may well be.

"The Doctor's Horse" soon reverts to a more acceptable conclusion. By courtesy of fiction, the doctor, grown old, buys the same old horse. "He did not know him first," says the narration, but when the horse stops where they always used to stop, the doctor remembers: "The doctor stared at him. Then he got out and went to the animal's head, and man and horse recognized each other" (96). He who had forgotten, whose consciousness had been discontinuous enough not to know his old companion can suddenly reconnect with his youth and former self. Unlike the horse, who knew him from the start, the doctor needs the face-to-face encounter to regain an extended consciousness of himself. The tale ends with this moment of recognition that also heralds a backward move to the initial dynamics between man and beast, master and servant:

> He was once more the master, in the presence of that which he had mastered. But the horse was expressed in body and spirit only by the lines of utter yielding and patience and submission. He was again the doctor's horse. (96)

Not unlike the conclusion of "The Cat," the tale comes full circle—almost, that is. For something has happened in between; a story has developed, a story of a life—a horse's life—made possible, within the conventions of the genre of the story, by the acknowledgment of the horse's extended consciousness. The title of the story gives us a clue. "The Doctor's Horse" is neither the story of the Doctor nor exactly the story of the Horse, but the story of a relation that verges on interdependence, or "intra-action." In "The Doctor's Horse," neither the doctor nor the horse's identities are stabilized at the beginning of the tale; they emerge in and as relations, until in the end, disappointingly perhaps, both acknowledge their relative and relational selves—as master, as servant.

There are, of course, other ways of reading Freeman's understudies. "The Doctor's Horse," for one, reads like a failed emancipation story; the analogies with slavery—the mention of "unbreakable chains of servitude" (87), of "the assertion of freedom"(92)—are hidden in plain sight. The emergence of the relational selves of master and servant also signifies within the immediate context of its publication, the imperialistic turn of US national policy inaugurated by the Spanish-American War and the Philippine-American War.[7]

We should not be surprised, then, that at a time when magazines voiced the concerns of many about encountering others and other selves, Freeman, however obliquely, chose to change the templates and the coordinates of her regionalist tales accordingly. Adopting the perspective of anthropology and psychology in her turn-of-the century fiction was a way to try to come to terms with the broader issue of the existence, or not, of a continuum of interiorities that would radically challenge the geopolitical order, the imperialistic partition of the sensible. In "The Philippine Question" (1899), psychologist William James proposed: "If ever there was a situation to be handled psychologically, it was this one—We have treated the Filipinos as if they were a painted picture, an amount of mere matter in our way. They are too remote from us ever to be realized as they exist in their inwardness" (159). Freeman's *Understudies*, I suggest, uses the tools of fiction to do just that: it inquires into the other's inwardness and, betting on the continuity of interiorities that is at the heart of non-Western ontologies, handles the question "psychologically," as she herself admits in a letter to her editor,[8] as her fellow anthropologists and philosophers tried to do at the time, and as today's cognitivists, neuroscientists, and anthropologists also do. Her turn-of-the-century tales prompt us to pay attention, not only to (subjected) others, but to other modes of consciousness at large that fiction as a privileged means of encounter can best articulate.

In *Understudies*, Freeman's uncanny continuities ask that we accept the unreliability of our contours, the performativity of our "identities," and the untimeliness of the present itself that allows the deeper time of non-Western ontologies to seep into, and pluralize, the "now." Entering this world demands that we understand ourselves as co-agents in the relation between us and those who are no longer simply, and wrongly, referred to as "them." Her next collection, *Six Trees*, goes even further. It trades the ontological cut for a continuity with variations.

Vibrant Demarcations

About halfway through *Six Trees*, the narrative voice boldly asks:

> Who shall determine the limit at which the intimate connection and reciprocal influence of all forms of visible creation upon one another may stop? <u>A man</u> may *cut down* <u>a tree</u> and *plant* one. Who knows what effect <u>the tree</u> may have upon <u>the man</u>, to his *raising* or *undoing*? ("The Great Pine," 79–80, my emphasis)

Some readers have recognized here one of the last symptoms of Swedenborg's theory of correspondences, or a late transcendentalist penchant in Freeman's writing. And rightly so.[9] Reading Freeman as untimely, however, invites us to disjoin her questioning from her present, and let her meet ours. To do so it suffices to take her at her word, that is, to let her words do their office. Freeman's question is more than a formulaic device. Her text does what it does not yet dare say it does—figuratively and diegetically. Figuratively, the double chiastic structures interveave man and tree, and create a logical bond between the cutting down of a tree and the undoing of man, and conversely the raising of man with the planting of a tree. As such, the narration lexically performs the "intimate connection and reciprocal influence" between man and tree that it pretends to offer as a mere hypothesis—something that also comes to pass diegetically. The plot, indeed, turns the great pine of the tale into the transformative force whereby an irresponsible sailor (who has left his wife and family to see the world) becomes a caring community healer. A narrative agent, the tree changes the man's heart and ethical stance at the cost of its—or, shall we say, like Freeman, "his"—own life.

Freeman's question cuts through the pith of her book and opens an interpretive rift right at its center: we are asked to situate ourselves where the limit is, at the very place of connection between human and tree, and read from this unstable, if vibrant, demarcation. In other words, the text itself requires that we should dis-inhabit our narrative comfort zone on *one* side of "the impassable barrier" between species; that we shoot our readers' roots in the messy terrains resisting classification.

This is *not*, however, how the stories were received at the time of their publication. Cut the trees, the critics suggested, or at least cut them off the narration as so many disposable, even obstructive elements: "With all deference to the admirable technique of the author," wrote Eleanor Hoyt in *The Lamp* in 1903, "one feels that there is too much tree in her landscape" (253). *The Spectator* concurred: "We cannot help thinking that these six 'short stories' would be better, or a least as good, *without* the six trees" (Anon. 23). The trees, or so it seems, are a hindrance, at least an embarrassment.

No wonder the illustrators of the book version also chose to downplay the trees' importance. The frontispiece is a case in point, which shows the sailor of "The Great Pine," aghast in a Gothic chiaroscuro, confronting the consumptive bedridden man that has replaced him and the trembling children huddled in a corner. No tree whatsoever, not a branch, not even a leaf. But why? Why capitalize on the well-known melodramas of domestic life, when the trees beg for recognition? Why did the editorial *mise en scène* minimize, or even minoritize, them? In 1995, Shirley Marchalonis, who unearthed this collection of stories, also cast some doubt on the "intimate connection" between humans and trees, arguing that these "stories are not 'about' the Natural Other, but about people . . . what they do is widen the world Freeman writes about without changing the human predicaments she explores."[10]

True enough, despite promising titles and incipits using gendered personifications, the animistic beginning leaves the stage to the all-too-familiar regionalist tale: in "The Elm Tree," a destitute old man resists the selectmen who have decided to "uproot" him in the name of the welfare of the community; in "The White Birch," a rich old bachelor decides to marry a young money-grabbing girl, only to be jilted in the end. The trees may indeed appear as baits to catch our gullible attention, and the paratext and the story frame as yet another guise for an old story. I want however to time our reading differently, and consider Freeman's stories not from the perspective of her short-lived human characters, but from that of the deeper temporality of trees.

Reading from the tree's perspective requires that we revisit the old story that the tree frames, and allow it to be diffracted by its (non-human) paratext. What emerges when we do so is first a gradual transfer of agency from characters to trees. After all, it is the eponymous "elm-tree" that saves David Ransom from the violence of the selectmen. Once sheltered in the foliage, the old man is "inexpressibly changed" (33). By dint of a passive voice, agency has shifted from man to tree; or more accurately, the human (character) is now defined through his relationship to what is no longer, and maybe never was, an "Other."

What we might have taken to be a late manifestation of anthropomorphism is revealed to be one part of a two-part drama, where the becoming-human of the tree is balanced with the becoming-tree of the human. *Six Trees* does more than allocate possibilities for selfhood across the species boundary, like in "The Doctor's Horse"—what David Herman has called a "narratology beyond the human." The collection stands as a warning against an obsolete epistemic, and semiotic, regime based on the fallacious givenness of the differential categories of human and nonhuman. Here, trees and humans talk, and think, and feel, with and through the "other." The ending of "The Birch-Tree" may serve as an illustration.

Old Joseph Lynn, who has eventually decided to let go of his young lover, comes to sit under, or rather, *with* the tree:

> the silvery shimmer of the birches and their white gleam of *limb* caught his eye . . . the solitary birch which had been bereft of her sisters was very

near. He flung himself down beside her, and leaned against *her frail swaying body*, and felt *her silvery skin against his cheek*. ("The Birch-Tree" 64, my emphasis)

What we are witnessing here is not just another version of a regionalist critique that allows the "other" to look back, and gives some agency to those relegated to the margins. We may even suggest that reading these stories through the lens of 1990s feminist readings of Freeman has prevented us from attending to other modalities of critique. Reading against the grain of earlier criticism, even as we don't consign it to the dustbin of history, is a move that Freeman's late collections in particular invite us to do.

The end of "The White Birch" inquires into "other ways of being that might emerge from transmaterial"—and I would add cross-species—"affections" (Chen and Luciano 186). Categories "rub on and against each other, generating friction and leakage" (186), companion species dance cheek to cheek. The text concludes: "He loved the girl as he had never loved her before" (64–5). The girl? Which girl? Sarah, the lover that he lost to his younger rival? or the lonely white birch who stands so close to him, also referred to as "her"? The somehow hackneyed phrasing finds itself revitalized and destabilized by the shifting

Figure 14.2 "The White Birch." *Six Trees*, 1903. Image courtesy of Thompson Library Charvat American Fiction Stacks, Thompson Library Special Collections, The Ohio State University Libraries.

system of referentiation; the text prolongs the indeterminacy as much as it can, and toys with this emergent continuity between humans and . . . human trees, a continuity that only dismisses difference to conjure it up again as variation. Man and tree touch, and the body of the one responds to the swaying body of the other as the sibilants join the two in an erotic textual dance. But what do they say?

One of the problems addressed by anthropologist Eduardo Kohn is that no matter how hard posthumanist studies try to sidestep the anthropological binarisms of human/nonhuman, *because* nonhumans are devoid of linguistic abilities and capacities for symbolism, they will always be the passive objects of human cognition. One of Kohn's solutions, then, is to downplay the symbolic function of the sign and focus rather on its iconic and indexical value, something he borrows from Charles Sanders Peirce, a contemporary of Freeman. Monkeys know, Kohn notes, that when a tree crashes, it means—indexically—that they have to leave in haste: "Significance is not the exclusive province of humans because we are not the only ones who interpret signs . . . representation exists in the world beyond human minds and human systems of meaning" (Kohn 31). A more embracing semiosis brings together humans and other life forms. The beginning of "The Great Pine" offers an illustration of such enlarged semiosis.

> It was in the summer-time that the great pine sang his loudest song of winter, for always the voice of the tree seemed to arouse in the listener a realization of that which was past and to come, rather than of the present . . . The man who lay beneath the tree had much uncultivated imagination, and, though hampered by exceeding ignorance, he yet saw and heard that which was beyond mere observation . . . He did not know that he heard the voice of the tree and not his own thought, so did the personality of the great pine mingle with his own. ("The Great Pine" 69–71)

The tree's song—outside the linguistic realm—is not devoid of meaning. The man understands it, as if it were his own voice talking to him. The man is dumb, so is the tree which, unlike the horse, or even the cat of *Understudies*, "cannot project itself beyond its own existence to judge of it" (73). However, a message has traveled from tree to man—maybe through the mediation of the bird, casting a glance at the human figure "from an eye like a point of bright intelligence" (71)—a bird who, if we believe Kohn, has made the most of the indexical signs delivered by the tree and passed them on to the more vulnerable and weaker form of life—man that is. At the end of the story, Dick goes back to the mountain, a redeemed man, only to find the pine lying prostrate on the ground. Has he been able to read, on his way, what the text calls the "ice-*mailed* branches" of the trees (98, my emphasis)? We will never know. What we know, however, is that a larger semiosis than the one we humans have been confined to has done its office. The tree has transformed the human, at the expense of his own life. Reading *with* the trees of Freeman's book has forced us to read outside our narrative comfort zone, and invited us to share with her forest if not a language, at least an ensemble of significant signals—the "nodding" of leaves, the gleam of a white branch, the "rocking" of a bough—of which we have learned to make sense.

For the Runa of the Amazonian forest, Kohn explains, "all beings, and not just humans, engage with the world and with each other as selves—that is, as beings that have a point of view" (132). What Freeman's *Six Trees* teaches us is to engage with the leafy world of trees as selves indeed, yet not as the protectively bounded selves that we have inherited from our engrained dualisms. Paradoxically, then, the more sustainable selves—David, Dick, and Joseph—may well be those that accept some level of porosity, some quivering of their own borders, "the intimate connection with and reciprocal influence of" other selves. In between Freeman's leaves, there vibrate the premises, or the dream, both untimely, of a community of contingent and volatile selves—not so much a community, then, as a commons born of singular encounters, or combinations, *across* species.

Queer Assemblages, or Freeman's Oddkin

Staying with the trouble requires making oddkin; that is, we require each other in unexpected collaborations and combinations.
Donna J. Haraway, *Staying with the Trouble.*

Freeman's *Six Trees* takes stock of the age of extinction and deforestation that was as much hers as it is ours. In "The White Birch," the birch trees were a family, but only one sister has survived; "The Balsam Fir" takes place at Christmastime, a dire time for trees, while the beginning of "The Lombardy Poplar" resumes the same lamento, "Now they were all gone, except this one, the last of the sons of the tree" (131). In a context of devastation, when "families" and genealogies are going extinct, new forms of kinship need be reinvented. Freeman's *Six Trees* poignantly "speaks back" to us, as we read into her bold fictional oddkins a future that may not yet have come to pass.

"The White Birch" projects us into the spectral temporality of embodied loss, a disjuncted present that both vibrates with a deadly past and repeats the postcript that is our "now." Tree-kinship, as described in the incipit of the tale, relies on proximity and entanglement—what the devastated and lonely present is precisely missing.

> At one time the birch-tree had *sisters*, and they stood *close together* in sun and wind and rain, in winter and summer. Their pretty, graceful limbs were *intertwined*; their rustling leaves were so *intermingled* that

> one could not tell to which they belonged; . . . But all her sisters were gone; one or two had died of themselves, the others had been lopped down by the woodsman, and there was only the one white birch left. ("The White Birch" 43, my emphasis)

The elegy, however, soon yields to more uncanny developments: what the "tree alone" endures is less separation than a spectral embodied connexion beyond death.

> The white birch felt always, *as a man will feel a missing limb*, the old spread of the others' branches, the wind, and rain, and the sun in them. She never fairly knew that she was alone, that her sisters were not there. When the snows of winter fell, she felt them, soft and cool and sheltering, *weighing down her sisters' limbs as well as her own*; when the spring rain came, there was not a young leaf of the trees which were gone but was evident to her *consciousness* . . . (44–5, my emphasis)

An extension of the phantom limb syndrome that affected so many Civil War soldiers, the tree alone can feel what her dead sisters (would) feel.

Trees, scientists have recently shown, communicate through root systems that "intersect and grow into one another," with the help of fungi that "act as intermediaries to guarantee quick dissemination of news" (Wohlleben 10). But after they have died? To say it with Peter Coviello, Freeman, here, allows us to uncover "broken-off, uncreated futures" (20), something that science has not (yet?) unearthed—a postmortem kinship that prolongs the loving entanglement of sister trees well into the age of the Anthropocene. In that sense, our present is indeed haunted by "the ghost of future pasts" (Coviello 15), those "errant possibilities" of Freeman's present that have not yet come to pass. But these possibilities, in Freeman's time, were already both contemporaneous with her and redolent of a "premodern" "nonindividuated form of being" (Bentley 169).[11] Freeman's untimely present, then, meets ours, and recasts our "now" as irreducibly heterogeneous and open.

The postmortem kinship that opens "The White Birch" allows for more radical cross-species affections, still. As we have seen, the heteronormative plot—the marriage of old Joseph to young Sarah—will not obtain. Sarah will marry Harry—Harry Wyman ("why man" or "women," we will never know)— leaving the reader unsure about the reproductive futurity of this union. Joseph, on the other hand, will make up for the loss of Sarah with the birch tree he already loves, a love which, to take up Donna J. Haraway's words, "is a historical aberration."

> We are, constitutively, companion species. We make each other up, in the flesh. Significantly other to each other, in specific difference, we signify

in the flesh a nasty developmental infection called love. This love is a historical aberration and a natureculture legacy. (*When Species Meet* 16)

"The White Birch" is the story of this legacy that speaks back to us as an errant future possibility, distinct from the heteronormative plot—an oddkin, indeed. That Freeman's stories resist the heteronormative story is old news. But the alternative that *Six Trees* proposes is not. When Joseph decides to turn away from his fellow humans in order to hook up with . . . a tree, something goes amiss in the system that we call the world.

"The Lombardy Poplar," another story of extinction, also tells of the need to craft new forms of kinship. But this time the rewriting of the romantic plot verges on comedy. Starting with the dire observation that the Lombardy poplars are "all gone," except for one, "the last of the sons of the trees," the narration immediately pairs this with human history. Sarah Dunn is herself "the last of her" family. Sarah and Marah Dunn were twins. Marah died. And Sarah Dunn became closer to her cousin, also called Sarah Dunn and looking very much like her. There starts the comedy. "The Lombardy Poplar" is a tale of sameness and difference, a tale about how to order and classify amidst the confusion created by "unexpected collaborations and combinations." In botanical terms, the story raises the question of how to measure variation, how to draw lines between species.

Sarah and Cousin Sarah's first disagreement starts with the "popple-tree." While Sarah has a special tenderness for it—"it seems like my own folks, and I can't help it" (145)—Cousin Sarah regards such affection as sacrilegious. How can a tree replace a human? All the more so when the tree, *that* tree, does not even look like a tree: "It ain't a tree. It's a stick tryin' to look like one" (147). "That's why I like it," answers Sarah. "I'm sick of things and folks that are just like everything and everybody else. I'm sick of trees that are just trees. I like one that ain't" (148–9). The violence of Cousin Sarah is significant. She cannot deal with a tree that does not belong to any species, nor category, a tree that is one of its kind. She cannot understand Sarah's "'goin' on so queer'" (151), and taking risks indeed when she decides that her family, her kinship, no longer defines her.

> She was a creature of as strong race-ties as the tree. All her kin were dear to her, and the cousin had been the dearest after the death of her sister. She felt as if part of herself had been cut away, leaving a bitter ache of vacancy, and yet a proud self-sufficiency was over her. She could exist and hold her head high in the world without her kindred, as well as the poplar, the last. (154–5)

At the moment when whole species go extinct, when trees lose their kins and are turned into solitary units, or loners, Sarah shifts allegiances, and turns from her human kin to her "popple" oddkin; letting go of the advantages (and constraints) of a community of similarities, she chooses not to abide by the law of the category, and ally with a tree "that ain't a tree," so as to be free to be a woman that also isn't just a woman. "The Lombardy Poplar" ends with Sarah's coming out, her extravagant red outfit serving as a sign that she no longer belongs to the Dunn family as defined by the law of strict similarities, but is "a Dunn apart" (165). Sarah has not renounced *any* kinship; she has crafted her own, she has chosen her companion species—the "popple" that she loves.

"Making kin as oddkin rather than, or at least in addition to, godkin and genealogical and biogenetic family troubles important matters," writes Haraway. "What must be cut and what must be tied if multispecies flourishing on earth, including human and other-than-human beings in kinship, are to have a chance?" (*When Species Meet* 2) Freeman leaves us, and "them," whoever they are, that chance. *This* is her untimeliness. *Understudies* and *Six Trees* will give us no straightforward answers to the pending questions that are ours. As fictions of the early 1900s, they tell us neither of a world gone by, nor of a future, our present, of which they would be the harbingers. Rooted in a place, Freeman's New England, and in a time, the turn into the twentieth century, they uncannily echo the voice speaking at the opening of another fiction, written in another turbulent time, ours: "That's the trouble with people, their root problem," murmurs the voice that introduces Richard Powers's *The Overstory* (4). Against essentialisms and rooted selves, Freeman entreats us to listen to another story, and read her otherwise. Not unlike the voice that resonates in Powers's prelude, Freeman's texts sing to us: "If your mind were only a slightly greener thing, we'd drown you in meaning . . . Listen. There's something you need to hear" (Powers 4). Paying attention to Freeman's volatile selves and oddkins neither brings us *back* to a pre-modern episteme nor projects us into a desirable utopia; her fictional propositions are unforeclosed possibilities that open our present (reading) to broken-off futures and suspended designs. In that sense, she is our contemporary *because* she is untimely. Because her "now" is always out of joint, her present and ours may meet, time and again, in the staggered dischrony that we happily share.

Works Cited

Agamben, Georgio. "What is the Contemporary?" *What is an Apparatus, and Other Essays*. Translated by David Kishik and Stefan Pedatella, Stanford UP, 2009.

Alaimo, Stacy. *Undomesticated Ground: Recasting Nature as Feminist Space*. Cornell UP, 2000.

Anon. "Six Trees." *The Spectator*, 18 April 1903, p. 23.

Barad, Karen. *Meeting the Universe Halfway*. Duke UP, 2007.

Bentley, Nancy. "Clannishness: Jewett, Zitkala-Ša." *American Literary History*, vol. 31, no. 2, 2019, pp. 161–18.

Chen, Mel Y., and Dana Luciano. "Has Queer Ever Been Human?" *Queer Inhumanisms, GLQ*, vol. 2–3, 2015, pp. 183–207.

Coviello, Peter. *Tomorrow's Parties. Sex and the Untimely in Nineteenth-Century America*. NYU Press, 2013.
Damasio, Antonio, and Kaspar Meyer. "Consciousness: An Overview of the Phenomenon and of its Possible Neural Basis." *The Neurology of Consciousness: Cognitive Neuroscience and Neuropathology*, edited by S. Laureys and G. Tononi, Academic Press, 2009, pp. 3–14.
Descola, Philippe. *Beyond Nature and Culture*. 2005. Chicago UP, 2013.
Dixon, Terrell F. "Nature, Gender, and Community: Mary Wilkin's Freeman's Ecofiction." *Beyond Nature Writing: Expanding the Boundaries of Ecocriticism*, edited by Karla Armbruster, and Kathleen R. Wallace, UVA Press, 2001, pp. 162–76.
Fetterley, Judith, and Marjorie Pryse. *Writing Out of Place: Regionalism, Women, and American Literary Culture*. U of Illinois P, 2003.
Fleissner, Jennifer. "Historicism Blues." *American Literary History*, vol. 25, no. 4, 2013, pp. 699–717.
Freeman, Mary E. Wilkins. "The Balsam Fir." *Six Trees*. Harper & Brothers, 1903, pp. 101–27.
—. "The Cat." *Understudies*. Harper & Brothers, 1901, pp. 1–16.
—. "The Doctor's Horse." *Understudies*, pp. 83–96.
—. "The Elm-Tree." *Six Trees*, pp. 1–40.
—. "The Great Pine." *Six Trees*, pp. 67–99.
—. "The Lombardy Poplar." *Six Trees*, pp. 129–67.
—. "The White Birch." *Six Trees*, pp. 41–67.
—. "Letter to Harper's, 6 October 1900." *The Infant Sphinx: Collected Letters of Mary E. Wilkins Freeman*, edited by Brent L. Kendrick, Scarecrow Press, 1985, p. 244.
Griffin, Susan. "*Understudies*: Miming the Human." *PMLA*, vol. 124, no. 2, 2009, pp. 511–19.
Haraway, Donna J. *Staying with the Trouble: Making Kin in the Chtulucene*. Duke UP, 2016.
—. *When Species Meet*. U of Minnesota P, 2007.
Herman, David. "Narratology Beyond the Human: Storytelling and Animal Life." *Diegesis*, vol. 3, no. 2, 2014, pp. 131–43.
Hoyt, Eleanor. "Six Trees." *The Lamp*, vol. 26, 1903, p. 253.
James, William. "The Philippine Question (1899)." *Essays, Comments and Reviews*, vol. 15. Harvard UP, 1987.
Jewett, Sarah Orne. "The Foreigner." *Atlantic Monthly*, vol. 86, no. 514, 1900, pp. 152–67.
Kendrick, Brent L., ed. *The Infant Sphinx: Collected Letters of Mary E. Wilkins Freeman*. Scarecrow Press, 1985.
Kohn, Eduardo. *How Forests Think*. U of California Press, 2013.
Kuiken, Vesna. "Idiorrhythmic Regionality, or How to Live Together in Sarah Orne Jewett's *Country of the Pointed Firs*." *Arizona Quarterly*, vol. 74, no. 3, 2018, pp. 87–118.
Marchalonis, Shirley. "Another Mary Wilkins Freeman: *Understudies* and *Six Trees*." *ATQ*, vol. 9, no. 2, 1995, pp. 89–101.
Miller, Cristanne. *Reading in Time: Dickinson in the Nineteenth Century*, U of Massachusetts P, 2012.
Pattee, Fred Lewis. *A History of American Literature Since 1870*, D. Appleton-Century Company, 1915.

Powers, Richard. *The Overstory: A Novel*. Norton, 2016.
Rancière, Jacques. *The Politics of Aesthetics: The Distribution of the Sensible*. Translated by Gabriel Rockhill, Mansell Publishing, 2004.
Rogers, Carl R. "A Theory of Therapy, Personality and Interpersonal Relationships, as Developed in the Client-Centered Framework." *Psychology: A Study of a Science*. McGraw-Hill, 1959, pp. 184–256.
Roudeau, Cécile. "'Like Islands in the Sea': Intermingled Consciousness and the Politics of the Self in Sarah Orne Jewett's Late Stories." *William James Studies*, vol. 13, no. 2, 2017, pp. 190–216.
Sewell, Anna. *Black Beauty: The Autobiography of a Horse*. Jarrolds and Sons, 1877.
Stone, Susan M. "'A Woman's Place': The Transcendental Realism of Mary Wilkins Freeman." *Towards a Female Genealogy of Transcendentalism*, edited by Phyllis Cole, and Jana Argersinger, U of Georgia P, 2014, p. 377–98.
Walsh, Rebecca. "Sugar, Sex, and Empire: Sarah Orne Jewett's 'The Foreigner' and the Spanish-American War." *A Concise Companion to American Studies*, edited by John Carlos Rowe, Wiley-Blackwell, 2019, pp. 303–19.
Westbrook, Perry D. *Acres of Flint: Writers of Rural New England, 1870–1900*. Scarecrow P, 1951.
Wohlleben, Peter. *The Hidden Life of Trees*. William Collins, 2017.
Zagarell, Sandra A. "*Country*'s Portrayal of Community and the Exclusion of Difference." *New Essays on* The Country of the Pointed Firs, edited by June Howard, Cambridge UP, 1994, pp. 39–60.

Notes

1. I'm borrowing the phrase from Cristanne Miller's title, *Reading in Time: Emily Dickinson and the Nineteenth Century*, in which she forcefully defends a reading of Dickinson in the context of the Civil War.
2. Coviello uses the notion of the "untimely" in the context of the history of sexuality. He is interested in "the contours of a series of erotic possibilities that were not quite, not yet, legible in the terms of the century's impending sexual taxonomies" (11). I extend his use of the "untimely" to consider how Freeman's texts challenge other taxonomies as well, in particular our binary ontologies opposing animals and humans.
3. Fetterley and Pryse quote Carl Rogers who wrote in 1959: "The state of empathy, or being empathic, is to perceive the internal frame of reference of another with accuracy, and with the emotional components and meanings which pertain thereto, as if one were the other person, but without ever losing the 'as if' condition" (Rogers 210–11, quoted in Fetterley and Pryse 346).
4. There are also six plant stories, which I am not looking into here. For an analysis of "Arethusa," see Susan Stone's chapter in this volume.
5. "The neologism 'intra-action' signifies the mutual constitution of entangled agencies. That is, in contrast to the usual 'interaction,' which assumes that there are separate individual agencies that precede their interaction, the notion of intra-action recognizes that distinct agencies do not precede, but rather emerge through, their intra-action" (Barad 33).

6. See Vesna Kuiken for a study of how Jewett's *The Country of the Pointed Firs*, and especially the chapters around Shell-Heap island, "collapse the future and the past into one vast present." She writes: "[T]ime becomes a physical repository of simultaneous—idiorrhythmic—possibilities" (100). I argue here that contemporaneousness as untimeliness does just that.
7. The Spanish-American War and the Philippine-American War (1898–1902) came to represent a critical milestone in the development of the US as an overseas empire. The US was now ready to vie with other world powers to take up the "white man's burden." Many among Freeman's contemporaries, among them Mark Twain, William Dean Howells, William James, or Jane Addams, enrolled in the Anti-Imperialist League. The political and cultural work of acquaintance performed by regionalism was impacted by the racial plurality of selves that this turn to global imperialism made more visible. See Jewett's tale "The Foreigner" (1899); see also Roudeau, Walsh, Zagarell.
8. "Somehow, the flowers and the animals seem to me not to combine very well. They are so essentially different, one being symbolic, the other psychological" (Letter to Harper's, 6 October 1900; Kendrick 244).
9. See Susan Stone's article in Phyllis Cole and Jana Argersinger (eds), *Towards a Female Genealogy of Transcendentalism*. See also Stone in this volume.
10. In 2001, Terrell Dixon read these stories as a call for a displacement of focus, for the need to put back "nature" at the center of the stage in Freeman's studies. For Dixon, *Six Trees* could even be read as "a type of ecological teaching tale" (166). I argue that Freeman goes further. For an ecofeminist reading of Freeman, see also Stacy Alaimo.
11. For a thought-provoking exploration of alternative ("premodern") forms of kinship in Jewett, see Nancy Bentley.

AFTERWORD: WHY MARY E. WILKINS FREEMAN? WHY NOW? WHERE NEXT?

SANDRA A. ZAGARELL

Why Mary E. Wilkins Freeman?

The essays in this timely volume extend our view of Mary E. Wilkins Freeman well beyond the heyday of post-bellum regionalism, with which she has typically been associated. They showcase her as a writer who, over her fifty-year career, employed many forms of the short story and penned fourteen novels, almost all of them in conversation with major changes in the nation, often, but not always, as they played out in New England. At her best—and she was often at her best— she explored questions that were pressing when she wrote. Many continue to resonate. Some—but only *some*—of her subjects are gender, gender formation, and sexuality, the lives of the elderly, family dynamics and individuals' psychology, class, the conflicting interests of wage laborers and capitalists and the very nature of labor, all as they were informed by era, tradition, culture and place and affected by her characters' individuality. She wrote in an astonishing range of genres in addition to novels and short stories—a narrative of community, plays, poetry, essays. Her letters, collected by Brent L. Kendrick, offer insight into the life of a professional woman writer between 1875 and 1930.

Freeman's fiction is rarely as straightforward as it may seem. Much of it is staunchly undecidable, to adapt Elizabeth Meese's influential phrase.[1] Indeed, undecidability is a hallmark of an artistry that is indispensable to the pleasure of reading her and to the excitement that this new volume of scholarship offers. Because Freeman's artistry is often assumed rather than examined, I begin with an exploration of it, and hope that more extensive discussion will follow.

Assessing Freeman's artistry can be a challenge because it often confounds persisting assumptions about artistry itself. Freeman supported herself by her writing and wrote for the money she earned through it. As Brent L. Kendrick's chapter shows, she was adept at negotiating payment for her work. She tailored her writing for placement in specific magazines—*Harper's Bazar, Harper's Monthly Magazine, The Ladies' Home Journal, Woman's Home Companion,* to name a few—and for specific publishers, especially Harpers. She wrote for occasions like Thanksgiving and Christmas; she sometimes matched fiction to illustrations her publisher sent her or asked for illustrations to which she could match stories; she proposed writing tales that centered on particular subjects—trees, animals. Put somewhat differently, Freeman wrote what is often regarded as popular literature—literature that appealed commercially because it featured familiar subjects or themes and employed established convention. Though popular writing was once dismissed by literary historians and critics, and the distinction still holds in the awkward category "literary fiction," many scholars now acknowledge that "popular" and "good" need not be mutually exclusive, and that "good" itself is a relative category, as Susan K. Harris's "But Is it Any Good?" demonstrated thirty years ago. Many scholars also recognize that popular writing, whether or not we deem it good, warrants serious attention because it has wide appeal, tapping into and helping shape the culture in which it flourishes.

But *how* did Freeman work with popular conventions? Her 1913 essay "The Girl Who wants to Write: Things to Do and Avoid" offers some insight into her view of how she did. Here she suggests that being a popular writer, one who takes up familiar subjects and employs established conventions, and being a good writer can be synonymous. Expressing skepticism about the notion that the bona fide author is an inspired creator, she explains that while many a writer sits down to write without knowing what the ultimate outcome of her task will be, she does very good work because she follows "the law of sequence," which she also terms "the sequential order" and "the creative order." Writing is a "task" undertaken for a purpose—fame, money—and also good when it follows a logic, a law of sequence. These terms suggest the logic of established conventions at which Freeman herself excelled. She often favored popular formulas, plotting many tales around young women whose romances are initially thwarted or who resist marriage but do ultimately marry—or do not; she featured types and tropes common in regionalist writing about New England—young women, spinsters, widows, widowers, bachelors, ministers, village eccentrics.

Conventions inspired her. Although, as the editors of this volume note, she sometimes simply reproduced formulas, more often she was a virtuoso of established formulas, forms, character types, and other tropes. Her use of them contributes to the staunch undecidability of much of her fiction, for she at once embraces or references them and, by counterposing them with disjunctive elements, explores—and sometimes exposes—the values and lifeways in which they were invested. Many of her tales about heterosexual romance and marriage combine conventional narrative lines and unconventional ones, gesturing towards unconventional possibilities or an unconventional assessment of norms while also acknowledging the authority and, not infrequently, the benefits of a conventional life. Most familiar is her penchant for complicating formulaic stories with narrative lines or characterizations that offset formulaic teleologies while declining to resolve the tales' grounding tensions. "A New England Nun" exemplifies this. Her deformation of formulas, subjects, and types also often entails braiding together different registers or perspectives without dissolving one into the other. "The Amethyst Comb," for instance, devotes equal sympathy and understanding to dignified Jane Carew's embrace of her middle-aged unmarried womanhood and her friend Viola Longstreet's impassioned and destructive efforts to forestall the aging process and enjoy the rewards of youthfulness, especially heterosexual romance.

The staunch undecidability of much of Freeman's fiction is at once textual and extra-textual. It is founded on fault lines or cruxes—difficult or unresolvable issues—that marked the country. She keeps pace with, and often highlights, the real-world coordinates of conventions and counter- or anti-conventions she puts to use. Many tales bespeak her awareness of the shifting, often contradictory, discourse about white middle-class womanhood that accelerated after the end of the Civil War. She articulates this awareness tartly in her 1906 dismissal of William Dean Howells's objections to her depiction of a sexually attractive independent 34-year-old woman in her chapter "The Old-Maid Aunt" for the composite novel *The Whole Family*.[2] She is also alert to other cruxes. Shifts in the relationship of humans with nature—deforestation, species endangerment—inform the abiding tensions of several of the stories in *Understudies*, and *Six Trees*, while *The Portion of Labor* reflects on the potentially irreconcilable conflicts between emergent forms of factory production and of entrepreneurship on the one hand and the working-class exploitation and solidarity that these conditions generated on the other.

Freeman's complex use of conventions is inseparable from qualities more commonly associated with artistry: extraordinary powers of observation and an extraordinary imagination. Founded in her intense openness to the world around her, her power of observation was inspiring, though also alarming: not always conscious, willed, or even desired. Her awkward attempt to describe it in a letter to Sarah Orne Jewett, whose work she admired, suggests how unwilled it could be:

> I suppose you feel as I do, that everything you have heard, seen or done since you opened your eyes on the world, is coming back to you sooner

or later, to go into stories and things. And I never knew it at the time, and I think there is something awful about it, as if I had been scudding all the time before a high wind, instead of walking at my own gait. But I don't believe I am making you know what I mean.³

Certainly these almost uncanny powers informed Freeman's astute mastery of conventions of popular fiction and her imaginative play with them. They also surely enabled her to take up many popular genres and write about a wide range of subjects. They go hand in hand with the stylistic mastery—of description, syntax, imagery, focalization, narrative rhythm—that makes her psychological acuity, attention to social dynamics, renderings of daily life and of disruptions to its established patterns so compelling. And they are surely essential to her creation of fiction that could seem homogenous because so much is situated in rural New England, but is actually dynamic and changing, as I will suggest in the final section of this chapter.

Why Freeman Now?

The feminist recovery of Freeman which began in the late 1970s made previously unrecognized aspects of her artistry visible, especially her unconventional representations of women and incisive critiques of patriarchy. More recently, literary recovery and an ongoing push for changes in literary historiography, along with the flourishing of many new approaches to writing itself, are bringing the many-facetedness of Freeman's oeuvre into sharper focus. Of particular significance is literary recovery's attention not only to books—once reified as the most significant form in which literature appeared—but to writing published in magazines and newspapers.⁴ For Freeman, the expanded scope of recovery has been generative because, as the bibliography compiled by Jeff Kaylin shows,⁵ some of her magazine fiction was not republished in book form and some was put out by houses considered popular and therefore of little interest. *The Jamesons*, for example, was published by Curtis Publishing Company of Philadelphia and New York's Doubleday & McClure, then associated with *McClure's*. Moreover, contemporary tastemakers like F. Lewis Pattee and, until recently, literary scholars, took her at her word when she declared her novels inferior to her short fiction; this has contributed to commentators' general failure to consider her work in that most venerated of forms.

Literary recovery has entailed far more than adding writers and writing to American literature. It is pushing some literary historians to reconsider standard periodization and the concept of literature that periodization both relied on and reinforced. Not only, as I have suggested, does reconceiving what counts as literature encourage us to explore Freeman's artistry as well as her subjects and themes (this holds true for recovered writers as different as Alexander Posey, Alice Dunbar-Nelson, and Sui Sin Far). Undoing the constricting parameters of periodization also allows us to recognize incommensurate modes, strains, and registers within individual works and across the span of a writer's oeuvre. As Monica Elbert's chapter suggests, some of Freeman's later fiction is a cacophony of naturalism and modernism, and characters' isolation and desolation and the general pessimism of such tales as "The Cloak Also," which might once have been classified as belated regionalism, can be seen as philosophically modernist. Likewise, while most of Freeman's fiction is regionalist, applying that classification as though it were explanatory obscures the diversity of her writing about New England. Moreover, by assigning regionalism to the decades between 1870 and 1910, standard periodization implies that the regionalist fiction Freeman wrote after 1910 is anachronistic, thereby discouraging serious consideration of still-undervalued work like *Edgewater People* (1918). Sidelining the temporality of traditional periodization altogether can also be illuminating, as Cécile Roudeau's chapter on Freeman's untimeliness shows. Expanding Peter Coviello's work on the untimeliness of nascent sexualities that were suppressed by the regime of heterosexuality and homosexuality of the late nineteenth century, Roudeau showcases the untimeliness of *Understudies'* and *Six Trees'* blurring of Enlightenment-based dualities—human vs. nonhuman; culture vs. nature and others. Freeman's untimeliness is out of joint with her own time but not predictive of ours. Rather, it suggests futures that, while they have not come into being, are also not foreclosed.

Like Elbert's and Roudeau's, the other essays gathered here demonstrate how well Freeman's fiction rewards contemporary theoretical-critical methods. Taking a textual-contextual approach, many of the chapters examine the complex relationship between her fiction and aspects of the contexts in which it was written or appeared. Several reflect on her representation of gender as a cultural crux. Audrey Fogels situates fiction Freeman published in *Harper's Bazar* when Mary Louise Booth edited it to show how it echoes Booth's feminist views about women's independence while also encouraging consumerist and other conservative values to which the *Bazar* was officially dedicated. Aušra Paulauskienė discusses the actual practices of Catholic nuns and Catholic writers' portrayals of them to shed new light on the multivalence of Freeman's complex presentation of Louisa Ellis. Recovering the extraordinary tale "The Prism," H. J. E Champion uses queer theory to analyze protagonist Diantha's queerly sideways relationship to conventional femaleness—her autoeroticism and vibrant imagination—and the tale's overt troubling of conventionalities of womanhood. Susan M. Stone spotlights an ecological crux in Freeman's transcendentalist-inspired proto-ecofeminism fiction. A relationship with nature can, Emersonianly, transform a man spiritually ("The Great Pine") but it can also dissolve conventional forms of gender ("Christmas Jenny"). Stone's Freeman understood that nature was being affected by its relationship to humans. When Freeman wrote *Six Trees*, she was responding to the deforestation that was accelerating in and beyond New England, yet she continued to focus on the life-changing power of nature in a distinctly ecofeminist way.

In several chapters, textual-contextual approaches ground examination of Freeman's unconventional use of conventions. Daniel Mrozowski illuminates her skeptical take on popular themes, registers, and motifs that promoted domestic support of World War I. In the war stories in *Edgewater People*, conventions, especially those celebrating men who enlist, are challenged by characters' personal, sometimes selfish, and decidedly non-patriotic reasons for sending village boys off to fight, and tales end by reinforcing, not dissolving, the irreconcilability of their personal motives with patriotic discourse. Elucidating Freeman's use of conventional tropes—dolls, ghosts—unconventionally, Donna M. Campbell probes Freeman's focus on trauma, suffering, and violence, often as experienced by women, and the violence, extending to murder, which women commit. *The Portion of Labor* supports two somewhat divergent analyses both of which highlight its challenge to conventional thinking. Laura Dawkins brings the theoretical-historical work of Karen Sanchez-Eppler and other scholars to bear on her proposition that the novel rebuffs the prominent Progress-Era belief that working-class lives would be improved by the adoption of middle-class values of domesticity and child-rearing. For Dawkins, *The Portion of Labor* presents child labor in working-class families as a virtual inevitability because the family wage system of Freeman's era necessitated that everyone in a family work if it was to survive. Taking a queer and Marxist-historicist approach, Rogers-Cooper discerns both a queerly disruptive temporality that disturbs, but does not alter, the capitalist teleology of ongoing progress and the affiliative solidarity with other women which informs Ellen Brewster's unconventionally affective leadership of the workers in Lloyd's shoe factory. Mobilizing Amy Kaplan's work on realism's self-contradictions, he also teases out *Portion*'s suggestion of a possible future in which labor would achieve the equity which the novel seems to preclude.

Freeman's artistry is such that essays in which her use of conventions is not a focus also give us new purchase on her work. Offering a fresh look at Freeman's regionalism, Jana Tigchelaar sees in many tales a "project of neighborliness" in which "neighborly encounters" transform local cultures and communities by circumventing the power relations which allow village ministers and selectmen or the culture of an entire village to marginalize those who are odd or recalcitrant. Two chapters exemplify the value of abandoning the US-centric perspective that has narrowed our understanding of US writers. Myrto Drizou's transatlantic, intertextual approach places "Old Woman Magoun" within the matrilineal "lineage of deviant maternal figures" "epitomized by" the Central and South American figure of La Llorona. Comparing Freeman's tale and Greek author Alexandros Papadiamantis's 1903 novel *The Murderess*, Drizou points to a matrifocal global literature that, while foregrounding women's transgressive acts of retributive justice, also features their strengths and restorative powers, thereby calling for the establishment of women's full humanity in their respective countries and in the world. Uncovering Freeman's influence on the British writer Sylvia Townsend Warner, Stephanie Palmer reverses the standard view that influence traveled from the UK to the US. She establishes that Warner's sense of affiliation with Freeman was instrumental in her defense of realism at a time when modernism was fashionable and in her adaptation of Freeman's dualistic realist aesthetic, which mixed realism with romanticism and melodrama, to her own practice of mixing realism and fantasy.

Where Next?

Separately and together, these essays enrich our understanding of Freeman. Their scope and insights exemplify the value of cultural-literary interpretation at a time when the humanities are too often being discounted. The different routes they take illuminate Freeman's writing's multifariousness. They also open the way for further possibilities for Freeman scholarship, so many possibilities that I will limit myself to discussing only a few. In doing so, I suggest that exploring, as much possible, Freeman's sizeable oeuvre as well as continuing to engage with single works or groups of work will cast her artistry in even sharper relief, for, contrary to what many earlier commentators maintained, it persisted well into the twentieth century. Its hallmarks—the variety of the conventions she worked with and against, her changing treatment of subjects for which she is best known, including New England life, as the world in which they were embedded changed, her imaginative observation, the quality of her prose—all flourished in much of her twentieth-century fiction.

My first suggestion, inspired by Monica Elbert's proposal that in some of Freeman's twentieth-century tales, a modernist "malaise of isolation" predominates, is that we read other late Freeman in conjunction with the modernist Freeman. Doing so indicates that rather than consistently viewing life in the twentieth century as bleak, she explored it from several angles. In her last published volume of new fiction, *Edgewater People*, set during and after World War I, both modernity and tradition shape villagers' lives. Modern population expansion has led the original village to divide into four separate villages. Cars and trains provide increased mobility; some villagers are oriented outward, toward cities, toward the war in Europe; city people spend summers in houses purchased for temporary residence only; an antique shop sells village heirlooms. Traditions also persist. Old families retain their status; people live in their ancestral homes; ties of neighborliness and kinship continue for some Edgewater people. But, in contrast to Jewett's Dunnet Landing, where people are united across distances by "a golden chain of love and dependence" (Jewett 146), intra- and inter-village connections are often tenuous and must be created and re-created. The main character, Sarah Edgewater, exemplifies the tension between isolation and connection that are conditions of contemporary life for Edgewater people.

Alone in her home, Sarah experiences soul-harrowing loneliness, a description of which extends over four pages. She alleviates her isolation by forging meaningful connections—reuniting with family from whom she has been estranged, fostering ties across the four villages—but other people remain isolated. That Freeman develops the coexistence of isolation and connection in different ways in other twentieth-century work—"The Travelling Sister" (1908) is one—makes this a promising area.

Second, and related, I suggest continued scholarship on Freeman's regionalism. Despite the constraints that classifying Freeman as a regionalist once imposed, current recognition that regionalism is a many-sided, long-lived genre should encourage scholars to engage the complexity of Freeman's regionalism, including its alignment with her understanding that New England, far from being static, was always affected and partly shaped by national, even global, circumstances and conditions. June Howard's *The Center of the World* is particularly generative for this aspect of work on Freeman. Howard theorizes regionalism as both substantive and relational, simultaneously grounded in particular places and temporalities, as Freeman's work is, and reflecting, perhaps reflecting on, the larger world of which these places are always also part, as most of Freeman's work does.

My third suggestion is that the materialist-historical methodology of book history inform continued examination of relationships between Freeman's published writing and the material contexts in which it appeared. What kinds of relationships existed between Freeman's texts and their paratexts? How did covers, running headers, illustrations, *mise en page* form conditions under which her work might have been read? What can attention to the sequencing and interplay of pieces gathered in collections of her short fiction tell us about, say, her complicated representations of New England? In *Silence and Other Stories*, for example, conventions about heterosexual romance inform sharply contrasting versions of relationships between men and women in colonial and nineteenth-century New England. In the first tale, "Silence," men and women are devoted to each other and to sustaining the colonial village of Deerfield. The book's final tale, "Lydia Hersey, of East Bridgewater," centers on the battle of the sexes between independent Lydia and her fiancé, which she loses. Once he has subdued her, her now-husband uses a raucous village tradition to which she has objected—young men blow conch shells at weddings to which they are not invited—to put his triumph and her submission on public display.

My fourth suggestion is that scholarship on gender continue. Feminist critics—Josephine Donovan, Marjorie Pryse, Judith Fetterley, Mary Reichardt, Elizabeth Meese, Leah Blatt Glasser, June Howard, and others—show that in effect Freeman de-essentialized "woman" and troubled normative gender by featuring women who exceeded or obviated conventional types. Queer theory offers purchase on another way in which Freeman troubles gender, her unsettling of the "expected linear movement towards marriage, children and adulthood," in H. J. E. Champion's formulation. Using Elizabeth Freeman's concept of chrononormativity, Champion sees Diantha's relinquishment of her queer autoerotic life for heteronormative adult womanhood and marriage as a narrative choice Freeman may have made to concede to "market driven conventions of nineteenth-century women's writing." When we put Simone de Beauvoir's famous dictum that "One is not born but rather becomes a woman" into conversation with this queer reading, "The Prism" also comes into focus as Freeman's underscoring of culturally enforced conventions which mandate Diantha's transformation into a heterosexual adult woman, from the materialization of heterosexual love when she nears adulthood through marriage and her relegation to the home and its routines. Read this way, the ending of "The Prism" is not an about-face but an extension of its critique of heteronormative gender and the cultural conventions which enforce it.

Combining queer and feminist theory also backlights the gender radicalism of other tales. "The Reign of the Doll" emerges as a parodic telescoping of the chrononormative process of becoming a woman. The elderly Nutting sisters receive a doll clothed only in "coarse muslin undergarments" and thus insufficiently gendered. Referring to the doll as both "it" and "she" they spend a night and part of a day making clothes for it. The process, a sped-up version of the construction of womanhood, fixes the doll's gender; once they dress it the sisters "refer to the doll as she and her" ("The Reign of the Doll" 327). Because they do not recognize that they themselves have made her a woman, the process of becoming a woman seems natural to them. Making doll's clothes also reverses, in warp speed, the sisters' own lifelong process of becoming and remaining women. They immediately feel restored to their childhoods, when their attachment was to each other and they were only incipiently heteronormative, and they prolong their not-yet heteronormative identities by continuing to sew clothing for her. Bringing queer and feminist theory together will also be productive for work on "Billie and Susie, "Eliza Sam," "Louisa," and many other tales.

Finally, I suggest exploring a subject that has been addressed with regard to *The Portion of Labor* but only minimally for other fiction: Freeman's enduring attention to what qualifies as labor and what labor entails. As the chapters by Dawkins and Rogers-Cooper suggest, the 1901 novel correlated with widespread contemporary economic, political, and social thought. In fact, labor was a much-debated issue. Marx and Engels theorized labor's exploitation as the foundation of industrial capitalism and encouraged labor's resistance; Progressives wanted to reform the working classes in keeping with middle-class ideology; Christian socialists wanted to restore the dignity of labor; conservatives touted work as a social duty and warned that American society was being threatened by widespread laziness. Like *The Portion of Labor*, fiction by other American women—Harding Davis, Phelps—critiqued the condition of industrial laborers. But long before *Portion*, Freeman, who referred to her own writing as "brain labor," portrayed work that was not industrial and had nothing to do with coal refineries: the labor necessary to maintain life in rural New England. She was not unique. New England regionalist fiction and painting depicted activities like farming and knitting. Especially as regionalism converged with the Colonial Revival Movement, however, it tended to rely on hardened tropes to reify such activities as metonyms of an organic way of life that was being eradicated by an atomizing modernity (Conforti). The farmer might be portrayed as noble; women's domestic activities, a frequent focus, were expressions of virtue and pleasure and seemed to be achieved without effort. Freeman brought to life the labor that such tropes often elided.

Like Charlotte Perkins Gilman, Freeman was especially attentive to the labor that dominated white women's lives. If for Louisa Ellis domestic activities are gratifying ends in themselves, they are more typically endless and grueling. "Silence" pushes back at Colonial Revival nostalgia for an imagined Age of Homespun by dwelling on this work's arduousness. It is also a retort to the popular view of a 1704 French and Indian raid on the village of Deerfield, a view promulgated by John Williams's *Redeemed Captive*. The narrative centers on his captivity and his stout resistance to efforts to convert him to Catholicism. Freeman, by contrast, locates "Silence" in ravaged Deerfield during and after the attack. Women's labor, as essential as men's, occupies center stage. After the raid, the villagers gather in one of the homes that remains standing. There one woman "sat down and began to nurse her baby"; a second woman "hung the porridge-pot over the fire; another put some potatoes in the ashes to bake" (26). Two others clean and dress the bodies of a murdered woman and child and lay them out. Then "Eunice stirred the bubbling porridge, scowling at the heat; some of the women laid the table with [the murdered woman's] linen cloth and pewter dishes, and presently the breakfast was served up" (26–7). Women's labor continues to sustain the village as it rebuilds; they "[unflinchingly] toil at wheel and loom . . . for there was great scarcity of linen . . ." (41). Nor is all of the women's work conventionally domestic. During the attack, they build up the hearth fire, melt cherished domestic items—pewter plates, a silver cream mug—and make bullets (19).

Freeman also departs from prevailing conventions about colonial women by not suggesting that, given American progress, such toil became unnecessary. She often calls the ideology of domesticity, with its downplaying of women's labor, into question. As Elizabeth Freeman shows, in the antebellum era this ideology "naturalized women's labor into feminine influence through the angel in the house who magically kept things clean and people fed without seeming to lift a finger" (39). (In idioms and images that correlate with cultural and technological changes, especially those having to do with cleanliness, this naturalizing persists in our own day.) In tale after tale, Freeman portrays the domestic labor that women perform. She also presents activities that were supposedly natural for women—providing emotional support, caring for the sick and dying—as work, detailing them in the same realistic register in which she described food preparation. *Pembroke* takes pains to lay out how Charlotte Barnard, who often "watche[s] over the sick and [sits] up with the dead" (250), ministers to Barnabas Thayer when he is deathly ill. The unfinished tale "The White Shawl," which takes place during a blizzard, dwells on elderly Susy Dunn's care for her ill husband, and assurance that he die a good death while simultaneously—and miraculously—occupying a tower near their home to perform his job of assuring that trains do not collide.

Here too, moreover, Freeman did not take a uniform perspective. In *Pembroke* and "The Apple Tree" she features the obsessive, even destructive, potential of New England women's famed industriousness. *The Jamesons* spoofs contemporary enactments of colonial domesticity; "Dear Annie" and "The Selfishness of Amelia Lamkin" dramatize the deleterious effects of twentieth-century women's anachronistic insistence on performing all domestic labor rather than distributing it among family members; "Knitting Susan" centers on a village's dependence on a disabled girl's singular skill at knitting socks; "The Great Pine," "The Umbrella Man," "Eliza Sam," and others variously undo the conventional domestic woman/farming man dichotomy. Here, as elsewhere, a transatlantic lens is also worth considering. In Great Britain, where awareness of class was pervasive, novels by Elizabeth Gaskell, Charles Dickens, and Thomas Hardy associate women's labor with the industrial or agricultural poor, while Charlotte Brontë focuses on the work available to impecunious middle-class women: teaching or being a governess. These and other writers offer opportunities for comparing concepts of women's work on both sides of the Atlantic.

In this context, *The Portion of Labor* comes into focus as an extension of Freeman's interest in work and in prevailing discourses about it. Fulfilling her own 1891 prediction that the novel of the future "would be at once romantic and realistic," she employs these modes to present the condition of labor in two mutually exclusive registers, both of which had traction in her America.[6] Realistically and at length, she depicts the work, the working conditions, and the economic precarity of the women and men who labor in Lloyd's shoe factory, as well as their views of their own exploitation. Dawkins and Rogers-Cooper adroitly engage the complexity of this dimension of the novel. But counterposing the novel's realism, though alien to many twenty-first-century readers, is a Protestant-derived view, expressed in a romantic-religious register that labor is a good in itself, in effect its own reward.[7] That these incommensurate views and registers reflect a cultural-social crux is underscored by the novel's closing paragraphs, in which Ellen Brewster's father Andrew reflects on the portion of labor. Observing the physical toll which factory work has taken on his neighbors and kin—their "poor, knotted hands"—he implicitly rejects the possibility of upward mobility that America has promised industrious citizens, envisioning workers' lives as a journey along "the tracks which they had worn on the earth towards their graves with their weary feet" (562). Immediately before and after this grimly realistic account, though, Andrew gainsays it in romantic-religious language. Regarding comments on labor in Ecclesiastes as a spiritual celebration—"my heart rejoiced in all my labor, and that was the portion of labor"—he concludes that "labor . . . is for the growth of character in the laborer" (563). Reducing each perspective to its extreme (the laborer is only a body; only the laborer's soul matters), this ending resists resolution. It returns readers to their current moment and its conflicting discourses about the portion of labor.

That in *The Portion of Labor* opposing standpoints correlate so conspicuously with conflicting views of a major contemporary problem reminds us of the vitality of Freeman's artistry. In her hands, both urgent and seemingly banal subjects—the prescribed progress from girlhood to womanhood is one of the latter—emerge as literary and cultural cruxes that were at the center of American life. Her fiction is accessible; it feels familiar; it is appealing—and it disturbs custom and convention. *New Perspectives on Mary E. Wilkins Freeman* exemplifies the kind of consideration Freeman warrants. It assures us that she will continue to reward the attention of scholars, of students, and of what Virginia Woolf memorably called "the common reader."

Works Cited

Conforti, Joseph N. *Imagining New England: Explorations of Regional Identity from the Pilgrims to the Mid-Twentieth Century*. U of North Carolina P, 2001.

Freeman, Elizabeth. *Time Binds. Queer Temporalities, Queer Histories*. Duke UP, 2010.

Freeman, Mary E. Wilkins. "The Amethyst Comb." *A New England Nun and Other Stories*, edited by Sandra A. Zagarell, Penguin, 2000, pp. 286–99.

—. "The Apple-Tree." *Six Trees. Short Stories*. Harper & Brothers, 1903, pp. 171–207.

—. "Billy and Susie." *The Winning Lady and Others*. Harper & Brothers, 1909, pp. 103–21.

—. "Dear Annie." *A New England Nun and Other Stories*, edited by Sandra A. Zagarell, Penguin, 2000, pp. 250–85.

—. *Edgewater People*. Harper & Brothers, 1918.

—. "Eliza Sam." *The Winning Lady and Others*. Harper & Brothers, 1909, pp. 281–303.

—. "The Girl Who wants to Write: Things to Do and Avoid." *Harper's Bazaar*, XLVI, June 1913, p. 272.

—. "The Great Pine." *Six Trees. Short Stories*. Harper & Brothers, 1903, pp. 69–99.

—. *The Jamesons. A New England Nun and Other Stories*, edited by Sandra A. Zagarell, Penguin, 2000, pp. 79–142.

—. "Knitting Susan." *Youth's Companion*, vol. 66, no. 1, January 5, 1893, <http://wilkinsfreeman.info/Short/KnittingSusan.htm>(last accessed 27 December 2021).

—. "Louisa." *A New England Nun and Other Stories*, edited by Sandra A. Zagarell, Penguin, 2000, pp. 48–63.
—. "Lydia Hersey of East Bridgewater." *"Silence" and Other Stories*. Harper & Brothers, 1898, pp. 255–89.
—. *Pembroke. A Novel*. Harper & Brothers, 1906.
—. *The Portion of Labor*. 1901. The Gregg Press, 1977.
—. "The Prism." *The Uncollected Stories of Mary E. Wilkins Freeman*, edited by Mary R. Reichardt, UP of Mississippi, 1992, pp. 55–65.
—. "The Reign of the Doll." *Mary E. Wilkins Reader*, edited by Mary S. Reichardt, U of Nebraska P, 1997, pp. 317–32.
—. "The Selfishness of Amelia Lamkin." *The Winning Lady and Others*. Harper & Brothers, 1909, pp. 125–72.
—. "Silence." *"Silence"and Other Stories*. Harper & Brothers, 1898, pp 1–54.
—. "The Travelling Sister." *The Winning Lady and Others*. Harper & Brothers, 1909, pp.175–206.
—. "The Umbrella Man." *The Copy-Cat & Other Stories*. Harper & Brothers, 1914, pp. 239–65.
—. "The White Shawl." *The Uncollected Stories of Mary E. Wilkins Freeman*, edited by Mary R. Reichardt, UP of Mississippi, 1992, pp. 304–18.
Gilbert, Robert E. *The Tormented President: Calvin Coolidge, Death, and Clinical Depression*. Praeger, 2003.
Harris Susan K. "But Is It Any Good? Evaluating Nineteenth-Century American Women's Fiction." *American Literature*, vol. 63, no. 1, 1991, pp. 43–61.
Howard, June. *The Center of The World: Regional Writing and the Puzzle of Place-Time*. Oxford UP, 2018.
Jewett, Sarah Orne. *The Country of the Pointed Firs*. Houghton Mifflin and Co., 1896.
Kendrick, Brent L., ed. *The Infant Sphinx. Collected Letters of Mary E. Wilkins Freeman*. Scarecrow Press, 1985.
Meese Elizabeth. "Signs of Undecidability: Reconsidering the Stories of Mary Wilkins Freeman." *Critical Essays on Mary Wilkins Freeman*, edited by Shirley Marchalonis, G. K. Hall, 1991, pp. 157–76.

Notes

1. Meese's formulation is "staunch indeterminacy of view" (162).
2. In the letter to *Bazar* editor Elizabeth Jordan, Freeman emphasizes unmarried women's "voluntary celibacy" and says she can think of fifty women "who look as pretty and as up-to-date as their young nieces," adding that "men are at their feet" (1 August 1906. Kendrick, p. 313).
3. To Sarah Orne Jewett, 12 December 1889 (Kendrick, p. 99).
4. This also pertains to such work as short stories by Alice Dunbar-Nelson published in *Legacy*, vol. 33, no. 2, 2016.
5. Available at <http://wilkinsfreeman.info> (last accessed 22 July 2022).
6. "[In the novel of the future] romance and realism will be more equally combined than they have ever been before" (To Foster Coates, before 20 March 1891; Kendrick, p. 100).

7. As Lieutenant Governor of Massachusetts, Calvin Coolidge would take the spiritual dimension of the religious-romantic view to an extreme that would seem comic if it not for the fact that it resonated in 1916 and, in different ways, continues to resonate. "The man who builds a factory builds a temple," he proclaimed. "The man who works there worships there" (Gilbert 78).

INDEX

1877 general strike, 134, 143

Ackland, Valentine, 237, 240, 244, 245
activism, 44, 55, 80
adaptability, 47, 217
Afghanistan, 216–17
African Americans and/or Blackness, 90, 134
Agamben, Giorgio, 65, 67, 254
aging, 147, 184–7, 205–6, 217, 240, 246–7, 272
Alaimo, Stacy, 12
Alcott, Louisa May, *Little Women,* 83
Alpheus, 51
"Amanda in Love," 248
America in the War, edited by Louis Raemaekers, 213
American Academy of Arts and Letters, 5, 164
American Expeditionary Forces (AEF), 205
"The Amethyst Comb," 235n4, 274
Ammons, Elizabeth, 81
Anderson, Donald R., 114

Anderson, Sherwood, *Winesburg, Ohio,* 222
"angel in the house," 148
animals, 80, 83, 84, 92, 254–60
Ansley, Jennifer, 29, 41n9, 61–2, 64–5, 121–2
"The Apple Tree," 43, 53–4, 282
archetype, 102–3, 118
"Arethusa," 43, 49–51, 73
Atlantic Monthly, 3
autoeroticism, 62, 66–9, 75, 112

Bacheller, Irving syndicate, 174
"The Balking of Christopher," 226
"Balsam Fir," 51
Barthes, Roland, 253
Battle of the Somme, 246
Beecher, Catharine, 120
Behling, Laura L., 88
Bendixen, Alfred, 80
Bennett, Paula, 182–3, 190, 196
Berkson, Dorothy, 10, 147
Bernardi, Debra, 10
Best Stories of Mary E. Wilkins, 175–6

INDEX

Biblical references
  Ecclesiastes, 283
  Esau, 91–2, 121
  imagery, 66, 98, 103
  Matthew 5, 208–9
"Billie and Susie," 280
birds, 46, 49, 264
Blake, William, 163n1
Bloom, Harold, 237, 239, 243, 249
Bode, Rita, 237, 239
Booth, Mary Louise, 3, 37, 42n11, 169–70, 182–3, 184, 189, 195, 276
Borden, Lizzie, 88
Boston, 6
"Both Cheeks," 203, 208, 210
"Bouncing Bet," 55
boundaries, 44, 55, 62, 255, 243
Brace, Charles Loring, 147
"Brakes and White Vi'lets," 4
Brattleboro (VT), 2, 164–6, 168, 211
  Brattleboro Gas Light Company, 168
  Brattleboro Home for the Aged and Disabled, 176
bridge, 44, 99–100, 105–8
Bread and Roses strike, 134
Brodhead, Richard, 12, 12n10, 81
Brontë, Charlotte, 282
Brown, Alice, 4, 73
  "A Flower of April," 73
Brown, Bill, 81
Bruhm, Steven, 61, 66–7, 70
Budd, Louis J., 146n7
business
  business customs, 165, 168, 176
  businessmen, 169–73
  businesswoman, 15, 164–81
  estate value, 164, 169, 176
  financial success, 164, 169, 176
  investments, 168, 176
  royalties, 174–5
By the Light of the Soul, 175

"Calla-Lilies and Hannah," 225
Campbell, Donna M., 96, 98, 101–2, 132, 135, 142, 144, 147, 148, 149, 150, 239, 277
Campbell, Helen, 147
capitalism, 9, 49–50, 53–4, 98, 102, 132, 135, 222, 253, 272
"The Cat," 255–8, 264
Cather, Willa, 72, 147
  My Ántonia, 222
  One of Ours, 205
Catholicism, 82, 113, 114–27
Cavaliero, Glen, 245
Chamberlin, Joseph Edgar, 3, 6
Champion, H. J. E., 280
charity, 47, 184–7
child, 4, 46–8, 50, 53–4, 95, 104–7
childhood, 16, 82, 84–8, 95–6, 118
  child textile workers, 157
  cult of childhood, 154–5
  child labor, 15
Chodorow, Nancy, 7
Chopin, Kate, 50, 147, 236
  "Lilacs," 113, 117, 118, 120
Christianity, 34–5, 46–8, 66, 104, 107
"Christmas Jenny," 13, 27–8, 34–6, 38, 43, 45–8, 54, 61, 276
chrononormativity, 240, 253–4, 257
"A Church Mouse," 8, 32–3, 35–6
Civil War, 1, 4, 7
Clark, Kate Upson, 175
Clark, Michele, 7
class, 7, 10, 15, 272, 282
  middle class, 184–6, 190, 192
  lower-middle class, 15, 183, 193, 197n2
  upper-middle class, 15, 134, 182–6, 193, 196
  working class, 137, 139–40, 143, 144, 148, 152
Cleary, K. McPhelim, "The Stepmother," 113, 118–19
"The Cloak Also," 227, 230–1, 276
Cogley, John, 114
Cold War, 243, 249
colors, 47, 67–9

INDEX

community, 6, 8, 12, 14, 28–30, 36–40, 100
commodities, 1, 3, 9–10, 101–2
comparison, 97, 99, 107–8
"A Conflict Ended," 31, 47
consumer culture, 9, 15, 183–4, 191–2, 197n1, 222, 225
conservation, 44, 51–2
conventions or conventional, 16, 96, 105, 205, 216, 273–5, 277, 279, 280, 283
Cooke, Rose Terry, 4
Couch, Ben, 112
Council of National Defense, 212
Coviello, Peter, 266, 276
Crane, Hart, 3
Crane, Stephen, 163n1
crime, 14, 80, 84
cross-cultural, 97–9, 107–8, 239, 243
Cullinan, Elizabeth, *House of Gold*, 115
Curtis Publishing Company, 275
Cutter, Martha J., 112

Darwinism, 53, 104
Davis, Rebecca Harding, 147
Dawkins, Laura, 251n1, 277, 282
Dawley, Alan, 153, 157–8
death, 71, 102–3, 104–5, 106–7
d'Eaubonne, Françoise, 44
de Beauvoir, Simone, 281
deforestation, 49, 51–3, 55, 265, 290
degeneration, 205
Deland, Margaret, 147
Damasio, Antonio, 259
"Dear Annie," 282
dénouement
    ending, 13, 242–3, 258, 262–3
    conclusion, 242–3
dependence, 8–9, 13–14
Descola, Philippe, 255
determinism, 102
deviance, 33–5, 60
Dickens, Charles, 147, 163n1, 282
Diner, Hasier, 148, 152
Dixon, Terrell F., 12
"The Doctor's Horse," 258–60, 262, 264

dolls, 80, 81–3, 84–5, 92
domesticity, 12, 16, 44–6, 49–50, 53, 55, 61–2, 67, 205, 216, 225
Donovan, Josephine, 7, 98, 219, 279
Doubleday & McClure, 275
Douglass, Frederick, 143
dowry, 100–1, 105–7
Dreiser, Theodore
Drizou, Myrto, 10, 238, 277
Dublin, Thomas, 155
Du Bois, W. E. B., 92
Duvall, John N., 222
Dwight, Theodore, 175
Dyer, Richard, 61

Ebest, Ron, 114, 115, 120
ecocriticism, 2, 12
    ecofeminism, 12–14, 43–51, 54, 57n2, 58n15
    ecological stewardship, 44
    queer ecology, 12
economy, 98, 101–2, 105–6, 225, 237
ecosystem, 44
Eden, 54, 65–7
Edgewater People, 203, 227, 232, 276, 278–9
Elbert, Monika, 96, 98, 276, 278
Elfenbein, Andrew, 237–8
Eliot, George, 239
"Eliza Sam," 280, 282
"The Elm Tree," 51
Emerson, Ralph Waldo, 48, 51, 53–4, 57n2, 58n7, 58n13, 59n19
"The Emmets," 174
"Emmy," 174
empowerment, 54
Entin, Joseph, 151
environment, 43–4, 46–8, 51–2, 54–5
    environmentalism, 44, 46, 55
    environmental justice, 55
    see also nature
ethnicity *see* race and ethnicity
"Evelina's Garden," 225, 237, 247–8

Faderman, Lillian, 7
fairies, 68–9, 72

INDEX

family, 63–4, 272
Fanning, Charles, 115
Far, Sui Sin, 9
Farrell, James, 113
   "Jim O'Neill" 119
   "Mary O'Reilly" 117
fashion, 1, 3–8, 15
Fates, the, 102, 111n8
Fauset, Jessie Redmon, 205
female, 243
   female world, 7
female affiliation complex, 238
femininity, 47–8, 53, 184–9
feminism, 44, 45–6, 54, 80, 143
   feminist agenda, 183–4
   feminist critique, 7
fertility, 65–6, 101, 106
Fetterley, Judith, 4, 6, 12, 21n7, 26, 30, 61, 66–7, 279
Fields, Annie, 43, 57n5, 58n14, 220
Fisken, Beth Wynne, 9, 95
Flaubert, Gustave, "Un Coeur Simple," 83
Fleissner, Jennifer, 9, 143, 144, 253
Fliter, John A., 153, 155, 161
flowers, 49–51, 53
Fogels, Audrey, 276
Foote, Stephanie, 26, 29–30, 40n1, 41n4, 42n10
For France, edited by Charles H. Towne, 213
Forster, E. M., 243
"For the Love of One's Self," 225–6
Foster, Edward, 165
France, 211, 219, 232
Freeman, Charles Manning, 169, 171–3, 205
Freeman, Elizabeth, 62, 64–5, 72, 136, 280, 281
Freeman, Mary E. Wilkins
   childhood, 4, 147, 189, 253
   class, 5, 13
   criticism about, 79–80, 263, 275
   genre preferences, 1–3, 173
   marriage to Charles Manning Freeman, 2–3, 58n17, 172–3

   negotiations with publishers, 174–5
   on female relationships, 8, 80
   Puritanism, 5
   relationship with Mary Wales, 21n10, 170–2
   relationship with mother, 95, 163n2
   reputation of, 236, 239, 241
   Works:
   "Amanda in Love," 248
   "The Amethyst Comb," 235n4, 274
   "The Apple Tree," 43, 53–4, 282
   "Arethusa," 43, 49–51, 73
   "The Balking of Christopher," 226
   "Balsam Fir," 51
   Best Stories of Mary E. Wilkins, 175–6
   "Billie and Susie," 280
   "Both Cheeks," 203, 208, 210
   "Bouncing Bet," 55
   "Brakes and White Vi'lets," 4
   By the Light of the Soul, 175
   "Calla-Lilies and Hannah," 225
   "The Cat," 255–8, 264
   "Christmas Jenny," 13, 27–8, 34–6, 38, 43, 45–8, 54, 61, 276
   "A Church Mouse," 8, 32–3, 35–6
   "The Cloak Also," 227, 230–1, 276
   "A Conflict Ended," 31, 47
   "Dear Annie," 282
   "The Doctor's Horse," 258–60, 262, 264
   Edgewater People, 203, 227, 232, 276, 278–9
   "The Elm Tree," 51
   "Eliza Sam," 280, 282
   "The Emmets," 174
   "Emmy," 174
   "Evelina's Garden," 225, 237, 247–8
   "For the Love of One's Self," 225–6
   "A Gala Dress," 192–5
   "The Girl who Wants to Write: Things to Do and Avoid," 198n4, 273
   "The Great Pine," 13, 36–7, 43, 51–3, 262, 264–5, 276, 282
   "A Guest in Sodom," 227, 229–30
   The Heart's Highway, 175

Freeman Mary E. Wilkins *(cont.)*
  "An Honest Soul," 62
  "Humble Pie," 227–9
  "A Humble Romance," 62
  A Humble Romance and Other Stories, 3, 37, 42n11, 175
  "An Idyl of a Berry Pasture," 12
  "An Independent Thinker," 33
  The Jamesons, 29–30, 41n5, 41n6, 80, 221, 275, 282
  "The Liar," 203, 210–12, 213, 217, 227, 232, 233
  "Life-Everlastin,'" 33–5
  "The Little Maid at the Door," 9, 95, 110n2
  "The Lombardy Poplar," 55, 267–8
  "The Long Arm," 61, 80, 84, 88–9, 92, 168
  "The Lost Ghost," 8, 80, 84, 85, 86–8, 92, 95–6, 110n2
  "Louisa," 8, 14, 112, 120
  "The Love of Parson Lord," 82–3, 84, 92
  "Luella Miller," 80
  "Lydia Hersey, of East Bridgewater," 279
  Madelon, 11, 80, 84, 89–92
  "A Mistaken Charity," 4, 11, 15, 62, 184–7, 225, 246
  "A Modern-Day Dragon," 15, 187–9, 190
  "A New England Nun," 3, 9, 14, 61, 83, 91–2, 112–14, 116–22, 123, 126, 127, 274
  A New England Nun and Other Stories, 237, 240
  "Now Is the Cherry in Blossom," 173
  "The Old-Maid Aunt," 274
  "Old Woman Magoun," 8–9, 14, 80, 82, 87, 97–103, 105–8, 225, 251n
  "One Good Time," 225
  "The Outside of the House," 31
  "The Parrot," 83–4
  Pembroke, 3, 114, 115, 122, 123–7, 174, 248, 282
  "Peony," 31

The People of Our Neighborhood, 171
"A Poetess," 8, 41n8, 95–6, 107–8, 245–6
The Portion of Labor, 10–11, 15–16, 61, 80, 84–6, 92, 131–44, 147–62, 226, 251n, 274, 277, 280–3
"The Prism," 14, 174, 276, 280
"The Reign of the Doll," 8, 81–2, 96, 280
"A Retreat to the Goal," 227, 233
"The Return," 213, 216
"The Revolt of 'Mother,'" 8, 32, 34–6, 100
The Revolt of Mother and Other Stories, 79
"The Selfishness of Amelia Lamkin," 8, 282
"A Shadow Family," 173
"Silence," 279, 281
Silence and Other Stories, 279
"Sister Liddy," 15, 61, 189, 225
Six Trees, 12, 48, 51, 54, 254, 260–8, 274, 276
"The Slip of the Leash," 51, 235n3
"The Soldier Man," 203, 206–8, 210
"A Stolen Christmas," 191–2, 193, 225
"Sweet-Flowering Perennial," 227, 231–2
"A Symphony in Lavender," 62
"A Taste of Honey," 62
"The Three Old Sisters and the Old Beau," 122
"The Travelling Sister," 279
"The Twelfth Guest," 225
"Two Friends," 61
"Two Old Lovers," 2, 10, 224–5
Understudies, 12–13, 16, 31, 48–9, 51, 54, 83, 254–6, 260, 274, 276
"Up Primrose Hill," 61
"A Village Singer," 13, 32–3, 34–5
"Wake Up, America," 213, 214
"A Wayfaring Couple," 10, 174, 223–4, 241
"The White Birch," 262, 264–7

"The White Shawl," 282
"The Wind in the Rose-Bush," 95–6, 110n2
Wind in the Rose-Bush and Other Stories of the Supernatural, 10
French and Indian War, 90, 281
Fuller, Margaret, 43, 45, 47–50, 54, 58n8, 59n18
  Summer on the Lakes, 49

"A Gala Dress," 192–5
Gandel, Keith, 216
Gaskell, Elizabeth, 282
Garber, Marjorie, 236, 238
Garland, Hamlin, 3,
genealogy, 98, 101, 107–8
gender, 136, 272, 279
  dress, 47, 184–9
  identity, 46–8, 50, 54–5
  nonconformity, 45–7, 54–5
  performance, 185–8, 255
  roles, 43, 45, 47, 50, 52–5, 253
George III, 91
ghosts, 9, 16, 80, 84, 86–8, 92
gift, 81–2
Gilbert, Sandra, 237, 238, 249
Gilman, Charlotte Perkins, 281
  Women and Economics, 220
Gilded Age, 143, 149, 153, 155
Gilligan, Carol, 7
"The Girl who Wants to Write: Things to Do and Avoid," 198n4, 273
Glasgow, Ellen, 147
Glasser, Leah Blatt, 8, 3n3, 45, 50, 58n17m, 84, 158, 160, 198n4, 217, 225, 279
Gothic, 2, 8–10, 80, 89, 95–6, 98, 203, 206
Grasso, Linda, 9, 87, 101–2
"The Great Pine," 13, 36–7, 43, 51–3, 262, 264–5, 276, 282
Greven, David, 238
green woman, 45, 49–50, 54
Griffin, Susan, 83, 255
Gubar, Susan, 237, 238, 249
"A Guest in Sodom," 227, 229–30

Halberstam, Jack, 69
Halperin, David, 60
Hamilton, Gail, 190
Hanson, Ellis, 63
Harde, Roxanne, 9, 87
Hardy, Thomas, 282
  Tess of the D'Urbervilles, 92
Harper & Brothers, 171, 174, 273
Harper's Bazar, 15, 169, 173–4, 182–96, 273, 276
Harper's Monthly, 3, 97, 174, 273
Harper's Weekly, 174
Haraway, Donna J., 265, 266, 268
Harde, Roxanne, 96
Harris, Susan K., 113, 123
Harrison, Hubert, 143
Hawthorne, Nathaniel, 46, 51, 240
Hay, John, *The Breadwinners*, 145n1
The Heart's Highway, 175
Heininger, Mary Lynn Stevens, 154
Hindman, Hugh D., 161
Hines, Lewis W., 157–8, 159, 161
historicism, 7, 12, 204, 253–4
  anachronism, 6, 16
  queer historicism, 12
Hoeller, Hildegard, 82
Hollingsworth, Ellis, 169–70
"An Honest Soul," 62
Howard, June, 26, 137, 143, 221, 279
Howells, William Dean, 3, 3n4, 3n5, 25, 79, 145, 164, 212
Hoyt, Eleanor, 261
Hsu, Hsuan, 26
human/nonhuman, 9, 12, 14, 16, 79, 254–68
"Humble Pie," 227–9
"A Humble Romance," 62
A Humble Romance and Other Stories, 3, 37, 42n11, 175
Hurley, Natasha, 61, 66–7, 70

"An Idyl of a Berry Pasture," 12
imperialism, 4, 6, 80, 84, 92, 253, 260
"An Independent Thinker," 33

industrialization, 44–5, 55, 222, 224–5, 253
  health problems associated with, 156–7
industrial reform novel, 133–4, 148, 149
infanticide, 95–8, 103–4, 106–7
influence, 236–52
inheritance, 164, 168, 176, 248, 252n10
intertextuality, 238, 245, 277
Irish, 14, 112–123, 126
Iroquois (Haudenosaunee), 90
Irving, Katrina, 152
Irving, Washington, "Rip Van Winkle," 224
"Item, One Empty House," by Warner, 236–7, 240–3

Jagose, Annamarie 60–1
The Jamesons, 29–30, 41n5, 41n6, 80, 221, 275, 282
James, Pearl, 205, 216
James, William, 260
Jewett, Sarah Orne, 3–4, 7–8, 44, 58n14, 72, 169, 174, 220–1, 243, 258, 274
  "A Businessman"
  The Country of the Pointed Firs, 29–30, 72, 133, 271n6, 278
  Deephaven, 73
  "The Foreigner," 87
  "The Failure of David Berry," 221
  "The Gray Mills of Farley," 221
  "A White Heron," 46, 73
Johanningsmeier, Charles, 169, 174, 181n1
Johns, Barbara, 46
Jordan, Elizabeth, 174–5
Joyce, James, 240, 241
  Dubliners, 222

Kaplan, Amy, 277
Keene, Jennifer D., 204
Kendrick, Brent L, editor of *The Infant Sphinx*, 8, 37, 41n11, 59n19, 272, 273
kinship, 12–13, 265–8
Kipling, Rudyard, 3,
Kohn, Eduardo, 264

labor, 9, 219, 272, 280–3
Ladies' Home Journal, 273
Lady in White (*Die Weisse Frau*), 97, 110n4
Lamia, 96
Lamp, 261
landscape, 44, 50, 53
Lawrence, D. H., "A Rocking-Horse Winner," 222
lesbianism, 61, 236, 245
"The Liar," 203, 210–12, 213, 217, 227, 232, 233
"Life-Everlastin,'" 33–5
Lilith, 96
liminality, 28, 30–2
Limón, José E., 97–8
literary salon, 43–4, 58n14
"The Little Maid at the Door," 9, 95, 110n2
Llorona, La, 96–8, 100, 102, 104, 106–7, 277
Lockwood, J. Samaine, 12, 90, 132
Lodge, Sir Oliver, 212
"The Lombardy Poplar," 55, 267–8
London, Jack, 163n1
"The Long Arm," 61, 80, 84, 88–9, 92, 168
"The Lost Ghost," 8, 80, 84, 85, 86–8, 92, 95–6, 110n2
"Louisa," 8, 14, 112, 120
"A Love Match" by Warner, 246–7
"The Love of Parson Lord," 82–3, 84, 92
Lowell, James Russell, 175
Lowry, Richard S., 157, 158
"Luella Miller," 80
Lutz, Tom, 26, 40n1
"Lydia Hersey, of East Bridgewater," 279
Lynn strike of 1860, 134

McCarthy, Mary, 120
Macieski, Robert, 155, 161
McClure, S. S. syndicate, 174
McGill, Meredith, 239
Madelon, 11, 80, 84, 89–92

magazines *see* periodicals and individual names
Manning, Susan, 239
Mann, Susan, 44, 58n16
market forces, 82, 280
marriage, 45–6, 48–51, 54, 61–2, 64, 69, 70–2, 99–101
masculinity, 6, 45, 47–8, 51–3, 205, 226–7
Marchalonis, Shirley, 10–11, 240, 262
Marchand, Mary V., 10, 132, 147, 148, 243
Mary Wilkins Freeman Reader, 80
matriarchy, 7, 45, 50, 54, 98, 277
Matthews, John T., 211
Matthiessen, F. O., 52
Maupassant, Guy de, 240
Maxwell, William, 241, 243–4
Medea, 96, 104, 110n4
Meese, Elizabeth, 216, 272, 279
Mencken, H. L., 205
#MeToo movement, 55
Metuchen (NJ), 172–3, 211
Mignolo, Walter D., 97
"A Mistaken Charity," 4, 11, 15, 62, 184–7, 225, 246
mobilization, 203–5, 210, 212, 216
"A Modern-Day Dragon," 15, 187–9, 190
modernism, 1, 15–16, 79, 81, 203, 206, 219–35, 236, 237, 243, 253, 278
Moran, William, 156, 157
Morrison, Toni, 90
motherhood, 45, 47–50, 52, 64, 84–8, 95–8, 107, 115
mother-daughter conflict, 7–9, 248
mother-centered world, 7
Mrozowski, Daniel, 277
Mumford, Lewis, 204
Muñoz, José Esteban, 72–3
Murderess, The, by Papadiamantis, 99–100, 104–8, 277
Murfree, Mary Noailles, 3
mysticism, 46
mythology and mythical time, 96–9, 102, 107–8

National Institute of Arts and Letters, 164
naturalism, 1–2, 11, 15, 81, 132–3, 135, 138, 141, 143–4, 147, 148, 221, 239, 255
nature, 222, 227, 253–72, 276
  beauty, 48, 53
  commodity, 45, 49, 51, 53–4
  correspondence, 49, 58n13, 261
  exploitation, 49, 54, 265, 274, 276
  moral influence, 50–1, 276
  mother, 43, 46, 50, 52, 54
  reciprocity, 49, 55, 261–5
  spirituality, 46–8, 52
  teacher, 52
  see also environment
New England, 1–6, 12, 15, 87, 127, 183, 275
  Women's Club, 43, 57n5–n6
"A New England Nun," 3, 9, 14, 61, 83, 91–2, 112–14, 116–22, 123, 126, 127, 274
A New England Nun and Other Stories, 237, 240
New Woman, 144, 147
New Yorker, 236–7, 240, 241, 249
New York Herald Tribune, 244
Norris, Frank, 133, 135
non-violent activism, 44, 54–5
"Now Is the Cherry in Blossom," 173
nun, 112–23, 241, 276

O'Brien, Jean, 206
O'Dea, Dathalin, 222
"The Old-Maid Aunt," 274
"Old Woman Magoun," 8–9, 14, 80, 82, 87, 97–103, 105–8, 225, 251n
"One Good Time," 225
O'Neill, Ella Quinlan, 119
O'Neill, Eugene, 113
  Long Day's Journey into Night 118–19
Orr, Mary, 236, 238
O'Shaughnessy, Edith, 212
"The Outside of the House," 31

INDEX

pacifism, 54, 217
Palmer, Stephanie, 10, 111n6, 114
Palwekar, Sanjay D., 45
Papadiamantis, Alexandros, *The Murderess*, 99, 101, 106–7, 111n5, 277
"The Parrot," 83–4
patriarchy, 44–6, 49, 53–4, 81, 96–8, 102–3, 107, 238
Pattee, Fred Lewis, 4–5, 12, 173, 175, 205, 254, 275
Paulauskienė, Aušra, 276
Peiss, Kathy, 143–4
Pembroke, 3, 114, 115, 122, 123–7, 174, 248, 282
"Peony," 31
The People of Our Neighborhood, 171
Perez, Domino Renee, 97
periodicals, 12–13, 173–4, 275, 279; *see also* individual titles of periodicals
periodization, 13, 15, 203–70, 276
Phelps, Elizabeth Stuart, 147, 258
Philippine-American War, 260
Pierce, Charles Sanders, 264
place, 3, 6–7, 12
"A Poetess," 8, 41n8, 95–6, 107–8, 245–6
Politi, Gina, 104
Pondrom, Cynthia N., 238
Poole, Hester, 58n7
The Portion of Labor, 10–11, 15–16, 61, 80, 84–6, 92, 131–44, 147–62, 226, 251n, 274, 277, 280–3
Posey, Alexander, 275
Pound, Ezra, 206, 240, 241
poverty, 79, 81, 242, 248
Powers, Elizabeth, 239
Powers, Richard, *The Overstory*, 268
"The Prism," 14, 174, 276, 280
Progressive Era, 6, 203
"The Prism," 174
Pryse, Marjorie, 4, 6–7, 12, 21n7, 26, 30, 61, 66–7, 79, 121, 279
Puritanism, 5–6, 10, 14, 81, 82, 83, 113, 115, 121, 126, 127
and Catholicism 14

queerness, 2–3, 6, 8, 16, 60–1, 64–5, 66–8, 243, 245, 257–8, 277, 279, 280
queer child, 14, 49, 60–1, 65–7, 69–70
queer futurity, 14, 62, 72–3
queer historicism, 12
queer temporalities, 62–5, 132–3, 141, 265–68, 277
romantic friendships, 132–5
quest, 48, 50–1
Quiet Hour Club, 43, 58n7

race or ethnicity, 10–11, 14, 39, 86, 90–1, 105, 113, 114, 115–16, 118, 133, 136–42, 203
African Americans and/or Blackness, 90, 134
Irish, 14, 112–23, 126
Iroquois (Haudenosaunee), 90
whiteness, 11, 39, 138–9, 242
rainbow, 67–9
Randolph (MA), 2, 6, 157, 165, 170
realism, 1, 5, 15, 133, 206, 221, 239, 241, 243, 245, 278
moral realism, 147–9
rebellion, 7–8, 47, 50
Reconstruction, 143, 253
regionalism, 1–2, 4, 6, 10–11, 16, 26–7, 29–30, 61, 221–2, 239, 277, 279
local color, 1, 3–4
queer regionalism, 12
Reichardt, Mary R., 8, 21n10, 31, 58n17, 80, 88, 147, 279
"The Reign of the Doll," 8, 81–2, 96, 280
reproduction, 98, 101, 104–5
"A Retreat to the Goal," 227, 233
"The Return," 213, 216
"The Revolt of 'Mother,'" 8, 32, 34–6, 100, 165
The Revolt of Mother and Other Stories, 79
Reynolds, Guy, 222
Riis, Jacob, 147–8, 151, 152, 162
Rogers-Cooper, Justin, 251n1, 282
Roosevelt, Theodore, 4

Rosenblum, Nancy, L., 40n2
Roudeau, Cécile, 12, 276
Rousseau, Jean-Jacques, 154
Ryden, Kent, 221

sacred space, 47
Sanchez-Eppler, Karen, 154, 155, 158, 161, 277
Sanger, Margaret, 157
satire, 80
Saturday Evening Post, 208
Scahill, Andrew, 68
Scudder, Horace, 91, 92
Selected Stories of Mary Wilkins Freeman, 80
Selective Service Act of 1917, The, 212
"The Selfishness of Amelia Lamkin," 8, 282
self-reliance, 98, 100–1, 106
sentimentalism, 1, 15, 132–3, 144, 147, 148, 152, 154, 158, 196
Sewell, Anna, *Black Beauty,* 257
sexual harassment, 55
sexuality, 90, 112, 127
"A Shadow Family," 173
Shetley, Vernon, 238
Shih, Shu-mei, 97
short story structure, 242, 245, 262
"Silence," 279, 281
Silence and Other Stories, 279
Sinclair, Upton, 135, 145n1, 163n1
sisterhood, 47, 49, 243
"Sister Liddy," 15, 61, 189, 225
Sitwell, Edith, 238
Six Trees, 12, 48, 51, 54, 254, 260–8, 274, 276
slavery, 84, 98, 101, 102
"The Slip of the Leash," 51, 235n3
Smith-Rosenberg, Caroll, 7
social justice, 54–5
social reform and labor reform, 10, 15–16, 43, 47–8, 54–5
"The Soldier Man," 203, 206–8, 210
solidarity, 132, 136, 141
Spanish-American War, 260
species, 16, 83, 261–7, 274

Spectator, 261
spinsters, 46, 237, 240, 243, 249
  old maids, 5
Steinbeck, John, *In Dubious Battle,* 145n1
Stein, Gertrude, 238
Steinman, Michael, 240
Stockton, Kathryn Bond, 61, 65, 67, 74–5n3
"A Stolen Christmas," 191–2, 193, 225
Stone, Susan, 12, 276
Storey, Mark, 26, 221
Stowe, Harriet Beecher, 3, 15, 58n7, 239
sustainability, 53, 55
Swedenborg, Emanuel, 261
"Sweet-Flowering Perennial," 227, 231–2
"A Symphony in Lavender," 62

"A Taste of Honey," 62
Tarbell, Ida, 212
Thompson, Charles F., 168
Thoreau, Henry David, 45, 53–4
"The Three Old Sisters and the Old Beau," 122
Tigchelaar, Jana, 82, 277
Tolman, Isaac, 169, 170
Tolman, Nathan, 169, 170
transatlanticism, 14, 16, 96, 239, 261, 277, 282
transcendentalism, 1, 12–13, 43–4, 48, 51, 53–4, 226
  transcendental realism, 43, 48, 53–4, 58n9
transgression, 96–8, 107–8
trauma, 80, 81, 92, 253
"The Travelling Sister," 279
Trout, Stephen, 204
trees, 9, 12, 49, 51–5, 220, 261–5
True Womanhood, 49, 55
Turner, Victor, 28, 30, 34, 41n3, 41n7
Tuxbury, Willis, 165
"The Twelfth Guest," 225
"Two Friends," 61
"Two Old Lovers," 2, 10, 173, 224–5
Twain, Mark, 164
Tyler, Thomas Pickman, 165, 189

INDEX

Understudies, 12–13, 16, 31, 48–9, 51, 54, 83, 254–6, 260, 274, 276
"Up Primrose Hill," 61

Vassar, 85, 137
Vermont Phoenix
"A Village Singer," 13, 32–3, 34–5
violence, 3–4, 13, 79, 80, 81, 89–92, 248

Wachman, Gay, 245, 246
"Wake Up, America," 213, 214
Wales, Mary, 3, 170–2
Warner, Michael, 60
Warner, Sylvia Townsend 236–52, 278
  "Item, One Empty House," 236–7, 240–3
  Lolly Willowes, 243, 245
  "A Love Match," 246–7
  Mr. Fortune's Maggot, 243, 245–6
  "The View from Rome," 246
Watts, Edward, 26, 40n1
"A Wayfaring Couple," 10, 174, 223–4, 241
Webb, Mary, 243
Weeks, Kathi, 141
Weir, J. Alden, 3
  The Factory Village, 219, 220
Westbrook, Perry, 5, 9, 12, 51, 81, 114, 217, 254
Wharton, Edith, 5, 8, 21n6, 79, 147, 205, 220, 221, 236
  A Backward Glance, 21
  Ethan Frome, 222
  The Fruit of the Tree, 251n1
  The House of Mirth, 251n1
  Summer, 235n1

"The White Birch," 262–3, 264–7
White, Elizabeth Wade, 237, 244–5
whiteness, 11, 39, 138–9, 242
"The White Shawl," 282
Wide Awake, 173–4
Wilkins, Eleanor, 2, 163n2
Wilkins, Mary E. *see* Freeman, Mary E. Wilkins
Wilkins, Warren, 2, 165, 166–8, 176
Wilson, Woodrow, 203, 204, 211
"The Wind in the Rose-Bush," 95–6, 110n2
Wind in the Rose-Bush and Other Stories of the Supernatural, 10, 80
witchcraft, 46–8, 75n8, 96, 104, 245
woman, 80, 81, 237, 279
Woman's Home Companion, 174
Woolf, Virginia, 206, 283
world literature, 98–9, 107–8
World War I, 15, 203–5, 222, 227, 278
  American Expeditionary Forces (AEF), 205
  Battle of the Somme, 246
  mobilization, 203–4, 206, 213
  propaganda, 204, 210
  Selective Service Act of 1917, The, 212
World War II, 247

xenophobia, 46

The Youth's Companion, 174

Zagarell, Sandra A., 2, 10–11, 13, 26, 29–30, 38, 41n5, 41n6, 80, 81, 133, 221
Zieger, Robert H., 211